Greater than Emperor

STYLUS
Studies in Medieval Culture

Mirabile Dictu: Representations of the Marvelous in Medieval and
Renaissance Epic, *by Douglas Biow*

Ami and Amile: A Medieval Tale of Friendship, Translated from the
Old French, *translated by Samuel N. Rosenberg and Samuel Danon*

At Play in the Tavern: Signs, Coins, and Bodies in the Middle Ages,
by Andrew Cowell

Greater than Emperor: Cola di Rienzo (ca. 1313–54) and the World of
Fourteenth-Century Rome, *by Amanda Collins*

This interdisciplinary series is devoted to that millennium of Western
culture extending from the fall of Rome to the rise of Humanism that
we call the Middle Ages. The series promotes scholarship based on the
study of primary sources and artifacts within their social and discursive
contexts. With its emphasis on cultural studies, the series favors
research that considers how the psychological, ideological, and
spiritual dimensions of the medieval world converge in expressions of
individual experience and in perceptions of material events.

Greater than Emperor

Cola di Rienzo (ca. 1313–54)
and the
World of Fourteenth-Century Rome

Amanda Collins

Ann Arbor

THE UNIVERSITY OF MICHIGAN PRESS

Copyright © by the University of Michigan 2002
All rights reserved
Published in the United States of America by
The University of Michigan Press
Manufactured in the United States of America
♾ Printed on acid-free paper

2005   2004   2003   2002   4   3   2   1

A CIP catalog record for this book is available from the British Library.

Library of Congress Cataloging-in-Publication Data

Collins, Amanda, 1968–
    Greater than emperor : Cola di Rienzo (ca. 1313–54) and the world of
fourteenth-century Rome / Amanda Collins.
        p.   cm. — (Stylus)
    Originally presented as the author's thesis (Ph. D.—University of
Oxford, 1996) under the title: Cola di Rienzo (1312–1354), the
revolution in historical perspective.
    Includes bibliographical references and index.
    ISBN 0-472-11250-3 (Cloth : alk. paper)
    1. Rienzo, Cola di, d. 1354   2. Rome (Italy)—History—476–1420.
3. Revolutionaries—Italy—Rome—Biography.   4. Rome (Italy)—Biography.
I. Title.   II. Series.
DG811.6.C65   2002
945'.63205'092—dc21   2001007708

Acknowledgments

My interest in the relationship between Roman antiquity and the Italian
Renaissance began at school; I owe a particular debt to the classics and
history staff of Clifton High School, Bristol, who inspired me to pursue my
interests further than I would ever, then, have thought possible. Once
again, at university, encouragement came from a wonderful tutor and
excellent Roman historian, Miriam Griffin of Somerville College, Oxford,
and from a proper Renaissance man, Gervase Rosser, at St. Catherine's,
Oxford, who went on to become an inspiring and imaginative thesis
adviser. Academic assistance in Rome was not so easy to come by; archival
staff across Rome and Lazio, by contrast, have been extremely helpful.
Dottoressa Dommarco and Dottoressa Collega of the Sopraintendenza
Archivistica per il Lazio deserve particular thanks. Dottoressa Lanconelli
at the Archivio Storico di Stato also provided assistance and some not
inconsiderable rule-bending; the staff of the Archivio Capitolino and the
capo of the Vatican Sala dei Manoscritti, Dottore Alvise Burriola, also
warrant a mention here. Those Italian *professori* of the archives to whom
I owe special thanks are Isa Lori-Sanfilippo, Paolo Cherubini, and the late
Renzo Mosti, each of whom made helpful suggestions and contributions
at vital stages in my research. I would pay tribute, too, to the late great
Prefect of the Vatican Library, Father Leonard Boyle, who gave me a personal tour of his premises and personnel—and thereby a useful imprimatur—when I first arrived on that hallowed ground of medievalists. I
owe most, nonetheless, to an excellent historian and personal friend, Mar-
garet Hunt of Amherst College, Massachusetts; without her timely critical
input the doctoral thesis might never have been completed; without her
warmth and support, before and since, I might never have become a historian at all.

I would also like to thank all those institutions and organizations whose financial support, great or small, between 1991 and the present has enabled me to complete this study: Somerville College; the British Academy; St. Hugh's College, Oxford; the Taylor Institute, Oxford; the Modern History Faculty of Oxford University; the British School at Rome; the Institute of Historical Research at London University; the Leverhulme Trust; the Etruscan Foundation of the University of Michigan. Since 1997 I have held the Hornik Junior Research Fellowship in Intellectual History at Wolfson College, Oxford; Wolfson has been a truly excellent employer, both supportive and noninterfering!

I have also been privileged to enjoy a huge range of personal and practical support from family and friends alike. My parents, paternal grandmother, my on-line buddies and "real life" friends have been excellent and consistent in their encouragement over the years. Particular thanks go to my brother Adam Collins for help, at a much earlier stage, with bibliographical editing; to my two special academic mentors and historian-heroines, Marjorie Reeves and Brenda Bolton, for their constant backing; to Philip Ditchfield for frequently putting me up, and putting up with me, in his flat in Rome; to Claire Bowden-Dan for an incomparable reading and correction of the manuscript; and to Carol Flemming for just about everything else.

I should have liked to offer the dedication to Marjorie Caines, my maternal grandmother; sadly I may only do so, now, in her memory. Yet history and memory are connected forever.

Grateful acknowledgment is made to the following individuals and institutions for permission to reprint previously published illustrations.

Figure 1 is from a private collection. Figure 2, Mss Royal 6.E.IX, folios 21v–22r, is reprinted by permission of The British Library. Figure 3, MS FR 4274, folio 10r, is reprinted courtesy of Bibliothèque Nationale de France—Paris. Figure 4 is reprinted courtesy of Staatsgalerie Stuttgart. Figure 5, NG4762, is reprinted courtesy of the National Gallery, London. Figure 6 is from the author's collection.

Contents

Figures

Abbreviations

A.C.	Archivio Capitolino, Rome
ARC	Giuseppe Porta, ed. *Anonimo Romano: Cronica.* Milan: Adelfi, 1981.
A.S.R.	Archivio Storico di Stato, Rome
ASRSP	*Archivio della Società Romana di Storia Patria*
B.A.V.	Biblioteca Apostolica Vaticana (Vatican City, Rome)
MEFRM	*Mélanges de l'École Française de Rome (Médiévale)*
R.I.S.	*Rerum Italicarum Scriptores.* 1st and 2d eds. (2d ed. = Raccolta degli Storici Italiani: Istituto Storico Italiano per il Medio Evo)
S.A.P.	S. Angelo in Pescheria

The Life and Afterlife of
Cola di Rienzo

But for that event the future liberator of Rome might have been but a dreamer, a scholar, a poet—the peaceful rival of Petrarch—a man of thoughts, not deeds.

The event in question was the death of the younger brother of Cola di Rienzo, an accidental casualty of a running battle on the streets of Rome between the young barons of the hostile Colonna and Orsini factions. The story is recorded by his near-contemporary "biographer" and has been retold, in one elaboration or another, for nearly seven hundred years, to explain the motivation and circumstances of a daring political revolution in a dangerous medieval city. There is, however, no evidence that this event ever took place; Cola himself, in all of his sometimes disingenuous attempts to justify his early actions, never once referred to such a tragedy.

Nonetheless, the stirring sentiments quoted above appear in the earliest of the three English-language "studies" that describe Cola's revolution of 1347: Bulwer-Lytton's novel *Rienzi, Last of the Tribunes,* completed in 1835. Bulwer-Lytton was the first to admit that the story was, in fact, dense and complex: indeed, as his novel's preface informs us, Bulwer had to place the haunting fate of *Rienzi* to one side in order to compose *The Last Days of Pompeii.*[1] This gives us an ironically fitting insight into the unique niche that this brow-striking novel *Rienzi* occupies in the history of

---

1. Edward Bulwer-Lytton, *Rienzi, Last of the Tribunes,* 2d ed. (London: Routledge, 1848), ix. The second chapter is tartly entitled, "A historical survey—not to be passed over, except by those who dislike to understand what they read." *Rienzi* the novel and its world-wide influence significantly assisted in the distortion of the modern historical reception of Cola and late medieval Rome.

English prose. The most bizarre modern epiphenomenon of Bulwer-Lytton's *Rienzi,* and thus of Cola himself, is the annual Californian "Bulwer-Lytton Contest": literary cynics submit opening paragraphs (to imaginary novels), composed of the most astonishingly convoluted purple prose.[2] Yet in its day *Rienzi* became swiftly an immensely popular tale, soon translated across all media, in most European languages. Bulwer-Lytton's immediate heirs were near-contemporaries: the composer Richard Wagner, the philosopher Friedrich Engels, and the Pre-Raphaelite Brotherhood artist William Holman Hunt. Both the libretto for Wagner's opera of 1841–42 and Engels's unpublished play of 1842 were based on scripts condensed from Bulwer-Lytton's novel. Holman Hunt placed my opening Bulwer-Lytton quotation below his painting (see fig. 1) entitled *Rienzi vowing to obtain Justice for the death of his young brother, slain in a skirmish between the Colonna and Orsini factions,* at its first exhibition (Royal Academy, London, 1849); his first painting, interestingly, to carry the initials *P-R B.* The range of artistic formats that these three examples encompass is typical, in microcosm, of the extraordinary and fascinating *Nachleben* of the Tribune of Rome.

The various positions assumed by Bulwer-Lytton, Wagner, Holman Hunt and so on are also, however, indices to the distance between the events of the Roman Trecento and their treatment throughout the subsequent centuries. The quotation in point suggests that Cola was a bookish recluse before turning to politics for personal revenge: the *vendetta* image medieval Italy conjures up, familiar from Shakespeare to the present day. Clearly Bulwer-Lytton bypassed the historical evidence of Cola's professional and political career in favor of a story about the fate of Cola's younger brother and the results of that one "accident" for Rome's history. Indeed, as a "historical figure" of the later Middle Ages, calling for the people's liberation from the tyrants and justice for the oppressed, Cola's career and personality have offered a most convenient peg on which politicians and ideologues have hung a series of anachronistic identities: he has been hailed as a Jacobin hero, a prophet of Italian nationalism, a herald of German fascism, and a prototype for Russian Communism.

---

2. The competition was started in the early 1980s by an assistant professor of English literature at San Jose, who cited the opening line of *Rienzi* as an example of the most appalling prose conceivable: Scott Rice, *"It was a dark and stormy night": The Best (?) from the Bulwer-Lytton Contest* (London: Abacus, 1984), ii–iii.

Fig. 1. William Holman Hunt, *Rienzi vowing to obtain Justice* (1849)

The isolation of Cola, which has permitted such fallacious comparisons, is partly also a result of the influence of his "biography," the *Vita di Cola di Rienzo*.[3] The Chronicler, we have seen, was responsible from the start for giving a rather simplistic, and ahistorical twist to the reasons behind Cola's inspired seizing of power in May 1347. However, it is the format itself of the record that has done the most damage. The *Vita* did not appear in print until 1624, although it is in fact an authentic near-contemporary account of Cola. In the seventeenth century it was excerpted from a longer, but now fragmentary chronicle of Trecento Rome (1327–54) that includes the Cola episode. The very form of the *Vita*, therefore, jolted Cola from his historical context, rendering him an archetypal biographical subject, and displacing him immediately from the Trecento Roman realities of familial allegiances, political networks, and cultural referents. The historiographical stage was thus set from the start. The fate of the account between its composition (ca. 1358) and the appearance of several sixteenth-century manuscript copies is unknown. Cola would seem to have undergone a form of *damnatio memoriae* in the fifteenth century. A rare exception is the evidence of a butcher, Giuliano, who in 1444 asked the Araceli Franciscans to bury him below the arms of the Tribune, above the door;[4] presumably where the tombstone of Flavio Biondo may now be seen. Evidently imitators of Cola no longer posed a political threat by the time of the pontificate of Sixtus IV; historical accounts were not uniformly hostile. Platina's account of events in his *Lives of the Popes* is intriguingly objective;[5] that of Machiavelli in his *Storie Fiorentine* is positively favorable.[6] The ecclesiastical historians and annalists of the sixteenth and seventeenth centuries—Baronius, Bzovius, and Baluze; Rainaldi and Duchesne—were, by contrast, full of censure for Cola's rebellion against the papacy. However, after the reworking and translation of the tale in 1733 by the French Jesuit Du Cerceau, Cola's star began once again to rise; he

---

3. See chapter 4 for an analysis of the Chronicler and his biographical account. Quotations are generally taken from the English translation of John Wright, *The Life of Cola di Rienzo* (Toronto: Pontifical Institute of Mediaeval Studies, 1975), although I have felt free to interpolate my own alternatives where relevant. Those translated from earlier parts of the chronicle or cited in Roman dialect are from the 1981 text edition—Giuseppe Porta, *Anonimo Romano: Cronica* (Milan: Adelfi, 1981) (hereafter, *ARC*)—which is excerpted from his excellent critical edition of 1979.

4. Noted by Anna Maria Corbo, *Artisti e artigiani in Roma al tempo di Martino e di Eugenio IV* (Rome: De Luca, 1969), 77.

5. B.A.V. Vat. Lat. 2044, 182v–184v.

6. Chapter 31, in Laura F. Banfield and Harvey Mansfield Jr., eds., *Florentine Histories by Niccolò Machiavelli* (Princeton: Princeton University Press, 1988), 43.

became a model revolutionary for the great nationalist movers and shakers of the nineteenth century.

The little French handbook was the first popular biography of Cola. The story that a copy was found among the baggage abandoned by Napoleon after Waterloo is probably apocryphal, but acts as an early indication of the heroic and dictatorial identity already attached to the memory of Cola. It circulated and was translated widely, inspiring both Schiller and Byron: the latter, in high Romantic splendor, described Cola as a "leaf" from "the tree of freedom's withered trunk."[7] The account of Edward Gibbon, written in 1787,[8] combined with Byron's poetic posturing, inspired the so-called Tragedy of Rienzi by the redoubtable Miss Mitford, despite protests from critics in 1828 that the subject was hardly suited to the pen of one of the fairer sex.[9] But Bulwer-Lytton's reworking of the tale was to have the broadest impact: his version of Cola di Rienzo's story was reproduced in no fewer than eighteen plays based on his life staged between 1791 and 1938. In addition to this, a silent film was made in 1912, and an illustrated children's version of Cola's life appeared in 1946. Novels have been legion, and generally dire: yet they continue to appear.[10] Most recently Cola has enjoyed a cameo appearance in a bawdy little romp based on the story of his contemporary, Joanna, Queen of Naples.[11] Thus the tendencies of poets, novelists, artists, and dramatists, over the centuries, to comment on Cola's own ambiguous and charismatic personality, have also, inevitably, contributed to the process of his decontextualization.

Cola's near-mythical status in European literature has passed, and his Roman regime is largely forgotten even in Italy. However, in Rome itself there is still a powerful popular tradition: visitors frequently pass the marble bust on the Pincio in the Garden of Heroes, the untitled bronze statue to the left of Michelangelo's steps up to the Capitol piazza, and the eponymous piazza, cinema, and road that runs between the Piazza della Libertà

---

7. *Childe Harold's Pilgrimage*, in *Childe Harold's Pilgrimage*, ed. John D. Jump and Frederick Page, rev. ed. (Oxford: Oxford University Press, 1970), canto IV, verse 114, p. 242.

8. Edward Gibbon, *The Decline and Fall of the Roman Empire* (London: Penguin, 1994), 3:1022–42.

9. The play was first performed at Drury Lane (1828) and then transported to the American stage: see William J. Roberts, *Mary Russell Mitford: The Tragedy of a Blue Stocking* (London: Andrew Melrose, 1913), 244–58.

10. E.g. Francesco Mazzei, *La Fantastica Vita e l'Oribile Morte del Tribuno del Popolo Romano* (Milan: Rusconi, 1980); Sigrid Grabner, *Traum von Rom. Historischer Roman um Cola di Rienzo* (Berlin: Buchverlag Der Morgen, 1985); Ugo Reale, *Cola di Rienzo* (Rome: Newton Compton, 1991).

11. Alan Savage, *Queen of Night* (London: Warner, 1993).

and the Piazza di Risorgimento (by the Vatican City). Until 1997, when the shop relocated to the more prestigious shopping district around the Corso, the *Via di Cola di Rienzo* even housed an exclusive gentleman's outfitters with the Roman dialect name *Rienzi,* corresponding to the oldest local traditions of Cola's story.

A series of jingoistic articles in the 1870s and 1880s, in the aftermath of the reestablishment of Rome as the national capital, sheds light on the development of Cola's legend; this new "scientific" and political interest revealed the existence (while disputing the verity) of local myths relating to the location of the Tribune's house and his tomb (despite the Chronicler's assurance that Cola's body was burned and his ashes tossed into the Tiber).[12] Descent from the blood of the Tribune claimed by Pope Leo XIII in the eighteenth century was debunked;[13] a direct genealogical connection was also claimed by the explorer G. L. Domeny Rienzi, who named two islands in the Philippines after Cola (the Isola Rienzi and the Isola del Tribuno, southwest of Mindanao). The legendary childhood home of Cola in Anagni was still, in 1994, being pointed out by the fierce nun who escorted parties around Boniface's papal palace. It is even possible that the "Di Rienzo" family survives in Rome, as owners of a *tabacchi* on the Salita dei Crescenzi between Piazza S. Eustachio and the Pantheon.[14] Indeed, searching the World Wide Web supplies a range of echoes of "Rienzi" beyond the wildest dreams of a *Nachleben* enthusiast.[15]

---

12. Fernando Gori, *La torre del Monzone presso il Ponte Rotto di Roma non fu mai casa del Tribune Cola di Rienzo e nuova spiegazione d'una tavola enigmatica del XII secolo* (Rome, 1872); Filippo Porena, *Due Parole in Difesa di Cola di Rienzo* (Rome, 1873); Domenico Tordi, *La Pretesa Tomba di Cola di Rienzo* (Rome, 1887); *Tribuno e Pontifice* (Rome, 1890).

13. Tommaso Gabrini, *Osservazioni storico-critiche sulla Vita di Cola di Rienzo* (Rome, 1806). Gabrini himself claimed to be an heir of the Tribune.

14. This has not been, however, a particularly uncommon name in Rome since the Middle Ages: in Cola's own time sons of Lorenzo (dialect: *Rienzi*), even sons of Lorenzo called Nicola ("Cola"), appeared two or three times in the surviving notarial material: one example of May 29, 1354, mentions a witness, a tailor: *Cola Laurentii, sutor:* see Renzo Mosti, *Un notaio Romano del '300 (1348–1379). I Protocolli di Johannes Nicolai Pauli* (Rome: École Française, 1982), 76.

15. I list here the strangest tributes to the Tribune: the lively little town of Rienzi, Mississippi, founded not long after Bulwer's novel and now boasting a population ca. 340; the Union general Sheridan's horse (who died in 1878, and is still preserved in the Smithsonian); a long-distance steamship that left Dublin for Australia in 1858; and a smart yacht available for charter today on Lake Michigan, all called *Rienzi.* Also to be found are a U.S. pasta distributor, a New Jersey–based health care marketing firm, and the newly opened decorative arts wing of the Houston Museum of Fine Arts, in a converted private villa of the name. My personal favorite is Rienzi, the kosher fish restaurant at 10, King David Street, Jerusalem. One way or another, one might say, Cola realized his ambition to reach both the Holy Land and a New World.

The same process—the extraction of Cola from his proper historical environment—became as true of Cola's political reputation as of his heroic literary image or of his memory in popular culture. Cola has indeed provided a curiously variable totalitarian model: in 1928 Wagner's *Rienzi* overture opened the Tenth Congress of Soviets in the U.S.S.R.,[16] but the original score of the opera disappeared along with Nazi supreme command in 1945. Many articles praising the supposedly protofascistic regime of the Tribune appeared in the 1930s; and there were several—equally anachronistic—reactive attacks on Cola immediately after the Second World War.[17] Historians have found it hard to resist making comparisons with subsequent "dictators," whose intense personal ambition and even semidivine self-perception have not prevented their pragmatic, effective government of nations or empires. Over the last two centuries, comparisons have been drawn between Cola and other charismatic leaders such as Caesar, Nero, Napoleon, Garibaldi, Hitler, and Mussolini.[18]

The combination of these factors—the nature of the events and Cola's powerful personality, plus the nature and form of the record of his life—has served to embroider Cola's image beyond reason and recognition as a fourteenth-century ruler. Of course, this is not, per se, a new assertion; the complaint has been reiterated by the present generation of historians.[19] Such treatments of Cola have been exacerbated by a comparative absence of evidence for the civic life of Trecento Rome (an archival dearth relative, that is, to the documentary holdings of other major cities such as Florence). The balance of historiographical interest has tipped all the more easily, therefore, in the direction of this one man's career and fate, and the events of "his" decade (1343–54), a period for which a broader range of sources survives than for much of the rest of the century. The most importance collection of sources is Cola's own correspondence of 1343–54, edited and described by Konrad Burdach and Paul Piur, along with a variety of other relevant sources, between 1912

---

16. Iris Origo, *Tribune of Rome* (London: Hogarth, 1938), 13.

17. Including the somewhat agitated English monograph of Victor Fleischer, *Rienzo: The Rise and Fall of a Dictator* (London: Aiglon Press, 1948).

18. This remained as true in 1967 as in 1821: see G. W. Meadly, "Two Pairs of Historical Portraits: Octavian Augustus and William Pitt; Rienzi and Buonaparte," *Pamphleteer* 18, no. 35 (1821): 129–41; Gabriele D'Annunzio, *La Vita di Cola di Rienzo* (Florence, 1905); Luigi Barzini, "Cola di Rienzo or the Obsession of Antiquity," in *The Italians* (London: Hamish Hamilton, 1964), 117–32.

19. The newer historiography of Cola, especially the articles by Massimo Miglio since 1974, is generally impressive, although there has been no single, serious critical study of Cola or the Tribunate since the 1930s.

and 1929.[20] Burdach was widely reviewed, and not always favorably:[21] criticism was frequently directed not so much at Burdach's editorial skills as at his relentless positivism, and/or his unerring propensity to view Cola as a sort of medieval *Übermensch,* the *fons et origo* of both the Italian Renaissance and the German Reformation. Apart from the Romanesco chronicle and the correspondence, several other accounts survive; those of Petrarch, Hocsemius (a canon of Lièges), a number of German chroniclers, and no fewer than fifteen contemporary Italian civic chronicles also provide evidence of Cola's period in power.[22]

Nevertheless, the last thirty years have seen the gradual discovery and publication of material relating to a broader sweep of fourteenth-century urban life in Rome.[23] Perhaps understandably, however, the overemphasis on Cola in the past has tended to have the effect that recent studies of Trecento Rome contain little reference to the sources for the Tribunate: but this could be a case of throwing out the baby with the bath water. The present study, while not claiming to offer an exhaustive study of "Rome during Avignon,"[24] does attempt to redress this imbalance, by repatriating Cola within the context of the social and political history of the city of Rome in the century of the pope's absence. It will also seek to correct a number of historiographical misconceptions about the nature of Cola's

---

20. Konrad Burdach and Paul Piur, *Briefwechsel des Cola di Rienzo,* 5 vols., Vom Mittelalter zur Reformation. Forschungen und Geschichte der Deutschen Bildung, pt. 2 (Berlin: Weidmann, 1912–28) (see bibliography for full references). The majority of Cola's own letters appear in the third volume, and those of his correspondents or commentators in the fourth (and fifth); these will be abbreviated as e.g. III:40 (volume 3, letter no. 40), with line numbers following.

21. G. Buzzi, "Konrad Burdach und Paul Piur, Briefwechsel des Cola di Rienzo. Dritter Teil," *ASRSP* 35 (1912): 638–42; Pietro Fedele, "Konrad Burdach und Paul Piur— *Briefwechsel des Cola di Rienzo.* Kritischer Text," *Giornale Storico della Letteratura Italiana* 44 (1914): 386–405; Paul Joachimsen, "Vom Mittelalter zur Reformation," *Historische Vierteljahrsschrift* (1920–21): 426–70; Carl Brandi, "Konrad Burdach. Vom Mittelalter zur Reformation," *Göttingen Gelehrte Anzeigen* 7–12 (1923): 187–98; Bernhard Schmeidler, "Bemerkungen zu Konrad Burdach, *Vom Mittelalter zur Reformation,*" *Zeitschrift für Kirchengeschichte* 49 (1930): 64–73.

22. These are described in chapter 4.

23. Other contemporary evidence relating to Cola, his career, and the supporters of his revolution, found in the course of this research among the scattered archival sources of the city, is also treated in chapter 4; a full complement of notarial, statutory, and necrological *fondi* is listed among the primary sources.

24. The best modern account of medieval Rome was first published in 1974: Robert Brentano, *Rome before Avignon: A Social History of Thirteenth-Century Rome,* 2d ed. (London: British Museum Press, 1991). Significantly enough, this fascinating study of Duecento Rome nevertheless uses fourteenth-century documentary material throughout.

regime and indeed, the confusion concerning his own attitude to the City and its government. The frequent assumption that Cola's revolution was a short-lived affair, with wider consequences for nineteenth-century literature than for the Trecento society that evidently consented to and participated, up to a point, in the regime, particularly needs to be reexamined: this is treated in chapter 5.

The even more common assumption that Cola was insane must be repudiated at the outset, as prejudicial, pejorative, and ultimately irrelevant. The fact that his "biographer," the Roman Chronicler, states that some men in 1347 saw Cola as "a fantastical madman"[25] is hardly an adequate endorsement of the claim. It is undoubtedly true that his ambitions, particularly in terms of the restoration of Roman hegemony across the Italian peninsula, were unrealistic in the context of the contemporary Italian world of civic autonomy and in the absence of a political mechanism for such an *all'antica* restoration; Cola did not share the apparent political realism of some of his Roman (or Italian, or Bohemian) peers. If his Chronicler, failing to comprehend the symbolic gestures Cola made toward other cities, suggests that he might have been mad, then we should look for an explanation in the Chronicler's own political agenda and his own perceptions of Rome (we have already noted the Chronicler's preference for a simplistic—but entirely unproven—explanation for Cola's early motivation in the death of his brother). Giovanni Villani, in contrast, noted that the councilors thought Cola's aims were "fantasy" and likely to fail swiftly; but, believing he understood Cola's political intentions, he felt no call to stigmatize him with the accusation of insanity.[26]

Again, the image has been further slewed by "modern" approaches. The heavy emphasis on Cola as a patriotic hero and romantic individualist met, at the turn of the present century, the development of psychiatry and the new analyses of psychohistory. The madness theory thereby gained further credibility. Indeed, Cola has enjoyed the dubious privilege of a study by Lombroso, the notorious pioneer of social and criminal psychology. The title of his study—"Cola the Obsessive"—sets the tone for its contents.[27] Regrettably, despite dispensing with outdated psychobiographical theories in the abstract, many modern historians (particularly British or English-speaking historians) still choose to dismiss the Tribune

---

25. Wright, *Life,* 73.

26. Giuseppe Porta, ed., *Giovanni Villani. Cronica* (Parma: Ugo Guanda, 1990), 2:495–98, book 13, chapter 90, henceforth cited as, e.g., 13:90.

27. Cesare Lombroso, "Cola di Rienzo monomane," *Fanfulla della Dominica* 46 (1880).

as mad.[28] More circumspect (German and Italian) historians[29] have certainly seen Cola as anomalous and his actions as visionary and bizarre, but have avoided highlighting the taint of mental instability that carries with it a danger of taking Cola less than seriously; crucially, it diverts attention from the attempt to find an overriding coherence in Cola's ideas, and blinds scholars to the real long-term effects of his regime. Instead the present study seeks to understand, so far as possible, the aims, ambitions, and expediencies of Cola's Tribunate, without resort to perceived flaws in his character that are, ultimately, unknowable.

Not only have Cola's ambitions been misunderstood, but the role he saw himself as occupying in Rome has suffered a similar fate. Some have reduced Cola to the convenient identity of a manipulative petty bureaucrat;[30] no one has fully examined the implications of Cola's background as a notary and his career within the municipal financial administration of Rome. This study provides such a examination. Others have seen him as a scholar thrust into the political limelight, reminiscent of Bulwer-Lytton's grandiloquent phraseology quoted at the head of this introduction. Few, surprisingly, have seen him as a signore within the pattern of contemporary Italian city-state politics: chapter 4 will demonstrate that Cola manifested many signorial characteristics and was indeed perceived as such by outside commentators, even though the anomalous ideological nature of Rome itself, in terms of the heritage of its past and indeed its promised apocalyptic future, makes comparison with other Italian cities necessarily circumspect.

Rome, ultimately, was the location, the cultural context and the final point of departure for all of Cola's activities, both the visionary and the pragmatic. Following an introductory sketch of the events of Cola's career, the first half of this study focuses on the imaginary Roman world Cola inherited. His reliance on the cultural and political models of the long

---

28. E.g. Paul Hetherington, in *Medieval Rome: A Portrait of the City and Its Life* (London: Rubicon, 1994), 26, refers to a "vein of insanity" that he sees running through Cola's actions; John Larner's description of Cola's "limitless faculty for fantasy and self-delusion" only narrowly avoids the term *insane* (*Italy in the Age of Dante and Petrarch 1216–1380* [New York: Longman, 1980], 55).

29. Walter Ullmann claimed that Cola's personal fate did "not in the least detract from the importance of this episode," that is, its importance to Ullmann's subject, *The Medieval Foundations of Renaissance Humanism* (London: Elek, 1977), 139.

30. One particularly scathing phrase comes to mind: "A fat little lawyer . . . on whom too much ink has been spilt." Peter Partner, *The Lands of St. Peter* (London: Eyre Methuen, 1972), 333.

Roman past are examined in the first chapter; his debt to apocalyptic imagery and notions of the prophetic future of the Eternal City itself is the subject of the second. The third chapter tracks the contemporary importance of these cultural points of reference in Cola's broadest conceivable spatial and chronological context, positing, ultimately, that he was by no means as unusual or bizarre as has sometimes been thought. His position in the contemporary social hierarchy of Rome (the "real" Rome of his day and age), the profile of that hierarchy, and his relationship with the different groups in a period of change are explicated in the second half of this study, with a full introduction in situ.

The division itself is a slightly ironic commentary on Cola's historiographical reception: modern writers have tended to perceive, and exacerbate a binarizing contrast between such styles of rule (accountancy as opposed to apotheosis, fiscal or fantastical, Henry VII of England versus the Holy Roman Emperor Frederick II). In the case of Cola's self-identification, however, these were merely the ends of a spectrum of self-presentation across which he moved with speed, ease, and frequency throughout his career. But a false dichotomy of this nature is, essentially, the result of anachronistic perspectives; of artificial and inappropriate historiographical categorization. In response to this failure to comprehend the range of his positions, therefore, this study provides a series of new perspectives on the career and regime of Cola di Rienzo. This book is intended to offer a new examination of Cola's own perception of the history of Rome, with regard to the classical past, the municipal present, and the apocalyptic future, and his role with regard to each. Older literary and newly studied archival sources are then used to establish a better contemporary perspective on Cola. The ways in which such sources illuminate and augment the much better known account of the Chronicler are a central facet of the argument. New information based on archival research is used in the latter half of the book to rebuild the contemporary municipal, administrative, professional, and prosopographical context of Cola's revolution. In theoretical terms, conversely, this study will appreciate and incorporate the contributions of earlier research while circumnavigating previous ideological biases, particularly seeking to avoid the cult of personality that has grown up around Cola. Above all, I have sought to understand Cola di Rienzo on his own terms, as a product of a distinct social, political, and historical context, and not as a patriotic herald of modern Western democracy.

PART I

FROM ANCIENT BABYLON TO THE NEW JERUSALEM

The "Life and Times" of Cola di Rienzo

Although I have foresworn a biographical approach to Cola's career, the following introductory section provides an outline of Cola's career, to avoid burdening later analytical chapters with narrative. The latter half of Cola's career, after 1347 particularly, is not well known and deserves careful reconstruction. The broader political, cultural, and religious context of Rome—and certain ostensibly obscure references—will come into focus in the main body of the study.

Cola was born the son of an innkeeper in late 1312 or early 1313, in the *rione* Regola.[1] He spent his childhood in Anagni, a town around fifty kilometers—a day's journey—to the southeast of Rome. When he returned to Rome, notionally around 1333, he became a notary and married into a family of notaries.[2] During the following years his oratorical skills must have come to the attention of men with considerable standing in the communal government of the city: in 1342, just after the aristocratic city rulers had left for Avignon to pay their respects to the new pope, Clement VI, a sudden antimagnatial revolution in Rome put the *popolo* regime of the Thirteen "Good Men" in power.[3] In the very wake of the baronial delegation to Avignon, they dispatched Cola as an ambassador to request (unsuccessfully) Clement's return to Rome and to press (successfully) for a Jubilee in 1350.[4] Cola's impact in Avignon varied: castigating the barons

---

1. Rome inside its ancient walls was, and is, divided into thirteen of these (dialect) *rioni* or (Latin) *regiones*.

2. Cola's family connections are examined in chapter 6.

3. *Popolo* politics and Cola's connections therewith are examined in chapter 5.

4. See H. Schmidinger, "Die antwort Clemens VI. an die Gesandtschaft der Stadt Rom vom Jahre 1343," *Miscellanea in onore di Monsignore Martino Giusti* (Vatican City, 1978), 2:342–50; "Die gesandte der staat Rom nach Avignon vom jahre 1342/3," *Romische Historische Mitteilungen* 21 (1979): 15–33.

for their ill-government in the past and their perpetual lawlessness, he impressed the audience with his rhetoric but incurred the anger of the Colonna and was dropped from court circles. In the meantime, the revolution at home failed and Cola's future looked far from secure. Somehow, nevertheless, he regained the favor of both the Colonna and the curia in general; scholars have suggested that his new acquaintance with Petrarch may have swung the balance. He requested and received appointment as Notary of the Roman Civic Chamber, supervising the income of Rome; a post subordinate only to the Chamberlain himself and the ruling Senators and judges of the City.

After his return to Rome, with the purse strings of the City at least partly in his hands, for the next three years Cola's animus against the Colonna had the opportunity to evolve from a personal vendetta into a political mission. This was, ultimately, to hasten his downfall, and in the short term it exposed him to attack: his attempts to criticize the current baronial Senate (of two) met with abuse: the Colonna chamberlain even slapped him in public. His threats that he would take over Rome and bring the lawless to justice were scorned by barons, but the restoration of justice, via a "popular" government similar to that of 1343, was high on Cola's agenda. During 1346, in the buildup to his own revolution, Cola's meetings with his conspirators produced a series of impressive public warnings. One day, up above the political and commercial heart of the city—the market below the senatorial palace on the Capitol—appeared a vast image, frescoed on the wall of the senatorial palace, which showed female personifications of the great empires of the world, drowned, and *Roma* under threat. It also portrayed the corrupt ranks of the rulers and administrators, being watched by an image of the apocalyptic Christ in judgment between Peter and Paul, the patron saints of Rome. Soon after, Cola held a public rally in the Lateran, where he illustrated and analyzed an ancient tablet describing the grant of supreme power from the Roman people to the emperor. He then brought home the urgent message regarding political stability by reminding Romans that their economy was in no fit state to withstand, let alone benefit from the influx of pilgrims expected in 1350 for the Jubilee. Shortly after, another great *pittura* appeared, this time above the busy fish market in front of the church of S. Angelo in Pescheria: similarly metaphorical, it represented the corrupt rulers of the Capitol image as dead or dying and *Roma,* although badly burned, being rescued from a blazing church by an armed angel as Peter and Paul looked on; a notice attached declared that the "time of great justice" was imminent. A further message appeared on the door of S. Giorgio in Velabro, that Romans would soon be restored to their ancient "Good Estate," *Buono Stato;* a term that Cola was to use throughout 1347 to describe his beneficial regime.

These events show Cola and his fellow conspirators putting the pieces in place for a coup, and indeed the very swift imposition of reforming statutes after his seizure of power suggests that the Tribunate had been worked out in advance in considerable legal, financial, and military detail. The conspirators, on May 20, 1347, used the opportunity of the baronial militia's absence from the City,[5] to lead a rival militia up from S. Angelo to the Capitol, and to seize power and announce the new Ordinances. By popular acclamation Cola and the papal Vicar, Raymond of Orvieto, were elected Rectors of the City; soon after Cola requested and received the title of Tribune. The barons of the *Destretto* (Rome's political dependent urban hinterland, or *contado*) and the judges of the City were all obliged to swear obedience to the regime. Those who did not—Giovanni di Vico, signore of Viterbo and hereditary Prefect of Rome, various Colonna, a Gaetani baron in the far south of Lazio, the Stefaneschi di Porto near Ostia, and, later, the Orsini of Marino—were ruthlessly hunted down and brought to heel (or executed) during the next months by the reformed militia of Cola's Ordinances. In the City, a new age of justice, as Cola declared, had certainly dawned; the new regime did, temporarily at least, provide peace on the streets, a viable climate for commerce, and a new public faith in the mechanics of the judicial system. Barons, monks, and commoners alike paid the penalties of theft and robbery, so that Rome was, for a short time, *Ye Solace of Pilgrimes* rather than the *spelunca latronum* (den of thieves) widely advertised by medieval writers.[6] Cola also introduced impressively successful measures to ensure both the income of the Camera Urbis and the grain supply; he let the populace participate in the splendor of the regime in a series of public triumphal processions throughout June and July. The dedication of his regime to the Holy Spirit as well as to the reestablishment of ancient Roman glory gave his rhetoric powerful sacral overtones in addition to nostalgic fervor.

---

5. They were marching to Corneto, up the Latian seaboard; the town had blocked Rome's grain supply, which happened regularly, until Cola reached an accord with the coastal towns.

6. C. A. Mills, ed., *Ye Solace of Pilgrimes: A Description of Rome, circa 1450 A.D. by John Capgrave, an Austin Friar of King's Lynn* (Oxford: Oxford University Press, 1911). For the *spelunca latronum* trope, see for example Giuseppe Porta, ed., *Matteo Villani. Cronica* (Parma: Ugo Guanda, 1995), 2:358–59, 411–12.

Once the City was safely becoming the *Buono Stato* of his rhetorical promises, Cola began a series of diplomatic initiatives, on three "rising" levels. The first of these zones of influence stretched across an area broadly coterminous with the Papal Patrimony, that is, beyond the *Destretto* to the boundaries of Lazio and into the southern parts of Umbria and Tuscany. The loyalty of this area was achieved quickly and efficiently. Second, he dispatched ambassadors beyond these boundaries to rulers of city-states in the remainder of the Italian peninsula. Thirdly, he sent communiqués to the rest of the princes of Christendom, among whom—as soon became clear—he ranked himself. By late summer, he had dropped Raymond of Orvieto as "co-Rector," and sat alone in visible splendor to hear embassies sent from the signori of the north and from the various factions then in competition for control of Naples. In the latter case, Cola claimed the authority, as ruler of Rome, to judge the case. He was also to claim the right to jurisdiction over the princes of the north, ordering the participants in the Hundred Years War to appear for arbitration, and summoning to Rome the rival claimants—Lewis of Bavaria and Charles of Bohemia—and the electors to the Holy Roman Empire.

He offered little challenge, however, in real terms, to the autonomy of the latter figures. His claim to jurisdiction over the cities of Italy was felt much more keenly, but as a policy met with limited success.[7] Though able to impose the authority of Rome on towns within and just beyond the *Destretto,* Cola faced a much greater challenge when it came to his restoration of what he chose to describe as *Italia Una* and the "ancient union" of Rome with the rest of the peninsula. This, as the representatives of Florence and Todi rightly surmised, was a thin smoke-screen for Roman hegemony. It was less than feasible, however, in terms of the mechanics of administration and lines of communication from Rome. Moreover, the intensely particularist historical development of the urban entities of Italy since the end of ancient Roman authority rendered such an ambitious project impossible. Cola clung, however, to the dream, despite the explicit rejection of his overtures by Florence and other important central Italian towns at the very time of his knighting and coronation in August.

During the same months, July and August 1347, Cola staged a series of spectacular performances and exhibitions of power. On the first day of August, he received his spurs. After a vigil in the Lateran, and bathing sacrilegiously in a relic, the baptismal basin of the emperor Constantine, he

---

7. Cola as an Italian *signore* in his own right is described in chapter 4.

was knighted as *Cavaliere dello Spirito Santo.* He followed the buckling-on of the sword with a grandiose ritual gesture signifying his inheritance of the imperial and holy mantle of Constantine, and went on to feast alone on a high table in the Lateran palace: a symbolic act reminiscent of the coronations of both emperors and popes.[8] On August 15 he completed the sequence of ceremonies with his own multiple coronation as Tribune, by six senior prelates of the City, in a ritual both evoking the splendor of the classical past and invoking the future protection of the Holy Spirit over the new earthly government of Rome.

Cola's regime, however, swiftly slipped from these empyrean heights. He had begun to incur the suspicion, and gradually earned the wrath, of Pope Clement at Avignon. Snubbing the new Papal Legate in October did not assist Cola's case, and the downturn in Cola's fortunes around now may be partly attributed to the attempts by Clement to persuade the towns and barons of the *Destretto,* and the populace of the City, to abandon the Tribune. He was finally excommunicated at the end of the year.

Meanwhile, during the autumn, Cola's attempts to hold together an increasingly fragile alliance of interests led to an event with unfortunate ramifications, both ideological and practical, for his regime. He imprisoned the most dangerous barons overnight and threatened to execute them, but in the morning allowed himself to be persuaded by a less radical group of advisers that he should release them and restore them to municipal office. Not only did this expose a central flaw in Cola's base of support, it also implied chronic indecision.[9] Crucially it permitted a number of barons, particularly the Orsini of Marino and the Colonna of Palestrina, to escape to their strongholds and plan military raids on the City.

Already by September the expense and the never-ending military campaigns demanded by Cola's judicial and antimagnatial policies were straining the resources he had accumulated. Orsini Marino was taken during October, but at great cost, while the Colonna mustered for an attack on the City itself. This came on November 20; the Colonna and their allies came down the Via Tiburtina and grouped at S. Lorenzo *fuori le Mura,* while the populace, and Cola's new militia, fortified the Porta S. Lorenzo. The defenders, in the event, won an overwhelming victory and slaughtered a great list of barons. Reading between lines of the Chronicler's account, it seems that the victory was achieved despite Cola's vacillation rather than with his intrepid leadership. This did not stop him claiming the glory, how-

---

8. And discussed more fully in chapter 1.
9. The episode is discussed in chapter 5.

ever, and, in an ill-chosen gesture, he dubbed his son *Cavaliere della Vittoria* in the blood of the Colonna fallen. This act disgusted his own knights and lost him their support.

The Chronicler's account describes Cola's swift descent into political isolation during the next three weeks, making the claim that he had become one of the very tyrants his regime had been designed to suppress. A number of disruptive factors coincided in early December to undermine the remaining shreds of Cola's confidence: the presence of the Papal Legate, agitating against him in the City's council; the continued hostilities of the Colonna, whose power he had damaged but not destroyed; their cooperation with the powerful Savelli, who decided to enter the fray; and the distracting activities of a Neapolitan baron in exile, Giovanni Pipino. Pipino's men killed one of Cola's constables in a skirmish at the barricades around the Colonna zone in Rome.[10] The bells tolled for the Tribune, as the Chronicler tells us; Cola promptly fled into the arms of Orsini allies in the Castel S. Angelo.

The events before and during 1347, Cola's period of supreme power in Rome, are well known and readily accessible through the account of his Chronicler. But, generally speaking, historians, following the Chronicler's lead, have spent much less time considering the vicissitudes of Cola's life between the end of his Tribunate and his death, after a second period in power, on October 8, 1354.[11] Certainly the Tribunate presents a temptingly glittering and mysterious subject for analysis. However, a framework of events after 1347 is required in order to locate the further geographical—and ideological—movements of the erstwhile Tribune.

After making his so-called (but not very) triumphal descent from power in December 1347, Cola di Rienzo began his wilderness years. For a few months he hid in the Castel S. Angelo, stronghold of one branch of the Orsini clan that had previously supported his rule. Using this Roman fortress as his base of operations, Cola began negotiations with Lewis of Hungary, who had arrived in central Italy to avenge the murder of his brother Andrew, former consort of Queen Joanna of Naples. These negotiations may have involved discussions with regard to the loan of Lewis's mercenaries, to put Cola back in power in Rome. However, the Hungarians retreated swiftly in the face of the plague of 1348, leaving Cola to face the wrath of Joanna, a former ally. Then it seems that the money that Cola

---

10. Roughly coterminous with the modern *rione* Colonna.

11. Even less again, on the seven years between Petrarch's coronation on the Capitol in 1341 and Cola's in the Lateran in 1347.

raised for the troops was stolen by his brother.[12] He returned to the safety of the Castel S. Angelo.

It appears, however, that the castellans—an uncle and nephew who had held office in Cola's government—were, by the first months of 1348, planning the sale of Cola to his enemies. Fortunately for Cola—he was subsequently to cite this as evidence of God's support for his continued venture—both barons died of plague in September 1348. They had received rival offers for Cola's skin from the Papal Legate and their kinsmen, the Orsini of Marino, but had not yet decided to whom they would betray the ex-Tribune.

The sequence of events is not clear, but Cola may then have spent time—at least until early 1349—on the island of Ponza; he then fled rising Inquisitorial pressure by disappearing into the Monti di Maiella (the other side of Abruzzo, almost the opposite side of the peninsula to Rome).[13] Here he joined an eremitic, possibly "Celestinian" community living in isolation and refuge from persecution. A visit to the City in the Jubilee Year, and an attempt to ambush him, reinforced his decision to retreat from this-worldly strife. Having assumed a new identity, he was therefore astounded to be greeted by one Fra Michele, or Angelo, di Monte Volcano who knew Cola's real name, his political background, and he claimed, the purpose of Cola's life.

"Fra Angelo" told him that a heavenly voice had spoken: Cola had done enough penance in the wilderness. God had a new mission for Cola, which was all there in Fra Angelo's favorite prophetic text, the so-called Angelic Oracle of Cyril. Now identified as the future imperial counselor in Rome, Cola was, on divine authority, to seek the assistance of the emperor and an "angelic Pope"[14] to bring off the long prophesied and now imminent reform of the world order.

In the summer of 1350 Cola traveled north to the court of the emperor elect, Charles of Bohemia, at Prague. He did not reveal his identity at first, simply announcing publicly that the plague and earthquakes currently devastating Italy were precursors to the final expression of divine wrath,

---

12. Burdach and Piur, *Briefwechsel,* vol. 2, *Kritische Darstellung der Quellung zur Geschichte Rienzos* (1928), 147.

13. This account is reconstructed tentatively from Cola's own letters between 1350 and 1354 (III:49–80), contemporary and retrospective, and compared against Burdach and Piur, *Darstellung,* 148–49.

14. See chapter 2 on the *pastor angelicus,* usually translated as Angelic Pope (though occasionally the term *pastor* is used, in medieval prophecy, to denote a mysterious "leader" or "shepherd").

heralding the punishment of the corrupted Church and its leadership, and the imminent advent of the Age of the Spirit. The new pope, a "pious man," would be persecuted at first; but with the worldly treasures of the Church, he and the emperor would erect a new temple to the Holy Spirit in Rome, where Christians, Jews, and pagans alike would come to worship.

Charles soon uncovered the ex-Tribune's identity, but assured Cola that he would not be punished for the imperial presumptions of the Tribunate. Cola announced that Rome and all Italy would welcome the emperor with open arms. He also requested Charles to consent to his own reinstatement, now as regent, in Rome, claiming that all lay rectors who controlled Rome *imperio non vacante,* without Charles's permission, were "adulterers."

Had Cola pronounced all this to Lewis the Bavarian's court at Monaco, with its outlaw theologians and rebel Franciscans, he might have met with more sympathy and enthusiasm. The Prague court, however, where even the grave young emperor—pious, orthodox, and a former pupil of Clement VI—was well versed in theology, listened carefully, but more critically. The Chronicler claims that "Cola stunned these Germans." The link, however, between Cola's political attack on the moral bankruptcy of the Avignon curia, and the radical ideas of the Spirituals, was all too heretically obvious. Only recently had Ockham at Monaco violently attacked Charles's imperial election. For the Bohemian king it could not have been worth jeopardizing relations with Avignon for an unrealistic venture proposed by an excommunicate rabble-rouser. Charles had Cola repeat his prophetic plans before prelates and theologians. A brief interrogation yielded the court's decision that Cola's opinions were indeed heretical; a message was sent to Avignon, and Cola was imprisoned. Clement replied urgently, first with instructions to use "articles" enclosed in his communiqué as the basis for an inquisition, then to send Cola to Avignon.[15]

Charles, however, currently in the middle of delicate diplomatic negotiations with Avignon over other contested issues, retained Cola as a useful political pawn. Cola was confident, at first, that this was merely one of the temporary afflictions predicted on the silver tablets of the Cyril Oracle. After September 14, 1350—the date of his proposed triumphal return to Jubilee Rome—passed, however, with no indication of the end of this

---

15. IV:53, 25; IV:55, 32; IV:56, 11.

tribulation, Cola started to employ his persuasive capacities in letters both to Charles and to the Prague archbishop, Ernst von Pardubitz. His first letter, to the emperor, was confident in tone, relating the story of his supposed imperial parentage as public knowledge in Rome, and describing the homage offered him by other rulers. He described his role in the Holy Roman Empire as parallel to that of St. Francis, buttress of the tottering Church.[16]

Charles's response was a long and clever sermon that avoided the subject of Rome, emphasizing instead a biblical theme of rebuttal, and encouraging Cola to give up his unorthodox beliefs. Cola replied vehemently in letters addressed to Ernst and to Charles respectively, which subsequently circulated in the Prague chancery under the titles "The true manifesto of the Tribune against matters schismatic and erroneous," and "The Tribune's oration in reply to Caesar on the eloquence of charity."[17] These urged Charles to reconsider the prospect of an Italy united and loyal to him by Pentecost, the Feast of the Holy Spirit, 1351, and pictured him entering Rome in triumph alongside the twin consort of "widowed" Rome, the pope. Cola's "instruction" of the emperor continued with a contrast between the life of the true disciples of Francis and the worldliness of the Avignon curia: had Francis been among contemporaries, Cola claimed, he would be ridiculed as a "fantastical, beastlike idiot"[18] by the corrupt and worldly clergy.

Charles did not reply to this last impassioned plea. Instead, he handed over the case to his archbishop for investigation. Ernst was, in fact, as much a political as an ecclesiastical adviser to Charles and was familiar with Italian politics, having studied canon law at Padua and Bologna. He had begun the process of reform of the Bohemian church in 1349 and was not so rigorous as Avignon in the punishment of popular preaching on reform. He therefore responded less harshly to Cola's critique of the contemporary church. Ernst nonetheless condemned Cola for his past presumptions. However, he concluded with the famous statement of Gameliel on the legitimacy of prophecy:[19] if these opinions really had come from

---

16. III:50, 355–62; III:58, 201.

17. III:57, III:58: the titles appear in the earliest manuscript of Cola's letters, a late-fourteenth—century Bohemian chancery formulary, now at B.A.V. Vat. Lat. 12503.

18. III:58, 91.

19. III:61, 43–46; from Acts 5:38 (biblical references are from KJV unless otherwise indicated).

God, men could do little to prevent the truth from being spread; a compliment to Cola, since by analogy it placed Ernst and the Prague court in the role of the Sadducees and Pharisees persecuting the preaching apostles.

Cola was, nonetheless, not to be liberated. In early September 1350 he had been moved to the fortress of Raudnitz; he only gradually realized the hopelessness of his situation. He refused to take back his prophetic opinions, but drew attention to the fact that before abdicating in Rome he had publicly withdrawn his summonses to the emperor, and put off his more pretentious titles. He argued that he had already repented the sins now imputed to him. Cola's judge was God and not the archbishop; God who had commissioned him to rule Rome.[20]

Despite his bravado, Cola's spirits sagged. In late September a letter to Fra Michele (or Angelo) described the wreck of the mission, and the likelihood of his execution or extradition to Avignon. He begged the hermit to guard his son, and to oversee the distribution of his estate and his library. If he failed to return by the end of the year, Michele was to inform Cola's supporters in Rome that they and the Roman consuls should choose his successor.[21]

During winter Cola slid into apparent depression. Ernst, meanwhile, left for Avignon in January 1351, to discuss details of Charles's visit to Rome for his coronation (he had no plans to remain there in power, of course). The trip was less than successful, possibly due to the continued possession of the Tribune by the emperor. As the envoys left to return to Prague, Clement gave them a letter to Charles, demanding that Cola be sent to Avignon forthwith. However, Charles then learned of ongoing negotiations between Clement, the Florentines, and the Visconti, who were holding up his imperial coronation arrangements; Cola was retained, still under guard.

During these bitter northern months, Cola's dreams and prophecies were eclipsed by the harsh circumstances of his situation. He came to prefer the prospect of death to slow deterioration and seems to have had the scales drop from his eyes. In spring 1351 Cola described himself scathingly to Johan von Neumarkt, the imperial chancellor, as a "dreamer" *(sompniator)*.[22] Charles IV promptly recommenced correspondence with the ex-

---

20. III:60, III:62, especially III:63.

21. III:64, 165–74. The Roman People did act on this, in effect, selecting Giovanni Cerroni in 1351, then Francesco Baroncelli in 1352; see chapter 4.

22. III:68, 2–3.

Tribune, granting Cola a backhanded honor: he had Cola exercise his rhetorical talents on a written response[23] to Petrarch's demand, that the emperor reinstate the glory of the Empire by making his permanent residence in Rome. This humbled Cola by forcing him to explain how unwise and unrealistic it would be for the German emperor to reside in Rome, albeit the city that was nominally the seat of his empire. Charles had declared, to Cola's indignation, that the ancient Roman Empire would never be reconstituted except by a miracle from God;[24] but now Cola was being obliged to promote that very line.

After this, the Bohemians showed no further interest in prosecuting Cola's heresies. In spring 1351, Cola backtracked on his accusations of Clement VI himself, merely admitting to having castigated corruption in the curia. He claimed his "sins" stemmed from too great a love of the Roman People, whose sufferings had been ignored in Avignon. Cola, like the Romans themselves, he begged, deserved pity and exoneration. Both pope and emperor had rejected him and would not allow him to disappear to Jerusalem; or even go on to Avignon, perhaps to his death, but where he could at least make a public defense.[25]

Months later Charles IV finally sent Cola into the custody of Avignon. The Chronicler described Cola's journey from Prague in glowing terms, with a triumphant entry to Avignon; the reality was better assessed by Petrarch.[26] He described the former glory of the Tribune of Rome—whom he, Petrarch, had heralded as the Prince of the Romans—and Cola's present disgrace, in Cicero's ponderous terms: "He was being sent to the Roman Pontiff by the King of the Romans! Strange traffic indeed . . . *O tempora, o mores.*"

By now Cola was prepared, on the surface at least, to prove his orthodoxy at all costs. When a secret message from Fra Angelo—that is, Fra Michele—was smuggled to him, Cola declared publicly that Michele was an *angelus sathanicus* who had "inebriated him with apples of temptation."[27] Cola was not executed, but remained—silenced, of course—in the darkest prison available to Clement VI, who was presumably sick of the Tribune's all-too-persuasive rhetoric.

23. III:71.

24. III:50, 353–54.

25. III:63, III:64.

26. *Familiari,* 13.6, August 10, 1352; Mario E. Cosenza, *Petrarch: The Revolution of Cola di Rienzo* (1913; reprint, New York: Italica Press, 1986), 187.

27. III:73, 19–20.

Clement VI died in the following year, 1352, however, and his successor, Innocent VI, was of a rather different disposition; ascetic but energetic, committed to clerical reform and to peace in the papal territories around Rome. To combat the anarchy in the City and *Destretto* of Rome, he appointed as Legate the Spanish cardinal Gil d'Albornoz, a soldier-priest of the Iberian *Reconquista* with, therefore, considerable experience of recovering Church lands. Innocent was not, however, immune to Cola's rhetoric. Cola presumably had to abjure, fully and openly, all his heterodox opinions and activities before gaining papal absolution, and the reversal of his excommunication. This was a lengthy process, which may explain why Cola was still in prison until September 1353. But once released, Cola was awarded yet another new role in Rome: both his rehabilitation and his expendability[28] were reflected in his appointment as Papal Senator.

The post was given partly at the request of an envoy from the *Populus Romanus,* and partly following a report from the Papal Nuncio on the terrible conditions in the City. These conditions were particularly due to the Prefect Giovanni di Vico, Cola's old enemy, who had seized two-thirds of the *Destretto* and was aiming for control of Rome. The only opposition available to the Church, before Albornoz, had been the expensive *condottiere* Fra Moreale.

Cola was sent off in the wake of Albornoz in late 1353, although a further popular revolution in Rome, combined with Albornoz's reluctance to grant Cola funds, prevented Cola's official reinstatement at the head of the City until August 1354. According to papal pay-records, Cola saw service as a knight in the army of the Legate from April to July 1354: he commanded a company against di Vico in May under the leadership of Giovanni Conti of Valmontone.[29] This military service may have eased Albornoz's doubts; but in any case, Cola managed to raise the cash for the attempt by his own rhetorical devices.[30]

Cola's return to Rome was pulled off in considerable style, as Albornoz reported to Innocent. In a speech on the Capitol, Cola told the crowd that he was like Nebuchadnezzar, divinely returned to power as a vassal of the true Lord, after six years of exile and humiliation. However, in the end, his

---

28. Legates and Senators alike had died in the Roman tumult since Cola's abdication.

29. Great-nephew of Bishop Ildebrandino Conti of Valmontone, who may have been patron of the Roman Chronicler (see chap. 4). Evidence of Cola's military service is presented in Burdach and Piur, *Briefwechsel,* 5:41–43.

30. See Wright, *Life,* 131–33 for Cola's rather devious behavior.

new regime lasted less than six weeks. Both a new campaign against the Palestrina Colonna for their failure to arrive and pay homage, and the execution of Fra Moreale for threatening to seize Rome, demonstrate the lack of security Cola felt (probably not without reason).[31] He never regained the broad range of support he had enjoyed in 1347. When, in October, in order to pay his troops, Cola instigated extra wine and salt taxes, he was felled by a riotous mob, incited by agitation from enemy barons and led by hostile individuals whose identity is discussed in chapter 6; his body was torn to pieces and burned, and Rome, at least for the moment, slid back into the anarchy for which it was so famous among contemporaries.

The events of Cola's life and career, however, do not explain his success in the short term, nor his personal failure to reform the City within his lifetime. To appreciate the full significance of Cola's "mission" we must also understand the anomaly that was, and still is, the city of Rome. We will begin our study by examining the past and the future of the *Caput Orbis* as these were imagined by Cola and in contemporary Roman cultural circles; in the latter half of the book we will see how these perceived roles of Rome meshed with real events in Rome both before and after his Tribunate.

---

31. O. Coccanari, "Cola di Rienzo e la congiura di Fra Moriale," *Bolletino di Tivoli e regione* 18 (1936): 2693–95.

Chapter 1

The *Sacra Res Publica:* Antiquity and Apotheosis in the City of Rome

Cola di Rienzo's political journey began with the dream of resurrecting the ancient classical glory of Rome at the center of a world empire, within its postclassical global role as capital city of Christendom. A powerful dream and a passionate ideal indeed, but in Rome itself the presence of the past, in the fourteenth century, still had—as indeed it retains today—tremendous power. However, the fourteenth-century reality was somewhat different, and so were the actual policies Cola put into place, for all the grandeur of his dream. The real action he took was less globally ambitious, and even that localized campaign—the restoration of civic autonomy, civil authority, and economic security across a small zone of central Italy—was not to be easily achieved. And yet while operating on a lower level in the real world, he never gave up the rhetoric of the classical global dream.

This fascinating dissonance runs right through the career of the Tribune. What Cola thought—or said—he was doing and what he managed to do were far from the same thing; a division which is echoed by the separation of this study into two parts. There survive no "mission statements"—overall policy documents—for Cola's period in power; and having failed in the attempt to bring about a restoration of the past glory of Rome, the motivation cannot be deduced from the success of the result: one may only reconstruct Cola's perspective on, and use of, Rome's great past from his own statements, set against the evidence of influences from the perceived past upon his rhetoric, his self-presentation and his governmental praxis.

What was the past that Cola saw, then, from the perspective of the Trecento? Where did Cola claim to find (and where did he really find) his precedents, his sources, and his imagery for the so-called Holy Roman Republic? The ancient Republic of Cato and Cicero; the classical Empire of the Julio-Claudians; the Christian Roman world of Byzantium? The Holy Roman Empire of Charlemagne and Leo, the less-than-holy enterprises of Barbarossa and the Germanic kings? This chapter will examine Cola's apparent reliance on political models, literary forms and legal precedents of the ancient world, mediated as these were, inevitably, through later readings of their meaning, and filtered through an ideal, even an idyll, of the past.

The People's Liberator: "I burn with a passion as great for the Republic as for the Empire, if not greater"

Writing of his regime and his position in 1347, Cola tried later to convince his readers that the aim had been purely to restore the "republic" of Rome. Of course, exactly the same claim was made of and by Rome's first emperor, Augustus. The letter in which Cola made this assertion was addressed to a "genuine" imperial figure, the Holy Roman Emperor Charles IV: no wonder, then, Cola was stressing his own nonimperial ambitions. Yet it is true that the first title Cola took, upon seizing the reins of power on May 20, 1347, was "Liberator of the Republic," and he followed it up with the announcement of his new role as "tribune," an ancient military-political office, nominally representative of "the people." It was precisely the kind of slightly obscure, grand-sounding quasi-juridical title that would back up Cola's typically demagogic and antimagnatial rhetoric throughout his period in power. The titles, and the powers these carried, fed Cola's concept of the Republic restored: but from where did these titles and this concept derive?

The overwhelming authority of Livy's history of ancient Rome, and the dry, encyclopedic works of Valerius Maximus on classical forms and norms, were Cola's main literary touchstones, according to his Chronicler.[1] Cola's later letters demonstrate an impressive and wide-ranging knowledge of the classical and patristic heritage of the later medieval period, containing references to Cicero and Plato, Livy, Sallust, Lucan, Vergil, Valerius Maximus, Seneca, Symmachus, Macrobius, Jerome,

---

1. Wright, *Life*, 31.

Gregory, Augustine, Justinian, and Boethius, with allusions to Juvenal, Persius, and Prudentius.[2] When the *Populus Romanus* first encountered Cola, in 1343, it was in a jubilant public letter, proclaiming the pope's promise (empty, as it happened) to return to Rome, comparing Clement VI to the heroes of the ancient Republic:

> For what Scipio, what Caesar, what Metellus, Marcellus, Fabius— names of ancient renown, whom we deem worthy of unperishable memory as liberators of their country. . . .—which of them ever adorned their country with so much glory?[3]

The notion of liberator here is clearly associated with Rome before the imposition of the Julio-Claudian dynasty. Another apparently republican statement lurks in a letter to a friend in Avignon in 1347, shortly after his takeover of administrative control of Rome, where Cola compared himself to Livy's classical republican hero Cincinnatus, called from the plough to govern Rome briefly, and keen to return to the fields once the crisis was averted.[4] By 1350 he had built up a significant library that also consisted of many postclassical and ecclesiastical books. But he was not alone: though it was not Montecassino, neither was Rome the wasteland declared in humanist rhetoric.[5]

In fact, mid-Trecento Rome also had its quota of scholars and thinkers (though obliged to share many of them with Avignon), all of whom discussed ardently the Roman past. Cola was not so exceptional as Petrarch's complaint, "Who knows Rome less well than the Romans?" would have us believe.[6] Cola's near-contemporary Giovanni Cavallini, for example, divided his time between Avignon and Rome and composed his encyclo-

---

2. Burdach and Piur, *Briefwechsel,* 5:322; III:64, 126.

3. Ibid., III:2, 57–62.

4. III:18, 126; see also III:28, 117–20. Also in Dante, *Convivio,* 4:5 (*Convivio* and *Monarchia* references are from *Opere Minori,* ed. Domenico de Robertis and Gianfranco Contini [Milan: R. Ricciardi, 1984]), and in Petrarch's *De Viris Illustribus* (see Luigi Razzolini, *Petrarca: Vite degli Uomini Illustri* [Bologna, 1874], 1:57–58).

5. Cola, nonetheless, was equally capable of resorting to the *spelunca latronum* trope (e.g. III:18, 26). There was a thriving library tradition and book trade in Rome even before 1400: see Massimo Miglio, "Cortesia romana," in *Alle origini della nuova Roma. Martin V (1417–1431),* ed. Maria Chiabò et al. (Rome: Istituto Storico Italiano per il Medio Evo, 1992), esp. 321 n. 42.

6. Massimo Miglio offers a useful discussion of the points of reference of Trecento Roman high culture: "Et rerum facta est pulcherrima Roma," in *Per la Storia del Trecento a Roma,* vol. 1 of *Scritture, Scrittori e Storia* (Rome: Vecchiarelli, 1991), 11–53.

pedic treatise on ancient Roman culture, *Polistoria,* on the joint bases of firsthand knowledge of Roman topography and classical authors, particularly Valerius Maximus.[7] Cavallini provided innumerable reflections on the Roman cultural points of reference of his day, and operates as an important gauge of the intellectual sphere in which Cola moved.[8] The standard of intellectual life in Rome and its environs is also evident in the work of the Roman Chronicler,[9] who may have hovered upon the fringes of Petrarch's own circle of acquaintance.[10] The range of references in this vernacular account[11] is easily as wide as that of Cola's own correspondence and demonstrates a particular attachment to Livy.[12]

It is also recorded that at the height of his career in municipal office, after 1343, Cola attended banquets with Giovanni Colonna;[13] but certainly he knew the elder as well as the younger "Janni." The elder Giovanni was a patron and correspondent of Petrarch and mentor and companion to the poet during Petrarch's visit to Rome in 1337.[14] Giovanni

---

7. *Polistoria* is supposed to have been composed around 1345–47, although the absence of references to Cola cannot be said to provide a secure *terminus ante quem:* Marc A. Laureys, "An Edition and Study of Giovanni Cavallini's *Polistoria de virtutibus et dotibus Romanorum,*" Ph.D. diss., Harvard University, 1992, 29, 57–58 (now published as *Iohannes Caballini de Cerronibus Polistoria de virtutibus et dotibus Romanorum* [Stuttgart: Teubner, 1995]).

8. There is no suggestion of an intellectual "circle," however, contra Enrico Guidoni, "Roma e l'urbanistica del Trecento," in *Storia dell'arte italiana. Dal Medioevo al Novecento,* vol. 1, *Dal Medioevo al Quattrocento,* ed. Federigo Zeri (Turin: Einaudi, 1983): 309–83 (see also Isa Lori-Sanfilippo, "Roma nel XIV secolo. Riflessioni in margine alla lettura di due saggi usciti nella storia dell'arte italiana Einaudi," *Bulletino dell' Istituto Storico Italiano per il Medio Evo* 91 [1984]: 281–316 and Laureys, "Giovanni Cavallini's *Polistoria,*" 47).

9. See Gianfranco Contini, "Invito a un capolavoro," *Letteratura* 4 (1940): 3–6; Miglio, "Et rerum facta est"; Gustav Seibt, *Anonimo Romano: Geschichtsschreibung in Rom an der Schwelle zur Renaissance* (Stuttgart: Klett-Cotta, 1992), 47–49, 66–84.

10. See chapter 4, and especially Giuseppe Billanovich, "Come nacque un capolavoro: La 'cronica' del non più Anonimo Romano," *Rendiconti dell'Accademia Nazionale dei Lincei,* 9th ser., 6 (1995): 195–211.

11. With Latin interjections, possibly the result of the unfinished translation of the Chronicle from its Latin version.

12. The Chronicler describes Cola as "nutricato de latte de eloquenzia" by such authors as Livy, Seneca, and Cicero (Wright, *Life,* 31; *ARC,* 104). Cola used an identical phrase: "ex . . . ipsius lacteo eloquencie fonte manantis Titi Livii, Tullii quidem et Senece" at III:58, 420–21. For ancient and Trecento Roman precedents, see Miglio, "Et rerum facta est," 41–43, citing Giuseppe Billanovich, "Gli umanisti e le chronache medioevale. I: *Liber Pontificialis,* le *Decadi* di Tito Livio e il primo umanesimo a Roma," in *Italia Medioevale e Umanistica* 1 (1958): 123.

13. Wright, *Life,* 35.

14. The younger "Janni," grandson of the cardinal, was an early colleague and later sworn enemy of Cola, and also "one of the most clever and magnificent men of Rome" (Wright, *Life,* 35).

was also cardinal-deacon of S. Angelo, the forcing-ground of the revolution in 1347, and is known to have spent most of the last years of his life in or around Rome.[15] Giovanni certainly enjoyed a high profile within the intellectual landscape of mid-Trecento Rome: he produced a De Viris Illustribus in Avignon in the 1330s, and then a universal history, Mare Historiarum.[16]

Other unknown Roman contemporaries who may have been more actively associated or acquainted with the Tribune showed off their classical erudition: the author of a letter of 1343, contemporary with Cola's own cited above, announced Clement's decision to allow a Jubilee with the "Astraea" imagery of Vergil's Fourth Eclogue.[17] There is further evidence of the cultural standards maintained by certain of Cola's political associates: one of his ambassadors, Pandolfuccio di Guido dei Franchi, addressed the Florentines in two speeches full of Dantean language;[18] another, Francesco dei Baroncelli, paraphrased Petrarch's canzone VI.5 in his appeal.[19] Another colleague and fellow notary, one of Cola's protonotaries in 1347, Cecco (short for "Francesco") Rosani, was to become a

15. 1338–48, according to Georg Waitz, ed., Giovanni Colonna: Mare Historiarum, Monumenta Germaniae Historiae (Scriptores), vol. 24 (Leipzig, 1879), 262–84, which confirms Cola's own account at III:57, 859–76.

16. The cardinal never once mentioned Cola, nor indeed contemporary Rome, although it was Colonna restoration (after withdrawal) of favor in Avignon that gained Cola his civic post in 1343 (Wright, Life, 32). Cola later claimed that God and the archangel Michael avenged him for Giovanni's accusations in 1347 of heresy: allowing him to slaughter Giovanni's family on November 20, 1347, thereby causing the cardinal's near-immediate death, following a bout of fury-induced violence (III:57, 875–76).

17. Burdach's argument for Cola's authorship of III:1 was overwhelmingly rejected in Fedele's review in 1914 ("Konrad Burdach und Paul Piur," 388–93), and also by Monike-Beate Juhar, "Der Romgedanke bei Cola di Rienzo," Ph.D. diss., Kiel University, 1977, 17. Cola uses the same Vergilian imagery in 1350 (III:70, 265), but the tag was circulating widely and may be found at Dante, Purgatorio, 22.70–72 (the version of the Divine Comedy used throughout is the three-volume Temple Classics edition-translation of 1900; reprint, London: J. M. Dent and Sons, 1924); at Monarchia, I.13; and in his letter to Emperor Henry VII (Paget Toynbee, ed., Dantis Alagheris Epistolae [Oxford: Clarendon Press, 1920], 101). There are similar evocations of the Saturnian Golden Age in Petrarch's sonnet 106 (G. Mestica, Le Rime di Francesco Petrarca [Florence, 1896], 210–11); in Seniles, VI.8 and XV.3 (Aldo S. Bernardo, Saul Levin, and Reta Bernardo, eds., Francis Petrarch: Letters of Old Age (Rerum Senilium Libri) [Baltimore: Johns Hopkins University Press, 1992], 1:211, 2:562); and in his Invettiva (Guido Martellotti et al., eds., "Petrarca: Invettiva contro un uomo di alta condizione ma senza dottrine e senza virtù," in Petrarca: Prose [Verona: Ricciardi, 1955], 702).

18. IV:4, 30; in IV:5, 7–11 Pandolfuccio paraphrased a story used by Dante in his letter to Henry VII (see Toynbee, Dantis Alagheris Epistolae, 87–106), originally from Lucan, Pharsalia, ed. R. Mayer (Warminster: Aris and Phillips, 1981), I, 280.

19. IV:4, 39–49.

friend and correspondent of Salutati.[20] Finally, an anonymous letter of 1354, composed by a open supporter of the regime, bemoaned Cola's untimely death and the fickleness of the Roman mob, in the rhetoric of the classical funeral oration, and cited Vergil, Lucan, and Seneca.[21]

The civic institution with which knowledge of the past might best have been associated, that is, the Roman Studium, founded by Boniface, is usually thought to have been in decline during the fourteenth century.[22] There is, however, evidence for its continued existence in the civic statutes of 1363, which restate emphatically the importance of the *Studium generalis* by confirming salaried positions for *doctores* to teach law, grammar, and medicine.[23] However, these posts already existed: Cola had himself sponsored the appointment of one of his diplomats, Giovanni dei Giudici, for a similar position in 1347.[24] In its award, Clement VI referred to the "Studium that flourishes in the City."[25] Was Cola, described by the Chronicler as a *buon grammatico, megliore rettorico,* and *autorista buono,* also an alumnus?[26] He certainly kept up his scholarly interests, even while pursuing his professional career. While acting as Notary of the Camera Urbis between 1344 and 1347, "Spurning all other studies, I gave my attention entirely to the reading of the deeds of the ancient empire and to the memory of those most virtuous men."[27]

---

20. IV:17B, 14–15. His relationship with Cola's regime is described in more detail in chapter 6.

21. IV:75.

22. See David Chambers, "*Studium Urbis* and *Gabella Studii:* The University of Rome in the Fifteenth Century," in *Cultural Aspects of the Italian Renaissance,* ed. Cecil H. Clough (Manchester: Manchester University Press, 1976), 68–110; Gemma Puscheddu, "La fondazione dell'Universitaria di Roma," in *Roma e lo Studium Urbis: Spazio Urbana e Cultura dal Quattro al Seicento,* ed. Giovanni Cherubini (Rome: Quasar, 1989), 11–15.

23. Camillo Re, *Statuti della citta di Roma dal secolo XIV* (Rome, 1880), 244–46; book III, chapter 87 (= III:87). Noted by Carla Frova and Massimo Miglio, "*Studium Urbis* e *Studium Curiae* nel Trecento e nel Quattrocento: Linee di politica culturale," in *Roma e lo Studium Urbis: Spazio Urbana e Cultura dal Quattro al Seicento. Atti del convegno. Roma, 7–10 giugno 1989,* ed. Paolo Cherubini (Rome: Istituto Storico per il Medio Evo, 1992), 26–39.

24. Giovanni dei Giudici is discussed further in chapter 6.

25. Noted by Burdach and Piur, *Briefwechsel,* 5:19.

26. Porta, *Anonimo Romano: Cronica,* 104. Miglio, "Et rerum facta est," 41, notes these as standard terms of reference for a university lecturer (they are also used of Dante by Giovanni Villani). At III:74, 9–11, dedicated to an unknown Avignon prelate, Cola wrote of the "historical rhymes" he was about to compose. Petrarch was mistaken to scoff (*De Rebus Familiaris,* XIII.6: Cosenza, *Petrarch,* 191–92); Cola may well also have composed the *volgare* rhyming verses of the public allegories of 1346–47.

27. III:50, 183–85.

Were these virtuous men ancient republican heroes, however, or classical emperors, by 1347? His Cincinnatus reference also defines the republic only by omission, or antithetically: that is, the fact that a republic only really exists when a dictator does not rule it. This is very telling: more Caesar than Brutus. In fact, it was Dante and his emperor who seemed to offer Cola a more compelling model than Petrarch's republican hero, as we will see below.

Rome's civic authority in 1347 revolved around Cola's own role, and he did not elaborate on his idea of what made a, or the, republic. In fact, the Republic Cola organized and ran was quite clearly not a hark-back to the ancient world; rather it owed its governmental structures and its administrative practices to that powerful tradition of communal autonomy that developed in cities across the Italian peninsula—confusingly, often referred to as city-republics and ruled by "consuls"—after the twelfth century (this type of republic was inevitably less successful in Rome because of its peculiar domination by papal-baronial and papal-imperial politics, described in the introduction to part 2). The contrast between Cola's new Republic and Petrarch's reform proposals of 1351,[28] which offered Rome an idealized blueprint for a new republican constitution based on the moral quality of ancient *virtus,* was the difference between pragmatic politics and academic rhetoric.

Indeed, the "concept" of republic and much of the apparent classical metaphor in Cola's run-up to and pursuance of power is more evident, we can see, in the language of his supporters and commentators than in Cola's own words. Classical references abound in the later letters—in his debates in 1350 with the worthies of the imperial court at Prague in particular—but references to classical authors overall, and particularly the Republican past, are lacking for the period of power itself in 1347. Cola can be said to have coasted along the surface of a new interest in the past, deriving political benefits from new cultural trends in the *studia humanitatis.* Rather than participating in new humanistic discourses, however, Cola was busy welding all these disparate ideological elements into a working nexus behind what was mostly an impression, a facade of the authority of antiquity. Cola's classical powers were not entirely illusory, as we will see, but he attempted to cast the legitimating aura of antiquity around his regime as much through rhetorical and aesthetic impression as through real restoration. As to the precise ideological details of his regime, Cola was

---

28. *Familiari,* 11:16–17 (Cosenza, *Petrarch,* 155–70).

not essentially loyal to one political philosophy or another, ancient or contemporary.

Cola's selections from the sources, in fact, ranged well beyond the world of classicizing, elite culture. His plebeian origins exposed him to the very rich urban mythology and popular legends of medieval Rome.[29] His public performances clearly relied on visual imagery familiar to the broadest conceivable audience. The literary and dramatic manifestations of ancient Rome were well known and loved: the Chronicler notes that, alongside his classical authors, the young Cola loved to hear *le magnificentie de Julio Cesare;* and that while in prison in 1350, Cola had with him his Livy, the Bible, but also his medieval *Storie de Roma.*[30] The *Magnificentie* is identifiable as an early fourteenth-century Italian text, the *Fatti di Cesare,* a version of the thirteenth-century French "best-seller" *Li Fet des Romains.*[31] The *Storie,* which circulated widely in both Latin and Romanesco versions,[32] was a "universal history" compiled in the late twelfth or early thirteenth century.[33] Elsewhere, Cola and Cavallini both refer to *cronicae Romanae:* most probably conflations of the accounts of postclassical authors[34] or compilations such as the *Liber Pontificalis.*

Paying tribute to the classical heritage was not the unique preserve of scholars and intellectuals, but also part of the civic power-game, in Pisa with its eleventh-century "consuls" and certainly in late medieval Rome. Beyond and before the new interest in antique forms and language of the early Renaissance had existed a long urban tradition of *Romanitas.* The unique governmental heritage of Rome is evidenced in the language of the "restoration" of the Senate in 1143, as are many of the cultural facets of the twelfth-century's so-called Roman Renaissance.[35] A twelfth-century

---

29. For which see Arturo Graf, *Roma nella memoria e nelle imaginazione del medioevo,* 2 vols. (Turin, 1882); Cesare D'Onofrio, *Un popolo di Statue Racconte. Storie, Fatti, Leggende della Città di Roma antica, medievale, moderna* (Rome: Romana società editrice, 1990).

30. *ARC,* 104, 178.

31. Louis-Fernand Flutre and K. Sneyders de Vogel, *Li Fet des Romains,* 2 vols. (Paris, 1937–38); Jeanette M. Beer, *A Medieval Caesar* (Geneva: Librarie Droz, 1976).

32. Ed. Ernesto Monaci, *Storie de Troja et de Roma* (Rome: Società Romana di Storia Patria, 1920).

33. III:50, 188.

34. Mélanges for the most part drawn from the late antique and early medieval accounts of Isidore, Dares Phrygius, Orosius, Solinus, Paulus Diaconus, Eusebius, Florus, and Eutropius.

35. See Robert L. Benson and Giles Constable, eds., *Renaissance and Renewal in the Twelfth Century* (Oxford: Clarendon Press, 1982); and Robert Folz, *The Concept of Empire in Western Europe from the Fifth to the Fourteenth Century,* trans. Sheila A. Ogilvie, 3d ed. (London: Edward Arnold, 1969). The idea of the political restoration of Rome's ancient

ordinance for the protection of ancient buildings for the glory of contemporary Rome was reiterated in 1363.[36] Frederick II brought his own imperial classicizing imagery—implying his pan-Italic, if not worldwide powers—to the Capitol, in the shape of the Milanese *carroccio* in 1235 and its accompanying verses.[37] The "republican" ideology of Ptolemy of Lucca, publicist of the Orsini citizen-pope Nicholas III (1277–80) harped on the ancient glory of the *Populus Romanus,* despite the fact that, in reality, this period saw a peak in papal rather than civic control of medieval Rome.[38] The political culture of the *Urbs,* then, was deeply imbued with grandiose classicizing language and imagery.[39] In 1299 the baronial governors had Latin verses celebrating Rome's governmental mission painted on the walls of the Capitol palace (where Cola later erected his own vernacular verses and images) with no reference to the papal or even the Christian identity of the City.[40]

This, then, was the long civic tradition of *renovatio* into which Cola inserted himself in the 1340s. It is quite different from the moral and intellectual themes, based on the personal qualities of ancient figures drawn from literary sources, stressed by later Renaissance humanists. The

hegemony was already evident in the imagery of Otto III (ca. 1000); the theme of Roman "civic" rejection of the non-Roman usurper was already present in the rebellion of Otto's opponent Crescentius.

36. See Re, *Statuti,* 188; II:191: "Ancient edifices should not be destroyed, lest their ruins spoil the appearance of the City and so that such buildings act as a symbol of honor to the City." The early ordinance of 1163, that the buildings of the ancients should be left standing, for the glory of the City, "so long as the world endures" is noted by Cristina Carbonetti and Marco Venditelli, "Rome (Moyen Age): gouvernment," in *Dictionnaire Historique de la Papauté,* ed. Philippe Levillain (Paris: Fayard, 1994), 1463.

37. Brentano, *Rome before Avignon,* 83; Ernst H. Kantorowicz, *Frederick the Second,* trans. E. O. Lorimer (London: Constable, 1957), 448–49.

38. See Charles T. Davis, "Roman Patriotism and Republican Propaganda: Ptolemy of Lucca and Pope Nicholas III," in *Dante's Italy and Other Essays* (Philadelphia: Pennsylvania State University Press, 1984), 224–53.

39. The same practices extended beyond the governmental context into the culture of all Rome. For a succinct account of the conservative and classicizing tendencies of ecclesiastical architecture in the thirteenth century see Angiola M. Romanini, ed., *Roma nel Duecento. L'arte nella città dei papi da Innocenzo III a Bonfacio VIII* (Turin: Edizioni Seat, 1991), 147–48. For the conservatism of fourteenth- and fifteenth-century private and domestic architecture, see Jean-Claude Maire-Vigueur and G. Broise, "Strutture familiari, spazio domestico e architettura civile a Roma alla fine del Medio Evo," in *Monumenti di architettura,* Storia dell'arte italiana, vol. 12 (Turin: Einaudi, 1983), 159–60.

40. It did, however, refer to the defense of the City's revenues, and rights of the underage, of widows, and of the poor: see Gian-Battista De Rossi, "La Loggia del Commune di Roma," *Bulletino della Commisione Archaeologica Communale di Roma* (1882), 133–37; A. Salimei, *Senatori e statuti di Roma nel medio evo* (Rome: Biblioteca d'Arte, 1935), 89.

emphasis on justice recurred in the tenets of, and supplied one of the central justifications for, Cola's regime. More importantly, the reference in the verses to the care of the income of the commune, and to the protection of the poor and of widows, is distinctly reminiscent of the earliest positions Cola assumed in his rise to power. In 1343, Cola went to Avignon as the self-styled "consul of orphans, widows and the poor" (a role he retained, in fact, throughout 1347);[41] in 1344 he returned from Avignon with a senior cameral magistracy, controlling the administration of the City's revenues.

If "Consul" in 1343, may we regard Cola's 1347 title "Tribune" as more authentically "antique"?[42] *Tribunus* unlike *consul* appears at first sight to be unique in Trecento Italy, as if it were indeed selected by Cola on the basis of a direct reading of classical precedents. A model has been suggested from Livy's account of the evolution of popular representation in the patrician Roman government of the fourth century B.C.[43] There is certainly a notable similarity between the description of the *tribunus plebis* Gnaeus Flavius, an ambitious, antimagnatial scribe-turned-revolutionary of humble origin with native ability and eloquence, and the Chronicler's description of the notary Cola.

Cola, however, never mentions such a precedent. And it is essential to note that the classical use of the term *tribunus* was not restricted to Livy's ancient republican heroes. It was also an imperial role: one of the vital governmental powers "selected" by the early emperors was the *tribunicia potestas.* Perhaps more tellingly, however, while Cola knew his Livy, he was also a reader of contemporary versions of the thirteenth-century *Fet des Romains,* as we have noted. One version actually mentions Augustus Caesar's exercise of power via the post of military tribune.[44] Finally, beyond the literary sphere, there were even medieval political and govern-

---

41. Wright, *Life,* 53: "The following day the Tribune gave audience to the widows, orphans and paupers."

42. Ibid., 44.

43. Amy Schwartz, "Images and Illustrations of Power in Trecento Art: Cola di Rienzo and the Ancient Roman Republic," Ph.D. diss., State University of New York, Binghampton, 1994, 28; Livy, *History of Rome,* ed. and trans. Aubrey de Sélincourt (London: Penguin, 1960, 1982), 9.46. Such a model might conceivably have been suggested to Cola by Petrarch, who used the example of Gnaeus Flavius in the letter (slightly later, in 1351) to the cardinals appointed to reform the City; *Familiari,* 11.16 (Cosenza, *Petrarch,* 164–65).

44. Though without explaining the title (Monaci, *Storie de Troja et de Roma,* 270). In the dialect version, tribunes at one point are described as knights (118); this would have accorded with Cola, "Tribune" and knight as he was to become. See also Flutre and Sneyders de Vogel, *Li Fet des Romains,* 714, 722; Beer, *A Medieval Caesar,* 100–101.

mental precedents for Cola's use of the title Tribune.[45] The title had been associated historically with posts in the paleo-Christian bureaucracy. From the fourth century there is evidence for the school of the *primicerius*,[46] head of the civil and military documentation center of the Roman Empire, and his subordinates: following the *primicerium* is his *tribunus ac notarius;* then the *secundicerius;* then more *notarii ac tribunii,* and then *domestici et notarii.* The connection of these two occupational titles—notary and tribune—is highly reminiscent of Cola's own position.[47]

Cola's "tribunate" may be regarded, then, as paradigmatic of his relationship to classical republican models; his choice of titles did not rely exclusively upon ancient precedent. The confounding factor is that Cola had both the classical training and the rhetorical talent of the new humanists, and the capacity to work politically within the *all'antica* tradition of medieval Roman urban leadership. His understanding of "the Roman republic" was both classical and literary, and thus far Cola participated on the fringes of Petrarch's intellectual world; but his understanding of the concept of republic was also contemporary and political within the tradition of communal government in Italy and in the particular context of medieval Rome. In Cola each of these streams of thought—the classicizing-humanistic "republican" and the medieval communal "republican"—met, because of a peculiarly Roman tradition of imitation of the antique. Cola simply chose to emphasize different precedents and to display the different influences at different times in his career. In this sense it is not Cola who represents an anomaly in fourteenth-century Italy, but Rome's urban culture itself, based on memories of a past power within the Italian peninsula that was the exception and not the rule. Rome was not just a city, but the City; and capital not just of Italy but of the world.

---

45. No near-contemporary commentator such as the Chronicler, the Villani, nor even later Renaissance historians such as Platina or Machiavelli appear to find the term surprising. An interesting usage survives in a late-thirteenth-century document of the monastery of SS. Cosma e Damiano (transcribed by the eighteenth-century bishop and scholar Pier-Luigi Galletti at B.A.V. Vat. Lat. 8054, vol. 1, 58r), where eight men's names appear, six followed by the title *tribunus,* the last written as "+ Et ego Adalgisi tribunus tabellio civitatis Sutrine."

46. Curiously there was a contemporary family of Roman notaries with the name *Primicerii* (and also *Scriniarii,* "scribes").

47. The title *Tribunus* had a meaning to Cola's advisers; at III:18, 55, Cola referred to his temporary constitutional role, and to the plan, mooted in council, of electing a new Tribune every three months.

August Tribune: "I began to despise the plebeian life"

Dante, the great exponent of the *vita activa*—ambassador, civic governor, imperial idealist, and soldier-knight, as well as a political theorist, Latin *litterato,* and *volgare* poet—offered, it may be argued, a more potent role model than Petrarch, for Cola, who was himself a citizen-soldier, Latin political theorist, *volgare* poet, visionary, *rhetor,* and civic administrator. The influence of Dante's oeuvre on Cola's peers in mid-Trecento Rome is easy to trace: the Chronicler dedicated an early (lost) chapter to Dante;[48] Cola's ambassador Pandolfuccio dei Franchi paraphrased Dante; and another contemporary, if not Cola himself, quoted Dante on the award of the laurel, in reference to Cola's own coronation in 1347.[49] Cola never, in fact, names Dante, but a close reading of both Cola's correspondence and the evidence for his concept of Rome and the past provides striking evidence of Dante's direct influence on his language, imagery, and phraseology.[50] One example from Cola's allegorical verses, a plea addressed to the *summo patre, duca e signore mio,*[51] is readily comparable to *Inferno* 2.140: *Tu duca, tu signore e tu maestro.*[52]

The larger question of the leadership of Rome—the resurrection of the glory of its past and the anticipation of its eschatological future—is addressed by Cola in terms far more clearly reminiscent of Dante than of Petrarch. In theoretical terms, Cola's allegiance to Dante's imperial Roman mission may be seen in his positive commentary on Dante's *Monarchia.*[53] In a practical sense, Cola responded to the clarion call of the political "prophecy" at *Purgatorio* 33.37–45. Despite the failure of Henry VII's Italian mission (ca. 1311–13), Dante continued to predict the advent

---

48. See *ARC,* 10.

49. IV:14, 19–27, from *Paradiso,* 1.28–30.

50. See Raffaello Morghen, "Il mito storico di Cola di Rienzo," in *Civiltà Medievale al Tramonto,* Biblioteca di cultura moderna, vol. 708 (Bari: Laterza, 1971), 162 n. 35; his second appendix (187–88, 194) has another six examples of suggestively Dantean terminology in Cola. A similarity not explored fully by Morghen involves Cola's use of the term *pomerium,* Dante's understanding of the same concept as *pomarium,* and the Roman Chronicler's conflation of the two as *jardinio;* see Amanda Collins, "Cola di Rienzo, the Lateran Basilica, and the *Lex de Imperio* of Vespasian," *Mediaeval Studies* 60 (1998): 170 n. 22.

51. *ARC,* 107.

52. Also noted by Miglio, "Et rerum facta est," 25.

53. See Pier Giorgio Ricci, "Il commento di Cola di Rienzo alla *Monarchia* di Dante," *Studi Medievali,* 3d ser., 6 (1965): 665–708. Cola's authorship of the commentary is less convincingly disputed by Juhar, "Der Romgedanke," appendix 2, xxv–xxx.

of a mysterious, messianic "DVX," the heir to the new Roman Empire who would overturn the corrupt Avignonese papacy. In 1350 Cola combined his own Joachite imperial imagery with an intriguingly "imperial" explanation of his poses of 1347.[54] He claimed, astonishingly, to be the product of the seduction of his mother by Henry VII, Dante's hero, demonstrating that he considered himself heir (at least in 1350) to an imperial rather than republican idea of the ruler.[55]

Still, Dante's uncompromisingly Caesarian language does not approach the complexity of Cola's attempt to weld civic, republican, and imperial rhetoric. Cola's antique forebears offered more subtle models of ideological manipulation; hence the *tribunicia potestas.* Caesar's heir Octavian (i.e., Augustus) cleverly assumed the ancient republican role of *Tribunus Plebis,* "protector of the people," for its power of veto in the senate, effectively crippling opposition to his imperial polity. Did Cola realize this? Certainly no ancient historian spelled it out. The Latin version, however, of the thirteenth-century *Storie* Cola read, concerning Octavian, does imply that the author understood the ambivalence of the *tribunicia potestas* by which Augustus exercised *imperium.*[56] Cola explicitly "upgraded" his title from Tribune of the People in May to *Tribunus Augustus* in August,[57] crowning himself with six different crowns.[58] Augustus had styled himself founder of a new age and restorer of the Republic, of its religion, its army, and its social mores; on both issues, Tribunate and restoration, Cola might well, therefore, be seen to be emulating the pseudorepublican rhetoric and gestures of the first emperor of Rome: "I am not afraid to imitate their mores," as he wrote of his antique forebears in power.[59]

But Cola also imitated Augustus much more explicitly. Up until August, his "tribunician" title had been "Tribune of peace, liberty and justice," or, as the Chronicler put it, "Tribune of the people."[60] Cola had shared this earlier title with his co-rector, the bishop of Orvieto. The new

---

54. Joachim and Cola's Joachite Trinitarian imagery (endorsed, if not inspired by its appearance in the *Divine Comedy*) is discussed at the start of chapter 2 and notes ad hoc.

55. Cola never assumed the republican identity of a "new Brutus," awarded him by Petrarch (Cosenza, *Petrarch,* 19–20).

56. Monaci, *Storie de Troja et de Roma,* 270. It is not known, however, whether Cola's version was in Latin or Romanesco.

57. III:28, 196–99; III:40, 164–66; III:57, 1026–40; III:63, 63–66.

58. III:35, 11–25; also IV:13, IV:14.

59. III:18, 131–32.

60. Wright, *Life,* 44; *ARC,* 115.

title, which rang quite differently, was his alone.[61] Cola knew the meaning and implication of both term and title *Augustus,* from *augere,* to increase or enhance:

> The Holy Spirit has, in my reign, liberated and enhanced *(auxit)* the Republic, and so on the aforesaid Kalends of August my humble state was promoted to that of a knight, and to the title and name Augustus.[62]

> Just as Augustus *augmented* the temporal Republic, my reign shall bring forth and *augment* its spiritual goods.[63]

Yet there are, too, clear postclassical precedents for the use of the title *Augustus* in the "real" political arena of medieval Italy and elsewhere;[64] the classicizing poses, activities, and patronage of Frederick II are archetypal.[65] The title *Augustus* appears throughout the coronation rituals of the Middle Ages, as a standard term of reference for emperors of both the present and of the past; Cola later used it to and of Charles IV of Bohemia, Holy Roman Emperor-elect.[66] The title was even used by local signori with serious pretensions; Castruccio Castracane in Lucca, for example, built a citadel that he named the "Augusta."[67] Just as Cola's knowledge of Augustus and Augustus's role in the history of Rome was drawn from a range of sources, ancient and "modern," so his political use of the title could also have been influenced by much more recent imitative use.

The best example of this postclassical "contamination" was Cola's treatment of a much more tangible early imperial source of authority: a set of constitutional measures inscribed on an extant bronze tablet from the principate of Vespasian (A.D. 69–79). Cola's exposition of this tablet, in a

---

61. Juhar's account tries to prove Cola's move toward direct rule without consultation of his council after this point ("Der Romgedanke," 99–100). However, Cola did nod to the elective principle (III:18, 55; III:64, 168), even calling an imperial election for Pentecost 1348 (III:27, 54–71; III:28, 174ff.; III:41, 51–67).

62. III:28, 196–99.

63. III:40, 164–66; see also III:63, 63–66.

64. The thirteenth-century *Li Fet des Romains* was composed within the orbit of the French king "Philip Augustus."

65. Brentano, *Rome before Avignon,* 83–84; Kantorowicz, *Frederick the Second,* e.g. 448–49; also 221–27 on Frederick's overlap between Augustan titles and "Justinian" legislation.

66. Cola refers to Constantine as "Augustus" at III:50, 209–11, and III:56, 33.

67. Louis Green, *Chronicle into History* (London: Cambridge University Press, 1972), 105.

bizarre ceremonial event in the Lateran in 1346, a year before seizing power, was possibly the most symbolically charged act of his career. He wove a dense web of meaning, power, and precedent around its interpretation, fully comprehending both the legal nature and the political potential of the *lex de imperio*. In addition to his ability to interpret the content of the tablet, Cola also demonstrated that he could manipulate the original form, that is, the appearance of the tablet. But, most importantly, Cola was even capable of adapting the original purpose of the law—the grant of supreme power by the *Senatus Populusque Romanus* to the Emperor—to his own schemes for the resurrection of the power of the *Populus Romanus* and their chosen representative.[68]

In his concern that the message should reach beyond the legal *cognoscenti,* indeed beyond even the literate, Cola translated the tablet into Romanesco dialect, reading the points of the tablet from a list and explaining the contents of the law, stressing the former glory of the people of Rome. In addition he then had painted around it "a picture showing how the Roman Senate conceded authority to the Emperor Vespasian."[69] So for those unable to read the tablet, perhaps not even able to understand Cola's summary and analysis, the basic message was still clear: that the people of Rome had once had the authority to rule the world, or, at least, to choose an emperor to rule for them.

Merely in terms of its "form" Cola's use of the written document and inscribed tablet, erected within a painted tableau, provides a superb example of *Wort als Bild* in action.[70] It is central to Cola's entire ideological thrust toward the restoration of Rome; his props here were "the real thing." By elevating the power of the people and the emperor in the heart of papal power in medieval Rome, he was, literally as well as symbolically, resurrecting something of the power of the past. As Cola spoke the words, translating and interpreting, the Senate of the tableau behind him was depicted in the moment of conceding the tablet, that is, power, to the emperor. The words of the text of the tablet are brought to life simultaneously through the media of the ear, that is, Cola's speech, and of the eye,

---

68. This episode is treated in further detail elsewhere: Collins, "Cola di Rienzo," 159–83.

69. Wright, *Life,* 36.

70. See particularly Hans Belting, "The New Role of Narrative in Public Painting of the Trecento: Historia and Allegoria," *Studies in the History of Art* (National Gallery, Washington, D.C.) 15–16 (1985): 151–68. For the methodology involved in this discussion see Serena Romano's detailed account: "*Regio dissimilitudinis:* Immagine e parola nella Roma di Cola di Rienzo," in *Bilan et Perspectives des Études Médiévales en Europe* (Louvain-la-Neuve: Fédération Internationale des Instituts d'Études Médiévales, 1995), 329–56.

that is, the artistic mise-en-scène of historic events, where the tablet "played itself" within the narrative of the tableau. With the *lex* tablet Cola, the new ruler of Rome, was able to combine the charisma of antiquity with an injunction for the future, invoking the classical equivalent of the biblical tablets upon which God's law was transmitted to Moses. So the *lex* tablet, one could say, was a secular relic, from the past, of the power of the Word, and yet at the same time a veiled prophecy for the future, concerning the power of the people. Once Cola had reerected, illustrated, and expounded on the *lex* tablet, the writing was, truly, on the wall.

In terms of "content" Cola's use of the tablet becomes even more prodigiously complex. The content of the inscription has attracted extensive attention from modern scholars.[71] If the terminology involved is examined closely, a clear connection can be made between the clauses of the surviving part of the *lex,* and the Chronicler's account of the clauses Cola had read out.[72] But the extant tablet does not tell the whole story. It is in fact only the second, or final, part of a longer inscription that originally listed more fully the powers granted to Vespasian. Meanwhile the account in the Chronicle obviously contains clauses that are not found on the surviving tablet. This has lead some to suggest that Cola possessed both original tablets. It is in fact the case that the authoritarian clauses contained in the original *leges regiae* of the ancient world[73] correspond explicitly with certain of the rights described in the paraphrase of Cola's speech; indeed each of the clauses that the Chronicler attributes to Cola's account of the content of the *lex,* even where these clauses do not appear on the surviving *lex* tablet, can be explained in terms of the surviving information for *leges regiae* in general.[74] But this is not the end of the story.

Despite long scholarly debate concerning Cola's ultimate ambitions, no one has attempted to relate the clauses of the *lex* tablet to the actual evidence there exists for the conception and construction of Cola's own authority. Cola evidently envisaged his own powers as analogous to Vespasian's, which he had read out in the Lateran several months before his

---

71. See e.g. Michael Crawford, *Roman Statutes,* 2 vols. (London: Institute of Classical Studies, 1996), 2:549–50; François Hurlet, "La *Lex de imperio Vespasiani* et la légitimé augustéenne," *Latomus* 55 (1992): 261–80; Peter A. Brunt, "Lex de Imperio Vespasiani," *Journal of Roman Studies* 62 (1972): 95–116.

72. Wright, *Life,* 36; Crawford, *Roman Statutes,* 2:551.

73. Reassembled by Otto Karlowa, *Römisches Rechtgeschictes* (Leipzig: Von Veit, 1885–1901), 1:494–501.

74. See Collins, "Cola di Rienzo," 169–72, for a detailed account of these rights and their analogues in the Chronicler's account and/or Cola's correspondence.

assumption of government. A distinction must be drawn, however, between the rhetoric of 1346 and the positions assumed in 1347: the purpose of the event in the Lateran was to stress not Cola's power, but the sovereign authority of the Roman People. Only after 1347 did Cola talk of how the assembled people of Rome had conceded to him their "absolute and unlimited power and authority."[75] In an interesting and barely noted passage,[76] the Chronicler provides some of the missing detail. After his ascent to the Capitol, Cola read out a list of undeniably "contemporary" legal ordinances, followed by a further list of suggestively "Vespasianic" powers.[77] This was quite obviously not a spontaneous transfer, by the assembled people, of a collection of ad hoc powers: Cola had this list drafted well in advance. These early "parliaments" of the Tribunate were heavily stage-managed, combining *laudes regiae* with *leges regiae.* His powers were conceived before he came to power; with only the inappropriate local model of the papacy to hand, the new authority was constructed in analogy to the powers conferred by the old *lex regia.*[78] Hence, before he took over the Capitol, Cola was at pains to ensure the Roman People's resumption of their universal power, in anticipation of the moment when they would then hand over their sovereign power to Cola as their chosen representative.

Yet how "antique" were these powers? Were they really based on classical *leges regiae,* drawn from ancient constitutional formulations? The answer is no. Cola would not have needed even one tablet, let alone both original tablets[79] in order to draw upon the *leges regiae* of Roman law. To put it bluntly, in Trecento Italy anybody with reasonable legal or philosophical training knew what a, or the, *lex regia* meant or could mean. It was bound up with the great questions of the sources, worldly and divine, of world authority. The central issue for medieval glossators, postglossators, and jurists was the striking of a balance between God's input and man's contribution in the creation of emperors. God's role in the divine ordination of temporal authority could be countered, or even bypassed, by

---

75. III:7, 8, 105–7; also see III:27, 24–26.

76. Seibt, *Anonimo Romano,* 125, has also picked it up.

77. Wright, *Life,* 43; *ARC,* 114.

78. A criticism of Karlowa is his failure to elaborate on the *tribunicia potestas* among the list of imperial prerogatives and titles the *lex regia* was designed to confer. If this element is added, it throws into yet sharper relief Cola's assumption of the title "Tribune."

79. Cola did not stand in front of the tablet and read it out; as the Chronicler says, he read out the chapters from a preprepared *carta.*

the authority of the Roman *lex regia,* since in accordance with its mandate the people, that is, the people of Rome, had the right to make, and possibly even to break, the emperor. This theoretical dilemma became ever more pressing after the *lex regia* was put back into political practice in the twelfth century, in the Roman People's constitutional relationship with Frederick Barbarossa.[80] Did the original *lex regia* represent the permanent alienation, the *translatio,* of the sovereign authority of the Roman People? Or had it been a one-off grant, a *concessio*[81] designed to be reinstituted when necessary with the accession of new emperors? And if so, could the *lex regia* be revoked by the Roman People?[82]

Let us not forget: Cola was a lawyer and politician as well as a scholar and ideologue. Contemporary legal political theory may have completely dominated his reading of the Vespasianic *lex de imperio* tablet. Cola was also very familiar with Justinian's codification of Roman law, including the *leges regiae.* There are direct references to Justinian himself and to the law codes, and also quotations from the Digest particularly, throughout Cola's correspondence.[83] Cola certainly used contemporary legal sources, as we may deduce from the intriguing report of a papal spy in Rome, Cochetus de Cochetis, referring to the grand ceremonies of August 1, 1347. Following the knighting, Cola declared the forthcoming election, for Pentecost 1348, of the Holy Roman Emperor, summoning the claimants themselves, and those who claimed the right to elect them, namely the German Electors, to attend his court in Rome.[84] Cochetus told Clement VI:

> After he received his knighthood . . . he had various legal arguments set out against the German Electors: [1] that they would have to come to the City and into his presence to explain why they thought they had the jurisdiction to elect the emperor . . . [2] that the election of the emperor

80. Robert L. Benson, "Political *Renovatio:* Two Models from Roman Antiquity," in Benson and Constable, *Renaissance and Renewal,* 356.

81. Seibt, *Anonimo Romano,* 124 n. 88, draws out the general difference in implication of *translatio* and *concessio;* the Chronicler, it should be noted, uses the Romanesco term *concedeva,* rather than a derivative of *translatio.* Cola, it hardly requires saying, favored the interpretation of a revocable *concessio;* he was to be the recipient of precisely such a "concession."

82. Legal scholars and political theorists were divided: see Collins, "Cola di Rienzo," 177–78.

83. III:58, 113, 376, 626, 740; and III:60, 22.

84. Lewis the Bavarian, then still alive, who had been crowned in 1327, and Charles IV of Bohemia, legitimate grandson and heir of Henry VII.

had devolved to the Roman People; and this he intended to prove in law.[85]

Clement VI disagreed violently:

> He [Cola] presumes to revoke those concessions made since the time of the foundation of Rome, but only *de facto,* because he cannot do it *de iure.*[86]

So Clement, a lawyer and scholar himself, did not think that Cola could prove his case in law. Cola, however, knew of a written legal precedent for the *concessio.* In another barely noted passage, following a description of Cola's summons to the Electors, the candidates, and also the Pope and cardinals, the Chronicler says:

> He [Cola] said that he had found it written that after the lapse of a certain amount of time, the election fell to the Romans.[87]

Regrettably, the Chronicler does not tell us precisely where Cola found this written. This *lex regia* "expiry date" is not in evidence on the classical tablet Cola manipulated; nor does it appear in the *Corpus Juris.* Yet this very argument, regarding the time lapse factor, does exist in contemporary jurists. For example, Bartolo di Sassoferrato claimed that the Roman People did retain their legal sovereignty after the grant of power in the *lex regia,* but that specifically over the course of time and events these powers were lost (so a temporary *concessio* slid into a permanent *translatio*).[88] His pupil Baldo degli Ubaldi, however, took a similar line to that of Cola, that is, that the Roman People could always revoke their *concessio.*[89]

It is impossible to establish exactly what Cola knew of contemporary juristic literature, but he certainly knew many jurists;[90] there are also several passages where he talks of his consultation, in 1347, of a legal advisory

---

85. IV:8, 52–57.

86. IV:40, 118–22.

87. Wright, *Life,* 72; *ARC,* 138.

88. Diego Quaglione, *Politica e Diretto nel Trecento italiano: Il De Tyranno di Bartolomeo da Sassoferrato (1314–57)* (Florence: Olschki, 1983), 208–9.

89. Joseph Canning, *The Political Thought of Baldus de Ubaldis* (Cambridge: Cambridge University Press, 1987), 57.

90. See chapter 6 on Paolo Vaiani and Matteo dei Baccari particularly.

body.[91] It is also very much the case that while the powerful aura of antiquity lent glamour and legitimacy to Cola's constitution, the realities of Cola's construction of executive power are also readily comparable to Bartolo's near-contemporary *De Regimine Civitatum.*[92]

In 1346, then, Cola di Rienzo marched into the heart of Christendom's debate over popular sovereignty and the authority of the Roman People. Cola did not believe that the Roman People had lost their supreme power for good; he held that the People retained the right to revoke those powers granted to the emperor. Thus around a year after the Lateran *lex de imperio* reading, via Cola, the People of Rome were back in control of the world. On the advice of the Roman college of judges and the *sapientes* of all Italy, Cola claimed, that with the authority of the Roman People, in their parliament,

> Revoking all authority, jurisdiction, power and all alienations of the dignity of imperial power and authority, we have reconferred the ancient legal rights of the same Roman people upon ourselves and on the people.[93]

This edict was to be recorded in proper classical style, just as the Vespasianic law had been, "on tablets of bronze as was the custom in antiquity."[94]

It may be asserted, therefore, that Cola knew, better than any of his contemporaries, the original *lex de imperio* tablet; but he also knew the tradition of the *lex regia,* from Justinian to Bartolo. Cola's interpretation, therefore, of this ancient artifact with its classical constitutional content was given a hefty contemporary bias: a politicized reading only fully comprehensible in the context of medieval lawyers' debates concerning the authority of the Roman People and the postclassical *translatio imperii.*

Cola's emulation of ancient imperial power did not stop with the titles of Augustus and the powers of Vespasian. Cola never explicitly referred to

---

91. III:7, 8, 192; also III:27, 80–85.

92. Bartolo's commentaries on the Digest and the Codex regarding the full legislative sovereignty of the autonomous city are described by Walter Ullmann, "*De Bartoli sententia: Concilum repraesentat mentem populi,*" in *The Papacy and Political Ideas in the Middle Ages* (1962: reprint, London: Variorum, 1975), 712–15. For Cola in the role of contemporary *signore* see chapter 4.

93. III:41, 39–51.

94. III:41, 118–19.

the *lex regia,* and yet, as we have seen, he constructed an entire discourse around its application to his own pretensions. A similar process may be seen at work with a much more notorious relic of antique power: the so-called Donation of Constantine. Here Cola was obliged to tread more cautiously, because of the apparent direct challenge to Avignon. Nevertheless throughout 1346 and 1347 Cola's activities in the Lateran Basilica—Constantine's palace and the medieval heart of western Christendom—can be read as undermining papal supremacy, and asserting his own sacro-imperial majesty.

The most important ceremonial occasions Cola staged, apart from the *lex* episode, were his knighting and then coronation of August 1 and 15, 1347 respectively. The knighting ceremony in particular brought Constantine's image into sharp relief.[95] Following grandiose festivities, Cola heard Mass in the Lateran Baptistery. He was then ritually bathed in the semiprecious stone bath where Silvester had baptized and miraculously purified Constantine of leprosy. The next morning, Cola was knighted as *Cavaliere dello Spirito Santo* and announced the resumption of the Roman People's ancient rights regarding the election of the Roman Emperor.[96]

Cola's relationship to the emperor Constantine was a little more complicated than has often been assumed: he enjoyed one relationship with Constantine as the refounder of the Roman church, but quite another with Constantine as its "donor" and thus corrupter. Yet this double-think was not so straightforward as the antithesis "love the sinner, hate the sin" that Dante expressed so vehemently.[97] Cola did not claim that the Donation per se was wrong, merely the way the Church chose to interpret it: worldly possession was not evil; the corruption and violence of Avignon *was.* As the new semisacral imperial ruler of the Holy Roman Republic, Cola's attitude toward both the papacy and the legacy of Constantine's Donation was therefore crucial to conceal.[98] The letters he sent and received from Avignon from May to November 1347 display Cola's attempts to main-

---

95. Wright, *Life,* 70–73, especially 71. The chronicle lacks a full description of the second ceremony.

96. IV:13, 12.

97. *Paradiso* 20:57; also note Dante's Constantinian "dualism" at *Inferno,* 19:115–17.

98. Cola's attitude to the papacy has been the source of much debate (see bibliography for the protracted quarrel of Brizzolara and Filippini between 1899 and 1907). In fact his attitude varied expediently: theoretically, Cola (like Dante) did not seek the abolition of the papacy; and both held that the *Romanitas* of the papacy gave it its supremacy over other bishoprics; see Diana Wood, *Clement VI: The Pontificate and Ideas of an Avignon Pope* (Cambridge: Cambridge University Press, 1989), 79. There is no evidence for his creation of an antipope in 1347 (an accusation Cola vehemently denied).

tain the deceit: stonewall, smoke-screen, and bluff. They also reveal the pope's increasing scepticism and anger.[99] By September 15, Clement had made up his mind that Cola was not to be trusted, telling his local cardinal-legate, Bertrand de Deux:

> For all the aforesaid Nicolas claims to act in all things for my honor and that of the Church, his words do not match his deeds.[100]

Clement probably had before him the report of his Roman spy Cochetus, who described Cola's baptism and purification in Constantine's *concha* in telling words: "As though he were the emperor, or something greater than emperor."[101] In early November, Cola put the final touches to his reputation, responding to a summons from Bertrand:

> [Cola] went with his knights to St. Peter's, entered the sacristy, and put on the imperial state Dalmatic over his armour. The emperors wore this Dalmatic at their coronations. . . . [He] appeared before the Legate, his sceptre in his hand, his crown on his head. He looked terrible and fantastic.[102]

The pattern is clear: in 1346, Cola had claimed the reversal of the *translatio imperii* in the name of the *Populus Romanus,* suggesting the symbolic secular repossession of the Lateran, with no reference at any stage of the proceedings to the Church. It was as though Rome had already returned to that "pristine" age before Constantine "donated" the Lateran and thus awarded temporal power to popes. Then, in May 1347, the People granted Cola supreme power as their representative. By locating the ceremonies of August 1347 in the Lateran, accepting the symbolic "purging" of Rome in his own person, and on August 15 announcing his own elevation to "Augustus," Cola was symbolically reversing the Donation of Constantine.

The Donation and its legacy, legal and political, was a much-discussed issue.[103] Cola's take on this "antique" source of imperial power (ironically

---

99. E.g. III:35, 1, 15–20; III:40, 76–86; III:43, 70–84.

100. IV:22, 12–14. See also IV:40, 78–81.

101. IV:8, 37: "ut esset imperator, et plus quam imperator" (see chap. 2 and title of the present study).

102. Wright, *Life,* 80.

103. Baldo described it as illegal; Ernst H. Kantorowicz, *The King's Two Bodies: A Study in Medieval Political Theology,* 2d ed. (Princeton: Princeton University Press, 1981), 177 n. 270 (see also 328 n. 46, 358 n. 158).

enough, not knowing it to be medieval forgery) was politically radical, but hardly evidence, nonetheless, of an uncontaminated relationship with the past. Still, Cola's simultaneous attempt to set up Constantine as a positive role model—the newly purified Christian reformer of Rome and herald of a new age—was unusual. Was that one case where Cola forged a unique relationship with the past? The answer must still be no, because of Cola's saturation in the works of Dante. The image of Constantine as a "good" emperor to imitate already had a *Nachleben* beyond literature, in imperial politics.[104] Constantine and the Lateran were consciously imitated by Charlemagne at Aachen and by his successors; the Constantine parallel was even applied to Charles IV of Bohemia, Cola's "nephew."[105]

Cola's claim to be Charles's uncle dated from 1350, when he told the story of his mother's seduction by Henry VII (Charles's grandfather, and Dante's hero) during Henry's months in Rome in 1312.[106] This was when, Cola claimed, he "began to despise the plebeian life" and started to read only the deeds of the great emperors of the past. This is retrospective reconstruction: in 1347, Cola had not yet invented a personal excuse for his imperial mandate. Yet clearly his mission to return Rome to its ancient power and glory was couched in terms of Augustus's titles, Vespasian's autocratic powers, and Constantine's miraculous conversion and renovation of the Christian church; very much, then, in terms of the supremacy of the imperial, rather than the papal, right to administer justice to the world. Even before the Tribunate began, Cola had made his quasi-imperial ambitions clear. The *lex* exposition in 1346 was not Cola's personal manifesto, but a claim on behalf of the Roman People that later dovetailed into his constitutional leadership. However, according to the Chronicler's account, shortly after this occasion Cola let slip a telling phrase. When mocked by the Colonna, he announced, ominously:

---

104. In terms of the staging of Constantinian power there were powerful visual precedents available to Cola: in the Silvester chapel at the Quattro Coronati (see John Mitchell, "St. Sylvester and Constantine at the SS. Quattro Coronati," in *Federigo II e l'Arte del Duecento italiano,* ed. Angiola M. Romanini [Rome: Galatina, 1980], 2:15–32; on the Lateran facade and Benediction loggia (see Stephan Waetzoldt, *Die Kopien des 17. Jahrhunderts nach Mosaiken und Wandmalereien im Rom,* Römische Forschungen der Bibliotheca Hertziana, vol. 18. [Vienna, 1964], 36, reproduced in Romanini, *Roma nel Duecento,* 272–73); and in the Hamburg manuscript of the *Storie de Roma.*

105. See Herwig Wolfram, "Constantin als Vorbild für den Herrscher des hochmittelalterlichen Reiches," *Mitteilung des Österreichischen Instituts für Geschichtsforschungen* 68 (1960): 226–43; R. Chadabra, "Der 'Zweite Konstantin': Zum verhältnis von Staat und Kirche in der Karolischen kunst Böhmes," *Umeni* 26, no. 6 (1978): 505–20, esp. fig. 2.

106. III:50, 179.

I am going to be a great signore or emperor. I shall persecute all of these barons.[107]

"From Roman chronicles . . . for five hundred years": The Medieval Precedents

Cola, then, cut a grand and deliberately "imperial" figure, but his reading of Augustus's tribunician role, Vespasian's autocracy, and Constantine's spiritual renovation was also and inevitably based on imagery condensed from the ideology and iconography of the medieval heirs of antiquity. While appealing, ironically, to a German emperor to return to Rome, Cola commented that he knew, *ex Romanis cronicis,* that for the previous five hundred years no Roman citizen had been able to defend Rome from tyrants.[108] It was, of course, five hundred years since Charlemagne's supporters had been the first to chant, "Blessed is he who comes in the name of the Lord," a line incorporated in the *ordines* of medieval imperial coronation, and heard by all successive imperial claimants, including Cola himself.[109] He chose to stage the procession to his own coronation in 1347 on one of the most sacred festivals of the early medieval Roman calendar. On the feast of the Assumption, August 15, ever since the eighth century, an ancient acheiropitic icon of Christ was carried through the streets to the cry *Ecce salvator! veniat Imperator!* (Lo the Savior! The emperor comes!)[110] By the fourteenth century a confraternity—mainly drawn from the new social groups whose support was crucial to Cola—had formed around this relic.[111] The significance of the imperial-messianic equation was not to be lost on observers of Cola's ascendancy: "As though he were emperor, or something greater . . ."

There is considerable evidence to suggest that Cola's rituals and symbols owed as much, if not more, to early and high medieval precedent, derived perhaps from five hundred years of chronicled impressions of the past and reinvented rituals of imperial power, than to the fragmentary imagery of antiquity. Cola's gestures and poses show remarkable continu-

---

107. Wright, *Life,* 37 (*ARC,* 109).
108. III:50, 188.
109. Wright, *Life,* 135.
110. Hans Belting, *Likeness and Presence: A History of the Image before the Era of Art,* trans. Edmund Jephcott (Chicago: University of Chicago Press, 1994), 313–14, talks of the procession as well established by the eighth century.
111. The Confraternity of the Savior is described in chapter 4.

ity with certain aspects of the imperial *ordo*,[112] drawn from the *Liber Censuum* of the eleventh century and elaborated in the twelfth century into the most explicit statement of medieval secular supreme power, the so-called *Libellus de Caeremoniis:*

> The emperor alone after God has all power, and dispenses all judgment and law, and holds the reins of all things, and thus must be waited on by all on earth.[113]

This text is one of three components of a twelfth-century collection called the *Graphia Aurea Urbis Romae;* this text was known in fourteenth-century Rome to Giovanni Cavallini, who notes it on two occasions.[114] The *Graphia* text seems to have had a profound influence on Cola's self-presentation, in terms of his ceremonial vestments, his titles, and, particularly, his coronation.[115] The section on imperial coronation lists ten crowns, each with a short explanatory note regarding precedent and meaning, or with a historical figure as illustration; there are stunning similarities with the six crowns Cola took and their respective implications.[116] Multiple coronation was by no means uncommon in ancient literary sources,[117] but the particular choice, order, and variety of Cola's crowns ostensibly owes more to the medieval imperial rite.

An alternative source of medieval ritual and power, the papal *ordines* (or "Pontificals"), may also be argued to have influenced Cola's symbol-

---

112. There is insufficient space to examine all aspects here. See Amanda Collins, "Cola di Rienzo: The Revolution in Historical Perspective," D. Phil. thesis, Oxford University, 1996, 68–79.

113. Roberto Valentini and Giuseppe Zucchetti, eds., *Codice Diplomatico della città di Roma,* Fonti per la Storia d'Italia 81, 88, 90–91 (Rome: Istituto Storico Italiano, 1940–53), 3:100.

114. See Laureys, "Giovanni Cavallini's *Polistoria,*" 448. Elsewhere in an annotation to his manuscript of Valerius Maximus (a text also familiar to Cola, the Chronicler, and Petrarch) Cavallini also glossed the meaning of the term *nomenclator:* "an official of the City of Rome . . . he had the duty of caring for widows, orphans, and all foreigners . . . as is mentioned frequently in the *Graphia*" (Vat. Lat. 1927, 84v: see e.g. Valentini and Zucchetti, *Codice Topografico,* 3:96). In 1343 Cola chose the title *consul;* but he assumed the same duties (III:2, 84–85). The same notion appeared in the "rhyme" of 1299, as noted.

115. The crowns are discussed by Percy E. Schramm, *Kaiser, Könige, und Päpste* (Stuttgart: Hiersemann, 1968–71), 4:42.

116. Valentini and Zucchetti, *Codice Diplomatico,* 3:98–100 and 4:14, possibly scripted by Cola or a follower.

117. E.g. Aulus Gellius, *Noctes Atticae,* 2.11 (ed. Peter K. Marshall. Oxford: Clarendon Press, 1968); Pliny the Elder, *Natural History,* 22.3.6, 22.5.9 (ed. and trans. John F. Healy, London: Penguin, 1991).

ism. Here is just one example from the Pontifical of approximately 1300 scripted by the curialist Guillaume Durand, relating to the power of the sword traditionally awarded the secular ruler by his superior, the spiritual ruler of the world:

> When the sword, blessed, has been replaced in its sheath, the pope buckles them onto the emperor, saying, "Buckle this your sword upon your thigh, most powerful one."[118]

Cola used this very phrase of the emperor, repeating it over and over in 1350 to the Bohemian king, whom he also addresses as Augustus.[119] The phrase derives ultimately from Ps. 44:4, but that Cola pulled the reference from the Pontificals may be suggested by an even closer correlation of one passage with Cola's own actions:

> Once it is buckled on, the emperor himself draws the sword from its sheath and brandishes it in his hand three times, naked, *viriliter* . . . knighted as a cavalier of the blessed Peter.[120]

The reference to the sacred knighthood is interesting; in the Pontificals, emperor and knight were given exactly the same distinctive triple sword-swinging gesture. The fullest ceremonial description surviving for Cola is his knighting, rather than his "imperial style" coronation as Tribune:

> Then the Tribune drew his sword from its sheath and waved it in the air toward the three divisions of the world, saying, "This is mine; this is mine; this is mine."[121]

Cola's version involves word as well as deed; words that do not appear in the pope's imperial investitures of the later Middle Ages. But the spoken element, in fact, like so much of Cola's self-construction, has a clear legal,

---

118. Michel Andreiu, *Le Pontifical Romain au Moyen Age,* Studi e Testi 86–88 (Vatican City, 1940), 3:431.

119. III:50, 380; III:57, 378; III:58, 972, from Ps. 44:4.

120. Andreiu, *Le Pontifical Romain,* 3:431. Another section reads, "We beseech you, O Lord, to hear our prayers and bless this sword . . . this your servant desires to be knighted . . . that he may be a defender of the Church, of widows, orphans and of all the servants of God" (Andreiu, *Le Pontifical Romain,* 3:447–44); a phrase that is echoed closely by Cola's self-proclaimed title in 1343.

121. Wright, *Life,* 72.

imperial, Roman origin: in the *Corpus Juris* (Digest 14.2.9). That this passage was, moreover, known in fourteenth-century Roman intellectual circles may be deduced from Cavallini's comments in *Polistoria* regarding the emperor's arrival in Rome from Monte Mario. He paraphrases the same Digest passage:

> Today it is called *Mons Marius,* where the Roman emperor ascends, and turning himself in each direction says: "All that we see is ours, and the whole world obeys our commands."[122]

The only imperial coronation that Cola could, conceivably, have witnessed was that of Lewis the Bavarian in 1327; and also, interestingly, a "popular" knighting of the same year, with distinct classicizing overtones.[123] Such evidence, however, reveals that *all'antica* posing could also take place on urban municipal terms, by civic magistrates, and not just as an imitation of emperors. Medieval Rome was a city particularly rich in processions, symbolic occasions, rituals, and feasts, as befitted both its classical imperial heritage and its subsequent papal identity, but also echoing the traditional status of the *Populus Romanus.* Public celebrations of the past and present importance of the City were expected by visitors and inhabitants alike; these formed part of Rome's unique mystique, a city of service and show. These did not simply evaporate in the fourteenth century, despite the absence of the curia and a paucity of evidence for the period. In fact a number of occasions are recorded in fragmented surviving documentary sources, though their authenticity has not been proved beyond all doubt. A rare manuscript account pertains to senatorial processions in Rome and has the suggestive, probably anachronistic title, "the Order and Magnificence of the Roman civic magistrates during the period

---

122. Laureys, "Giovanni Cavallini's *Polistoria,*" 463. Also see Valentini and Zucchetti, *Codice Diplomatico,* 3:36–37 n. 2 for the same expression in a pre-1348 (probably ca. 1329–30) *Tractatus de coronatione imperatoris* and in a so-called Provinciale Romano of the same general period.

123. The Roman Chronicler briefly describes the event (*ARC,* 9) but in fact a fuller account of this and other pageantry derives from the fragmentary chronicle of Lodovico Monaldeschi, dating 1327–40, the imagery and language of which is reminiscent of Cola's knighting in 1347 (Lodovico A. Muratori, ed., *"Fragmenta Annalium Romanorum.* Ludovico Bonconte Monaldesco," in *R.I.S.* [Milan: Societas Palatinae, 1728], 12:530–42). It should be noted, however, that Filippo Clementi, *Il Carnevale Romano* (Rome, 1899), 50–51, claimed that Gregorovius suspected the authenticity of this source (Ferdinand Gregorovius, *The History of the City of Rome in the Middle Ages,* trans A. Hamilton [London: G. Bell and Sons, 1894–98], 6:687 n. 2, 708 n. 1).

that the Papal curia resided in Avignon."[124] Enthusiasm for *all'antica* form and show alike was particularly noticeable among those who had a stake in proving the antiquity of their office or their family.

The public and ceremonial life of Rome was full of reminders of Rome's ancient glory, existing in a tradition extending so far back as to be believed continuous from the ancient world, and they were sponsored by medieval popes, emperors, local barons, international scholars and municipal officials (they were often the same men, of course). The plebs also participated by constructing arches for the processions, chanting the responses, attending the ceremonies, transmitting the stories of the ghost of Nero, the *salvatio Romae,* the myths of the Sybils and Augustus, his buried wealth and his future return, the once and future king;[125] and by acclaiming those who came in search of power, from the north, or from much closer to hand, within the City itself.[126]

In terms of Cola's potential sources, however, we have now come full circle, from the ancient republican to the classical imperial, to the medieval imperial, to the civic and popular; finally, however, it is possible to argue the case that Cola owed a strand of his self-construction to the grand ideology and, more cogently, to the humanist aesthetic of the hero of the new Republic. Cola was, I suggest, influenced with regard to his imagery, if hardly his polity, by Petrarch's poetic re-elevation of coronation and triumph to the finest expression of Roman cultural authority. Cola's own actions still have a flavor of imitation of the ancient triumph despite the many examples of postclassical contamination that undermine his claim to have restored ancient glory. His coronation specifically with laurels, for example—rather than the precious metals of the imperial and Pontifical

---

124. B.A.V. Vat. Lat. 6823; Lodovico A. Muratori, ed., "Ordine e Magnificenze dei Magistrati Romani nel tempo che la Corte del Papa stava in Avignone," in *Antiquitates Italicae Medii Aevi* (Milan: Societas Palatinae, 1739), 2:831–62. The title suggests a *terminus post quem* of 1368. Another description of fantastical, explicitly *all'antica* outfits is found in an ostensibly 1372 account of the Testaccian games (A.C. Archivio Boccapaduli, *Mazzo Supplementario,* 4 and 5). Again this is not an entirely reliable fourteenth-century source. It is partially edited by Clementi, *Il Carnevale Romano,* 39–44, and copied as authentic by Beatrice Premoli, *Ludus Carnevaleschi. Il carnevale a Roma dal secolo XII al secolo XVI* (Rome: Guidotti, 1981), 9. Premoli fails to take into account Clementi's footnote (*Il Carnevale Romano,* 39 n. 1), which suggests that the account is a later forgery, probably based on the Roman Chronicler's account of Cola's processions.

125. Graf, *Roma nella memoria,* 1:308–33; N. Cilento, "Sulla tradizione della *Salvatio Romae:* La magica tutela città medievale," in *Roma Anno 1300,* ed. Angiola M. Romanini (Rome: "L'Erma" di Bretschneider, 1983), 695–703.

126. See the introduction to the second part of this study for an account of late-medieval popular revolutions in Rome.

rituals—and his symbolic deposition of his arms upon the altar of the *Arx,* the Araceli in the Middle Ages, were both distinct elements within the ancient *Mos Triumphalis* for which there is only clear medieval precedent: the example of Petrarch, not in his writings but in the "real" terms of his own coronation on the Capitol in 1341.

Petrarch focused the disparate elements of a vague *all'antica* laureate coronation tradition into a glorious ceremony celebrating the Eternal City, the power of poetry, and his own brilliance, on Easter Day 1341.[127] There are a series of parallels in the coronation document that describes Cola's crowns: Petrarch's coronation poem cited Persius on Parnassus, the exact phrase applied in 1347 to Cola's laurel crown, "the custom of poets."[128] Petrarch also referred to Vergil's *Georgics* and Lucan's *Pharsalia,* both of which later appeared in Cola's coronation description.[129] Cola's deposition of arms on the Araceli, following his victory over the Colonna at the battle of Porta S. Lorenzo on November 20, 1347,[130] is an even more deliberately archaic gesture than Petrarch laying his laureate crowns on the high altar at the Vatican in 1341.[131] Even as Cola's Tribunate collapsed about him in December 1347, he was not prepared to let the occasion pass without a final "triumphal" gesture:

"Now in the seventh month I descend from my dominion." When, weeping, he had spoken these words, he mounted his horse and, sounding the silver trumpets, with the imperial insignia . . . he descended triumphally.[132]

Thus Cola's Tribunate even ended on a very typical note, recalling both the medieval imperial symbols, with their messianic overtones, inherited from an earlier period, and the newer, emphatically triumphal imagery of his humanist acquaintance.

---

127. See Joseph B. Trapp, "The Poet Laureate: Rome, *Renovatio,* and *Translatio Imperii,*" in *Rome in the Renaissance: The City and the Myth,* ed. P. A. Ramsay (Binghampton: Center for Medieval and Early Renaissance Studies, SUNY, 1982), 93–105.

128. IV:14, 5–9.

129. IV:14, 10–16, 1–3.

130. Wright, *Life,* 87; III:57, 586–97.

131. Petrarch, *Epistolae metricae,* in *Poëmata Minora di Francesco Petrarca,* ed. Dino De Rossetti (Milan, 1829–34), 2:94–105. See also Petrarch's *Africa,* 9:323–47 (Thomas Bergin and Alice S. Wilson, eds., *Petrarch's Africa* [New Haven: Yale University Press, 1977], 231–32).

132. Wright, *Life,* 93; *ARC,* 154. The Chronicler left the phrase *triumphaliter descendit* in Latin.

Cola stood at the confluence of two modes of thought regarding the past: *renovatio,* the revival of an ongoing tradition, however far in decline, and rebirth ("renaissance") following a break with the past. He clearly privileged *renovatio,* with concrete, "Dantean" political aims, putting the latter—the Petrarchan literary and aesthetic culture of *Romanitas*—very much to the service of the former. Cola acknowledged the *esemplarità* and moral *imitatio* stressed by Petrarch (and by the Chronicler),[133] but more cogently imitated the actual, ritual precedents set by Roman rulers of the not-so-distant past. A neat paradigm of Cola's attitude toward the Roman past was his attachment to the Neoplatonic philosopher and military liberator of sixth-century Rome, Boethius Severinus. Cola once again played down the direct imitative aspect of his personal self-construction, employing, instead, a more oblique reading of Boethius—as with Augustus and Constantine—as exemplary (and, curiously, "holy").[134] However, as Clement VI said, *non sunt verba consona factis:* his words do not match his actions. This was true beyond the context of his correspondence with Avignon: Cola's notions of *renovatio* assumed continuity, involving the use of such figures as direct political models; his writings, however, tended to invoke them as literary *exempla,* whose political context mattered less than their moral stature.

Typically, too, it would seem that Cola's knowledge of Boethius was "according to Roman chronicles,"[135] that is, later medieval accounts; even though he was directly acquainted with Boethius's *Consolation of Philosophy.*[136] Boethius was widely discussed; again, Cola's interpretation of the past may have been filtered through much more recent, even near-contemporary readings.[137] Cola also used his notional personal "Boethian connection" not merely in reference to the past, but also to suggest the apocalyptic imagery of future time.[138]

Indeed, time did not matter. Cola made no temporal distinction between Cincinnatus returning to his plough in the second century B.C., and Boethius the "philosopher-prince" of the sixth century A.D., as models, implying or assuming a continuity into his own day, seven hundred years on. Indeed Cola borrowed models, with chronologically indiscrimi-

---

133. See chapter 4.
134. III:50, 239–48.
135. III:50, 245.
136. Cola quotes it at III:50, 329–30; III:58, 420; III:70, 280.
137. Boethius was much discussed by Giovanni Cavallini, Cola's contemporary: Laureys, "Giovanni Cavallini's *Polistoria,*" 499.
138. See chapter 2.

nate abandon, from every century of the Roman past. Only his later disillusionment in prison forced an admission, reminiscent of the cultural
shifts inherent in Panofsky's theory of disjunction,[139] that his notion of
continuity with the classical past was untenable: "It was a vain idea to try
and bring back those days of old to the people; that world is gone."[140]
Moreover, despite a sincere reverence for the figures of the past, ultimately
Cola's use of antiquity was symbolic, for the legitimization of his own politics. For him the real power lay in the law. His early discovery of the *lex*
tablet was therefore a godsend; this law, or at least the ceremony he staged
around it, encompassed every rhetorical and performative technique that
was later to inform the regime, from the emphasis on popular power and
vernacular communication, to a message to the intellectual elite inviting
their participation in a universal scholarly debate. In Cola's *lex* spectacle,
present imagery and a past "relic" combined to promote a new Roman
dispensation for the immediate future.

In concrete terms, however, Cola found the resurrection of "popular"
legal power impossible to sustain. In theory Cola and his legal advisers
revoked the *translatio* or *concessio* to the Germans. But the attempt at the
practical application of the *antiqua jurisdictio* of Rome broke down in the
very first stage, with Cola failing to persuade other Italian communes to
accept symbols of their "union" with, or subordination to, as they cor-
rectly saw this union, Rome herself.[141] A near-contemporary jurist, Cino
da Pistoia,[142] glossing the *lex regia* in the context precisely of the *concessio-
translatio* debate, could have told Cola the facts of the matter:

> Make what choice you like from these opinions because I do not care.
> For if the Roman People were in fact to make a law or custom, I know
> that, in reality, it would not be observed outside the City.[143]

It is possible that by the end of the Tribunate Cola had understood the collapse of his pan-Italic vision. The last surviving letter of the Tribunate
(III:48) demonstrates a distinct scaling down of Cola's ambitions; in this
he appointed governors to several minor towns in the Sabina area, well

---

139. Erwin Panofsky, *Renaissance and Renascences in Western Art* (Stockholm: Almqvist
& Wiksell, 1960), esp. 106–13.
140. III:70, 295–96.
141. See chapter 4.
142. One of Cola's closest advisers, Matteo dei Baccari, knew Cino's work well: see chapter 5 and notes.
143. Cited in Latin by Canning, *Political Thought,* 57.

within Rome's communal jurisdiction, which had already voluntarily submitted to Cola's regime. This suggests Cola's ultimate acceptance of "contemporary," typically communal or signorial, limits to Roman power.[144]

"I am going to be a great emperor or signore": in fact, within jurisdictional limits more typical of a contemporary Italian signore, Cola's revolution did have certain long-term effects for both the City and *contado,* as chapter 5 in particular will demonstrate. But his attempt to restore the power of imperial classical Rome across and beyond all Italy was, of course, doomed to failure. The only tools available to reconstruct the power of the past were those of a contemporary, local world; tools that proved inadequate to construct Cola's timeless, global entity, the Holy Roman Republic.

---

144. See also Massimo Miglio, "Il progetto politico di Cola di Rienzo ed i comuni dell'Italia centrale," in *Per la Storia del Trecento,* 98.

Chapter 2

Plus Quam Imperator: King of Kings, Lord of Lords?

When Cola, newly invested "Knight of the Holy Spirit," brandished his sword in the air three times, each time crying, "This is mine!" he was not simply placing himself in the tradition of the imperial coronations of the past and summoning the symbolic image of a tripartite division of the medieval *mundus*. Cola's rhetoric and gestures, while based in historic precedent, also reveal the distinctively metaphysical dimension to his thought. Gesturing with his sword, Cola surveyed backward, sideways, and forward, to assert his role in the third and final age of Rome and of world history, which, he believed, was about to begin. These three divisions of time, reflecting in turn Cola's perception of the past, present, and future of Rome, recall the Joachimist division of history into three ages: the past, age of the Father; the present, age of the Son; the future, age of the Spirit.[1] This was represented visually in Joachim's manuscripts as the Trinity of three interlocking circles of red, green, and blue, an image that

---

1. Joachim of Fiore, the twelfth-century Calabrian abbot, scholar, and mystic whose symbolic divisions of time and divinity were held in suspicion by conservatives, but used by radical political and religious activists as springboards into antipapal and often antiecclesiastical theological speculation. Joachim's most influential innovation was the interpolation of his prophecy of the "new" *pastor angelicus* (or "Angelic Pope," as this was often understood) and the *viri spirituales* into a much older eschatology, which emphasized the theme of the three divisions or *status* of world history with the Age of the Spirit imminent. Joachim's teaching on the Trinity created difficulties, however, by questioning the centrality of the role of Christ—and thus the Petrine Church—in the context of the anticipated advent of the Spirit. The institutional implications of his doctrinal revolution were potentially cataclysmic; the doctrine was duly condemned in 1215. Joachim's interpretation of the Apocalypse, however, with its heightened emphasis on the Spirit, did remain canonical. Cola's "third age" imagery is supplemented by his similarly Joachite, Fraticellan conviction that the world stood at the end of six out of seven ages: III:58, 142–43.

Cola may have known from Dante's description of those whirling circles, the Trinitarian Godhead at the conclusion of his sublime journey.[2]

The present chapter discusses Cola's use of prophetic and apocalyptic material, its content in his writing, its influence on his political outlook, its effect upon his career in office and upon his movements and machinations in exile. In fact it has been often presumed that Cola assumed his prophetic garb only after the collapse of his "real" authority. There is certainly no doubt that his attachment to prophecies then circulating among contemporary religious radicals is most evident and only truly explicit in the correspondence of 1350. Even so, historians have been divided on the issue of the importance, the extent, and the timing of Cola's debt to the prophetic heritage of the Middle Ages: this chapter, therefore, will discuss Cola's use of the material in question, while chapter 3 will focus on more broadly conceived contextual influences upon Cola's thought.

In general, political historians have given little attention to the fact that Cola was already weaving overtly eschatological elements into the autocratic identity he constructed in 1347. Intellectual historians have been more circumspect. Kristeller hints that Cola's prophetic ideas were in play before his abdication and flight;[3] Marjorie Reeves draws a finer distinction between the apocalyptic and eschatological language of 1343, and the explicit Joachite imagery of 1350; but she describes Cola's "expectation of the outpouring of the Holy Spirit"—which we may already see in his 1343 letter from Avignon—as "deeply Joachite."[4] Moreover, she describes the Fraticelli of Monte Majella as a source of inspiration for Cola, without attaching a *terminus post quem* to his assumption of those ideas. It is possible to push her case further and argue that it is likely that Cola—who

---

2. *Paradiso*, 33.115–20. For Cola's use of Dante see chapter 1.

3. Paul O. Kristeller, *Renaissance Thought* (New York: Harper and Bros., 1961), 154–55 n. 28.

4. Marjorie Reeves, *The Influence of Prophecy in the Later Middle Ages: A Study in Joachimism* (Oxford: Oxford University Press, 1969), 318–19, 420–21; *Joachim of Fiore and the Prophetic Future* (London: SPCK, 1976), 70–71. The view that Cola met Joachite ideology well before his arrival in the Abruzzi is endorsed by Michel Mollat, *The Popes at Avignon, 1305—78,* trans. Janet Love, 2d ed. (London: Thomas Nelson and Sons, 1963), 242; Michel Mollat and Philippe Wolff, *The Popular Revolutions of the Later Middle Ages,* trans. A. L. Lytton-Sells (London: Allen and Unwin, 1973), 99; but not by Bernard McGinn, *Visions of the End: Apocalyptic Traditions in the Middle Ages* (New York: Columbia University Press, 1979), 239–45. It is also disputed by Jean-Claude Maire-Vigueur, "Jean de Roquetaillade ou la rencontre de l'imaginaire," *MEFRM* 102 (1990): 385–86, who claims that Cola's prophetic language in 1350 is no more than retrospective self-justification for primarily political activities; he falls into the trap of seeing these modes of action, the political and the prophetic, in antithesis.

clearly knew where to run when his political career collapsed—had already had some contact with, or knowledge of, this group and its ideas, in or even before 1347.

It is therefore a mistake to see Cola's postures in 1350 as the only evidence of his attachment to prophetic modes of thought.[5] The present chapter hypothesizes Cola's much earlier acquaintance with multivalent forms of prophetic imagery, language, hermeneutics, and of political interpretation and analysis. The prophetic mentality may be traced to the earliest evidence of Cola's political activity, that is, his writings of 1343. From here the argument moves on into the Tribunate itself to explore the thematic and iconographic apocalypticism of Cola's regime; a reconstruction of Cola's self-identification attempts to pinpoint the aim of his translation of apocalyptic imagery into political reality. Then we will turn to the 1350 language and present a detailed analysis of Cola's newly re-created prophetic role; finally, even after his admission of disillusionment in later 1351, it is worth asking: how attached was Cola, still, to his apocalyptic schemes? Cola ostensibly abjured his prophetic heresies in Avignon in 1352–53, but he still used the glittering rhetoric of jubilant, apocalyptic expectation of an age of worldly glory to come in his journey back toward power—and death—in Rome in 1354.

The Mission of 1343

Cola's letter to the People of Rome from Avignon in 1343 had as its central theme the City of Rome as the "spouse" of the pope, rejoicing at Clement's promise to return.

> May the Roman city . . . cast off the garment of widowhood and mourning, and put on the bridal purple! Let her head be adorned with the diadem of liberty. . . . Let her resume the sceptre of justice, and . . . show herself to the bridegroom![6]

The classical image of *Roma* as woman and wife regained favor among fourteenth-century writers (it was never lost, in fact), but now she had

---

5. One passage from 1351 has been overlooked: Cola implied that the prophecies he had brought from Italy served only as a confirmation—a source of encouragement—rather than a source of ideas themselves, which by implication he had held for rather longer: III:62, 31–35; III:64, 69–72.

6. III:2, 1–9.

aged and become haggard.[7] Indeed she is overtly portrayed as the injured party, widowed by an absconding spouse, in Dante and Petrarch inter alia, as we will discuss. However, this bridal imagery was also scriptural and, most importantly to this argument, apocalyptic.[8] The identification of the bridegroom as the metastasis of the Spirit is echoed in Cola's letter, which refers to Clement repeatedly in conjunction with the Holy Ghost:

> For behold, the heavens are opened, and the glory of God . . . sheds on us the rays of the Holy Spirit. . . . Behold, indeed, the most merciful Lamb of God, confounding our sins, the most holy man, the Roman Pontiff, Father of our city, the bridegroom and Lord.[9]

The extraordinary optimism of this message contrasts starkly with the later tone of Cola's "woes"; in 1347 and 1351 Cola's messages emphasized the image of Rome not as joyous bride but as a grieving widow, awaiting a *renovatio mundi* yet to come, after a time of tribulation. Back in 1343, on the other hand, the distinct impression readers receive is that Rome had already experienced its woes, and that the new pope would swoop in promptly on the wings of reform, eschewing the "scandal" of Avignon.[10] This was the message Cola had understood from Clement's own words in 1343; the new pope had prepared an extensive sermon in reply to the Romans' plea that he should return to his Roman bride. The pope admits to wishing, rather engagingly, "to gaze upon her ample bosom,"[11] but argues his need to be in Avignon to negotiate the war between the French and English, at least until the anticipated Jubilee of 1350; a clear implication, though no promises are made, that he will return to Rome. This early sermon also gives a fair impression of the apocalyptic repertory of the fount of doctrine himself, the prince of prelates;[12] this was as much Clement's reply to more general accusations of adultery and desertion of his apocalyptic bride, as a direct answer to the Romans' request for his return.

---

7. E.g. Lucan, *Pharsalia*, 1:183; visual illustrations of medieval *Roma*, widowed, are found in Fazio degli Uberti's *Dittamondo;* see Silvia Maddalò, *In Figura Romae. Immagini di Rome nel Libro Medioevale* (Rome: Viella, 1990), plate XII (= Bibliothèque Nationale, Paris, Ital. 81, fol. 18r) and cover/figure 56.

8. Rev. 19:7–11, 21:1–2, 22:17; Dante quoted the first verse of Lamentations, on the widowed Jerusalem, as the opening line of his eighth letter (Toynbee, *Dantis Alagheris Epistolae,* 121–47).

9. III:2, 15–20.

10. III:2, 81.

11. For a partial Latin quotation see Wood, *Clement VI,* 77 n. 16.

12. The Avignon environment is discussed in chapter 3.

So far Cola may be seen within a highly "prophetic" but clearly legitimate, orthodox, even curial milieu, and we have no other evidence of
Cola's thought in 1343. Yet at least the clues to Cola's attachment to
prophecy generally, and his readiness to use it, are there. Moreover, Cola's
perception of the end of world as involving a worldly *renovatio,* rather
than the swift progression from tribulation to Last Judgment, had a distinctly Joachite flavor, as did his tendency to see eschatological *renovatio*
in terms of human, rather than divine, agency.

Given his declaration that Clement was a greater hero than Caesar or
Scipio, Cola was in for a disappointment. Clement made no move to
return to Rome, despite the oratorical overtures of 1343. The political situation of the City was permitted to deteriorate until Cola moved into
power in 1347 and reminded the Romans of the need to prepare for the
Jubilee and, of course, for the restoration of Rome's glory. His decision to
lead a revolution secretly may be read as an indication that he now
believed his "most clement" patron was not the prophesied great instiga-
tor of reform and renewal. Cola's letters to Clement in 1347 insisted that
he was still the *fidelissimus* son of Mother Church. However, between the
disillusionment of 1344 and the first evidence of his revolutionary intentions in 1346, Cola had shifted from an ideological position in which the
pope was all powerful, to a position under the terms of which the pope was
nominally supreme, but where the real power would lie with Rome's "liberator." Cola took Raymond, bishop of Orvieto, as co-rector in the first
days of the new regime of May 1347: this was window dressing. The sub-
servient tone of Cola's letters to Clement VI in 1347 conceal a very different reality. Cola had moved from praise of Clement as redeemer in 1343,
to 1347, when he said one thing with respect to papal authority, but acted
quite otherwise, as Clement realized: "His words do not match his
deeds."[13]

Clement, by not hastening back to Rome in 1343, by failing to meet the
needs of his people and their future, embodied just the type of "false
prophet" later vilified openly by Cola in 1350, in terms used traditionally
by Fraticellan radicals and prophets. Clement's "persecution" of Cola,
toward and after the end of the Tribunate of 1347, resulted in 1350 with
Cola blasting the contemporary papacy with the full force of his rhetoric.
By failing to support Cola, the instrument of God, Clement must—obvi-

---

13. IV:22, 12–14.

ously—be the enemy of God. By 1347, Cola clearly had developed enough of an antipapal stance to keep Clement deliberately misinformed. Following the disillusionment of 1343–46, Cola improved his acquaintance with the literature of both the past and the future, concerning the renewal of the world, seeking a new prophetic hero: by 1347 he had discovered himself.

The Tribunate of 1347

Cola as "Tribune" enjoyed a somewhat elevated view of his position vis-à-vis world rule. He cast himself as supreme adjudicator between kings and emperors, as his pronouncements regarding Naples, England, France, and the imperial election demonstrate: behaving "as though he were emperor, or something greater than an emperor."[14] Yet who or what could be "greater than an emperor" without being pope? Cola never claimed the papal role; the sacral powers he assumed and the rituals with which he assumed them were imperial rather than papal, as argued in chapter 1. The temporal sword was to be fixed incontrovertibly in the hand of the secular authority—his own—in 1347. And yet his self-perception has a strong flavor of the supernatural. Cola portrayed himself not merely as king, and thus mediator for his people with the priestly caste, the representatives of God; nor strictly as priest, that is, mediator between divine and earthly authority. There are elements of both, some of which verged on the blasphemous: in 1350 he talked of his downfall in 1347, when his "ministry" had only just begun, and of his hopes for resurrection:

> Just as Christ, in the thirty-third year of his life, having cast down the tyrants of hell and freed its souls, ascended, crowned, to heaven, I, in the same year of my life, as victor over the tyrants and as sole liberator of his people, desired to be raised to the laurels of the Tribunal.[15]

The evidence to be reviewed in the following section suggests that Cola had moved beyond the conventional dualism of the "Second Age," the orthodox view of the power structure of the Christian world. By 1347 Cola faced the world, it will be argued, as the special envoy of the third manifestation of God, the herald of the new age of the Holy Spirit. Later in Prague he was to propose himself as the third part of an "earthly" Trinity:

---

14. Noted in chapter 1; IV:8, 37.
15. III:57, 514–18.

emperor, Tribune, and pope. This was not an idea he culled from one particular source; this was, rather, Cola's own synthesis of Livy's heroes, Constantine's leadership of the Church, and post-Joachite speculation about the holy leader (not necessarily a cleric, of course) to come. Cola made the leap from a rejection of the contemporary leadership of "Rome" (by the aristocracy, but also, technically, and in an earthly sense, by the papacy) to self-identification as the new leader or *pastor.* Rome was the *caput mundi,* and Cola was now head of Rome, the Holy City on earth. He would assume his powers, with their semidivine trappings, and reform the world.

The language used by his associates in power also demonstrates that Cola's prophetic interpretation of Rome's contemporary circumstances belongs to his cultural context, and not just to his own imagination. The words of Francesco Baroncelli, who was to revive Cola's polity in 1353 as *Tribunus Secundus,* are highly suggestive.[16] Sent in 1347 as an ambassador to Florence, Baroncelli's surviving speech is more explicit in its apotheosis of Cola, and general millenarian tones, even, than Cola's contemporary letters:

> Our Lord, seeing these things and understanding them to be the doing of the Holy Spirit . . . [shall determine that Cola's] fame shall never perish, so long as the universe itself does not fail. . . . He has made great signs and miracles among us.[17]

The problem is that the nature of Cola's Tribunate, and his powers—legal, bureaucratic, or miraculous—were never defined, either by Cola, his partisans, or the Chronicler. There are few clues in 1347 as to the metaphysical implications of the titles Tribune and then Knight and Candidate of the Holy Spirit; Cola certainly invoked no *specific* prophecies until after the Tribunate. For clues to the interplay of influences on Cola, we must examine in detail, therefore, the attributes Cola took upon himself in 1347, and the imagery he used, from the allegorical beasts of his frescoes to the apocalyptic symbolism of his role in Rome, in order to demonstrate the "prophetic" side—with both conventional and radical elements—of Cola's self-construction in 1347, that is, even before his new role of 1349.

---

16. Baroncelli is discussed in chapters 1 and 6.

17. IV:4, 76–82; a direct paraphrase, as Burdach's notes point out, from Petrarch's sixth *canzone,* which itself is drawn from Acts 6:8 concerning the deacon Stephen, inspired by the Holy Ghost.

The Birds and the Beasts

"Bestial" analogies are among the most straightforward elements of medieval culture upon which Cola drew, very widely appropriated by politicians and ideologues, but also extensively drawn into the complex world of prophetic symbology and hermeneutics. Cola was already demonstrating the slippage between prophetic and political imagery in his own concept of Rome's status in 1346, painting the Capitol palace with rows of illustrations composed of lions, wolves, monkeys, pigs, dragons, lambs, and foxes, and captions explaining which social group these represented; then placing these in the presence of otherworldly saints and saviors.[18] The images were part of a common currency: Petrarch introduced identical images in the sonnet *Spirito Gentile,* also addressed to a Roman political reformer.[19] However, Cola's sacred sources of inspiration were usually more obscure. At the time of his abdication, Cola had depicted (at S. Maria Maddalena, then near Castel S. Angelo) an angel trampling an snake, a lizardlike creature, a lion, and a dragon. This was in fact a direct illustration of Ps. 91:13: "Thou shalt walk upon the asp and the basilisk: and thou shalt trample underfoot the lion and the dragon." However, there exists a yet more immediate visual inspiration for this image, and in a civic context it may still be seen today on the inner arch of the Porta S. Sebastiano: a sculpted low relief of 1327, recording a minor civic victory over hostile troops, shows an angel "trampling" a serpentlike monster, and plunging his spear into its mouth.

Cola's symbolic birds also deserve description. The dove on the top of the cross borne by the angel at S. Maria Maddalena is one such; others feature in the following passage:

> Then he predicted his ascendancy. . . . on the wall of S. Angelo in Pescheria . . . he had a picture painted [that] showed many falcons, looking as if they had fallen from heaven; . . . [and] a beautiful white dove, with a crown of myrtle in its beak, which it was giving to a tiny sparrow-like bird; then the dove drove the falcons from heaven. The little bird was carrying the crown and placing it on the head of the old woman.[20]

---

18. Wright, *Life,* 35.

19. Cosenza, *Petrarch,* 44–47; see also 88 (and notes on 96) for a similar passage in Petrarch's Fifth Eclogue.

20. Wright, *Life,* 38.

The falcons are easily explained as the birds favored for sport by the nobility. The sparrow, the little plebeian bird, may be Cola, hero of the poor and needy, restoring to Rome her "ancient good estate," with the assistance of the Holy Spirit. The dove is an easy image to gloss, because of its orthodox identification as a symbol of the Third Person of the Trinity. Nevertheless it was an image associated with a brand of devotion that veered dangerously close to heresy, a sort of iconological *imitatio Christi*.[21] Thomas of Celano compared Francis to the nesting dove; this was close to declaring Francis to be somehow more than human. Doves feature widely in the radical prophetic literature of later Fraticellan-Celestinian circles (including in the Angelic Oracle). We may note also the Chronicler's account of 1335, when the young Cola had just returned to Rome, which describes the pilgrimage to Rome of Venturino of Bergamo and his followers, the *Palombelli*. These "Doves," an itinerant flagellant movement, bore images of white doves with olive twigs on their red and white robes.[22]

The dove was the symbol of a new world because of Noah's ark in Gen. 8:11; but it was a also a symbol of peace used extensively in classical Roman iconography, visible still throughout the City. Cola claimed both peace and the new age as features of his regime. Like Augustus, he instigated a new *saeculum;* the new dating began with his assumption of power. The olive carried by the dove in Noah's story was also, in classical Rome, a sign of victory like the palm and the oak, or of triumph, like the myrtle. Cola's image of a dove bearing a crown was both a classical and a Christian symbol of both victory and peace. Moreover his self-proclaimed inauguration of a new age, combined with the dove imagery, together add up to more than the classical past and Christian present: they suggest the incipient Age of the Spirit.

The Woman

Another frequent element in the public art Cola commissioned in 1346 was the female personification of a city or of a concept. After Cola's disillu-

---

21. There is no clear dividing line between orthodox iconography and the imagery used in criticism of the papal establishment, although many contemporaries were tuned to the subtlest of semiotic inferences; the merest taint of association with heterodoxical ideology could attract the attention of the Inquisition.

22. *ARC,* 18–20. See Domenico Corsi, "La 'crociata' di Venturino da Bergamo nella crisi spirituale di metà Trecento," *Archivio Storico Italiano* 147 (1989): 697–747; Chiara Gennaro, "Venturino da Bergamo e la peregrinatio romana del 1335," in *Studi sul medioevo cristiano offerti a Raffaello Morghen* (Rome: Istituto storico italiano per il Medio Evo, 1974), 1:375–406.

sionment with Clement's promise to return to his bride, the joyous personification of Rome, the maiden bride, vanished, and she is depicted as a grieving, vulnerable widow:

> Cola further admonished the rulers and the people with a *similitudine* . . . of a tremendous sea, with horrible waves, storming violently. In its midst a ship was foundering, without rudder or sail . . . in [which knelt] a widow woman, dressed in black, bound in a belt of mourning, her gown ripped from her breast, her hair torn, as if she would weep. . . . The inscription said, *This is Rome.*[23]

Other personifications inhabited the tableau: four sunken ships—the fate awaiting *Roma* above—contained four lost women named Babylon, Carthage, Troy, and Jerusalem. Two islands appeared to the left; on one sat "Italy," bowed in shame; on the other, the cardinal virtues, four women grieving. All addressed *Roma* in dialect couplets, bemoaning the fate of empires. The storm-tossed ship was a familiar metaphor, particularly in Rome, where Giotto's famous *Navicella* mosaic occupied the portico of the Vatican basilica, showing Christ calming the storm as an allegory of faith.[24] The ship was the Church, filled with souls facing destruction, insecure in their faith, requiring Christ's intervention.[25] Cola had simply adapted the theme to portray God's city, the lady *Roma,* praying for her savior.

In the next tableau Cola ordered, at S. Angelo, a figure would indeed come to pull her from the brink of doom:

> In this fire was an aged woman . . . there was a church, out of which an armed angel, dressed in white, [and] scarlet vermilion, . . . carrying a naked sword; with his left hand he was taking the aged woman by the hand. . . . At the top of the bell tower . . . Sts. Peter and Paul were standing, as if they had come from heaven, saying, *Angel, angel, help our lady host!*[26]

---

23. Wright, *Life,* 33.

24. Mark 4:36–39.

25. See McGinn, *Visions of the End,* 244–45, for the prophet-saint Brigit of Sweden's similar image. Brigit arrived in Rome for the first time in 1355, shortly after Cola's death. The image was also used by Dante (*Purgatorio,* 32.129) and by Clement VI in 1343 (Wood, *Clement VI,* 81–82 n. 31).

26. Wright, *Life,* 37–38.

Petrarch's contemporary rhetoric of mother Rome and her savior-to-come is interestingly similar:

> Your mother . . . now rests securely on her son's breast. All classes swear allegiance to him; and although a youth, he is burdened with the cares of an aged statesman and stands alert with drawn sword.[27]

The imagery of Petrarch's *Spirito Gentil,* closely related to his "exhortation" to Cola and the Roman People, is highly suggestive of the Chronicler's description of the S. Angelo tableau:

> The weeping women, and the unarmed crowd
> Of children, and the old who cannot fight . . . cry aloud,
> Saying: *O kindly lord, help us, help us!*
>
> . . . .
> . . . look at the house of the true
> God, that now blazes . . .
>
> . . . .
> On the Tarpeian height, my song, you will see
> A knight whom all Italy admires.[28]

In fact, though, Petrarch's poems postdate Cola's early public commissions.[29] Was there a shared precedent for these violent scenes involving Rome and her downfall by fire and by water? Again, we should consult the Book of Revelation; although in this context, it is the suggestive iconography of illustrated versions rather than the terminology that is relevant. The iconographic canon usually contains the Fall of Babylon, which is frequently glossed in medieval Europe as a precursor of the vicious degeneration of medieval Rome before the papacy migrated to Avignon (and created a new "Babylon" there). Rome in the fourteenth century was a victim of fire, flood, war, famine, and destruction, earthquake, and plague; a city already full of ruins, and manipulated by diabolical tyrants, recalling (per-

---

27. Fifth Eclogue (Cosenza, *Petrarch,* 88); note also Dante's *Purgatorio,* 6.112–14.

28. Cosenza, *Petrarch,* 46–47; compare *Variae* 48, ca. June 24, 1347 (Cosenza, *Petrarch,* 15–32).

29. The Chronicler's account, however, may, deliberately or unconsciously, echo Petrarch's addresses to Cola and Rome. Billanovich's recent work suggests the Chronicler moved in circles similar to those of Petrarch (discussed in chap. 4).

haps even inspiring) the Sienese *Malgoverno* fresco of 1337–39; easily reminiscent of fallen Babylon illustrations. Petrarch waxed eloquent on the theme, in letters of 1350–51.[30] As noted in chapter 1, for the people of Rome under Cola, in true prophetic style, the writing—and its illustration—was, already in 1346, on the wall.

Various illustrations of the Apocalypse show people being led from the arched city gate out from the burning city, reminiscent of the description of the S. Angelo tableau.[31] One striking image, from the thirteenth-century Dublin Apocalypse,[32] shows a disheveled woman, tearing her hair, burning in a tower, as the city around her collapses in flames. The tower stands to the left of the picture, at the edge of the sea, in the midst of which a ship tosses wildly on the stormy waves; the mariners implore the woman, their arms outstretched. Shipwreck was a theme to which Cola returned in 1351,[33] talking of the wreck of Italy, floating without a pilot. In 1347, however, all four previous world empires of Babylon, Carthage, Troy, and Jerusalem were depicted, along with the threat to Rome, the fifth supreme city (echoing, of course, the five world empires represented metaphorically in Daniel's apocalyptic vision of the idol with the feet of clay).[34] A near-contemporary manuscript gives an idea of the appearance of these super-women (see fig. 2).[35]

Yet Cola's Rome was Jerusalem, not Babylon, and would rise anew at the end of the world. Most importantly, this tableau informed viewers that

---

30. E.g. *Familiari*, 11:7, to "Socrates," June 1351; Cosenza, *Petrarch*, 174–77.

31. E.g. Getty Museum, Getty Apocalypse, 37v.; British Library, Add. 17333, 36v.; Add. 35166, 21v.

32. See Montague Rhodes James, *The Dublin Apocalypse* (Cambridge: Cambridge University Press, 1932), fig. 56.

33. III:71, 2–4.

34. Dan. 2:31–44; the prophet was one of Cola's favorite sources: see III:58, 50.

35. In terms of precise stylistic sources for Cola's imagery, attention has been given—justly—to the so-called Anjou panegyric of 1335–40, dedicated to Robert of Naples, by the citizens of Prato, illustrated by an unknown Neapolitan artist; British Library, Royal 6. E. IX; *Roma* grieves on fol. 11v; see Schwartz, "Images and Illustrations," 98–99; Philippe Sonnay, "La politique artistique de Cola di Rienzo," *Revue de l'Art* 55 (1982): 35–43. An unusual feature of the manuscript, startlingly analogous to Cola's tableaux, is not just *Roma vedova* herself, but the multiplicity of other monumental female personifications in the text: Florence, Italy, Faith, Hope, and Charity (see Sonnay passim for illustrations of these); two cardinal virtues, Philosophy, the seven Liberal Arts and the nine Muses. Figure 2 offers a selection. Another strikingly close similarity, not given due weight by the art historians, is that the cities all speak rhyming verses, appealing to Robert, just as the verses in Cola's tableaux appeal to God.

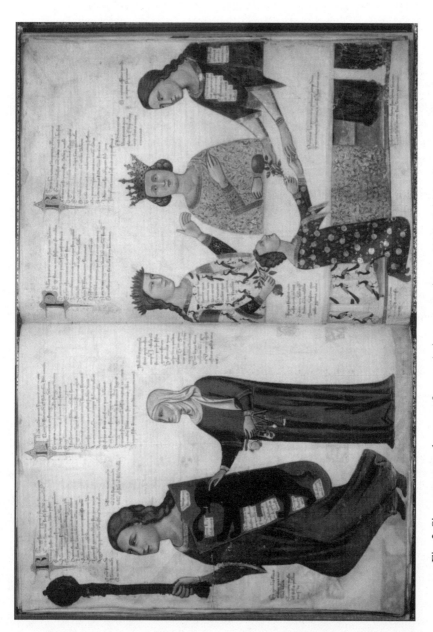

Fig. 2. Six monumental women figures, Anjou panegyric (ca. 1330). British Library, Mss Royal 6.E.IX, fols. 21v–22r.

it would not be the Church that would survive; it would be *Roma* herself. Rome was to be saved as the home of the Spirit; not as the Temple, nor as the Church, the manifestations of God's presence in the two previous ages. After her prayers in the unsafe ship of the Church, and then her torment in the burning Church, *Roma* was to be pulled free: God's Holy City would be led to safety by the armed angel at S. Angelo. The City would be protected by the angel near Castel S. Angelo, who trampled the inimical beasts: the asp and the basilisk, the lion and the dragon.

The Angel

In December 1348 the Porta S. Sebastiano sculpture of 1327 acquired a companion at S. Maria Maddelena. Yet the fact that Cola's last foray into visual propaganda was immediately vandalized suggests that the image held powerful resonances, provoking defiance and defilement from certain partisan elements.[36] Psalm 91 actually addresses "You, God's People," calling the people to trample the beasts that we have seen used as metaphors for the corrupt baronial and administrative personnel of the city. The image of the armed angel was already associated with *popolo* self-assertion in Rome in 1327; later, in 1378, the Florentine Ciompi adopted the image of an angel with a sword and a cross and described themselves as the *popolo di Dio,* closely echoing both the political overtones and iconographic features of Cola's public angels of 1347.

Frederick Antal claimed that Cola's angel was a representation of himself, as the champion of the People of Rome.[37] This accords with the elevated nature of Cola's self- perception, but underestimates the multivalence of the image for the city—ever since Gregory's sixth-century vision of Michael above Hadrian's mausoleum, prompting its renaming as the Castle of the Archangel.[38] The armed angel was a common occurrence in popular myth, as well as orthodox theology; and this was particularly true in Rome, the New Jerusalem. He also will return at Armageddon, where, with the power of God, he will fight the Devil and cast him into the bottomless pit for a thousand years. It is this episode that explains the traditional iconography of Michael with his spear in the dragon, "that old ser-

---

36. Wright, *Life,* 125; *ARC,* 176.

37. Frederick Antal, *Florentine Painting and Its Social Background* (New York: K. Paul, 1947), 264.

38. See Schwartz, "Images and Illustrations," 214–26, on the particular importance of the archangel in Rome.

pent, which is the Devil."[39] Michael the archangel had a traditional part to play in the hierarchy of heaven, as the avenging angel, and also defender of Israel and Jerusalem[40] and therefore of the apocalyptic New Jerusalem, Rome.

Cola's confessions in 1350 of his earlier hubris do not suggest that he identified himself as Rome's archangel. Michael was certainly a sponsor of the 1347 Tribunate,[41] and therefore enemy of its enemies, especially of the Colonna. Giovanni Colonna, Cardinal-Deacon of S. Angelo in Pescheria, accused him falsely of heresy, schism, and invocation of demons, according to Cola's public speech to the People on St. Michael's Day (September 29, 1347). Therefore Michael punished the Colonna for their offense against him, Cola: hence the Porta S. Lorenzo slaughter, on St. Martin's Day.[42] Cola again alluded to the assistance of the archangel when he thanked God for his escape from the clutches of the Castel S. Angelo Orsini in January 1348: God struck them down of plague "in their very own Castel S. Angelo itself, where Michael, as it is written, appeared to Gregory."[43]

The imagery of the armed archangel is, of course, ancient. An example from fourth-century Rome, the so-called Joshua Roll, sets an early iconographic precedent; a winged and armored figure in classicizing *contrapposto,* bearing sword and bow.[44] The evolution of the figure in Byzantine, and then south central Italian iconography, tends to show a figure with a spear,[45] transfixing the serpent. After the Duecento, however, the hitherto relatively small number of examples of Michael with a sword increases.[46]

---

39. Rev. 12:7, 20:2 (also Jude 9).

40. See Norman Cohn, *Cosmos, Chaos, and the World to Come: The Ancient Roots of Apocalyptic Faith* (New Haven: Yale University Press, 1993), 215.

41. III:57, 861–70.

42. Cola had already claimed (III:46, 108) to have adopted the symbol of the dove because of his victory on St. Columba's Day, i.e., November 20. Martin's feast day was November 11, not the twentieth, but in this context Cola evidently preferred to stress the martial aspects of the knight and tribune's son Martin—more akin to Michael the slayer—to the pacific dove of Columba, even at the expense of the truth.

43. III:57, 1153–60; in the guise less of Rome's savior than of the slaying archangel of 2 Chron. 21:16.

44. B.A.V. Pal. Gr. 431.

45. Schwartz's investigation of the iconography of Michael is useful. She fails, however, to give appropriate weight to the alternative canonical image of Michael wielding the lance. This was, after all, the format chosen by Cola for his "final" angel at Castel S. Angelo; it is also represented in Pietro Cavallini's ca. 1300 *Last Judgment* at S. Cecilia.

46. Schwartz, "Images and Illustrations," 266, notes other fourteenth-century examples, none of which, unfortunately, correspond with her "sword" description. She fails to note the illustration of Dante's *Purgatorio,* 8:26, "two angels both with flaming swords" at British Library (London) Add. 21965, 73r.

One such example, and important in the context of this investigation, is the Brancacci Tabernacle from S. Maria in Trastevere. Unfortunately, the only surviving illustration is a seventeenth-century ink drawing.[47] It shows very clearly, nonetheless, Michael trampling the dragon underfoot but carrying, instead of a spear, a sword and an orb. The dating is uncertain, between 1294 and 1385 (the only two recorded dates of Brancacci cardinalates). The inscription describes him as "Archangel, Defender of the Church, Protector of Rome, head of the world."

The Brancacci angel and the "angel-savior" at S. Angelo in Pescheria painted for Cola in 1346, both distinguished by the naked sword and orb, clearly belong to the same context. A last near-contemporary example of a sword and orb-bearing Michael the archangel, from the very period of Cola's regime, was discovered in the Lateran hospital circa 1900.[48] Paradoxically, the only sword-bearing angel that acts as a potential textual source is the angel who chastises, but thereby purifies, David's Jerusalem, as well as destroying its enemies.

The angels designed by Cola seem to represent Michael, then, guardian of the City, in different, but in neither case unprecedented, guises. The later angel was left behind by Cola to guard the people from those evil animals, the nobles and corrupt officials, allegories by extension of Satan, the serpent. The earlier angel, of the S. Angelo tableau, bears a sword before him: this was of course the traditional symbol of justice, very heavily emphasized in Cola's post-1347 language, as we will see. In 1347, however, this message was already clear: "Below . . . was written, *The time of great justice is coming, and you await the time.*"[49]

Cola did not claim to be Michael himself but was happy to attach "angelic" attributes, and intervention, to his own regime and his own identity. Particularly the sword, the sword of justice, attracted Cola's attention. We may note in this context the interesting and bogus connection in Cola's account of Michael with the knight (and tribune's son) St. Martin (the events of whose feast day are discussed above). Cola also retained a special interest in St. George: like the archangel Michael, a slayer of dragons, though always with a spear; like St. Martin, Cola was also a knight. Cola's "predictions" about justice, above, appeared on the door of

---

47. Waetzoldt, *Kopien*, fig. 285. Also noted with later dating by Schwartz, "Images and Illustrations," 84.

48. Laura Filippini, *La Scultura del Trecento in Roma* (Turin, 1908), 98 (fig. 29): commissioned, interestingly, by the man who (according to the Chronicler) struck the first blow against Cola in 1354 (see chap. 6).

49. Wright, *Life*, 38.

S. Giorgio in Velabro; the ancient banner appeared in two of Cola's cere-monies;[50] "Finally, the aforementioned nobles, inspired by the Holy Spirit, confessed, and afterwards . . . celebrated a solemn Mass to the Holy Spirit where the head and banner of St. George is kept."[51]

The Holy Spirit, the theme of purification, the idea of renovation, the exercise of justice, and the assumption of a sacred "knighthood"; all these constitute the range of elements at the interstices of Cola's self-representa-tion:

> He was made a knight of the bath on the vigil of the Assumption in August. . . . Before the Tribune came a man who carried in his hand a naked sword; . . . in his own hand he was carrying a staff of steel. . . . When morning came, . . . his sword was bound on by Messer Vico Scuotto, along with spurs of gold as a sign of knighthood. Then the Tri-bune drew his sword from its sheath and waved it in the air toward the three divisions of the world, saying, "This is mine; this is mine; this is mine."[52]

Cola's familiarity with the traditional imperial coronation procedure, dur-ing which the emperor is invested with a sword, has been discussed, as have the pontifical regulations for the investiture of a new knight; another curious passage may be cited:

> Bless this sword, through the invocation of your holy name and by the grace . . . of the Holy Spirit . . . that it may be buckled on and lead to victory over the invisible enemies underfoot. . . .
>
> Holy Lord, you have desired the institution of the military order, for the protection of the people.[53]

The elements "borrowed" by Cola are startling clear; the suggestion that the grace of the Spirit will bring victory is particularly striking. Cola took the title *Cavaliere dello Spirito Sancto* for himself; rather gruesomely, after the victory at Porta S. Lorenzo, he knighted his son Lorenzo in the blood of Stefano Colonna.[54] By becoming a warrior-knight of the Holy Spirit, of the Last Age, when Antichrist would be brought to justice, Cola added a

---

50. Ibid., 38, 41.
51. III:40, 49–54.
52. Wright, *Life*, 72.
53. Andreiu, *Le Pontifical Romain*, 3:447–48.
54. Wright, *Life*, 90; *ARC*, 152.

new element into an already vividly eschatological Roman political gestalt.

Yet this strange spiritual knighthood was also, to an extent, a product of Cola's context and not just his imagination. The notion of the imminence of the events of the Apocalypse, heightened by Joachite notions of Age of the Spirit, held vast appeal. From contemporary Naples a request concerning membership of an elite *Ordo Sancti Spiritus* was sent to Clement VI in 1352.[55] The knight dressed in white and bore the device of the dove on his chest; banners in battles were to be silver or white with a dove symbol. During chapter meetings, knights also combined the apocalyptic with the antique, wearing a laurel wreath in conscious imitation of the triumphal honors of antiquity. A Neapolitan manuscript detailing the statutes of the so-called Order of the Knot (ca. 1354–55) probably describes, instead, the Angevin "Order of the Holy Spirit"; the iconography of its illustrations seem to echo the descriptions of Cola as knight (see fig. 3).[56] Cola might have provided the order with a impressive precedent: or perhaps he was already a member—or even its founder—back in 1347: "As Knight of the Holy Spirit, I arranged to be crowned . . . with the tribunician laurels."[57] In the event—his coronation as *Tribunus Augustus* on August 15, 1347—Cola did not draw the line at a single laurel crown, but was awarded six crowns, of various leaves and of silver, which, as he claims, "I took devoutly, in memory of the six gifts of the Holy Spirit."[58]

The multiple crowns, the insignia and the sword of justice, the knighthood, and the titles all demonstrate Cola's classicizing tendencies, as described in chapter 1. To use them, however, in the context of the Holy

---

55. Burdach and Piur, *Briefwechsel,* 5:202.

56. Bibliothèque Nationale, Paris, Fr 4274, fol. 10r; more illustrations in Ferdinando Bologna, *I Pittori alla Corte Angioina di Napoli (1266–1414)* (Rome: Ugo Bozzi, 1969), figs. 47–51. This manuscript, probably illustrated by the miniaturist Cristoforo Orimina, has yet to be compared in detail with Cola's imagery, both verbal and iconographic. The areas of overlap are considerable, however: the order evidently gave a high priority to embarking for the Holy Land, which Cola himself claimed to desire after his failure in Bohemia. Sacro-secular feasts and banners, real battles (fig. 3) against men bearing the evil device of the scorpion (the "scorpioniti," interestingly, as we have seen, are also described the enemies of the Sun of the Angelic Oracle), and a ubiquitous paraclete, symbol of the Holy Ghost, also feature, in the same way as they appear in word, image, dream, and deed in Cola's Tribunate. Pentecost was of course the day Cola chose to stage his revolution, and also the day Clement was made pope. Joanna chose Pentecost 1352 as the date for her wedding to Andrew's replacement, Lewis of Taranto; on the same day Lewis founded, or perhaps only refounded, the so-called Order of the Knot (or Order of the Holy Ghost).

57. III:18, 129–31.

58. III:35, 20–21.

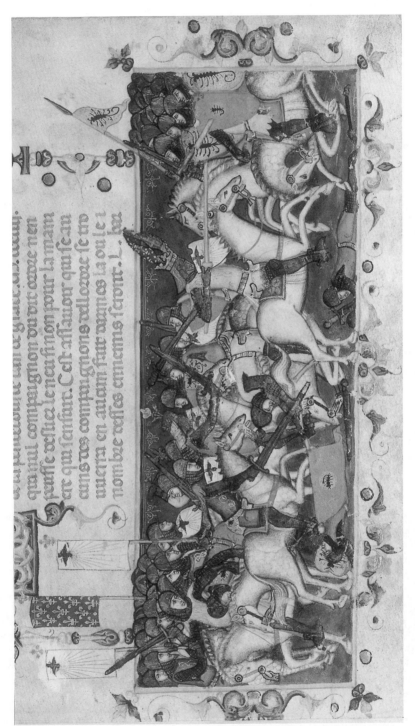

Fig. 3. Cristoforo Orimina, Statutes of the Order of the Holy Spirit (or "Knot") (ca. 1354), Spiritual Knights versus Scorpionites. Bibliothèque Nationale, Paris, MS FR 4274, fol. 10r.

Ghost was distinctly "unclassical." The same process may be observed with reference to the arms that, as a new knight, Cola assumed:[59]

In his right hand he carried a brightly polished steel rod; on its summit was an apple[60] of gilded silver, and above the apple a little cross of gold. . . . The field of [his] standard was white, with a sun of shining gold in the middle, surrounded by silver stars.[61]

These arms, Cola claimed, he had copied from his hero Boethius Severinus, sixth-century "rector and prince" of Rome.[62] As the Christian-visionary defender of the Sacred Roman Republic, Cola's claim of parity with Boethius is logical. These arms, however—Cola actually described them as a golden sun against an azure field, surrounded by seven silver stars—may also be interpreted as more powerfully symbolic than merely a display of homage to a late antique hero: Cola's imagery was apocalyptic.

And he had in his right hand seven stars . . . and his countenance was as the sun shineth in its strength. . . . The seven stars are the angels of the seven churches. . . .
And a great sign was seen in heaven; a woman arrayed with the sun, and the moon under her feet, and upon her head a crown of twelve stars.[63]

Cola's appearance and his garments constantly evoked the imagery of both past and future: "He was dressed in a white silk robe, astonishingly bright, decorated with threads of gold."[64] This certainly recalls his title, *Candidatus;* but it also echoes the Book of Revelation:[65]

---

59. Cola's arms, painted on the walls of the Capitol facing into the Forum, were still apparently visible in 1646; see Sonnay, "La politique artistique," 43 n. 32.

60. Surely a globe or an orb; a typical attempt to resolve the mysterious and symbolic with rather prosaic explanation (see the discussion of the Chronicler in chap. 4).

61. Wright, *Life,* 52.

62. III:50, 329–30; also III:58, 413–77; III:64, 155–56; see chapter 1. Among Boethius's greatest philosophical source of influence was Cicero's *Somnium Scipionis,* with the Neoplatonic commentary of Macrobius, although a case has been made for the additional influence of early apocalypses such as the *Visio Sancti Pauli:* Michael D. Cherniss, *Boethian Apocalypse: Studies in Middle English Vision Poetry* (Norman, Okla.: Pilgrim Press, 1987), 12, 34–35.

63. Rev. 1:16–20, 12:1.

64. Wright, *Life,* 71; *ARC,* 136.

65. Rev. 4:4, 15:6.

I saw four and twenty elders sitting, clothed in white raiment; and they had on their heads crowns of gold . . . And the seven angels came out of the temple . . . clothed in pure and white linen, . . . their breasts girded with golden girdles.

For Cola, the garments of white and gold were connected to his role as Knight of the Holy Spirit:

There was a festival of St. John in June. . . . The Tribune rode, with a great company of knights, mounted on a white war horse, dressed in white vestments lined with silk and decorated with gold laces. He looked beautiful and terrifying.[66]

On another occasion, when Cola dressed after the night of his vigil, for the assumption of the insignia of knighthood, he did not dress in white, but in scarlet; the interplay of these colors too is significant.[67]

The visual and symbolic impact of Cola's clothing, and its statements regarding not just the past but the future of Rome, matches the powerful messages of the other insignia he appropriated: the crowns and the sword. It is interesting that Cola felt entitled to use both crown and sword in late 1346, even before he had been elected Tribune by popular acclamation, let alone before the ceremonies in which these symbols were awarded to him. It suggests he believed already in his superhuman role. The Lateran exposition of 1346 is archetypal:[68]

He was dressed in a cloak . . . and a hood of fine white cloth; on his head he wore a white hat, with a circle of golden crowns around the brim; from the upper part of the hat arose a naked silver sword, the point of which went into the foremost crown and divided it in the middle.

---

66. Wright, *Life,* 51. Note the prophet's vision of a man "clothed in linen and girded in gold, his face as the appearance of lightning and his eyes as lamps of fire" (Dan. 10:5–6).

67. The "savior-angel" of S. Angelo is dressed "in white . . . his cloak of scarlet vermil- ion." St. George's colors, obviously, fit the paradigm. The combination, interestingly, was endorsed by both flagellant penitentials (hence Venturino's *Palombelli; ARC,* 19) and civic officials (a fresco in the Tarquinia cathedral crypt shows three civic officials in red and white fur and silk, with a similar pennant; Serena Romano, *Eclissi di Roma. Pittura Murale a Roma e nel Lazio da Bonifacio VIII a Martino V* [Rome: Argos, 1992], 248). Note also Cola's threat to execute nobles in 1347: "He commanded that the audience hall should be decorated with red and white silk bunting, and it was done. This he did to symbolise blood" (Wright, *Life,* 76; see also 46).

68. Wright, *Life,* 36.

Cola, it seems, had already in 1346 decided on the messages that his outfits were to proclaim, even before he was in a position to assume, with due ceremony, the realities of power in 1347. Once he had this opportunity, his appearances dazzled spectators with the complexity of the grandeur and symbolism. It was beyond many of his peers: a number, including his own biographer, described him as mad.[69] A similar incomprehension has gripped historians attempting to explain his pose—and his clothes—in terms of his dedication to the Holy Spirit. There is, however, one curious apocalyptic character whose attributes appear to match very closely Cola's symbolic gestures and appearances. An examination of this figure may move us toward unraveling the mysteries of Cola's self-perception.

The Rider and the Judge

> And behold I saw the heavens opened; and behold, a white horse, and he that sat thereon, called Faithful and True; and in righteousness he doth judge and make war. And his eyes are a flame of fire, and upon his head are many crowns. . . . And he is arrayed in a garment sprinkled with blood; and his name is The Word of God. . . . And out of his mouth procedeth a sharp sword, that with it he should smite the nations: and he shall rule them with a rod of iron. . . .
> . . . And he hath on his garment and on his thigh a name written, KING OF KINGS, AND LORD OF LORDS.[70]

We have seen how Cola fought for liberty and justice—and the people of Rome had to fight, too, under his banner—against the tyranny of the evil beasts and the treachery of Antichrist; that is, against anarchic barons, the papal adulterer, and his persecuting legates. Cola required a military role in the other world to complement his campaigns in the real world: the Rider Faithful and True of the Apocalypse offers an incomparable model. Cola was inspired by the Logos of John, the "spiritual" Gospel, the *Verbum Dei;* the word of the mouth that would be a sword,[71] the sword of justice. With this sword Cola would avenge the ills done to the People of God by the false leaders, and to the Bride by her adulterous spouse. He would

---

69. The Chronicler's attitude is fully examined in chapter 4.
70. Rev. 19:7–16.
71. Note Heb. 4:12: "The word of God is quick, and powerful, and sharper than any two-edged sword."

wield the sword to arbitrate—as *plus quam imperator* (King of Kings? Lord of Lords?)[72]—as judge over Rome, but also over the world, styling himself *Amator Orbis,* Lover of the World. He would call to appear before his judicial tribunal—merging the roles of Tribune and judge—the claimants to power in the Neapolitan kingdom, the German Empire, the Anglo-French conflict, and Constantinople—and even Babylon—in the east;[73] just as the Rider "in righteousness . . . doth judge and make war":

> Then he [Cola] had the Tribunal crown, which I [the Chronicler] shall describe later, placed on his head . . . and said, "I will judge the entire world in justice, and the people in equity."[74]

The original phrase is from Ps. 9:7–8 (Douay version): "The Lord . . . hath prepared his throne for judgement. And he shall judge the world in righteousness, he shall judge the people in justice." Moreover, as judge but warrior-knight too, Cola would also carry his sword before him, lead his mounted knights and his Holy Militia into the field, and return with the crowns of victory.

Can Cola's other titles be squared with this apocalyptic identity? *Candidatus* could suggest the gleaming white robes of either the political or the spiritual neophyte. The classical *tribunus,* moreover, could be either a representative of the People in the Senate, or a military officer. Under the Julio-Claudians, the office was swallowed up into the duties and titles of the emperor, and the office of the *tribunus Augusti,* the imperial tribune as protector of his people, came into being (as described in chapter 1). In the postclassical world, "the tribunal" became (and remains) the place for judges to sit in judgment.[75] Cola's title, *Tribunus Romanus,* later *Tribunus Augustus,* draws these diverse "tribunician" themes—themes of the shift from Republic to empire, of battle, of protection and of judgment—back together. However, one patristic interpretation of this very classical title, Tribune, by Gregory the Great, is almost universally overlooked.[76] Gregory provided a curious etymological derivation of *tribunus* from *tribus,* in the process claiming that tribunes must be understood to be "spiritual

---

72. Interestingly, "Joachim" uses this very appellation in his response to Cyril and in the commentary on the first chapter of the Oracle; Burdach and Piur, *Briefwechsel,* 4:246.

73. Cola's claims to world influence are especially explicit in III:50, 289–304.

74. Wright, *Life,* 66.

75. Cola himself uses the term in this sense in III:57, 10.

76. Except, of course, by the omniscient Burdach: see *Briefwechsel,* 5:377–78 for full references.

men, simple in knowledge, inflamed by love of God." Interestingly, *spirituales viri* was exactly the phrase later employed by Joachim to describe his future reformers of the world. And the use of the term *simplex,* its identification with the "celestial" reformer, and a mistrust of the new Aristotelian *scientia,* is found throughout pseudo-Joachimist literature; and in Cola's letters of 1350.[77] Cola's Tribune was thus the representative on earth of God's new dispensation, *liberator rei publicae,* protector of the people, *candidatus et miles Sancti spiriti,* Gregory's *vir spiritualis,* ruler of the New Jerusalem, who will sit in judgment upon the world.

Cola was hardly unique among rulers and prophets in adopting quasi-messianic attributes, or claiming to represent God on earth. This was by no means a non- or pre-Christian notion: the idea of divine rulership was, for example, far more crucial to the Christian Frederick II, *stupor mundi,*[78] than to the first Augustus, who rejected worship in his lifetime.[79] The phrase from Psalms and Revelation ("I shall judge the world") is also found in some of the earliest postclassical constructions of the emperor's duties. The seventh-century Isidore of Seville, for example, declared that the king's *ministerium* was "to rule with equity and justice and to ensure peace for the people." Other prophetic figures were granted superhuman status by their followers: the scholar-prophet Olivi was seen by the Beguines as an angel of the Apocalypse and messenger of God.[80] Significantly, he was also identified by Clareno (see chap. 3) as the *Sol* of the Angelic Oracle, as Cola was years later. Francis, with his stigmata and apostolic poverty, veered extremely close to identification as a new Christ, the Christ of the Second Coming. He was cast as the sixth angel of the Apocalypse, breaking vials at the end of the world, by John of Parma in 1247. Cola, comparing himself to Francis buttressing the Church, also accepted Francis as the sixth angel; in one particularly explicit pseudo-Joachite passage he commented on the present world as being "at the end of the Sixth Age."[81] Cola clearly envisioned himself among the *dramatis personae* of those who heralded the Last Judgment.

---

77. E.g. III:58, 149–54, 534.
78. Nicholas of Bari addressed him in the manner of Gabriel's Annunciation to Mary: "Hail, Lord Emperor, full of the grace of God. The Lord is with you, that is, was and will be."
79. Augustus as precedent is discussed in chapter 1.
80. See Raoul Manselli, *Il sopranaturale e la religione popolare nel Medioevo* (Rome: Edizioni Studium, 1985), 183.
81. III:58, 142, 201.

On the theme of the Just Judge, Cola's Capitoline image of the drowning women and the evil beasts also contained a greater personage:

Above was Heaven; in the middle stood the Divine Majesty, as if come in judgement. Two swords came out of his mouth, in one direction and the other.[82]

In many medieval commentaries on the Apocalypse, the Rider *Fidelis et Verax* with his mouth- sword is glossed as Christ himself, presumably on the basis of the initial vision of John:

I saw one like unto the Son of man . . . he had in his right hand seven stars: and out of his mouth proceeded a sharp two-edged sword. . . .
   These things saith he that hath the sharp two-edged sword: . . . Repent therefore; or else . . . I will make war on them with the sword of my mouth.[83]

Christ as the Rider, therefore, was a logical—and by the later Middle Ages, already traditional—identification. Yet Cola shared these attributes, that is, the sword, the clothing, the horse, the symbols of justice. However, not every glossator fixed the identity of the Rider as Christ.[84]

To him will I give authority over the nations: and he shall rule them with a rod of iron . . . He that overcometh, the same shall be dressed in white raiment. . . . I will write upon him the name of my God, and the name of the city of my God, which is new Jerusalem.[85]

The speaker here is the Son of Man, Christ, not predicting his own return as the crowned ruler of nations with the iron rod, nor himself as the white-clothed champion of the New Jerusalem, but, essentially, foretelling the worldly rewards of "him that overcometh." The grammatical object of the passage is not Christ himself, but the Rider Faithful and True, who, nev-

---

82. Wright, *Life*, 35.
83. Rev. 1:12–16, 2:12, 16.
84. Frederic van der Meer, *Maiestas Domini: Théophanies de L'Art Chrétien* (Rome, 1931), 413, lists those of the Rider's features that are shared by God's various other incarnations.
85. Rev. 2:26–28, 3:5, 11–12.

ertheless, bears Christ's double-edged sword in Rev. 19:15: a figure who was truly *plus quam imperator,* greater than emperor. Cola had his sword carried before him in his processions; in his hand, he carried a "rod of iron."[86]

It may be asserted, then, that where Cola had depicted "the Divine Majesty, as if come in judgement," he was not trying to indicate that he, Cola, was the Son of Man of the Apocalypse. Rather Cola was presenting himself as the emissary of the Spirit, the crowned knight on the white horse wielding the sword of justice, the judge on the Tribunal of the Capitol in the *caput mundi,* New Jerusalem. Moreover near-contemporary depictions from Naples of the Rider (S. Maria Donnaregina circa 1330; Apocalypse panel paintings ca. 1330;[87] see fig. 4) show this sword-spitting King of Kings also wearing seven crowns above his head, even though this is not specified in Revelation; it is a vivid and provocative reminder of Cola's multiple coronation.

And this symbolism was by no means lost on his contemporaries in Avignon. A letter of September 1347 serves to demonstrate how close to the edge of heresy Cola had veered, when he was forced to defend himself angrily against accusations regarding his use of the image of the double-edged sword: "What they are saying of us concerning the 'sword sharp on both sides' is absolutely false; but we shall leave vengeance to God . . . May he judge them!"[88] Regrettably, we do not have the precise accusation in point; but the nature of the objection may be inferred from the vehemence of the denial.

In late 1347 Cola still cared to be considered as a faithful son of the church (though he was hardly behaving as a loyal subject of the Vicar of Rome). This, of course, was about to change, with the collapse of his power, his persecution and flight over the mountains.

---

86. Wright, *Life,* 52, 126; *ARC,* 121, 177. Cola refers to his *virga ferrea* at III:57, 1071. The woman clothed in the sun of Rev. 12:1, whose attributes match Cola's Boethian arms, has a son, who will rule all nations with a rod of iron (12:5). Neatly enough, Cola compared Boethius's mother, who was Bohemian, with his own Bohemian "imperial" birthright. Cola also gave his son (Lorenzo?) the (additional?) name "Boethius" (III:50, 245–47).

87. Sometimes claimed as a work of Giotto, these panels, now in Stuttgart, have recently been exhibited in the Accademia in Florence (summer 2000). See Luisa Castelfranchi, "Le storie apocalittiche di Stoccarda e quelle di Giusto da Padova," *Prospettiva* 33–36 (1983–84): 33–44, for a description and illustrations.

88. III:40, 87–93.

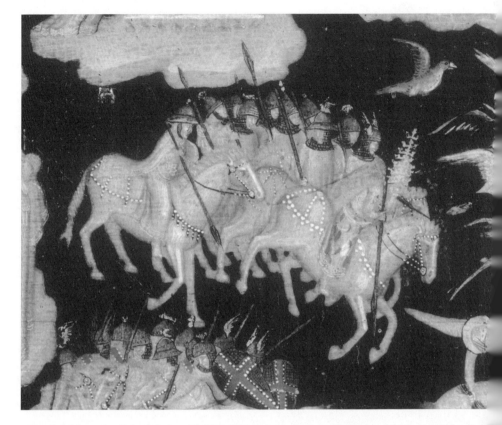

Fig. 4. Meister der Erbach'schen Tafeln, *Scenes from the Apocalypse* (ca. 1330), the Rider Faithful and True (with multiple crown and mouth-sword). Courtesy of Staatsgalerie Stuttgart.

The Mission of 1350

It was not until his lengthy apologia of August 15, 1350, that Cola openly stated his dependence on the "Angelic Oracle";[89] in the follow-up letter he explicitly declared that his downfall and imprisonment had been predicted by heaven, referring to Cyril, Joachim, and Gilbert.[90] What had happened in the meantime?

After December 15, 1347, when Cola's authority collapsed, he abdicated; in early 1348 he escaped both his enemies and the Plague to begin a

---

89. III:57, 944–1150.

90. III:58, 241–45. Only the briefest hint of the language of the Oracle appears at III:50, 451–52, dated less than a month before.

peculiar peregrination taking him first south into Campania and then east into the Abruzzese mountains. Here he received new impetus from a prophecy regarding the resurrection of Roman power, which eventually drove him to Prague in 1350. This prophecy, the remarkably named Angelic Oracle of Cyril, seemed to Cola a blueprint of his life and career. At least, that was how it was presented by the Oracle's greatest fan, the mysterious leader of the mountain band of spirituals that Cola joined: Fra Angelo, "Brother Angel."[91]

The Angelic Oracle itself follows a well-known pseudo-Joachite pattern: a heroic, saintly redeemer faces mysterious symbolism and diabolic tribulation in his attempt to reform the exercise of spiritual and temporal power in this world; ultimately he succeeds.[92] The reader, meanwhile, faces as many tribulations attempting to comprehend the extant Oracle text, with its range of peculiarly arcane symbols and abstruse language. Even the structure is incredibly complicated: first, the "great English theologian" Gilbert introduces the text of the Oracle, claiming to have discovered it in Cluny. The text describes a divine revelation, during mass, to Cyril, a twelfth-century Carmelite abbot in Jerusalem. An angel brought Cyril two silver tablets, upon which prophecies were engraved, which Cyril was instructed to copy onto parchment. Gilbert describes Cyril's confusion over the obscure predictions, and that he sent the Oracle to Joachim of Fiore, for an explanation. Gilbert then presents the subsequent correspondence of Cyril and the pseudo-Joachim as a preface to the text proper, while each of the eleven chapters is followed by pseudo-Joachim's exegesis. The Oracle thereby claims eleventh-century origins (Joachim died in 1202), but in reality both the pseudonymous commentary and the Oracle itself probably date from the 1290s, a fertile period in manufacturing of pseudo-Joachite prophecies. Such prophecies were used by political agitators for centuries to come, first but not least by the ex-Tribune.

For literally hundreds of lines in his two vast treatises of 1350 Cola focused precisely on the application of the content of the Cyril prophecies to his career, effectively producing a commentary to rival that of the so-called Joachim. The central figure, a "Sun," not identified by pseudo-Joachim, conquers the "Scorpion" and its offspring, the agents of the evil simoniac papacy, as Cola's gloss agrees.[93] Fra Angelo had identified

---

91. His possible identity is discussed in chapter 3.
92. The *Oraculum Cyrilli* is edited by Paul Piur in Burdach and Piur, *Briefwechsel,* 4:221–327.
93. III:57, 1143–50.

Cola as *Sol,* the past and future redeemer of Rome, the "poor and greedy City."[94]

The prophecy claims that the Sun would rise from obscure beginnings and drive out the *scorpioniti,* but then be captured: "He shall sit in the dust alone, groaning, humiliated throughout the time of the Jubilee."[95] The Jubilee reference must have seemed very convincing. Who else could this mean but Cola and Rome, in 1350? Cola linked the Oracle events to his Tribunate in such minute detail as to defy full exposition here. Elements such as the flying dove, sceptres, violent dogs, astrological positions, and so on, were fully glossed in Cola's treatise, retroactively, for their application to the Tribunate of 1347.[96] Cola was so convinced that the early chapters applied to his past, that he was ready to believe that the rest of the Oracle, the escape and resurrection of the Sun, described his future; a perfect case of *vaticinium ex eventu.* The events of the fourth chapter were now in progress, in 1350: he had fought the *fortes stimuli,* the "harsh goads," interpreted already by pseudo-Joachim as the nobles and potentates; he had escaped the "hunters of the simple," that is, the Inquisitors, who had harassed him following his abdication;[97] and he had risen again, though the "crowns and symbols of justice" were gone.[98] Cola spent considerable time discussing the "crowns of Arrogance" of the third chapter of the oracle: these were the six crowns granted him on August 15, 1347, of course.[99] God then punished Cola for his presumption, with the exile and disgrace predicted in the Oracle.[100]

Cola's self-appointed role as consul of widows, orphans, and other needy parts of contemporary society in 1343 has been demonstrated to have had both a past literary and a "real" political precedent in Rome. In pseudo-Joachim's introductory notes to Cyril, however, the same duty arises in a prophetic context: pseudo-Joachim stresses that precisely this task, "That is, provision for widows, wards, and others in need,"[101] has

---

94. *Oraculum Cyrilli,* chap. 1, line 36 (= Oracle 1:36); Burdach and Piur, *Briefwechsel,* 4:252.

95. Oracle 1:16–18 (Burdach and Piur, *Briefwechsel,* 4:252); III:64, 10–12.

96. III:57, 944–1150. Philip Jacks, *The Antiquarian and the Myth of Antiquity: The Origins of Rome in Renaissance Thought* (Cambridge: Cambridge University Press, 1993), 59–61, is the only scholar to focus on Cola's astrological interests.

97. Oracle 11:12 (Burdach and Piur, *Briefwechsel,* 4:315). At III:58, 608 Cola claims that these are the words of Cyril, Joachim, and Merlin.

98. Oracle 2:14 (Burdach and Piur, *Briefwechsel,* 4:260).

99. Oracle 3:1 (Burdach and Piur, *Briefwechsel,* 4:262).

100. III:49, 19–23; III:57, III:62.

101. Oracle, Joachim to Cyril, 90–91 (Burdach and Piur, *Briefwechsel,* 4:249).

been neglected by the contemporary church, implying that it would be the role of the messianic reformer to correct this; and adding yet a further potential dimension to the inspiration behind Cola's political stance of nearly a decade before.

The central section of the third chapter of the Oracle attacks the less than salubrious activities of the bridegroom and bride, *fornicantes* in various circumstances. Cola was convinced that this meant the scandalous behavior of the contemporary curia:

> What can we believe is more detestable to God's nostrils than the stink of our filthy uncleanness as it ascends to him from our altar? How many unclean priests and clerics . . . dare to . . . handle the Son of God and the Virgin with the same leprous hands that shortly before had handled a stinking whore?[102]

Such abusive language vividly recalls a later Oracle phrase: "the stench of the blood of the slaughtered shall rise to the nostrils of the Judge."[103]

Oracle 4 relied upon extensive animal imagery, including the *Coluber,* a large evil serpent, who "reenters his cavern, where the lion besieges it." The Dragon, the Lion and the *Coluber* come under attack from Cola, as they had in 1347, as "bestial" noble families who give their support to factions: "For the empire has snakelike enemies, subterranean mischief-makers, *colubros tortuosos.*"[104] Cola concurred with pseudo-Joachim on the identification of the Ram and the Cockerel; but he had his own ideas concerning the Dog, specifically attacking the "dog" tyrants of Italy (Canini, Mastini) and their hostility to the emperor.

Other language that recalls the posturing of 1347 includes the glossator's term *candidatus,* which Cola in turn glosses very specifically,[105] and the reference to that essentially antique Roman concept, the *pomerium,* which appears in the sixth chapter of the Oracle, and is thence defined by

---

102. III:58, 487–500.

103. Oracle 11:26–27 (Burdach and Piur, *Briefwechsel,* 4:316). Note also III:64, 85–87, where Cola speaks of "diverting this huge carnal stench from the nostrils of God." Petrarch used near-identical language of curial Avignon; e.g. *Familiari,* 13:8 of 1352 (Cosenza, *Petrarch,* 90–91); Dante used similar terms of Florence in his letter to Henry VII (Toynbee, *Dantis Alagheris Epistolae,* 104–5).

104. III:57, 162–63, for the "dogs"; III:50, 451–53; III:70, 19 for the *tortuosus coluber.*

105. Joachim's commentary on Oracle 6:6, line 35 (Burdach and Piur, *Briefwechsel,* 4:285). III:63, 64–66; note his more conventional usage at III:57, 532.

Cola: "The whole of Italy, which is called the *pomerium,* the sacred boundary, of the empire."[106] However, most importantly, it was Cola's mission to fulfil the prediction of the ninth chapter, where the Great Imperial Eagle with its black wings is exhorted to beware the evil, lying *Coluber* at its side.[107] God, Cola claimed, had humiliated him in 1347, to teach him that he was to be an imperial aide, rather than a ruler in his own right: the sheepdog rather then the shepherd.[108] The Holy Roman Emperor Charles, however, must recognize his duty:

> I beg that you, as God's chosen one, become the good leader of his people, laboring as they do in the stench of sins, in God's anger; you, just like Moses, must consult the divine tablets.[109]

Yet Cola did not envisage himself without influence in Rome in the near future; on the contrary, after this current humiliation, he would be "resurrected" like the Sun:

> I have continued to hope that in my coming you have sought a tribune for the New Jerusalem, that is, your Roman realm, . . . which by the will of its donor, Our Lord Jesus Christ, is the capital of the world.[110]

Evidently Cola's role as appointee, second-in-command to God's anointed, the faithful and true Tribune, rider-ruler, had not evaporated with the reality of power in December 1347.

One final element that is reflected in Cola's "prophetic" letters comes from Oracle Chapter 11: "Woe to one and all! We await the jests through which the *gladius biceps* shall slice!"[111] Joachim's attitude toward the papal exercise of both temporal and spiritual power was never stated explicitly; but Cola's line on this theme was clearly far removed from approval:

---

106. Oracle 6:1 (Burdach and Piur, *Briefwechsel,* 4:280); III:57, 645, 725; III:58, 720, 751. See chapter 1 and notes ad hoc on the technical contents of the *lex de imperio.*

107. Where "Joachim" interpreted the *coluber* as the Paleologan emperor, Cola saw a diabolic pope. Joachim could not possibly have known, after all, that Charles IV would grow up as pupil and protégé of Clement VI; thus readily interpretable as the serpent "at the side" of the emperor.

108. III:57, 704–13; even if the pastor joins the wolves and sinks his teeth into his own flock, bloodying his once *candidatus* status.

109. III:58, 502–5.

110. III:58, 915–18.

111. Oracle 11:7–9 (Burdach and Piur, *Briefwechsel,* 4:315).

Ah Lord! How much more honest and holy it would be, were the sword to be used to the proper ends of each. . . ; that which is God's should be rendered to God and that which is Caesar's, to Caesar . . . Ah Lord! The heir of the Apostle should obey the wishes of Christ, who forbade Peter the sword of bloodshed.[112]

The Oracle account stresses the sword "of double nature" and "with two sides" *(duplex, biceps)* at various locations; and Cola knew well "the double-edged sword" and its purpose: "[We are] working toward this worthy goal, with sweat and toil and with the *gladiis ancipitibus* in our hands: to release the hold of the tyrants."[113]

The image of two swords has, of course, an orthodox heritage. As one of the most widely used doctrinal metaphors for the exercise of temporal against spiritual power, the analogy had already reached maturity in the work of Bernard of Clairvaux. Over the next two centuries, however, the failure of the emperors to protect papal interests in central Italy had rendered it increasingly necessary—as tacticians and theologians alike argued—or the pope to employ his own troops, his own temporal sword. Cola was not convinced: "He should meet the People of God *in gaudio, non in gladio!*"[114] The Oracle reference to a single sword, however, sharpened on both sides, is significant: a distinctive feature of Cola's references *passim* is that the single sword is "the sword of justice," and its wielder (in 1350) is always the Roman emperor.[115] The *duplex* sword, as we have seen, was already playing a powerful part in the imagery of 1347.

To recap, Cola used the Oracle of Cyril very precisely, to explain the past events and future duties of his life and career. However, as, on the one hand, the Oracle itself drew on traditional imagery, to complement its obscure elements, just so, on the other, Cola had developed more than one string to his bow. His use of classical as well as biblical analogies, in the exegesis of theological, prophetic, and eschatological writings, demonstrates this well. One thinks of his extensive use—common, in a Roman context—of images of Paul. Simultaneously apostle and Roman citizen,

---

112. III:57, 415–35, 642; also see III:50, 380; III:58, 972.

113. III:57, 789–90.

114. III:57, 441.

115. There is one exception, rather telling in terms of Cola's continued hubris even in Bohemia; at III:57, 560 he refers to the death of the four Colonna *sub gladio meo divino iudicio.*

Paul traveled to Rome to seek justice. He is traditionally invested with the book, and, of course, the sword. However, in 1350 Cola also used more than just the Oracle of Cyril, in terms of unorthodox source material:

> If the prophecies of Merlin, of Methodius, of Polycarpos, of Joachim, and of Cyril are inspired by the evil spirit or are merely stories, why, then, do the pastors and prelates of the church keep them, so willingly, in beautiful copies bound in silver, among the contents of their libraries?[116]

Cola referred here to the oracle authorities, but also to Merlin and "Methodius," who do not belong in the Oracle. The latter pair stand, however, among the most important (and typically pseudonymous) exponents of medieval prophecy. Far from being tied to one specific set of prophecies—those of the Oracle—a close reading of his writings shows that Cola appropriated elements from a much wider range of contemporary prophetic material. Definite themes within Cola's "missionary" correspondence rely on "Merlin";[117] not the magician of the Arthurian court, but "author" of several Italian prophecies of the thirteenth century, reflections of the battle of the Hohenstauffen and the papacy. Cola owned an ancient book containing the prophecies of Merlin,[118] which set is, unfortunately, unknown. His references to Merlin invoke images not found in the Oracle:

> And perhaps the flaming sun and the bloody moon shall run together . . . and the stars shall fall from the sky, before any new heaven may come to pass.[119]

Cola referred to the bloody moon and also a "furtive beast" as "foretold by the British one."[120] However, he also talked of "Merlin" and his

---

116. III:58, 280–84; not an unreasonable question, and relevant to understanding the context in which Cola "prophesied." Robert E. Lerner, ed., and Christine Morerod-Fattebert, trans., *Jean de Roquetaillade (Johannes de Rupescissa), Liber Secretorum Eventum* (Fribourg: Éditions Universitaires Fribourg Suisse, 1994), 83, suggests Cola saw such libraries in Avignon in 1343.

117. See McGinn, *Visions of the End,* 180–85.

118. III:58, 650.

119. III:64, 89.

120. III:64, 117. A comparable image appears in Acts 2:16–20, a Pentecostal prophecy.

prophecy of the destruction of the stars, and a "virgin adorned with virtues" who, Cola explains, is the *Ecclesia Renovata;* not the whore of the Oracle.[121] And yet these images do not appear in any extant "Merlin" text; and gaps in present knowledge of the textual relationships make it impossible to identify clear sources.[122] One clue, however, may lie in Cola's reference to a *balista,* a sort of catapult based on the principle of the bow, set up "against the stars," predicted by Merlin while "speaking of the current *pastor.*"[123] Burdach notes that this term only appears in a sixteenth-century text called the *Mirabilis Liber;* but in fact elements of this work can be traced back, via the works of Telesphorus of Cosenza, to the early fourteenth century.[124] There is also a possible correspondence for Cola's term *bestia furtiva*[125] within the same related group; another early Trecento pseudo-Joachite work, *Horoscopus,* refers similarly to Boniface VIII, as the *bestia finitiva,*[126] the evil "present pope" of the 1290s.

The best evidence for the identity of Cola's "Merlin" references, however, is to be found in the language and imagery of a more notorious early Trecento compilation, the most famous of the "group"; the *Vaticinia de Summis Pontificibus,*[127] and another close textual relation, the *Liber de*

---

121. III:58, 636–43.

122. Burdach and Piur, *Briefwechsel,* 5:391–94, presents an inconclusive account. See also McGinn, *Visions of the End,* 181–85.

123. III:58, 634; also III:64, 165.

124. Though note the existence of *balestrieri* in contemporary Rome (described in chap. 5), also recruited by the Tribune. At III:58, 509 Cola described the *balistarii Ecclesie* preventing the pursuit of spiritual eremeticism. A document of 1321 shows that the commune of Anagni owned several *balistae* in the years when Cola was growing up there; Giuseppe De Magistris, "Un Inventario dei beni del commune di Anagni nel secolo XIV," *ASRSP* 7 (1884): 284.

125. III:64, 118.

126. Burdach and Piur, *Briefwechsel,* 5:420.

127. A compendium of fifteen descriptions of future popes, once thought to have been assembled ca. 1304 by a Fraticellan group in Perugia, led by Angelo Clareno. Relying *on vaticinia ex eventu,* the prophecies were manipulated into a systematic chronological survey of recent popes and predictions regarding their successors. To complicate matters, these fifteen predictions were supplemented, before 1356 (probably around 1342; see Marjorie Reeves, "Some Popular Prophecies from the Fourteenth to the Seventeenth Centuries," in *Popular Belief and Practice,* Studies in Church History 8 [Cambridge: Cambridge University Press, 1972], 107–34) with an additional fifteen prophecies. The *Vaticinia* may even have been prepared in the context of Orsini-Colonna political rivalry. The prophetic material is older, probably Byzantine in origin, before its application to popes.

Flore.[128] Cola's Merlin book, it may be conjectured, came from among this set of prophecies; the reference to the Celestine debacle is a case in point:

> A man as simple as Tobias has appeared in our times; Merlin and Joachim prophesied him most explicitly. By fraud and trickery he was deceived into abdicating from the papacy; finally he was imprisoned and killed. The prophets Merlin and Joachim clearly predicted before it happened how the King of Heaven would be angered by this sin; because of this the Church deserted its rightful, holy location for a brothel controlled by the archbishop of Bordeaux.[129]

Vaticinium IV, on Celestine, is readily comparable:

> By the fox's voice he will throw away the papacy. Blessed is he who comes in the name of the Lord of Heaven, one who contemplates *Coelestium* [all heavenly things] ; a simple, holy man, summoned from the ground.[130]
> . . . O how much will the bride weep for the destruction of her legitimate spouse, handed over to be eaten by the lion! Why, O Simple Man, have you left your Bride to be given over to savage dogs? Think upon your name and perform the first works, that you may be received in the East.

There is also a striking similarity to be drawn between a passage in the *Liber de Flore:* "Such a great scandal shall arise in the world . . . that it would be better to remain silent than to speak. . . . But I will briefly explain"; and the phrasing of a comment Cola made, after describing the scandals of clerics fornicating with the "stinking whore": "I would gladly be silent about them all, if God permitted me."[131] Another case centers on the image of the stars being knocked from the sky: the Oracle has many

---

128. A study and edition of the *Flore* fragment reveals its similarity with the *Vaticinia:* Herbert Grundmann, "Die *Liber de Flore*. Eine schrift der Franziskaner-Spiritualen aus dem Anfang des 14. Jahrhunderts," *Historisches Jahrbuch* 49 (1929): 33–91. Grundmann, in fact, suggests that Cola's "Merlin" source was the *Liber de Flore;* the *balista* citation proves that was not the case.

129. III:58, 478–86. See also McGinn, *Visions of the End,* 243.

130. Celestine the "simple man" also appears in the *Liber de Flore;* also in the early Trecento writings of Ubertino da Casale (noted at Burdach and Piur, *Briefwechsel,* 5:396) and in Angelo Clareno's interpretation of the Erithraean Sibyl (Burdach and Piur, *Briefwechsel,* 5:405).

131. III:58, 499–500.

astrological elements, but no such reference. *Vaticinium* XV reads: "This is the last beast, of terrible appearance, who shall drag down the stars."[132] It is not an image unique to "Merlin": "Behold, a great red dragon . . . And his tail draweth the third part of the stars of heaven, and did cast them to the earth . . ." (Rev. 12:3–4). It does suggest strongly, though, that Cola used sources, orthodox and otherwise, in 1350, besides the Oracle.[133]

Nonetheless, the images and themes of both sets of prophecies, in respect of many of their other features—brides and bridegrooms, swords, symbolic beasts[134]—are similar. Indeed *Vaticinium* VI, after the description of the Neronian pope, offers us the phrase "the proof of which lies in the Testament of the Angel"; probably a cross-reference to the Angelic Oracle. Finally, the illustration of *Vaticinium* IX shows a double-edged sword emerging from the mouth of its pope, while the *Liber de Flore* claims that the *stimulus*—as opposed to the *fortes stimuli* of the Oracle—that attacks the tyrants shall be *bis acutus.*[135]

Except where Cola specifically refers to the Oracle as a source, therefore, it may be concluded that he drew on a more extensive body of symbols and ideas; just as he did in 1347, in fact. On balance, his debt to the Oracle is greater, and most explicitly acknowledged; but there are many elements that overlap with, and some that only exist within, the *Vaticinia-Horoscopus-Liber de Flore* set, to which Cola's mysterious book of Merlin prophecies clearly belonged.[136]

The final example of the range of Cola's prophetic heritage demonstrated in 1350 is the theme of going east to Jerusalem to end his career and life in peace and devotion; this encompasses his reference to "Methodius," and will be treated shortly. Yet before such notional events could come to pass, Cola's life was to undergo yet another serious of trials and tribulations perhaps more humiliating than any hinted at in the Angelic Oracle, as he was handed over to Avignon in 1352 for examination. Yet even then,

---

132. III:57, 455.

133. However, as the *balista* reference makes clear, Cola's Merlin book was not synonymous with the *Vaticinia;* the term does not appear there.

134. The Cockerel, the Eagle, the nesting Dove, specifically "truculent dogs," the false clerical figure ("pseudoprophet" in the *Liber de Flore* and Cola; *pseudopontifex* in the oracle), bears, angels, and various flowers, a Sun and Moon, fertile-infertile imagery, and crowns and sceptres. A "candid" term recalling Cola's *candidatus* also appears in *Vaticinium* X. Both prophecies contain images of the City of Rome.

135. Grundmann, "Die Liber de Flore," 91.

136. Burdach suggests that Cola's direct quotation of "Merlin," "You shall raise a *balista*" at III:58, 635–43, which does not correspond with any of the Vaticinia, may represent a "lost" pope prophecy or text.

even after two further years of prison, we must question his claim to have given up the heretical prophetic notions of his past. In a strange reversion to events a decade past, in 1353 he was awarded the post of political and military envoy of the pope and returned to Rome in a style reminiscent, once again, of both classical triumph and apocalyptic splendor.

From *Sompniator* to Senator; 1351–54

Clement VI, as we have seen, had trusted neither Cola nor his rhetoric. As soon as he had control over the ex-Tribune, in 1351, he threw Cola into his most secure prison, the Tour de Trouillas, postponing any opportunity of a trial. His successor, Innocent VI, pardoned Cola, but in order to obtain that pardon, Cola was required to abjure his "errors," as he did, also, in a letter of September 1352, to Archbishop Ernst.[137] He had already come to describe himself as a gloomy "dreamer" (hence *sompniator*).[138] Yet Cola still did not entirely discard his prophetic language and imagery. As soon as he left Avignon, in a letter to the Venetian doge, Andrea Dandolo, we find Cola discussing astrological conjunctions and the Apollonian oracle at Delphi;[139] hardly heterodox language, but certainly prophetically minded. Cola was set to return to Rome, after the collapse of the government of his former political associate, Baroncelli (whose own "millenarian" language has been noted), in terms as biblical-apocalyptic as ever: in 1352 he was still talking of the City as "spouse" and "the Holy Jerusalem."[140]

By summer 1354 Cola himself was back to his old pomp and circumstance, having reassumed his glorious costumes,[141] the heady, prophetic language of his Tribunate, and also his vendetta against the Colonna. He swiftly drew up his army and marched it off to besiege Palestrina, using the same quasi-apocalyptic "Boethian" arms he used in 1347.[142] Yet this was nothing compared to the manner of his triumphal return to Rome, on August 1, 1354, the anniversary of his knighting (also the feast of S. Pietro in Vincoli, and the date of Emperor Augustus's inauguration of an era of peace): "The Romans held a great festival for him [Cola], as the Jews did

---

137. III:73, 12–13, 30–34.
138. III:68, 2–3.
139. III:75.
140. III:80, 43.
141. E.g. Wright, *Life*, 132–33.
142. Ibid., 137.

for Christ, when he entered Jerusalem mounted on an ass. They honored him, singing: *Blessed is he who comes.*"

The account of the singing of the antiphon after victory over the Colonna in 1347—*Veni Creator Spritus*[143]—and Cola's personal analogy of 1350—"Like Christ in the thirty-third year of his life"—do show Cola verging on the blasphemous. Cola's own account of his triumphal return to Rome, in 1354, was scarcely more circumspect in terms of *imitatio Christi*: "The sacred Roman People itself came to meet Cola di Rienzo outside the walls of the city, with palms and olive branches and leaves . . . crying, as one, in voices of jubilation and to the sound of trumpets, *Long may he live!*"[144]

Even ultimate rhetorical flourishes of Cola's life, the *Re Giannino* letters of October 1354, if genuine,[145] seem typical of Cola's prophetic mindscape, invoking a final World Emperor in the person of the lost grandson—"King Johnny"—of Philippe le Bel. This young pretender, significantly, had plans to conquer the Holy Land and to reign from Jerusalem. The notion of an emperor-figure from Rome who would resurrect a Sacred Empire in the Holy Land has a clear prophetic heritage, with considerable points of comparison to Cola's imperial message of 1350. When his own failure in Prague became evident, Cola presented a new ambition: to give up his Roman (com)mission and become a Hospitaller;[146] to go to Old Jerusalem to merit the crown of martyrdom, for which purpose he had laid down his crown and arms in 1347 (or so he claimed in 1350, brushing the actual collapse of the regime under the carpet).[147] The notion of the ultimate trip to the East goes beyond the mentality of Crusader or Hospitaller, however: it is drawn from that last component of Cola's prophetic palette—the one prophet who, in fact, does not fit the thirteenth-century, papal, oracle-*Vaticinia* context—namely, "Methodius."

"Methodius" refers to a set of pseudonymous seventh-century *Revelations,* named after a fourth-century scholar-bishop. Transmitted into the gloomy predictions of Adso in the tenth century, and thence into virtually

---

143. A verse also borrowed by the Vaticinia authors to describe the then still future Pope Celestine V.

144. III:77, 22–28.

145. IV: 72–74. If these were not by Cola, but someone in his circle, instead, then they still act as a magnificent illustration of the all-pervasive nature of such prophetic language in contemporary Roman culture.

146. III:70, 329–35, 443–44.

147. III:57, 586–94.

all subsequent Western prophecy, the most dramatic and influential ele-
ment of "Methodius" was the concept of the Last World Emperor.[148] The
Adso version identified the precursors of Antichrist as political rulers, the
ministers of Satan. The king of the Franks[149] would become the Last
Emperor of the world, and place his sceptre and crown on the Mount of
Olives; then would follow the time of Antichrist, who would kill Elijah and
Enoch, but Christ (or the archangel) would kill him. Later variants
included the Erithraean Sibyl, where the figure of the Last World Emperor
was "the mighty lion" (recalling for us the Oracle's *Leo,* and the relevance
of the lion image to Rome). These Sibylline prophecies—sometimes
ascribed to Merlin—were roughly contemporary with the work of
Joachim, who bypassed the imperial reforming-messianic tradition, introducing, instead, the *pastor angelicus* (or "Angelic Pope") and *viri spirituales.* However, as may be seen in the Angelic Oracle, the Last World
Emperor myth pervaded Joachite speculation anyway; it certainly colored
Cola's perceptions both of a secular messianic figure, and the connections
between East and West.

The theme of the deposition of crown and sceptre, on the Altar of
Heaven—the classical and postclassical precedents for which are discussed
in chapter 1—suggests something else more important still. Cola's "post-
Oracle" description of the deposition of his arms (i.e., his account in 1350
of events of 1347 with the benefit of a hindsight colored by *vaticinium ex
eventu*) nonetheless tallies closely with the account of the Chronicler for
the same year.[150] His account in 1350 was not, then, in this case, a reinter-
pretation of events in 1347 based on a more recent exposure to the myth.
Cola, on the contrary, was already aware of the complex symbolism of the
gesture in 1347, before exposure to the prophecies of 1349. Partly he was
casting himself as the *triumphator* of the classical past, dedicating the
spoils of military victory to a patron god. However, he was also—already
in 1347—playing the role of a neoimperial savior of the prophetic future,
who, after having battled against the forces of Antichrist and his deputies,
would hand over the rule of Christendom to the returning Christ and disappear to the east. Cola was on a divinely inspired mission before his
regime collapsed in December 1347. Cola may be argued to have known

---

148. McGinn, *Visions of the End,* 43–44, argues that the concept may predate the seventh,
although not the fourth, century.
149. Later versions substitute their own "protonational" rulers.
150. Wright, *Life,* 93; III:57, 618–24.

already at least the prophetic image of the Last World Emperor and the theme of the deposition of arms, before retiring from the City in early 1348. Early in 1351 Cola claimed that the prophecies he retailed in Prague in 1350 were complementary, not fundamental, to his ideas regarding the future.[151] There are cases in 1347 where Cola looks to have already absorbed the material he only mentions later; how this could have happened will be discussed in the next chapter. There is, for example, a striking similarity between Cola's prophetic warning in 1346—"The time of great justice is coming; just you await that time"—and *Vaticinium* XXV: "Woe to you, City of the Seven Hills—your fate approaches, and the overthrowing of your potentates and of the judgements of the unjust. . . ; you shall see." It is also worth recalling here that already in 1343, Cola's heroic stance on behalf of the poor, widows, and orphans, for which a range of potential sources is discussed in chapter 1, echoes closely, nonetheless, both the language of *Vaticinium* XI and the introduction to the Oracle.

There are obvious factors that might have prevented Cola from overt ideological reliance on heretical prophecies in 1347. The sources of the events of 1347 are not very helpful in this regard: the Chronicler, although describing the occasions, rather prosaically ignores the prophetic strand in Cola's new Rome. This account, however, was written within parameters quite different from those of the world in which Cola believed he was operating.[152] It is also the case that Cola's diplomatic letters of 1347 betray no explicitly prophetic traits, beyond high-flown dreams for the future of Rome and Italy; yet these do have a distinct diachronic flavor in Cola's parallel vision of the contemporary and the eternal destiny of the City. Even that language was "suspect" enough. Yet surely Cola might well have chosen to conceal certain sources of inspiration, which smacked of heresy, in a period during which he wished, at least ostensibly, to keep the favor of the pope and his representatives in Rome.

---

151. III:62, 31–36; III:64, 69–72.

152. The Chronicler consistently refused to accept the apotheotic elements within the poses struck by his subject. He summarizes Cola's "mission" to Bohemia within one chapter, and the prophecy of *Fra Agnilo de Montecielo* in one phrase, "The eagle will kill the crows" (Wright, *Life,* 126), although it may be noted that this is curiously similar to, even appearing to provide a sequel to, *Vaticinium* VII, "The crows shall chase the dove" (Wright, *Life,* 125–27). It is also reminiscent of the birds of Cola's tableau at S. Angelo, which are described in the next subsection. The Chronicler's interest in dreams as portents draws on Aristotelian metaphysics (which Cola attacked in 1350) rather than prophecy (see Wright, *Life,* 60–62); his one accusation of Cola's supernatural meddling centers upon magic and demons, rather than prophecy or prediction (Wright, *Life,* 152).

Cola's correspondence with Clement, and with the rest of Italy, in 1343, then in 1347 and later, certainly demonstrates his capacity to dissemble regarding his ideas and their sources, when it came to his vision of Rome's future. As a postscript to this, and as an index of his deep and abiding commitment to such notions of time, the universe, Rome, and his own role, Cola, as we have seen, refused to avoid prophetic language and imagery, some of which veered close to a personal apotheosis more typical of 1347, even on his return to Rome as papal Senator in 1354. He was still at the end of his career, then, using the vocabulary of 1343, and the symbols of 1347: the double-edged weapon of God wielded by him in justice; the secularized *imitatio Christi;* the Boethian arms; possibly the image of the Last World Emperor; and the emphasis of the role of the Spirit in establishing the New Jerusalem in the earthly Rome of the mid-Trecento.

Chapter 3

Back to the Future: Anagni, Naples, Avignon, and Italian Prophetic Culture, 1200–1350

From the end of the world—Cola's world—in 1354, this study now turns back to the earliest stages of Cola's life, and before. The following chapter examines the broader context of the apocalypticism of late medieval Mediterranean culture, within which Cola's career found its context. The study moves from a comparison of the apocalyptic language and imagery of the struggle between the papacy and emperor in the early thirteenth century, to the dissemination of Fraticellan ideas in the later thirteenth century. The spiritual-political nexus is traced through the events of the pontificates of Celestine V and Boniface VIII in the 1290s, the removal of the papacy to Avignon in the first decade of the fourteenth century, and the simultaneous emergence and subsequent development of a radical theological climate in Naples. The spiritual-prophetic atmosphere of the south, carried along with growing political influence (and the absence of the papacy) during the first half of the century, had a considerable effect—though this is rarely studied—on local Italian religious culture from Sicily, to Tuscany, to Provence. One common element to emerge, as an area of crossover and exchange, is the region of Lazio, and thus this chapter draws together the evidence for the changing nature and profile of Latian "prophetic" culture in the later Middle Ages. Cola's spiritual convictions will be demonstrated to have belonged to the broad context of fourteenth-century radical mendicant culture and its prophetic politicization even before his flight to Abruzzo and the land of hermits and prophets.

It cannot be proved that Cola knew either the Angelic Oracle of Cyril or the Merlin-*Vaticinia* material before 1349. Yet, suggestively, much of the imagery he used in 1347 may also be found within these prophetic tracts. On the other hand, however, these prophecies themselves have many elements that are hardly "original." Chapter 2 uncovered numerous aspects of the imagery of these prophetic tracts in the light of their own inheritance from, inter alia, the first and finest Christian model, that is, the Revelation of St. John.

On the other hand, the Angelic Oracle's mysterious hero, the Sun, is closer in attributes than any other to the apocalyptic rider called Faithful and True. Cola "became" the Sun, in 1349–50. While the Rider of the Apocalypse—the Knight of the Spirit—in 1347 was entirely successful, Cola as the *Sol* of the Oracle was to undergo the time of tribulation and imprisonment (1348–52), before his predicted return as the adjunct of the "great Eagle."

However, these prophecies came from the thirteenth century, considerably predating Cola.[1] We have discussed the possibility that he knew these prophecies before 1347, even before 1343. Cola was certainly *au fait* with the language of the Christian apocalypse, which places him in a generally prophetic context; but this provides no evidence of Cola's exposure to less canonical prophecy in 1343 and before. The language, tone, and parameters of 1343 are arguably Joachite, but the terminology itself is "conventionally" apocalyptic. The same is true of Cola's own role in Rome's history, as it evolved 1343–47: in 1343 he already had a high opinion of his global role: "sole legate" of a newly reformed Rome. Cola's optimism in 1343, that the return of the pope was at hand, was to turn to disappointment. The monarchical, rather than papal, metaphysical authority suggested by the performances and imagery of 1346–47, and Cola's blasphemous flirtation with near-apotheosis in 1347, come into focus. Petrarch wrote to him after 1343 claiming to be addressing not a man, but a God.[2] Cola had already assumed the imagery of the crowns and the swords of his knighthood well before they were awarded to him—before his election by the Roman people as Tribune—in 1347. He was already well on his way toward creating a role within Roman eschatology that reflected strangely closely the attributes of the apocalyptic Rider Faithful and True; a canonical image, but a blasphemous stance for a mortal to adopt. Cola's heresies brought down the Inquisition upon his head. But could he have already adopted the overtly heretical ideas of the "spirituals"? Did he have access to sources of Joachite ideology before 1348–49, even before 1343?

---

1. Apart from "Methodius" and his last world emperor, a notion that emerged in the wake of the fall of ancient Rome.

2. *Sine Nomine*, 7 (Cosenza, *Petrarch*, 6–12).

An examination of the potential sources of Joachite-Fraticellan influence in Rome and its hinterland in the period should go some way toward resolving this crucial issue. Marjorie Reeves does not suggest that the antiecclesiastical, "radical" prophecies peddled by Cola in 1350 found their *origins* among the Majellan Fraticelli: she says, rather, that this group were his *source.* Writers on Cola seem to have failed to look beyond the—admittedly fascinating—intricacies of Cola's thought, or beyond the anarchic condition of the city, to the cultural milieu of Trecento Lazio. The following arguments will show, however, that Cola could readily have taken his apocalyptic cue from the political culture of central-south Italy over the previous century, and that, moreover, he might well have "imbibed" his radical ideas from an early age.

Burdach talks of "the religious atmosphere, which must have spoken emphatically to his spirit, already influenced as it was by Joachite ideas,"[3] but he does not expand upon the comment. He suggests several important, potentially heretical, centers within Cola's chronological and geographical range: for example the Franciscan convent attached to the Araceli church, adjacent to (and serving the spiritual needs of) the Capitol fortress (the friars also, rather interestingly, kept the records and documents of the guild of notaries, whose importance is discussed in chapters 4 and 6). Seemingly orthodox communities of Franciscans frequently harbored "Spirituals," radical elements who had slid over the edge into political and theological heresy. Rome's mendicant communities had a general reputation for orthodoxy, both political and spiritual:[4] there were, however, significant exceptions to this rule, which will be described later in this chapter.

Burdach's analysis of Cola's sacred knighthood also fails to draw out the connections between Cola's knighthood of the Spirit, and the order of the Knights Hospitallers.[5] Certainly the Knights of St. John flourished in fourteenth-century Rome: the brothers and prior of the Order of *San Giovanni gerosolimitano* appear in the Turin Catalogue.[6] Proof of their presence in Rome in the 1330s comes from the parchment archives of S. Maria Maggiore: parchment 114 contains John XXII's bull concerning the debts of the Order. They also appear in the protocols of the notary Francesco di

---

3. Burdach and Piur, *Briefwechsel,* 5:293.

4. On the Franciscans see especially Giulia Barone, "I francescani di Roma," *Storia della Città* 9 (1978): 33–35.

5. Burdach and Piur, *Briefwechsel,* 5:204.

6. A list probably drawn up by the "guild" *(universitas)* of regular clergy—the *Romana Fraternitas*—of the churches of Rome and their location, current condition, and staffing requirements, dating from some time after 1313.

Stefano dei Capogalli in the early 1380s.[7] Cola's desire to join them,[8] although he was already a knight of a different order,[9] may not have been the signal of his wish to leave politics altogether, however. The Jerusalemites certainly played their part in the government of Trecento Rome: in 1379 and in 1400, the Senator of the City was the prior of the Order of St. John.[10]

Perhaps one might see in Cola's Hospitaller ambitions a late attempt to render his anomalous spiritual knighthood more "respectable."[11] However, his interest in the Jerusalemites is most noticeable in his most radical phase: in September 1350 Cola asked Fra Michele, his Abruzzan mentor, to make an offering on his behalf at the oratory of the Jerusalemites in Rome.[12] He proposed leaving his money to assist fellow "brothers" in visiting the *Sepulchrum* in Jerusalem, referring to the precedent set by "the queen" for the "spiritual men" of Naples. Burdach's commentary[13] says that Sancia, wife of Robert of Naples, and regent after his death in 1343, set up such an oratory, for a group of Franciscan Jerusalemites, in 1342. The necrologies of the Vatican basilica reinforce the link between Cola's stress upon the role of the Holy Spirit, his idea of an order of knights bearing the title he had taken upon himself—the watchword(s) Cola chose for his sentries, on the eve of the Porta S. Lorenzo battle, was "Knights of the Holy Ghost"[14]—and the possible existence of an analogous order in Naples.[15] The *Liber Anniversorum* mentions Joanna, "Queen of Sicily," in various passages, including her donation of fifty florins for perpetual masses dedicated to the Holy Spirit.[16] The monastic-chivalric order may

---

7. Renzo Mosti, *Un notaio Romano del '300. Il Protocollo notarile di Francesco di Stefano de Caputgallis (1374–1386)* (Rome: École Française, 1994), 491.

8. III:57, 619–23, 822–27; III:64, 130.

9. III:58, 773.

10. Antonio Vendettini, *Serie cronologica dei senatori di Roma* (Rome, 1778), 66–67; Salimei, *Senatori e statuti,* 155–56.

11. Yet III:62 rings sincere: Cola even asked for news of the political situation in the north of Africa, as a port en route to the East. However, Cola had little time for Fra Moreale, the Hospitaller mercenary with ambitions on the *signoria* of Rome, employed by the Church in 1353. See chapter 6 on Moreale's fate.

12. III:64, 129–32.

13. *Briefwechsel,* 5:241.

14. Wright, *Life,* 82; note the plural form. Cola was not, then, the single Knight of the Spirit: perhaps he had handed out knighthoods to his men (though there is no surviving evidence for this); he certainly knighted his son.

15. Described in chapter 2 and below.

16. Pietro Egidi, *Necrologia e libri affini della provincia Romana,* Fonti per la Storia d'Italia 44–45 (Rome: Istituto Storico Italiano, 1908–14), 1:168, 192.

not, moreover, have been restricted to Naples: of considerable interest is a reference to four *Fratres* of an *Ordo Sancti Spiritus,* as witnesses to the will of another of the leading notaries of Trecento Rome, Francesco di Puzio, in 1363.[17]

However, it is likely that the religious order in which Cola's greatest personal interest lay was the Celestinians (or *Morroniti*), the brothers of the Order of St. Peter "de Morrone," the Abruzzan hermit-turned Pope Celestine V.[18] These brothers were dedicated to "spiritual" ends, similar to radical Franciscans—"Fraticelli"—in their rejection of the worldly papacy. The fact that Cola knew where among the wild mountain ranges of Abruzzo to track down one such branch of hermits suggests that he had contacts already before his departure from Rome: and that these brothers, in turn, knew what was going on in Rome. Certainly Fra Michele of Monte S. Angelo, a major influence on Cola during this period, was acquainted with the major politicians of Rome.[19]

Yet the Morroniti did not originate in Rome: Pope Celestine meditated in his cell in Angevin Naples in the 1290s, and his "cult" probably developed there in the radical environment tolerated, even sponsored by the royal court (he was sanctified in May 1313). Cola's reference to "spiritual men" in Naples is thus interesting, particularly where it smudges into a reference to the Knightly Order of St. John and then to Rome: the overlap between Franciscans and Jerusalemites, Spirituals and knights, Rome and Naples deserves careful explication. Chapter 2 described the near-contemporary order of the Holy Spirit in Naples, under Queen Joanna, Cola's contemporary; did it inspire—was it inspired by?—the actions of the Tribune-knight of the Holy Spirit of Rome?

The Neapolitan Connection

Cola's most notorious link with Naples, in fact, comes from 1347 rather than later, when he asserted the right to sit in judgment upon the rival claims of Joanna's consort, Lewis of Taranto, and Lewis of Hungary, brother of her murdered ex-consort Andrew of Puglia. Cola was much

---

17. B.A.V. S.A.P. 1/1363, 62v.

18. Both *Morroniti* and *Gerosalemiti* appear in the Catalogue of Turin (noted above). The *terminus ante quem* of the catalogue is 1313, i.e., Celestine's canonization.

19. In Cola's unhappy letter (III:64) of August 1350, he asked Michele to ensure that, should he (Cola) not be back in Rome by the end of the year, the "consuls and people" of Rome should appoint a successor, heeding the advice of the Chancellor and the Protonotary (Cola's military lieutenant, and his brother-in-law, respectively; see chapter 6).

involved in contemporary Neapolitan politics. Joanna is even said to have sent Cola's wife money and jewels.[20] Cola subsequently crossed theological swords with the Neapolitan ambassador, the Franciscan archbishop Giovanni Orsini, who, though impressed at the time with Cola's biblical scholarship, later betrayed him.[21] Burdach also mentions that Giovanni had played a part in Cola's August coronation; it seems probable that the court at Naples was aware, and in support, of Cola's Tribunate and its symbolic, "Spiritual" ceremonials.[22]

This would have been entirely consistent with religious policy in Trecento Naples. In the late 1340s the Neapolitan kingdom was embroiled in a bitter succession crisis. Until the death of King Robert, however, Angevin Naples had been a stronger political entity, than, arguably, Visconti Milan. In the first three decades of the century Rome lay well within the boundaries of Neapolitan fiat, and, on and off, came directly under the control of Angevin "vice-senators." One critical index of this strength was the Neapolitan court's ability to patronize not just the leading cultural lights of the period—Giotto, Pietro Cavallini, Simone Martini, Petrarch, Boccaccio—but also to shelter infamous Fraticellan scholars. Indeed this had been going on ever since the 1290s, when the Neapolitan court had "adopted" the most holy and angelic pope to date: Celestine V. It had also generated a recent royal saint, the Franciscan ascetic Louis of Toulouse, Robert's elder brother. One group of Franciscan radicals was based at L'Aquila, near Celestine's original hole in the rock; there were more again in Naples.[23]

Yet it was not only Franciscan radicals who reflected the apocalyptic tone of Neapolitan elite culture, but its more famous residents too, such as Petrarch and Giotto. One has only to consider Petrarch's language, and its visionary content, to conclude that his years at Naples (1341–43)—as an emissary of Benedict XII, ironically—were spent in congenial company. He went on, in 1343–44, probably to meet, in Avignon, and certainly to lionize, Cola. The similarity of Petrarch's imagery and Cola's illustrations has been noted. In the case of Giotto, the connection with Rome is less profound, but equally explicit: his *Navicella* mosaic in the Vatican was an

---

20. Wright, *Life*, 65–68.

21. III:57, 901–18.

22. At least until after the Tribunate, when Cola got involved with Joanna's Hungarian enemies.

23. Gian Luca Potestà, *Angelo Clareno: Dai poveri eremiti ai fraticelli* (Rome: Istituto storico italiano per il Medio Evo, 1990), 285; Renzo Mosti, "L'eresia dei fraticelli nel territorio di Tivoli," *Atti e Memorie della Società Tiburtina di Storia ed Arte* 38 (1965): 70.

obvious iconographic source for Cola's shipwrecked Rome, Italy, and Faith tableau. In Naples, Giotto's theme was more ambitious and more explicitly apocalyptic: Robert and Sancia commissioned him to fresco their great Clarisse foundation with the events of the end of the world (executed 1328–34).[24]

Only partial versions elsewhere hint at the appearance of the cycle, whitewashed in the seventeenth century: for example, Giotto's own abbreviated fresco of the Vision of St. John in the Peruzzi Chapel in Florence. Another "heir" is the "Stuttgart Apocalypse" panel,[25] generally attributed to a Neapolitan artist of the 1330s, which could hardly have been executed without reference to (and probably influenced by) Giotto's recent work. The same may be said of the apocalyptic imagery of the Neapolitan royal foundation of S. Maria Donnaregina.[26] These images are closest in time, place, and content to Cola's own apocalyptic tableaux. The loose narrative structure of the Stuttgart panel, particularly, recalls the physical attributes, the distribution of figures, and the symbolic foci of Cola's visual messages and personal exploits in and up to 1347.

The period of Giotto's stay coincided with the climax of the theological-ideological battle between Robert and John XXII. John warned the Neapolitans that their Spiritual sympathies would end in excommunication: sympathies so deeply felt that the Franciscan minister-general, Michael of Cesena, was exiled from Naples for attempting to compromise with John XXII. There even seem to have been plans to "depose" John, replacing him with Sancia's brother as the new and, of course, Angelic Pope.[27] The pope under threat probably recalled the heady atmosphere at Naples: Jacques Duèze, the future John XXII, had once belonged to the administrative staff of the Angevin king Charles II.

---

24. "What we wouldn't give for seeing what Giotto, of all people, made of the Book of Revelation," as Frederic van der Meer (*Apocalypse: Visions from the Book of Revelation in Western Art* [London: Thames and Hudson, 1978], 189) puts it, also noting Vasari's claim that the otherworldly episodes Giotto frescoed were planned by Dante.

25. See Luisa Castelfranchi, "Le storie apocalittiche di Stoccarda e quelle di Giusto da Padova," *Prospettiva* 33–36 (1983–84): 33–44; Schwartz, "Images and Illustrations," 106–12.

26. Schwartz, "Images and Illustrations," 108–9; *termini ante quem* of 1334 for the Last Judgment frescoes (possibly even 1323) are proposed in chapter 2 of the excellent new study by Janis Elliott, "The Last Judgement Scene in Central Italian Painting, ca. 1266–1343: The Impact of Guelf Politics, Papal Power, and Angevin Iconography," Ph.D. thesis, Warwick University, 2000.

27. See R. G. Musto, "Queen Sancia of Naples (1286–1345) and the Spiritual Franciscans," in *Women of the Medieval World: Essays in Honor of John H. Mundy,* ed. Julius Kirshner and Susan Wemple (Oxford: Basil Blackwell, 1985), 179–214.

Angevin Naples, particularly after Robert's Aragonese marriage alliance, also provided a haven for discussion of the unorthodox prophecies of Arnold of Vilanova. However, a more direct "prophetic" connection between Naples, the Avignon curia, and Rome was the radical mendicant Pietro di Fossombrone, known as Angelo Clareno.[28] After the election of John XXII and the onset of the apostolic poverty debate, which came to one of several climaxes in 1317, Angelo tried to found a new order, but was refused permission. So in 1318 he became a "Celestinian," and soon thereafter returned to central-south Italy. His influence at the court of Naples was, apparently, considerable.[29] In the 1320s Angelo composed the *Seven Tribulations of the Franciscan Order,* which included a specific exposition of the Oracle of Cyril; his subsequent career is described below.

Meanwhile, curial Avignon remained, paradoxically, both a focus of and magnet for heretical prophetic activity. In Avignon, of course, Cola met Petrarch, recently returned from Naples. Perhaps they met for the second time: only two years previously Petrarch had been crowned, under the aegis of Robert of Naples, on the Capitol in Rome. Cola, in 1341, on the verge of a political career, was probably active already within the upper echelons of his legal profession and perhaps even established in the Roman civic administration. It is unlikely that he "missed" the occasion to mix with Petrarch and the Neapolitan king, both of whom exhibited a complex interest in both classical and apocalyptic imagery Cola came to manifest even more powerfully. Like Robert and Sancia of Naples, Cola was both sincerely pious but well aware of the impact of prophetic imagery: he became just as good as the Neapolitans at using worldly power alongside otherworldly imagery to achieve political and religious ends.

The Avignon Connection

In a sense one may say the same for the "Avignon Papacy." If Cola's—and Rome's—exposure to prophetic ideas may be seen as a result of the shared

---

28. Angelo and Arnold may also have been connected through a mutual acquaintance, the Provençal Spiritual Bernard Delicieux, another Vaticinia adherent later tried for sorcery. For Angelo's possible connection with the production and circulation of the Vaticinia, see chapter 2 (notes).

29. See Decima L. Douie, *The Nature and Effect of the Heresy of the Fraticelli* (Manchester: University of Manchester, 1932), 64–65; McGinn, *Visions of the End,* 149–57.

cultural context of Rome and Naples, it must also be understood as a reflection of the world of Avignon the Whore. Indeed, this less-than-attractive female personification reflects the neat double-dialectic of the period: if Rome was the maiden bride and New Jerusalem of the Apocalypse, Avignon must be the raddled whore fornicating with the Kings of the Earth (France, England, and Bohemia inter alia, as Dante illustrated so graphically in canto 32 of *Purgatorio*). That the papacy "languished" in "exile" by the waters of Provence made the Babylon identification all the more cogent: it certainly fueled Petrarch's imagination.

The early years of Cola's residence in Rome (ca. 1332–ca. 1342) passed in an atmosphere of apocalypticized political tension; but the same atmosphere prevailed in both Naples and Avignon. Even Pierre Roger, Clement VI, bureaucratic expert and proto-Renaissance prince par excellence, was still indisputably a prelate and theologian, well acquainted with traditional and radical doctrine alike. As discussed in chapter 2, Cola felt no apparent call in 1343 for the antipapal dogma used by radical prophetic reformers. He believed Clement's promise; the pope, literally, spoke his language, using the same apocalyptic terms of reference. After 1347, of course, Clement came to use apocalyptic terminology in the violent execration, condemnation, and excommunication of Cola.[30] Over the next two years Cola was hunted and damned mercilessly, far more so than most "heretics."

This begs the question, what harm had Cola done? On a basic, material level, Cola had threatened the income and authority of the papacy; but, argues Wood,[31] he had also undermined the *fama,* the reputation, of Clement personally. The damage was also, even more importantly, ideological and theological, involving the different interpretations of the person of the *Sponsa.* Was this Rome, the personified city of Cola's tableaux? Or was she the *Ecclesia Romana*? Cola did not make this distinction: "He had confused Clement's two brides: he had made possession of the city of Rome a *sine qua non* for possession of universal authority."[32] Effectively Cola had turned the City of Rome into the essential constituent of the universal Church; then made himself the head of Rome; thus, by logical extension, he had usurped the papacy. For Cola, Rome was to be renewed, whether or not the agent of renewal was the pope. As under Augustus the

---

30. Between September 1347 and March 1352 Clement penned forty letters attacking that "Son of Belial" Cola (IV:19–IV:59).

31. Wood, *Clement VI,* 79.

32. Ibid.

first time, and Constantine the second time, the renewal would be effected by a figure who, mandated by the People of God, constituted supreme temporal and spiritual authority: thus he was indeed "greater than emperor."

Clement's apocalyptic language seemed to echo Cola's own accusations: Cola was the "schismatic . . . adulterer of the sacred body of Christ."[33] Cola had committed terrible sacrilege by undergoing baptism in the font of Constantine in the Lateran, the very heart of medieval Christendom, the New Temple of the Risen Christ. Cola had also staged a grand feast, as did popes at their inaugurations, in the Constantinian basilica, after his coronation. Clement compared this to the defiling of the Temple at the feast of Belshazzar (Dan. 5:1–5), an event interrupted by the proverbial writing on the wall.[34] But Clement's attack on Cola went much further, from the past to the future, into prophecies of the end of the world:[35]

Cola plunges downward rather than ascends . . . the precursor of Antichrist, man of sin,[36] revealed among the nations as the Son of Perdition . . . son of the Devil, enemy of justice,[37] monstrous beast, upon whose heads the names of blasphemy are written.[38] . . . [The Lord] has cast down the blaspheming beast into the lake of fire and sulphur, to be crucified,[39] so that the raised horn of *Nicolaus* may not gore[40] . . . he, whose wickedness slithers like a *coluber,* bites like a crab,[41] kills like poison . . . that Son of Belial, father of evilness. . . . He deserves to be condemned for heresy.

Clement was, evidently, a match for Cola in biblical and apocalyptic abuse. It is also hard to avoid the reference to the *Coluber,* that particularly unpleasant serpent, and the similar character that appears not in Revelation but in the Angelic Oracle. Such noncanonical prophecies were read and condemned. But, of course, they were read, as Cola himself

---

33. III:57, 355–60.
34. IV:29, IV:40.
35. IV:40, 107, 123, 171–75, 180–81; IV:51; and III:53–III:55. See also IV:50, 77.
36. 2 Thess. 2:3.
37. Acts 13:7.
38. Rev. 17:3.
39. Rev. 20:9.
40. Ps. 74:11.
41. 2 Tim. 2:17.

pointed out.[42] The similarities between Clement's announcements of 1343, and Cola's messages to Rome on the strength of those announcements, is an index of their shared cultural heritage. Cola's experience of Avignon in 1343 would have served to confirm and strengthen his impression of the potency of prophetic language, and its legitimizing capacity, within the sphere of traditional authority. As a postscript to this, it should be noted that such language was not the papal preserve and prerogative of Clement; in 1352–53 the diplomatic communiqués of Clement's heir, Innocent VI, may have refreshed Cola's acquaintance with painfully familiar apocalyptic rhetoric. The diabolic imagery of 2 Thessalonians resounds throughout Innocent's letters of 1353, as his lieutenant, with Cola in tow, tried to reclaim Lazio from the Viterbese baron, Cola's old enemy Giovanni di Vico: "Undertake, swiftly, our process against that Son of Perdition and pupil of damnation . . . [and] spiritual and temporal enemy . . . blunt the raised horn of the arrogant."[43] These are identical to the names and accusations leveled at Cola by Clement.

Curial Avignon also exercised a fascination for less than orthodox characters such as Angelo Clareno, who lurked in the area for some years, with his Oracle and, possibly, his papal prophecies. Indeed, the Occitan area, with its Beguin and Cathar heritage, had been attracting apocalyptic visionaries both long and immediately before the arrival of the papacy.[44] However, there is one "local" prophetic character in particular who seems to connect Cola, his Fraticellan-heretical literature, and his time in Avignon. Jean de Roquetaillade (John of Rupescissa) was born around 1310 (a close contemporary of Cola, therefore) and became a Franciscan at Aurillac.[45] Around 1340 Jean experienced a series of visions that brought him into conflict with his superiors; in 1344 he was imprisoned. In 1349 he was moved by Clement VI to the "Sultan's Jail" in Avignon, where he spent his last fifteen years. Not in great discomfort, apparently: it seems he had friends in high places. Nevertheless, his works appear to have been persistently radical. They are most readily accessible through the *Vade*

---

42. III:58, 280–84: noted in chapter 2.

43. IV:62, 26–32; IV:63, 25–36. Dante once accused Florence of raising its horn against the emperor Henry (Toynbee, *Dantis Alagheris Epistolae,* 104).

44. Bernard McGinn, *Antichrist: Two Thousand Years of the Human Fascination with Evil* (San Francisco: HarperSanFrancisco, 1994), 174.

45. McGinn, *Visions of the End,* 230–33; Jean Bignami-Odier, *Études sur Jean de Roquetaillade* (Paris: Vrin, 1952), 15–25.

Mecum in Tribulatione of circa 1356;[46] but this work was a synthesis of several earlier tracts, most clearly his *Liber Ostensor* and a commentary on the Angelic Oracle of Cyril.

There is no proof that Cola met Jean de Roquetaillade, or his followers, either in 1343–44, while Cola faced poverty in Avignon and Jean faced imminent arrest in Aurillac; nor even while they were both incarcerated in the Avignon papal palace in 1352–53. It is possible that Cola knew Jean's work, if a rare reference in the chronicle of Františka of Prague[47] to Cola's enthusiastic reaction on being shown the work of *Johannes hereticus* may be adduced as evidence. It is certain, however, that Jean knew of Cola, however, and quoted his letters.[48] Beyond quotation, though, Jean's prophetic imagery in his *Vade Mecum* contains elements startlingly familiar from Cola's own writings:[49]

> The fifth instruction concerns the revelation of the horrible future events from 1360 to 1365. . . . The earth's worms will . . . most cruelly devour almost all the lions, bears, leopards, and wolves. The larks and the blackbirds and the owls, will rend the birds of prey, the hawks and the falcons. . . . Within these five years will arise a popular justice. It will devour the treacherous and tyrannical nobles with the two-edged sword in its mouth.

Plagues, famines, and floods will usher in the false messiah. In "instruction" 9, a reformer will gain the *imperium mundi.*

> The twelfth instruction concerns the proximate restoration of the men of the Church and of the world through the celestial reformer who is at hand. . . . He will make the ravenous wolves flee the flock, [and] will

---

46. Edward Brown, ed., *Jean de Roquetaillade (Johannes de Rupescissa): Vade Mecum in Tribulatione. Appendix ad Fasciculum Rerum Competendarum et Fugiendarum* (London, 1690), 493–508. The phrase is from Rev. 1:9.

47. Noted by Burdach and Piur, *Briefwechsel,* 5:298–300; his reading is tempting though not entirely convincing. Františka, the imperial court chronicler, has Cola say, "This is the book I have sought, and Lo! I have found it." (Josef Emler, *Kronika Františka Praského,* Fontes Rerum Bohemicarum, vol. 4 (Prague, 1884), 452–53; elsewhere Cola himself claimed not to have a copy of the Angelic Oracle with him in Prague (III:57, 1143).

48. Maire-Vigueur, "Jean de Roquetaillade," 381 n. 1, cites the three passages of the *Liber Ostensor* that mention Cola, and asks whether Cola and Jean, could have met. The passage quoted reveals that, according to Roquetaillade, one of Cola's letters was already in wide circulation by 1352.

49. See McGinn, *Visions of the End,* 231–33; Brown, *Jean de Roquetaillade,* 497.

restore collapsed justice. . . . God will generally subdue the whole world to him: West, East, and South. He will be of such sanctity that no emperor or king from the beginning of the world is his equal in sanctity, save the King of Kings and Lord of Lords . . . who will conquer Jerusalem . . .

We note here the birds and the beasts, the celestial reformer, the false messiah, the release of the *popolo* from the tyranny of the nobles and the justice of the two-edged mouth-sword and the tripartite division of the globe. Add to this the notion of a reformer greater than any emperor alongside the use of the given title of the Rider Faithful and True—"King of Kings"—and the similarities with Cola's imagery of 1347 are legion.

Of course, the dating of *Vade Mecum,* and the fact that he knew Cola's writings, suggests that, rather than drawing upon a shared body of symbols, Jean could have seen Cola's own synthesis of personal and popular prophetic imagery. But the same is not true of Jean's earlier work, from which *Vade Mecum* was patched together: the commentary on the Angelic Oracle was written between 1345 and 1349.

One aspect is very different from the subsequent emphasis in Cola. Jean's slant was French: the Sun of the Oracle would be a future French king, an Angevin; though were these not Neapolitans, too?[50] Cola (like Petrarch) believed in *Sacra Italia* and a Roman reformer. Yet Jean's work was not without its references to Italian characters; he even mentions the contemporary Fra Angelo in reference to Cola's adoption of prophecy. Fra Angelo had an international reputation, evidently: in 1362 he was known to be the head of one of the three significant groups of Fraticelli in Europe.[51] There are innumerable overlapping features: Fra Angelo's/ Cola's interpretation of the Angelic Oracle in 1350, and that of Jean in 1345–49, share elements not found in the "original" Gilbert-Cyril-Joachim text of the 1290s: most importantly, their references to Merlin.[52] In his *Liber Ostensor* Jean talks of "Merlin the Briton in his book on the popes,"

---

50. See Lerner, *Jean de Roquetaillade,* 59–63, on the subject of "national" loyalties in Roquetaillade.

51. See Burdach and Piur, *Briefwechsel,* 5:301.

52. Other "overlaps" include the fact that both refer to the Avignon church in terms of a specifically "stinking" whore, for example; see Bignami-Odier, *Jean de Roquetaillade,* 91. Both quote "Pax, pax, et non (est) erit pax" from Isa. 48:22 (also used in *Vaticinum* IX); Brown, *Jean de Roquetaillade,* 500; III:57, 456. Cola may also have borrowed elements from *Horoscopus* and the *Liber de Flore,* as discussed in chapter 2; Jean mentioned, and used, both sources.

and cites *Vaticinium* V.[53] In 1350–51 Cola also talked of Merlin and inter alia paraphrased *Vaticinium* IV, on the "simple man," *Coelestium contemplator*. Contemporary with Cola's political career and secret conspiracy, most interestingly, Jean's *Liber Secretorum Eventum* (1345–49) contained thirty *intellectus*—"expositions"—of the imminent descent of the Holy Spirit and the start of the Third Age.[54]

Jean's knowledge of Cola, and of Fra Angelo, demonstrates that a connection between Latian and Provençal spiritual ideology existed independently of the bridge made by Cola between Rome, Naples, and Avignon, though it is also reminiscent of the career of Angelo Clareno. Clareno's popularity in Naples has been remarked. Yet when he fled from Avignon in 1318, he and his group settled not in Campania but in Lazio, under the protection of the abbot of Subiaco. One chapter resided at S. Giovanni *ante Portam Latinam* in Rome; another was based in Cori, just south of Valmontone. Inquisitorial records show large pockets of Fraticellan sympathy among the populace and nobility of Rome.[55] During the 1320s, the sect was comparatively safe in the City, partly due to Neapolitan jurisdiction over Rome, although also due to the activities of Lewis the Bavarian, who drew off such papal fire as could be mustered. Lewis also actively protected Fraticelli and other heretical ideologues, receiving their prophetic loyalties in return. After 1331, however, papal pressure on the region was again rising: Angelo was hunted by the orthodox Franciscans of the Araceli, on John XXII's orders. In late 1334, therefore, Angelo left Lazio for good; one account suggests he settled in the far south.[56]

Certain outposts of Fraticellan and Celestinian activity remained, however, in Rome and Lazio; and here we return to Cola and his context. After the death of John XXII, papal control in Lazio, and in the City, slumped again. There is no direct evidence for a rise in Fraticellan activity, but the time and the place were certainly ripe for agitation. In 1335 the *Palombelli*,

---

53. Ergo the second set of *Vaticinia* has a *terminus ante quem* of 1356. See also Burdach and Piur, *Briefwechsel*, 5:392.

54. Bignami-Odier, *Jean de Roquetaillade*, 125; Lerner, *Jean de Roquetaillade*, esp. 202.

55. Douie, *Nature and Effect*, 67, drawing on Franz Ehrle, "Die Spiritualen und ihr verhältnis zum Franziskenorden und die Fraticellen," *Archiv für Literatur- und Kirchen-Geschichte des Mittelalters* 4 (1888): 1–190; Potestà, *Angelo Clareno*, 279–86. The notary who took down one heretical friar's Inquisition testimony in 1334, curiously enough, was one *Cecchus Vechi* (Mosti, "L'eresia dei fraticelli," 67); for Cecco's later career, see chapter 6. It is worth noting that Cola's archenemy, the prefect Giovanni di Vico in Viterbo, was a well-known harborer of Fraticellan dissidents.

56. Potestà, *Angelo Clareno*, 281; Mosti, "L'eresia dei fraticelli," 61–62.

with their spiritual imagery and self-imposed tribulations, enjoyed a relatively free rein throughout the central-south region. Although they met a hostile reception in Rome, they were not banned, as they had been from cities further north.[57] Benedict XII's death in 1342, and Robert's in 1343 accelerated the descent into anarchy in Rome and its *Destretto*,[58] provoking circumstances of tension typical of those that always stimulate the dissemination of prophetic hopes for renewal. In this case, such cultural malaise may have contributed to a political coup in Rome: the new regime represented by Cola in Avignon in 1343.

This begs another question. Could Cola, in his youth, have met, heard, or in some way been influenced by Fraticellan activists? Cola was sent away from Rome as a child, and returned at the age of twenty after the death of his father.[59] If born in 1312 or 1313, he must have been educated in Anagni while Clareno was still in Subiaco. Obviously it is unlikely that the young scholar would have met the elderly prophet. It is, however, undeniable that Cola spent the years from circa 1318 to circa 1332 in the eastern hill towns of Lazio, growing up in a cultural climate flavored by the local presence of radical religious activists (documented in Cori, Tivoli, and Subiaco); and it is clear that he knew where to run when fleeing from Rome in 1348. Is it possible, then, that Angelo Clareno, Celestinian monk, devotee of the Angelic Oracle who once awarded the "Sun" role to Olivi, resident in the Ciocaria in the time of Cola's youth, retreated in the 1330s to the Abruzzan mountains of the east rather than of the south? Was he the same heretic Brother Angelo, described in 1362 as one of three major Fraticellan leaders in Europe, who hailed Cola, after his arrival in the Monti di Majella of Abruzzo, as the Sun of the Oracle?[60]

This is, of course, hypothetical. The net must be cast back further yet, in order to complete this survey of the range of potential influences to which Cola was "exposed." His formative years, as we have mentioned, were spent in the town of Anagni, some thirty miles southeast of Rome along the Via Casilina, across the Ciocaria. Cola described his education as *rusticus inter rusticos.* But just how "provincial" was Anagni?

---

57. Account at *ARC,* 18–20.
58. Such instability was noted by Cola: III:57, 740.
59. III:50, 171.
60. Burdach and Piur, *Briefwechsel,* 5:302, hints at the possibility that the two are the same but does not adduce the textual evidence presented here.

The Anagni Connection

"Anagni, *nutrix* of our youth," as Rainaldo Conti, later Pope Alexander IV, eulogized in 1258.[61] A good education—good enough for a pope—was once available in Anagni; it may well have still had a bishop's school for the Conti of the next century, though evidence is scanty. The Conti populated the upper ranks of the thirteenth-century Church, though their secular domination of the region, as lords and bishops, was partially whittled away by the Gaetani after the 1290s. Still, scholars have not generally credited the importance of Ildebrandino Conti, local bishop and patron, contemporary of and commentator on Cola (see chap. 4). The importance of Anagni was not diminished by the Gaetani inroads on Conti regional autonomy: thirteenth-century ecclesiastical history ended as it began, with a great and powerful pope from Anagni: Benedict Gaetani, Boniface VIII—nephew, also, through his mother, of Alexander IV. Boniface's universalist statements demonstrate the central location of Anagni in the power struggles of contemporary Christendom. The French king's infamous lieutenant, Nogaret, marched into Anagni and in the Sala del Schiaffo (the "Room of the Slap") tried to cut the Pope down to size (the slap is probably apocryphal). Yet the event failed to damage Anagni's reputation as a safe retreat from Rome's dangers: on August 9, 1378, it was in Anagni that schismatic cardinals elected Robert of Geneva as Clement VII.

However, the importance of Anagni as a location of power predates even the rise of the Conti.[62] Between 800 and 1300, especially during the so-called Investiture Contest, more secular power brokers were anathematized from Anagni than from any other "papal" town outside Rome. The notion that a rarefied atmosphere of papalist ideology might offer an explanation of Cola's apocalyptic mentality would be somewhat farfetched, however. Even the existence—not proved—of the school that gave him his excellent grounding in Latin, in Roman literature, history, and law, still would hardly explain his exposure to apocalyptic thinking. So did Cola come into contact with apocalyptic political prophecy only after arriving in Rome?

This was not necessarily the case. The following argument will propose

---

61. Charles Bourel de la Roncière et al., eds., *Registres d'Alexander IV* (Paris, 1902–59), 2:822.

62. For a detailed history of postclassical Anagni, see M. Baudrillart, *Dictionnaire d'Histoire et de Géographie Ecclesiastique* (Paris, 1914), 2:1421–29.

that Cola was influenced visually, in his understanding of the power of images, and ideologically, particularly in his early, "pro-papal" imagery of 1343, by the prophetic, cosmic, and apocalyptic themes of thirteenth-century papal iconography in Anagni.

The frescoed cathedral crypt at Anagni contains three rows of seven vaults,[63] which form a narrative series. The first of the vaults contains a representation of the Platonic astrological Macrocosm, followed by the homocentric Microcosm; three further vaults illustrate the tetramorphs, angels, and prophets. The other two vaults and five scenes in the third row illustrate 1 Sam. 2–10: the loss and recovery of the ark of the Israelites, and the divine punishment of the sacrilegious who dared usurp it (plagues, giant mice, and hemorrhoids rain down upon enemy cities). This concludes with Samuel anointing Saul as king. Other vaults depict the ascension of Elijah in a chariot, and the offering of bread and wine to Abraham by the priest Melchisedec: two regular typological parallels for the ministry and ascension of Christ. In the remainder of the third row, and on the far wall and triple *conche,* an abbreviated Apocalypse cycle is executed; below this, finally, runs the story of the martyrdom and translation of Saint Magnus's relics to the crypt.

The frescoes convey the viewer along a linear, "horizontal" route from the creation of the world to its last days. In "vertical" terms, the frescoes negotiate the terrestrial-celestial hierarchy, incorporating Platonic cosmology, local hagiography, both Testaments, and the Apocalypse; from Man the Microcosm to the Son of Man in eternal glory. But there is also a third, typological, theme, which transcends the other, existential axes: the dispute between *regnum* and *sacerdotium,* and its solution: a bold statement of the cosmic supremacy of the pope.

Smith's theory was that the unifying feature of the frescoes was the central presence of the *arca* theme within the images of the Eucharist, the Apocalypse, the Israelites, the Virgin Mary, of Rome, and of the patron saint of Anagni, the martyr Magnus.[64] The frescoes were designed to warn the people of Anagni against the blandishments of false priests and sacrilegious men, such as the Saracens who desecrated Magnus's cask, or the Philistines who abused the Ark of the Covenant. The *arca* would be their bond to God until the time of the Last Things. Cola, of course, lived in the

---

63. A numerological structure strangely unnoted by the art historians who have discussed the frescoes.

64. M. Q. Smith, "Anagni: An Example of Medieval Typological Decoration," *Papers of the British School at Rome* 32 (1965): 1–47.

certainty that the dove, with its olive twig, would return to the ark, that the reign of the Spirit would renew Rome-Jerusalem; he also made reference to "the Ark of the Roman Republic."[65] Before and during the Tribunate Cola staged mass demonstrations in the Lateran, centered upon his own relationship to the future of the City; but Rome, and particularly the Lateran Basilica, seat of the papacy (like Anagni), was the home of the covenant with God, housing the relics of Jerusalem, including the ark.

Hugenholtz pays tribute to Smith's theory and methodology, but presents an irresistible overriding hypothesis.[66] This revolves around the dating of the frescoes, generally accepted as 1250–55.[67] Hugenholtz argues that the political circumstances of the decades leading up to 1250 entirely dictate the content of the frescoes and explain their conceptual integrity. These years saw the deteriorating relationship between Gregory IX, his successors, and Frederick II Hohenstaufen. The violence of Gregory's ideological attack on Frederick increased in proportion to his own political impotence. Frederick II had succeeded early on in claiming Jerusalem, thereby, arguably, fulfilling prophecies of the Last World Emperor, and he crowned himself emperor, bypassing the papacy altogether. After a brief lull in hostilities, Frederick's overtures to the Romans in the late 1230s earned him a second excommunication. Frederick's revenge was to block—physically—a general council of the Church in 1241. Gregory promptly died. After a long and unpleasant series of negotiations,[68] almost literally over Gregory's dead body, a Genoese was finally elected as Innocent IV, and spent much of his rule in the south of France. Nevertheless, in Rome, hostilities continued. Rainaldo Conti of Jenne, Gregory IX's nephew and future pope Alexander IV (and quoted above), then papal vicar in Innocent's absence, continued the pressure on Frederick in a series of publicized written attacks.

Around the same time Stefano Conti, cardinal of S. Maria in Trastevere, built (and Rainaldo Conti dedicated) the S. Silvestro chapel in the Quattro Coronati convent below the Lateran. A apocalyptic theme fills

---

65. III:64, 85; III:71, 85; a possible quotation from Dante's ninth epistle (Toynbee, *Dantis Alagheris Epistolae,* 148–59).

66. F. W. N. Hugenholz, "The Anagni Frescoes: A Manifesto," *Mededelingen van het Nederlands Institut te Rome* 41 (1979): 139–72.

67. Pietro Toesca, "Gli affreschi della Cattedrale di Anagni," in *Le Galleria Nazionale Italiane* (Rome, 1902), 5:116–87. The much earlier dating argued by Miklòs Boskovits, "Gli affreschi del Duomo di Anagni," *Paragone: Arte* 30, no. 2 (1979): 3–41, on stylistic grounds, is unconvincing.

68. During which another stopgap pope emerged and died.

the main tympanum, showing Christ in glory, with angels rolling up the sky and stars as if it were a scroll. This event took place, in the course of the Last Things, after the breaking of the sixth seal. It suggests that, in the minds of the designers of the frescoes, the world was reaching crisis point. The overriding theme of the chapel, however—Constantine's Donation and thus the inferior status of emperor to pope—could not be more explicit (it is even more clear than the Abraham-Melchisedek image at Anagni). One barely needs to "gloss" these frescoes in their contemporary context, that is, Frederick's arrogance and his usurpation of papal supremacy. Although Constantine was already emperor, Silvester had to crown him again because his secular coronation had only resulted in God's punishment, leprosy. Frederick had had the gall to crown himself in Jerusalem; but he also needed to be crowned again in Rome, the heavenly New Jerusalem of the chapel's tympanum.

This detour into the S. Silvestro chapel is relevant because the same painters were responsible for the execution of the frescoes at Anagni; the same ideology clearly informs the iconography of both. The political message is both less explicit and more complex at Anagni; but the crypt very probably acted as the official papal chapel of the Anagni residence, since the small chapel of the papal palace could not have held the papal entourage. It is not, therefore, surprising, that the frescoes were designed to engage with a learned audience; the history of a local saint present in the crypt was itself designed as a microcosm of themes that were truly universal. The narrative purpose of the Old Testament frescoes was the most overt, clearly reflecting the same message as the S. Silvestro chapel: sacrilege would incur divine punishment. When Frederick subverted the Ark, the symbol of the Temple, the altar of the New Temple of the New Jerusalem, that is, Rome, and the Israelites/Romans followed his lead, there was plague and death and destruction. Only the priest Samuel, that is, the Conti pope, was able to save the People of God, after the wicked kings had all died: priests had the power to create new emperors. Hence Abraham in armor receives bread and wine from Melchisedek; even the good father of his people is subject to the high priest, God's representative and ancestor of Christ's representative on earth. Samuel also exercised his power to depose Saul.[69] The narrative fresco series illustrated the papal

---

69. Samuel went on to anoint David of the "stem" of Jesse, prophet and forerunner of Christ; a clear message that the Hohenstauffen were not, contra Nicholas of Bari, a special dynasty appointed by God for his people. Cola uses the same biblical story metaphorically at III:64, 56–59; III:58, 389–92.

right to make and break emperors: and, indeed, Frederick was excommunicated and formally deposed.

Frederick's attempts to be *Divus,* and to concentrate ultimate royal and priestly powers on his own person, were not merely general sacrilege and blasphemy: he was, effectively, usurping God's order. He was, therefore, the Antichrist, in papal logic. Yet at Anagni, the theme is of triumph over the Antichrist: St. Michael has already trampled the dragon, to the right of the Son of Man. Just so, by the time of the completion of the frescoes, Frederick had died (in 1250): but his heirs were being warned in the strongest terms to preserve the proper balance of power in this world. Frederick's descendants, however, would be readily overcome. Rainaldo succeeded to the Roman see in 1254; in 1255, as Alexander IV, he reconsecrated the cathedral of his beloved Anagni.

And this is where the highly impressionable Cola di Rienzo grew up, eighty years later. If there was still a canon school in Anagni, under the influence of the local Gaetani and Conti families, the educational standard might well have remained high, in an environment suffused with papalist ideology. In any case, even without the benefit of formal exegesis, the Old Testament frescoes clearly championed, for any observer, the cause of the priest's superiority to the king in the terrestrial hierarchy. Now Cola's earliest statements, in 1343, just like the frescoes of the crypt, had an "upbeat" tone: a sense that tribulation has passed and that the redeemer figure would now rule in peace; in 1343, his hero was the pope. Later, however, in the Lateran itself, Cola was to bypass the message of the nearby S. Silvestro chapel, emphasizing the secular authority of Constantine, effectively revoking the Donation and assuming the mantle of reformer himself. He read the message of Peter and Paul to Constantine as a pledge of his own role in rescuing Rome, just as Cola's angel, at S. Angelo, saved the lady *Roma* under the eyes of Peter and Paul. The recycling—indeed, the ideological reversal—of these images, from pro-papal ideology to a buttress of the new regime, still, nonetheless, shows Cola working within the same iconographic matrix that had framed the debates of the century before.

There is a final twist to the story of Cola's early exposure to apocalyptic ideas. Chapter 2 argued that Cola came to cast himself in a role analogous to the Rider Faithful and True of the Apocalypse; but not until after the disillusionment of 1343–44. One would not expect, then, to find this figure (and indeed it is not) illustrated at Anagni. It was also suggested that Cola was under the influence of the prophetic imagery of Joachite/Fraticellan circles earlier than has been thought, but he did not use this imagery explicitly in 1343 because at that point it was superfluous. The prevailing religious culture of southeastern Lazio, during this period, was not the current orthodoxy of Avignon, and this may have had an effect on Cola's range of models. But just as significant is the fact that the orthodoxy of fourteenth-century Avignon was not necessarily that of thirteenth-century Anagni either. There is evidence, albeit limited, of Joachite influence on the papal iconography of the Anagni crypt, and the consequent infiltration of these ideas, into the vocabulary of Anagni popes; and, possibly, therefore, into Anagni's later son, Cola.

At the start of the thirteenth century, Francis of Assisi and Joachim of Fiore both challenged the Vicar of Christ to justify the distance he had moved from the messianic ideal. But both were to some extent drawn under the then more generous aegis of the Church. Joachim's teachings were by no means universally condemned; Francis was canonized in 1228 by Gregory IX. Ironically, Gregory was also the author of the bull *Quo elongatis* in 1230, which permitted the followers of Francis to depart from the strict ascetic Rule of their leader; resulting, ultimately, in the division of the Franciscan Order and the extremism of the Fraticelli.

Gregory's own apocalyptic mentality must also be viewed in light of the fact that Joachim's imaginative commentary on the Apocalypse had been accepted as canonical in 1215. In fact, Gregory proved himself a material supporter of the followers of Joachim. Early in his clerical career, in 1216, he founded one Florensian monastery, and in 1232 he set up another, S. Maria della Gloria, just outside Anagni. Dying in 1241, Gregory missed the decade during which Franciscan, Joachite, and papal streams of thought raced toward an inevitable clash.

The 1240s saw relentless pressure on, but also by, Frederick. The situation was exacerbated by the appearance of radical Franciscan texts, in the wake of *Quo elongatis,* flaying not only the emperor but the papacy too. Joachim's multivalent images were seized, swiftly embroidered upon, and supplemented, in the hunt for more powerful ammunition. The first, and perhaps most influential, pseudo-Joachite work to appear was the commentary on Jeremiah, which criticized the contemporary papacy considerably more vehemently than Joachim had ever imagined. It was, however, even more critical of the emperor:

You are the serpent on the roadside; your successor is the horned basilisk in the road. . . . Hence the Lord will restore the Church to life with a sword hard, large, and strong. . . . It is necessary that the Lord destroy [the German Empire] with the sword of the Spirit.[70]

The sword of the Spirit, clearly depicted above the altar at Anagni in the mouth of the Son, now crushing the basilisk, the serpent: one may see how the iconography of the Anagni crypt reflects the Apocalypse, but also incorporates a contemporary, and not necessarily orthodox, selection of imagery. The passage also points to the currency of certain images that continued into the next century: the rider, basilisk, and sword-Spirit had much the same visual potency and political implication in Trecento Rome, as Cola's iconography demonstrates.

The Anagni heritage was mixed: orthodox and Joachite. Moreover, in written terms (the broader context of the Anagni images) Conti papal ideologues were not miles away from their pseudo-Joachite contemporaries: the Isaiah imagery of the pseudo-Joachite Jeremiah commentary above[71] is very similar to a Conti circle letter, *Iuxta vaticinium Isaiae* of 1245, one of the apocalyptic attacks on Frederick. In turn, this was echoed later (in the 1260s) by the pseudo-Joachite commentary on Isaiah.

Another feature of Joachimist thought, echoed not just in the political context, but explicitly, visibly, in the Anagni crypt, is a clear mistrust of the new Aristotelian schools of the thirteenth century. The conservative Platonic cosmology of the crypt could be interpreted as a critique of the new radical theology of Aquinas and his followers, attacked by Joachimist thinkers generally: the doctrines of the *garrulatores,* according to the Oracle and to Cola's commentary. There is also a particularly emphatic depiction of the Pentecostal dove, on a jeweled throne, to the side of the vault of the Son of Man and the tympanum of the Apocalypse. More generally, there is an emphasis throughout on a politicized, contextualized, reading of Old Testament prophets, in many of the nonnarrative vaults, which locates the present (the Christian church) within the eternal and eschatological of the Apocalypse, as predicted in the past (the Old Testament).

Franciscan prophecy, tinged with Joachimism, and papal ideology, looking for prophetic and cosmic domination of the secular world, veered more closely to one another in the middle of the thirteenth century than ever previously or since. The identification of Francis as the apocalyptic

---

70. This argument draws upon material discussed and quoted in McGinn, *Visions of the End,* 168–79.

71. See Isa. 14:29.

angel of the sixth seal was widely mooted. If the Anagni frescoes were executed 1250–55, then they must have been designed in the late 1240s: in which case the vivid image of the dove—Celano's image for Francis—and the breaking of the sixth seal (Rev. 7:12), painted next to each other in the Anagni crypt, must have had a particular significance for observers; observers such as Cola, perhaps? In the S. Silvestro chapel the apocalyptic event that immediately follows (at Rev. 7:14) surmounts the Donation narrative, that papalist explication of Rome's political destiny.

The 1250s, however, represented a watershed in more ways than one. It was now that the long-term results of *Quo elongatis*—the conflict between the conventional and radical factions of the Franciscan Order—reached crisis proportions. In 1254 Gerardo di Borgo San Donnino produced his *Introduction to the Eternal Gospel,* an interpretation and summary of Joachim's works, which, as McGinn puts it, "made claims from which the abbot would have fled in horror."[72] According to Gerardo, the church of the Second Status was about to be utterly destroyed, along with all traditional Scripture and doctrine; in its place would be substituted the work of Joachim. The result of this announcement was universal uproar. Once again Anagni was the center of the debate. Just after the completion and dedication of the crypt in 1255, a papal commission was established—at Anagni—to assess the acceptability of Franciscan theology and the future of the Order. Under the terms of a swift resolution, the Protocol of Anagni, Gerardo was condemned. The Protocol thus heralded an explicit break between the established hierarchy of the Church, and the Franciscan imitators of Joachim. It did not, of course, affect the iconographic elements of the recently finished frescoes, nor their association with both the conservative-intellectual and the radical-prophetic language of the mid-Duecento. The Anagni frescoes possibly represent the most extreme statement of the interpenetration of orthodox and radical apocalyptic imagery before the clampdown of 1255, and this in the pope's own chapel.

The next decades saw the papacy's overtures toward France. The Angevin results of the culmination of French influence within the Curia, and Celestine's "possession" by Naples, have been described. Meanwhile, in later thirteenth-century Anagni, the Conti family ceded its hegemony to the Gaetani; once again the town came to the forefront of ecclesiastical polity. The calls for the return of the pope to Rome cast a different light on

---

72. McGinn, *Visions of the End,* 160.

Boniface's "persuasion" of Celestine to abdicate. What could be more Roman than a pope with Conti and Orsini connections, ruling from the heart of traditional papal authority, Anagni?

Unfortunately, however "Roman," Boniface's methods were not very "celestial," earning him excoriating treatment from most Fraticellan prophecy-makers, particularly in the *Vaticinia,* where he was clearly identified as Antichrist, or his precursor.[73] Cola's attitude toward Boniface is hard to pin down. It appears to move, curiously, from the positive image—of an Anagni education?—to the negative image of the Fraticelli, which, in fact, Cola could also have first encountered in that part of Lazio. The Anagni connection thus, in fact, suits both the pro- and the antipapal rhetoric of Cola, in 1343 and 1350 respectively.

Perhaps the best example of his Anagni heritage, however, relates to that most important theme in Cola's ideology, repeated in the iconography of his Tribunate, in dress, procession and fresco, namely the emphasis on the sword. The apocalyptic sword "sharp on both sides" of the Son of Man—and of the Rider Faithful and True—continues to appear throughout the letters of 1349–51. It may echo the *Vaticinia* image of the sword emerging from the mouth, or the *duplex* sword language of the Angelic Oracle, both of which echo the imagery of the Book of Revelation. On the other hand, Cola may have adopted the image straight from the vault before the altar at Anagni, where there still looms an immensely powerful visual formulation of the vision of the Son of Man.

This vault, it has been argued, was depicted around the time of the production of the first wave of pseudo-Joachite prophecies. A curious passage in the contemporary commentary on Jeremiah[74] speaks to Cola's, rather than a papal, political context: "The young men . . . will perish by the sword of the new republic." In Cola's case, this was the sword of justice; not the twin swords of the old dispensation, the battle of pope and emperor, but the sword of the judge, the sword of Michael Archangel, defender of the Roman People; the sword of the Spirit, the two-edged sword of the mouth of the Son of Man of the Apocalypse, the sword of the Rider Faithful and True.[75]

---

73. Douie, *Nature and Effect,* 58, describes their interpretation of *Benedicti* (i.e., Benedetto Gaetani) as "666."

74. A gloss on Jer. 11:22.

75. To Rev. 19:15, 19:21 we must also compare Eph. 6:17 and John 21:9–20. A certain iconographic confusion surrounds the relationship of the twin swords and the double-edged sword from the mouth. Examples exist of the conflation of these two images, and no art historian has put forward a satisfactory explanation. Louis Réau, *Iconographie de l'art Chrétien*

To understand the broadest, as well as the immediate, context of Cola's apocalypticism, this discussion has pushed back the focus to the 1340s and considered the *Vaticinia* in Italy, and Jean de Roquetaillade in Avignon. It has gone further back, to the 1320s and 1330s, to Naples, to the *Palombelli,* and to Lazio and Angelo Clareno. It has carried on back to the years around 1300, and to the early *Vaticinia* and their cognate prophecies; and back again to the 1290s, the Angelic Oracle, Celestine V, and Boniface VIII. Ultimately, however, I suggest that it is the imagery of the 1250s, the reflection of the political and prophetic world of Anagni, with its combination of apocalyptic, macrocosmic themes and local, contemporary events, its overlap between canonical iconography and provocative, suggestively Joachite elements, that stimulated the young Cola's imagination, and perhaps even provides a source for the imagery he used to illustrate his attitude toward Rome, the Eternal City.

Conclusion

Cola lived in an cultural environment in which the end of the world was always nigh. His own unique synthesis of canonical eschatology and personal apotheosis is intriguing. Yet the elements that fed his construction of a New Rome, under his rule as Tribune, may all be found in central Italy in the later medieval period. Cola grew up in the 1320s in a town with over a century at the center of power behind it, and a range of apocalyptic imagery as its cultural heritage, not far from Subiaco, a town that was in turn a contemporary nerve center of Joachite ideology (and artistic patronage). The clearest evidence that exists of Cola's reliance on Joachite

---

(Paris: Presses universitaires de France, 1957), 687, talks of an aesthetic shift in the depiction of the Son of Man vision: the sword comes to cross the mouth horizontally (i.e., no longer resembling a cigar). It may be hypothesized that in cases where the protrusion of the sword is equidistant, it is less clear that there is only one sword. Cases of the depiction of two swords coming from the mouth do not rely on a different tradition; I would suggest, rather, that they represent a contamination of the biblical text of one sword, by the more popular allegory of the two swords, exacerbated, after Réau's "aesthetic shift," by the absence of descriptive clarity in nontextual models. Visual examples of the depiction of two swords where the apocalyptic text requires one, but one sharp on both sides, may be found in various applicable contexts, but the most cogent contemporary version comes from the 1346–48 St. John chapel in the Papal Palace at Avignon, painted by Clement VI's Viterbese artist, Matteo Giovanetti. As a written example, there is the account of the Chronicler (see Wright, *Life,* 64), suggesting that Cola's own design—or designers—confused the doubly sharp sword with the double sword, despite Cola's emphatic written reference to one apocalyptic, i.e., double-edged, sword of justice.

prophecy comes from the period of his life following his 1347 Tribunate, which corresponds to the antipapal nature of his mission to Prague. A strong case, nevertheless, can be made for his use of similar, though less explicit themes in the immediate run-up to and duration of his own regime. Cola presented himself as the triumphal military leader of the classical past and of the apocalyptic future, (re-)created in the present through particularly symbolic titles and insignia, especially the motif of the double-edged sword of justice, which he attached to his unique position in Rome. Nonetheless his imagery, visual and verbal, then and later, drew on a bank of symbols that had been circulating and evolving for a long period; the same symbols that, a century earlier, just before Joachite and conventional apocalyptic ideology reached their watershed, had been expressed at Anagni. Perhaps he saw himself as Joachim's *dux novus:* after all, Joachim's "duke" was never exclusively identified as a pope (though, interestingly, attached to "Babylon"); the title traditionally referred to military leadership.[76] This left open the route for Joachim's followers to substitute a secular messiah, most notoriously Dante's Imperial "DVX" of *Purgatorio* 33.43. Scholarly consensus tends to affirm that Dante's *dux* was intended to signify Henry VII: the Henry who, of course, was Cola's "father," or so he claimed.

It is not impossible for the modern reader to appreciate the tense atmosphere of apocalyptic expectation in the thirteenth and fourteenth centuries. Harbingers of doom and seekers of utopian renewal continue to flourish with the advent of the millennium, in the Age of Aquarius—penultimate stage of a chronological and symbolic cycle—spirits in a material world, employing apocalyptic language and weaving complicated conspiracy theories around contemporary happenings. The danger always lies in the temptation to surrender cultural rules and restraint, as demonstrated by the fate of charismatics such as Fra Dolcino in the fourteenth century, or by David Koresh and his branch of the Seventh Day Adventists in 1993, or indeed, most recently, the tragic Ugandan doomsday 2000 cult, the so-called Movement for the Restoration of the Ten Commandments. The more skilled operators, however, have always worked for reform within their social context and often with very worldly tools. When Cola bewailed the moral bankruptcy of the Avignon curia, much of the complaint was couched not in the fiery language of apocalypse, but as a

---

76. E. Randolph Daniel, *Abbot Joachim of Fiore. Liber de Concordia Novi ac Veteris Testamenti* (Philadelphia: American Philosophical Society, 1983), 402.

lengthy extension of the more mundane metaphor of sheep, shepherd, and wolves. In the midst of Cola's otherworldly claims before the Bohemian court, he was still sharp and keen to expose selected cases of papal venality: the annual rental of a papal vicariate, for example, to Lucchino Visconti, for twenty thousand florins[77] (a particularly sore point for Charles, whose Italian diplomatic overtures were being blocked by the Visconti). Cola finished a long section of his mission statement to the emperor, in 1351, outlining prophetic reasons for Charles to return to Rome, with a more prosaic incentive: he gave assurances of Rome's current good economic standing (his field of expertise, of course), with the "inflated incomes" of the Jubilee Year; these would funnel straight into Caesar's coffers of course.[78]

It is, then, this combination of precedent, convention and idiosyncrasy, along with the engaging balance of pragmatism and prophecy in Cola's political career, which demonstrates how remarkably well he managed to bridge the active and contemplative lives. Cola was both scholar and soldier, the mystic knight, the once and future *plus quam imperator,* and yet, at the same time, undeniably a shrewd notary and capable administrator, whose career, contacts, and political context will be delineated in the next chapters.

---

77. III:57, 154–58.
78. III:58, 782–90. See also III:50, 462.

PART II
THE ETERNAL CITY LIMITS

The Roman Revolution

The late Richard Krautheimer dismissed Cola's regime as little more than a rhetorical exercise: "His dream of a rebirth of Rome collapsed as it was bound to after a few years."[1] Krautheimer's comment is not atypical of the historiography. Indeed, it is indicative of the fact that Cola's social context and political career have been neglected even in modern studies of Trecento Rome. In contrast, the following examination of the surviving archival sources will serve to relocate Cola's regime within a broader pattern of events. His measures were composed within the framework of local and contemporary government; in addition to Cola's own agenda, these measures reflected, to an extent, the political expectations of the dominant element among the supporters of his revolution.

The reconstruction of the social history of fourteenth-century Rome has been gaining momentum since the 1960s. Yet there has been an apparent reluctance to insert Cola and his revolution into this rich new context. This is, arguably, the result of a still-pervasive image of Cola as an anomaly and is regrettable on two counts: first, because new research can reveal a great deal about Cola and the causes and circumstances of his revolution, and second, because the course of Cola's career could be used to reveal much about fourteenth-century Roman society, the fourteenth-century exercise of power, and the use of contemporary political models and language within his regime.

The purpose of the second part of this book is, therefore, to use archival sources from within the City to establish a much broader perspective on contemporary Rome and the social and cultural context of Cola's revolution. But we should begin with a consideration of the point of overlap

---

1. Richard Krautheimer, *Rome: Profile of a City, 312–1305* (Princeton: Princeton University Press, 1980), 228. Of course, in fairness, Cola once described his own failed plans as those of as a *sompniator,* a "dreamer."

between the historical and imaginary, and the real and tangible: the theme and patterns of revolution itself.

Ronald Syme's masterly treatment of Rome in the first century B.C., *The Roman Revolution,* traced the evolution of ancient Rome from the decline of the Republic into the creation of the Empire.[2] A little more than a thousand years later (more precisely, from 1143 to 1451) the process was moving in reverse, with the frequent reassertion of the idea of the Roman Republic. Rome's municipal history may be traced from the so-called restoration of the Senate in 1143; the following brief survey will move through and beyond Cola's role in the continued pursuit of "republican liberty" (in medieval terms, effectively communal autonomy) by the citizens of Rome in the later Middle Ages.

The re-creation of the Senate in 1143, under the charismatic Arnold of Brescia, was achieved at a moment of rebellion against Innocent II. However, it was not until the thirteenth century that Rome's communal government established its military domination of Tivoli and other *Destretto* towns, in a typical expression of contemporary Italian communal self-assertion in the drive to regional hegemony, defying attempts by pope (or emperor) to curtail such activities.[3] In constitutional matters, the emphasis placed by Brancaleone degli Andolò, *capitano del popolo,* on the political influence of a junta of guildsmen in 1255,[4] may be seen as the Roman manifestation of the emergence of the *popolo*—in Rome's case, thirteen sets of twin guild consuls—into preexisting communal structures. This process was analogous to contemporary political developments in other Italian cities, although in Rome, because of the on-off temporal authority of the papacy, the foothold was harder to establish.[5]

The end of the "re-republicanizing" process in Rome was arguably the stifled revolt of Stefano Porcari in 1451. The election as pope of Nicholas V in 1447 marked an acceleration in the process, already begun under Martin V, by which *lu baron san Pietro* became a contemporary Renaissance prince in the style of the Medici, the Visconti, and the doges of Venice. The midcentury uprisings of the preceding era—Arnold of Bres-

---

2. Ronald Syme, *The Roman Revolution* (Oxford: Clarendon Press, 1939).

3. Carole M. Small, "The District of Rome in the Early Fourteenth Century," *Canadian Journal of History* 16 (1981): 193–213.

4. Eugene Dupré-Théiseider, *Roma dal Comune di Popolo alla Signoria Pontificia (1252–1377),* Storia di Roma, vol. 11 (Bologna: Capelli, 1952), 3–100.

5. Brentano, *Rome before Avignon,* 93–136, illustrates the confusion of Roman governmental authorities up to the 1290s, which can be extrapolated well beyond that date.

cia, Brancaleone degli Andalò, Cola di Rienzo, Porcari—would at last be prevented from recurring.

However, in focusing on these "peaks" of activity there is a danger of overlooking the territory that connects them. This has been a major distorting factor in the historiography of medieval Rome. Curiously, there exists a lacuna in the literature that no social historian has yet sought to fill, perhaps because of the traditional overabundance of biographical literature on Cola and the dearth elsewhere.[6] That lacuna is, precisely, an examination of Roman popular revolutions of the late medieval period both in chronological terms of events from the twelfth to the fifteenth centuries, and in thematic terms of the continuous reassertion of *popolo* ideology. A brief survey cannot hope to cover such a subject comprehensively; the narrowest *filo rosso* may be followed. Yet Cola's existence *must* be seen within the historical perspective of a sequence, during these years, of other, analogous political events and comparable if not identical ideologies.

Already by the turn of the fourteenth century, the language of popular ideology in Rome, which had not yet succeeded in translating rhetoric into power, was being appropriated by baronial senators who sought to an extent to satisfy the demands citizens placed on those in office. The precise echoes of this language—the declamation of the rights of the underclass—in the earliest oration of Cola di Rienzo have been noted;[7] already by 1299 one may see the fluidity of boundaries between rhetoric, ideological allegiance, and political action. Popular revolutions, in any case, were often led by disaffected, and not necessarily altruistic, aristocrats; this is as true of the years 1143–1451 in Rome as anywhere else. On the other hand, *popolo* self-manifestation also came from "below"; Cola's heritage, as a revolutionary demagogue, was a mixed one. He did not, for instance, claim the semimilitary title (although he intermittently assumed the powers) of a *capitano del popolo.* Yet, as we will discuss in chapter 5, many of the measures Cola introduced fed straight into the semimilitarized political regime of the Bandaresi in the late 1350s, which represented the final, if short-lived, success of the *popolo* in its Roman manifestation.

Cola's revolution did not, then, occur in any sort of a vacuum. The fourteenth century witnessed revolution all over Europe: the French

---

6. The nearest to a consistent account of political affairs in Rome in the period is that of Dupré-Théseider, *Roma dal Comune,* which contains much detail, but a frustrating absence of critical apparatus. Gregorovius's narrative is similarly well constructed but inadequately footnoted/sourced.

7. Discussed in chapter 1.

Jacquerie, the Ciompi uprising in Florence, the Peasant's Revolt in England[8]; a pattern of historical circumstances that was both the creation and the creator of new social classes. In this sense Rome belongs within the widest, that is, pan-European, context. On a local level, in Rome itself, between the agitation of Giovanni da Ignano, *capitano del popolo* in 1305, and the establishment of the antipapal Libero Commune of 1398, there took place no fewer than between fifteen and twenty "popular" demonstrations of political discontent directed at the magnatial Senate (this consisted of two barons, along the traditional medieval model of the dual "consulship") or at representatives of papal authority. Opposition to this model was usually articulated by (multiples of) thirteen city-district representatives (twelve, before the inclusion of Trastevere at the end of the thirteenth century) sometimes also associated with lesser guild leadership.[9] The Roman districts or *rioni* had existed for centuries, although the medieval *rioni* were hardly coterminous with the classical subdivisions *(regiones)* of the City.[10] By the fourteenth century each *rione* had its own militia (re-formed, but not "invented," by Cola in 1347), which could act either independently or in concert with other rional forces to repel invasions of the City; this happened in 1327.[11] However, the clearest articulation of rional identity was in the context of episodes of *popolo* rule in the City by thirteen, twenty-six, or fifty-two "good men."[12]

Cola's revolution in 1347 was, in many senses, just one of these episodes. Ignano in 1305 was followed in 1312–13, after the imperial chaos of Henry VII's visit to Rome, by another *capitano*, the Stefaneschi-related

---

8. See the dated but valuable Mollat and Wolff, *Popular Revolutions.*

9. Guilds, particularly the lesser guilds, in Rome were weak in comparison to those in other cities; even in 1363 they were guaranteed no constitutional role, and their own statutes privilege administrative and ceremonial, rather than regulatory, details (see especially Egmont Lee, "Workmen and Workers in Quattrocento Rome," in Ramsay, *Rome in the Renaissance,* 142).

10. See Etienne Hubert, "Le *rioni* de Rome," *Dictionnaire historique de la Papauté,* ed. Philippe Levillain (Paris: Fayard, 1994), 1459–60; Camillo Re, "Le regioni di Roma nel Medio Evo," *Studi e documenti di storia e diritto* 10 (1889): 349–81. Rional identities crystallized early; see Giovanni Cavallini's discussion in *Polistoria* of their historic origins, locations, and insignia for an idea of how *rioni* were regarded in Cola's period (Laureys, "Giovanni Cavallini's Polistoria," 482–500).

11. The angel at the Porta S. Sebastiano (noted in chap. 3) commemorates this victory. For other evidence of the Trecento militia, see Pietro Egidi, *Intorno all'Esercito del Comune di Roma nella prima metà del secolo XIV* (Viterbo, 1897).

12. Brancaleone degli Andalò's *cohadunatio artium* had fifty-two representatives in 1252; there is evidence from 1263 (see Salimei, *Senatori e statuti,* 80) of a set of *XIII Buoni Uomini.*

nobleman Jacopo Arlotti. In 1320 an Orsini of Montegiordano was acclaimed as "deputy" of the Roman People. In 1324, popular reaction to the imposition of vicars for the Neapolitan Robert of Anjou, then papal Senator, brought about the deposition of the vicars—who happened to be Roman magnates—in favor of two other magnates claiming to be representatives of the people. A similar sequence of events surrounded the upset caused by the arrival and departure of Lewis the Bavarian at the end of the 1320s. This is the point, in 1327, at which the Chronicler begins, describing the expulsion of Robert's vicar and a Savelli co-senator by the (Orsini and Colonna) syndics of the Campidoglio, followed by an act highly symbolic as a precedent for Cola's own "popular" ceremonies: their knighting as *cavalieri per lo puopolo de Roma* by a group of *Buoni Uomini,* "good men" of the people.[13] In 1328, another junta of thirteen *Buoni Uomini,* playing on the Guelf-Angevin Ghibelline-imperial dialectic, seized power and opened the gates to Lewis the Bavarian.

The early 1330s saw the resumption of the dreary routine of magnatial infighting and interference by papal legates. The appointment of Robert of Naples as papal "overseer" in 1333 made little difference. It is worth remembering that Cola returned to the City and became a notary at the age of twenty, that is, around 1333. Popular unrest, stimulated by events such as the destruction of the Ponte Milvio in 1335 in the ongoing Orsini-Colonna fight, raised its head more than once in the shape of Thirteen more Good Men. Roman politics continued in similar vein, including an attack by the Savelli, Orsini, and their allies on the Colonna cardinal's palace at S. Angelo in Pescheria in 1338.[14] In 1339, under another new Thirteen (which nonetheless disappeared as swiftly as it had appeared), as Giovanni Villani relates, the Romans dispatched a request for Florentine assistance in establishing an antimagnatial constitution.[15]

Imperial interference resurfaced in 1342: on the death of Benedict XIII ·in 1342, the imperial vicariate was awarded to Giovanni di Vico, Prefect of Rome and overlord of Viterbo and later bête noire of Cola (and of Innocent VI). In much the same way Lewis the Bavarian had used the Lucchese despot Castruccio Castracane as his vicar in Rome in 1328. The 1342 gesture was a failure; the familiar balancing act of two baronial Senators of

---

13. *ARC,* 9.
14. See A. Mercati, "Nell'Urbe dalla fine di settembre 1337 al 31 gennaio 1338," *Miscellanae historiae pontificae* 10 (1945): 1–84; Dupré-Théseider, *Roma dal Comune,* 485–516.
15. Porta, *Giovanni Villani. Cronica,* 3:205 (12:96).

opposing factions reemerged before the end of the year. The next year, 1343, saw another revolution, and another Thirteen Good Men. The representative they sent to Avignon—unsuccessfully—to gain recognition for the new regime was, of course, Cola di Rienzo.

Cola's location within the process of the self-assertion of the *popolo* is very clear. The precise measures introduced by his government will be examined in the following chapters, but within the present review of *popolare* politics in fourteenth-century Rome, it may be noted that, when Clement wrote to the Roman People on October 7, 1347, attempting to undermine support for Cola's regime (and specifically to condemn Cola for imprisoning barons without papal consent), he addressed his letter to "XIII Boni Vires."[16] This illustrates the continuity of a *popolare* representative structure in Rome during Cola's regime, despite Cola's own apparent moves toward signorial and quasi-imperial status. A reference by a contemporary Ferraran chronicler to the Papal Legate's imposition of thirty-nine "Wise Men"[17] upon Cola's council is further evidence that the rhetoric and constitutional structure of *popolare* government thrived in Rome among Cola's enemies as well as his supporters.

The aftermath of Cola's regime will be discussed more fully in chapter 5; briefly to summarize subsequent political events, the revolutionary impulse did not stop with Cola: in 1351 a popular initiative, possibly under the cover of a Marian confraternity meeting at S. Maria Maggiore, put in power the noble Giovanni Cerroni. This ended in disaster, and the Senator escaped to Campania, allegedly carrying off a part of the communal treasury.[18] Cola, at this point, was in the far north, although his continued correspondence with the ecclesiastical and financial power-brokers of Rome reflects the continuity of pressure by *popolo* agitators despite the attempts of the barons to recover their previous authority. Baroncelli's spell as "Second Tribune" in 1353 did not end in a bloodbath provoked by Cola's return to Umbria-Lazio, as a bogus Baroncelli *Vita* claimed.[19] Far from it; he died a natural death.[20] Cola was actually prevented from retaking the reins of government as papal Senator because of financial and military

---

16. IV:26.
17. See chapter 4.
18. See Dupré-Théseider, *Roma dal Comune,* 629.
19. This tale, popular—possibly composed—in the sixteenth century, exists in a number of manuscripts. It has also helped to create an image of Cola as a brutal megalomaniac, particularly in his second period of rule in 1354.
20. See the excellent account by Pietro Egidi, "Per la vita di Francesco Baroncelli," in *Scritti di Storia, di filosophia e d'arte* (Naples, 1908), 363–77.

obligations: he was a knight in the army of the Legate Albornoz (evidence from papal expenditure registers confirms the account of the Chronicler).[21]

Following Cola's death, the City's political world began to see the rising influence of the militia men, the Felice Società dei Balestrieri e Pavesati, under two leaders called *Bandaresi.* These men were not the *popolo grasso* who led the economy and staffed the government, but men from a less elevated social background. Matteo Villani's claim in 1360 that they were introduced by Tuscan constitutional advisers, as Roman versions of Florence's *gonfalonieri di giustizia,* is unjustified:[22] we will see later that the existence of the *balestrieri* and *pavesati,* if embryonic, can be traced at least as far back as Cola's Tribunate. After the institution of a single Senator in 1357–58 (Cola was a precedent for this, in 1354, though also like the communal military leaders, the *capitani* and *podestà* of other contemporary cities) and of the government of the Seven Reformers, there followed what seems, although the evidence is limited, to have been a *popolo minuto* uprising in 1362 *(minuto* in that it was led, inter alia, by the cobbler Lello Pocadota).[23] Its immediate failure, and the introduction of the Statutes of 1363, brought Bandaresi autonomy to an end; thus began a period of their cooperation with representatives of the *popolo grasso.* Following this, there was a partial reassertion of papal authority in 1368, and the introduction of the three papal-appointed Conservators. However, the Bandaresi and their lieutenants, although officially disbanded by Urban V, swiftly regrouped under the equally *popolaresco* but more traditionally Florentine title of *Executori della Giustizia.* They were to prove a thorn in the side of the schism-ridden papacy upon its definitive return to Rome in the 1370s. The year 1384 saw a flurry of activity around another Thirteen.[24] A lengthy fight, in the next decade, with Pope Boniface IX culminated in his expulsion and the establishment of the (albeit short-lived) Libero Comune in 1398. In 1404, the City again refusing to accept the rule of Innocent VII, a further reform of the statutes replaced the three papal Conservators with seven, echoing the Seven Reformers of the 1350s. Resistance to Martin V and the expulsion of Eugenius IV mark further points in the declining struggle for Roman municipal self-assertion. Nicholas V's international triumph over the Conciliarist threat to papal

---

21. See Burdach, *Briefwechsel,* 2:23–42, esp. 35.
22. *Matteo Villani, Cronica,* 2:358–59 (9:51).
23. Ibid., 2:623–24 (11:25).
24. Salimei, *Senatori e statuti,* 147.

autonomy was matched at home, in Rome, by the summary execution in 1451 of the rebel Stefano Porcari, a noble descendant of the powerful Trecento notarial family.[25]

Neither the principle nor the gritty reality of urban revolution, then, was unfamiliar to Romans of the later Middle Ages. This reality must transport us from the imperial ethos of the preceding section into the "contemporary" world of the civic *signoria* of Rome. The political and institutional history of the fourteenth century in Rome centered upon the establishment and subsequent assertion of the governmental prerogatives of the *popolo;* this was given both rhetorical coverage and yet also a genuine trial in 1347 during Cola's regime, and the results were consolidated in the next decade. Cola's role outside Rome, as Italian chroniclers—and his own correspondence—demonstrate (see chap. 4), was fraught with a lack both of definition and of the resources necessary to impose power across the peninsula. Cola was not a stereotypical Italian municipal despot; but then, Rome was not a stereotypical Italian city. However, insofar as Roman administration was like that of other cities, so were Cola's techniques in running that administration; his expertise and authority may be seen throughout 1347.

Cola, it is clear, belonged both to the ideology and the reality of Roman politics, and his homage to *popolo* themes is a part of a much wider trend. The extent of Cola's debt to the support of the *popolo* will be investigated in the chapters below. Chapter 4 surveys first the range of "external" chronicle accounts of the Tribunate, including a detailed examination of the most important contemporary evidence of all, that of the Roman Chronicler. Particular attention is given to the manner in which the Chronicler also reflected social conflict and the new *popolaresco* initiatives within contemporary Roman society and government. This analysis also draws out the reasons this account has been both fatal and, paradoxically, fundamental to later readings of Cola as a contemporary ruler. The chapter is completed with an examination of the surviving archival sources and discusses the significance of these sources in understanding Cola's regime. Chapter 5 describes the most important aspect of social evolution in the period, the rise of the so-called *popolo.* It delineates the various groups and explains their relative mobility in mid-fourteenth-century Rome and then

---

25. See Anna Modigliani, *I Porcari: Storia di una famiglia romana tra Medioevo e Rinascimento* (Rome: Roma nel Rinascimento, 1994). The terms *bovattiere, popolo grasso, minuto,* etc. are fully explained in chapter 5.

goes on to demonstrate the extent to which Cola was supported by various groups, outlining where conflicts lay within those groups and how these conflicts were reflected in, although not successfully resolved by, his regime. Chapter 6 describes the professional notaries of Trecento Rome, who themselves participated in the "rise" of these newer social groups. Their particular importance in Rome—political, social, and economic—is investigated. It is posited that Cola's career and his ideological motivation were products of the social, economic, and political aspirations of notaries in particular, but also of the various, and conflicting, groups of the *popolo* in general. The chapter ends with an examination of not only the social and economic status but also the precise identities of Cola's contemporaries, both those who ran his government and those who brought it crashing down.

Chapter 4

Bene me ricordo como per suonno: The Nature of the Evidence

Cola's imaginary world was, not surprisingly,[1] best reflected in his own subjective statements, and to a lesser extent in those of his personal correspondents. External evidence for and from the Tribunate, therefore, must be granted considerable weight in the objective reconstruction of the "real" parameters of Cola's exercise of power and justice within—and beyond—Roman society. The following chapter will move across the spectrum of evidence, from a description of the more "distant" observers of the Tribunate to an analysis of the most important contemporary source, the Roman Chronicler, whose account of the events of Cola's career is the fullest; so far so, indeed, that his work readily metamorphosed into a biography of the Tribune.[2] How others perceived Cola—in which categories of rulership he was placed, during an era of *popolo* self-assertion across the continent—helps toward a clarification of his position and politics within Rome itself.[3] The chapter ends with a section introducing the range of surviving documentary sources from the City itself in this period; material that will then be used in the following chapters to flesh out the internal economic and constitutional context of Rome in Cola's heyday.

Cola from Afar

Cola's commentators, from Abruzzo to the upper Rhine, shared an interest with him in both the past and the future history of Rome, the central

---

1. "I remember it well, like a dream"; the Chronicler describing events in Rome in 1328, at the very start of his "eyewitness" account (*ARC*, 8).
2. See the general introduction for a discussion of the biographical motif.
3. There were no fewer than twenty-nine chronicles or other contemporary accounts of the events of Cola's career.

city of the Christian world; they differed considerably in their assessments of the Tribune himself: prophet, lawyer, *signore,* fool? Starting from the furthest afield, we examine those aspects of Cola's political career that stand out from six accounts composed beyond the Alps. From here, we move back to Italian city-states; there are no fewer than fourteen Italian civic chronicles that describe the Tribunate, interesting in varying degrees for their attitudes—varying from contempt to respect—toward Cola's pan-Italic rhetoric and pageantry, but also for their responses to his direct military intervention and his assertion of the local hegemony of the City. These provide information complementary to the major sources for the regime, regarding Cola's government itself, and, of course, evidence for the reception and the success—or not—of his claims to rule not just Rome, but all Italy and indeed, the world. Finally we assess the accounts of Cola and Rome that emanated from the circles of the Roman curia in Avignon, and complete our survey with an analysis of the position taken by the Roman Chronicler, whose narrative account (1327–54) is the most important external source of all.

Imperial Reports

Cola never presented a threat to the Imperial authority of Charles IV; so much is clear from the chroniclers of Charles's household, and from other German commentators. The accounts relevant to this section center on the period Cola spent in Prague, which is, in comparison, glossed over by Cola's Italian narrative sources (the Chronicle included). A brief consideration of the possible sources for each of these accounts is provided in Burdach's second volume. Seibt's partial analysis of these sources, however, stresses that Burdach's image of Cola di Rienzo as a great *Epochefigur* cannot be justified in terms of the portrait created by the transalpine chronicles.[4] Something of the religious impact of Cola's propositions to the emperor appears to have filtered through, hence the curious apocalyptic sentiments triggered by the distant impression of events surrounding Cola—and Rome—in the vague accounts of Henrik of Diessenhoven, and the *Oberrheinische Chronist.*[5] More specifically, regarding the charges of

---

4. Seibt, *Anonimo Romano,* 118.

5. Henrik of Diessenhoven, *Chronica,* ed. J. F. Böhmer and J. Hüber, Fontes Rerum Germanicum, vol. 4 (Stuttgart, 1868). The Upper Rhine chronicle, a fascinating dialect account of far distant events, talks (for 1347) of the imminent realization of the prophecies of Hildegard and of the Second Coming; and, in this time, of a notary in Rome called "the Miller," who attacked the Colonna and Orsini (cited by Burdach and Piur, *Briefwechsel,* 2:66–67).

heresy Cola faced, Františka of Prague's account contains assertions by Cola identical to those that appear in the postscript to Cola's first letter to the emperor[6] (that the power of the worldly clergy would be overturned within eighteen months, for example). These postscript assertions are more explicitly—and conventionally—heretical than any other prophetic claim Cola was to make, at least in writing; it is possible that the postscript was added by one of the scribes of the Prague archbishop, Ernst, and copied into the Bohemian corpus of Cola's letters.[7] The lack of subtlety may indicate that Cola was being, in some way, framed; or that he may have allowed more heretical opinion to slip under verbal examination. Moreover, Mathias of Neuenberg accuses Cola of planning to elect a new pope. Cola always strenuously denied this accusation, though, interestingly, it also appears in the Roman chronicle, and was obviously widely believed to be a feature of his regime. Pope Clement, for one, did not believe Cola's assertions of loyalty, as we have seen.[8]

So, whether or not Cola planned to depose Clement and elect an antipope (as Lewis the Bavarian had done, in recent memory), Cola was believed, at a distance, to be going down that route. Little is to be learned from these transalpine chronicles of the nuts and bolts of the regime and its innovations, apart from one passage in the chronicle of Heinrich von Taube of Selbach, which mentions Cola's ordinance against feuding, associated with the use of the sectarian names Guelf and Ghibelline. Obviously, the political context of the composition of this set of chronicles is different from the situation south of the Alps; descriptions of Cola's assertion of republican, municipal autonomy are not to be anticipated. We would not expect to be informed of certain aspects—the antimagnatial, for instance—of Cola's polity.[9] However, the identification of Cola as a notary does reinforce the importance of this occupation and its perceived authority (see chap. 6), and, particularly, its association with the exercise of power in the City of Rome.[10]

---

6. III:49, 131–36.

7. A fourteenth-century Prague chancery codex, and probably a first-generation copy of a large number of Cola's letters; now B.A.V. Vat. Lat. 12503.

8. IV:22, 12–14.

9. One exception is found, in the account of Františka of Prague, possibly a *familiaris* of Archbishop Ernst (*Kronika Františka,* ed. Josef Emler, Fontes Rerum Bohemicarum, vol. 4 [Prague, 1884], 452). He claims that by smashing the Colonna, the "leading citizens" *(principales)* of the City, Cola "brought great advantage to the Republic and commune (*universitas*) of Rome."

10. Henrik of Diessenhoven's first sentence on Cola comments on the latter's financial resources (Henrik of Diessenhoven, *Chronica,* 57); this and another similar reference are discussed in chapter 6.

Signore of Rome or "Hero" of Italy *(Zelator Italie)*?

The various Italian city chroniclers who kept an eye on Rome sketched numerous episodes in the course of the Tribunate.[11] They provide further information for the obscure period between Cola's escape from the Castel S. Angelo following his abdication in late 1347, and his appearance at the court of the Bohemian emperor in 1350. In particular there is evidence to suggest that Cola forged a temporary alliance with the Hungarian forces, then en route for the internecine strife of the contemporary Neapolitan kingdom.

Italian civic sources also provide useful information regarding the culture and economy of Rome itself in the mid-Trecento, the center of Christendom, home of the faith and distant capital of an ancient empire. Clearly Romans possessed a cynical and grasping reputation—*chi paga, passa,* as St. Bernard deftly put it ("he who pays, gets in")—from long before the period of Cola's regime. But it is particularly well expressed in accounts of the Jubilee Year of 1350. Perhaps the most entertaining—and most critical—account is that of the Abruzzan chronicler, Buccio di Ranallo, whose intriguing dialect rhyme account describes the arrivals of the supply ships for the pilgrims, the expense of the amounts of wax being burned by pilgrims, deaths in the crowds, the price hikes, shortages in food and particularly, in lodging.[12] Buccio evidently experienced this in person: "The worst thing these wretched Romans do, I'll tell you, is when the innkeepers, who seem angels but are actually complete dogs, putting you up for the night, promise you a bed but give you bare boards; tell you you're sharing a bed with three or four, but when it comes to lying down, you're bedding down with six or seven or eight others. This happens all the time, but you put up with it so as not to make trouble."[13] A strong element of

---

11. These are too numerous to cite, but one irresistible passage in an account from Modena follows (on the spectacular celebrations of August 1, 1347): "They built an artificial castle of pasta, from which emerged vessels in which were living beasts, though how they had got in there no-one knew. Eventually the said luncheon castle *(castrum prandii)* was broken up and carried to the table for the feast" (Giovanni Bazano, *Chronicon Mutinense,* ed. Tommaso Casini, in *R.I.S.,* 2d ed., vol. 15, pt. 4 [Bologna: Nicola Zanichelli, 1919], 136).

12. Buccio di Rannallo di Poplito, *Chronicon Aquilana,* ed. V. De Bartolomeis, Fonti per la Storia d'Italia 41) (Rome: Istituto Storico Italiano, 1907), 192–94. *Plus ça change:* the considerable hotel price hikes in late 1999, in anticipation of the 2000 Jubilee (one central hotel charged 70,000 lire at Easter 1998 and 120,000 lire in October 1999 for the same room) highlight a less attractive aspect of economic continuity in the Eternal City. Interestingly, Buccio also commented on Cola's period as Senator in 1354, attacking Cola for executing the "great" Fra Moreale, before dying himself at the hands of his own fellow citizens (Buccio, *Chronicon Aquilana,* 227).

13. Buccio, *Chronicon Aquilana,* 194.

Cola's appeal in 1347 must have lain in his proven track record—namely, the successful "bid" in 1344 to Clement VI for the Jubilee of 1350—and with the economic benefits associated. He had kept up the pressure, in his powerful, enthusiastic speeches of 1346, presenting long-term economic projections and demanding Romans prepare themselves for 1350 by embracing an end to civic conflict.[14] The revival sponsored by Cola clearly paid dividends, in the Jubilee Year itself.[15] Romans with an investment clearly benefited, even if affairs were by no means so well managed as they had been for the first ever Jubilee in 1300;[16] complaints by Buccio and Matteo Villani regarding the dearth of provisioning and accommodation in 1350 make this very clear.[17] Cola's measures nonetheless encouraged local business to respond to the Jubilee; this is important in an assessment of his impact on Roman social history of the period.

The Italian sources cast new light on Cola's external position, that is, in terms of the contemporary political and economic context across the peninsula. Going back a few years, the famous Florentine chronicler, Giovanni Villani, recorded, with ill-concealed pride and glee, the arrival in 1339 of embassies from Rome requesting assistance in the construction of a new constitution.[18] He solemnly remarked on the contrast between "this century" and the ancient world, when it was the Romans who handed down laws to other cities (just a few years before Cola's attempt to do precisely the same thing). In his account of the Roman revolution of 1347 Giovanni was to cut through all the rhetoric of Cola's circular letters to the cities of Italy, revealing "how he [Cola] wished to restore the whole of Italy to obedience to Rome, as in ancient times."[19]

---

14. "Though in fact the Jubilee is approaching, you are not provided with food or provisions, and if the people who come . . . find no food here, in their ravenous hunger they will seize the very stones of Rome. And even the stones are not enough for such a multitude" (Wright, *Life*, 36–37).

15. The Chronicler, incidentally, provides very little information concerning the social impact of the Jubilee, except one offhand remark about the large numbers of people present. He provides, instead, a malicious account of the political failures of Annibale da Ceccano, the 1350 Papal Legate to Rome (Wright, *Life*, 97–103).

16. Giovanni Villani's account of the preparations made locally for the crowds expected at the 1300 Jubilee is complimentary (Giovanni, *Cronica*, 2:57–59 [9:36]), though he certainly mentions that both the Church and the Romans profited immensely. For prices in 1300, see Arsenio Frugoni, *Pellegrini a Roma nel 1300. Chronache del Primo Giubileo* (Casale Monferrato: Piemme, 1999), 60–61; for a brief but well-sourced account of conditions in 1300, see Debra Birch, *Pilgrimage to Rome in the Middle Ages: Continuity and Change,* Studies in the History of Medieval Religion (Woodbridge: Boydell Press, 1998), 197–202.

17. Matteo, *Cronica*, 1:57–58 (1:31).

18. Giovanni, *Cronica*, 3:205 (12:96).

19. Ibid., 495–98 (13:90).

Matteo Villani appears, on the other hand, more sympathetic to Cola's dealings with a fickle populace, though less explicit on Cola's antimagnatial legacy than his brother. The same Florentine-centric worldview prevails, of course: in his account in 1359 of the evolution of the popular regime of the Bandaresi in Rome,[20] Matteo comments on the formative constitutional debt that contemporary Romans, once the signori of the world, now inhabiting a "den of thieves," owed to the liberty-loving Tuscans. Florence participated intimately in the establishment of the regime of the Bandaresi, or so Matteo claims; we may note the continuity from Giovanni's account of 1339. As in his brother's judgmental account, the Rome-decline trope features heavily in Matteo, particularly, for example, in his account of the collapse of the popular revolution (partly) led by the shoemaker Lello Pocadota in 1362. However, his account does, thereby, firmly fix Cola's revolution within the Italian civic world of *popolo* agitation.[21]

The overwhelming impression—that is, of the perception of Cola's period of power by the majority of the Italian city chroniclers who comment—was one of suspicion. Cola was not regarded as a threat, within the northern zones of the empire, to imperial authority, but this was not so clearly the case in peninsular Italy, where his ambitions for the role of Rome, even more than for himself, were keenly felt. Thus Cola was treated by the nearest contemporary commentators with a mocking tone that only partially disguised real anxiety. Most of the accounts focus, at least implicitly, on Cola's attempts to forge *Italia Una,* under the sovereign rule of the City of Rome. The language used of Cola's efforts at "Italian brotherhood" was not always hegemonic per se, but mistrust seeps through the accounts; such mistrust was demonstrated explicitly by the refusal of major cities to accept Cola's symbolic and diplomatic overtures. On August 2, the day following his knighting, Cola proclaimed a celebration

---

20. Matteo, *Cronica,* 2:358–59, 411–12 (9:51, 9:87). For the relationship between Cola's polity and Roman politics a decade later, see chapter 5. See Marisa Mariani, "Il concetto di Roma nei Cronisti fiorentini," *Studi Romani* 4 (1956): 15–27, 153–66, for a comparison between Matteo and Giovanni; Giovanni's sharp critique of the Roman Tribune stands in contrast to Matteo's relatively respectful account. Mariani suggests that Giovanni's blunter feelings echo a threat to Florentine civic autonomy (or at least, to Florentine *fama*) posed by Cola in 1347, whereas the situation had changed by 1354. Note also Luciano Palermo, "Carestie e cronisti nel Trecento: Roma e Firenze nel racconto dell'Anonimo e di Giovanni Villani," *Archivio Storico Italiano* 142 (1984): 371–72, on Matteo's inaccurate view of Roman politics in the 1360s.

21. Matteo's account of Cola in 1354 praises his "harsh and rigid justice"; he uses *exactly* the same terms in reference to the rule of the "Tuscan-influenced" Roman Bandaresi of 1359: Matteo, *Cronica,* 1:504–7, 2:411–12 (4:23, 9:87).

of Italian "fraternity," awarding rings of union to the envoys of (supposedly) two hundred towns.[22] He then attempted to award, ceremonially, four grand banners, each bearing a device that could be read as advertising the ancient dominion of Rome over all Italy, to the towns of Florence, Todi, Perugia, and Siena; the Florentines walked away.[23] Siena then followed the Florentine lead; the Sienese chronicle talks of ambassadors from Cola who arrived in October 1347, "to establish treaties; and the Sienese did not consent to this." It continues: "And he made the same requests across all Tuscan territories; and they did not consent."[24] This explicit reluctance to participate reveals the reality of Cola's diplomatic relationship with the towns of central-north Italy. The Chronicler notes the refusal of the Florentines to accept the standard prepared for them; Cola's letters reveal the Florentine refusal to lend troops for Cola's use beyond the Roman *Destretto*.[25] Both these refusals testify to a process that comes into sharpest focus in the accounts of the Ferraran and the Bolognese chroniclers (rather than in Giovanni Villani, interestingly). The Ferrarans describe Cola simply and explicitly as "wishing to enlarge the state of the said City." Most Italian civic records, nevertheless, as Seibt points out, picked up on the distinctly high-handed tone of the circular sent out by Cola on September 19, 1347;[26] this is an index of the sensitivity of Italian cities to the signals of a challenge to their autonomy.

Much of the evidence in these sources is based on Cola's own correspondence with civic councils; chroniclers' information was culled directly from then recent archival records of the diplomatic exchanges circulating in contemporary governmental circles. Sometimes these sources were better informed than the Roman Chronicler, who has (otherwise) the fullest account of events. The Ferraran *Chronicon Estense,* for example—the second fullest external account—explicates Cola's alliance with Manfred of

---

22. Juhar, "Der Romgedanke," 95–100, offers a detailed description of the relationship between Cola and other cities (see also Miglio, "Il progetto politico").

23. From the very beginning of the Tribunate, in fact, increasingly frustrated requests for backup from Cola demonstrates that the Florentine priors' concept of military assistance was restricted to skirmishes within Rome's *contado:* III:29 (30), 33, 36.

24. Agnolo di Tura del Grasso, *Cronica,* ed. Alessandro Lisini and Fabio Iacometti, in *Chronache Senesi, R.I.S.,* 2d ed., vol. 15, pt. 6 (Bologna, 1939), 552; also quoted by Seibt, *Anonimo Romano,* 118.

25. The consequent frustration of Cola's schemes for the control of "rebel" entities beyond the traditional boundaries of Roman civic authority, incidentally, gives a sense of the limitations of a civic militia, even one as effectively constructed as that of Cola in Rome.

26. III:41; Seibt, *Anonimo Romano,* 120.

Corneto, appointed by Cola as Rector of the Patrimony.[27] The importance of Corneto's relationship with Rome, and the concomitant effects on the grain supply, was paramount; indeed Cola's revolution in May had been carefully timed to coincide with the political crisis (and military diversion) resulting from a breakdown in this relationship. Cola is also recorded in this source as appointing a *podestà*, or head of government, to Arezzo, following its submission to Roman hegemony.

In certain contexts the Estense chronicle also explains and qualifies Cola's actions more clearly than his Roman "biographer." For example, the fury and the violent, defiant posturing of Cola in the presence of the Papal Legate, Bertrand de Deux, late in the Tribunate, described in the Roman chronicle in such a fashion as to suggest that Cola had succumbed to megalomania, receives a more sophisticated treatment here. The Legate, according to this source, had been working for Cola's downfall with the Orsini of Marino, Cola's enemies, against whom Cola was operating, at that moment, in the field. Hence Cola's anger was justified; he meant to impress on the Legate his control over the Roman *Destretto*. Meanwhile—another interesting revelation—we have notarial evidence (see also chap. 6) that in 1372, the Roman notary Antonio dei Scambi drew up the formal betrothal pact of Francesco di Vico and Perna Orsini;[28] the Estense chronicle remarks that the plans for this betrothal were actually laid years in advance on December 12, 1347, under the aegis of the Tribune, in an attempt to reconcile the barons Giordano Orsini and Giovanni di Vico, then churning up the territory north of Rome in their fight.[29] The Estense chronicle also notes the participation in the sequence of events by Luca Savelli, son of Cola's own local "liege lord" Francesco; Luca was to assert his power in Rome directly after Cola's fall in December 1347.[30] In fact, the Estense chronicle gives a more detailed account of the complexities of the balance of powers in Rome, in November-Decem-

---

27. *Chronicon Estense,* ed. Giulio Bertoni and Emilio Vicini, in *R.I.S.,* 2d ed., vol. 15, pt. 3, 2d ed. (Città del Castello: S. Lapi, 1907).

28. B.A.V., S.A.P. 7/1372, 12v–16v.

29. An attempt somewhat undermined by Cola's reimprisonment of the young Francesco di Vico, that very night, as a hostage; and his sacking of Giordano's stronghold Marino the next day.

30. Luca hardly appears in the Roman account. Still, considering the extent of his influence in the City in the next year, and indeed over the next decades, perhaps such a reference might have been imprudent, or impolitic, on the part of a local chronicler. The peculiar axes ground by the Chronicler are discussed below.

ber 1347, as Cola's power waned, than the Roman Chronicler, who tends to give an impression of Cola's authority as basically unchallenged until a sudden crisis in the last days of the Tribunate.[31]

Along with its clone, the shorter *Polyhistoria* of Bartolomeo of Ferrara,[32] the *Chronicon Estense* even provides unique internal constitutional information concerning Cola's council and its composition, again with an emphasis on the period at the end of the Tribunate. It would appear, as suggested, that the influence of the Papal Legate was a force to be reckoned with, despite Cola's attempts at intimidation; in the *Chronicon Estense,* Cola is obliged to apologize to the Legate and offer to resign, because of violent conflict on the streets between the *popolares* [*sic*] and the supporters of the thirty-nine "Wise Men" newly introduced into Cola's council. In the *Polyhistoria,* the implication is more explicit: "The Legate, who imposed these thirty-nine men on the council, was extremely vexed"[33] (disgusted, presumably, at the brawling behavior of his appointees).[34] Cola, it would seem, himself originally a joint papal appointee with the then papal Vicar, Raymond of Orvieto, was now being forced to accept governmental reforms instigated by the Papal Legate.

With this apparent "insider" view of Cola's tenuous position, and the relative weakness of the Tribunate in early December, it may not be surprising that the Estense chronicle does not describe Cola as *signore,* the conventional term for a sole, dictatorial head of state in fourteenth-century Italian polities. Instead, Cola is described, nonetheless flatteringly, as "the magnificent knight, the lord Nicolaus, Tribune, rector, and governor of the magnificent city."[35] Other civic chronicles, however, do hang the

---

31. Seibt, Miglio, and Burdach, all of whom comment at some point on the "rival" chronicle traditions of other cities, do not draw out this evidence. Even Seibt, whose analysis of the Roman Chronicle is unrivaled, might have paid more attention to the very inconsistency and the lacunae of the Roman Chronicle, by a closer study of those accounts that supplement the information it provides.

32. Bartolomeo of Ferrara, *Polyhistoria (Libro di Polistore),* ed. Lodovico A. Muratori, in *R.I.S.* vol. 24 (Milan: Societas Palatinae, 1738).

33. Bartolomeo, *Polyhistoria,* 803A; the Estense account actually mentions thirty-eight (Bertoni and Vicini, *Chronicon Estense,* 157), but thirty-nine chimes better with the customary division of municipal representative offices into multiples of thirteen, the number of *rioni.*

34. Their disgrace redounded on the angry Legate, the account continues; and *therefore* Cola called another council where he apologized for the *popolo* and their "excessive zeal," even offering to resign his Tribunate. The conflict in Cola's regime between the interests of different sections of the *popolo* was crucial to events and is described in chapter 5.

35. Less stress, interestingly, is given to Cola's position of notary in the Italian sources; exceptions include the Modena chronicle of Giovanni Bazano (*Chronicon Mutinense,* 134),

term *signore* on their perception of Cola's regime: the Bolognese, Sienese, and Pistoian chronicles all use the *volgare* term explicitly, particularly the latter: "A great cry went up, Signore! Signore! and thus, hastily, with no further deliberation, [the Senate] elected as their signore Nicolas Tiberius . . . his cleverness had prompted him to use this method to make himself signore."[36] The Sienese chronicler Agnolo di Tura says the Tribune "signoregiava," that is, "was ruling" Rome;[37] both Villani brothers describe Cola as *signore,* and his regime as *signoria.*[38]

Cola di Rienzo more than superficially fulfilled the criteria of signorial leadership. He bore a mandate from the *popolo* to institute new constitutional measures; he created and led a civic army in the field, with explicitly antimagnatial designs.[39] He drew constantly on both historical imagery and religious authority, engaging a broad populace in public spectacles to legitimate the new regime. The rhetorical assumption of an autocratic, antimagnatial, ostensibly "republican" ideological position (in Cola's case, in both the classicizing and medieval-communal senses) suits the signorial paradigm. In a more negative sense, Cola's political fate also echoes that of other signorial figures: hamstrung by aristocratic counterattacks, and defeated ultimately by the need to impose unpopular fiscal demands on the populace.

Peter Partner once said, of what seemed to him to be the anomaly of Cola's exercise of power, "There is no other example of a tyrant who seized the signoria of an Italian city, not by mercenaries and menace but by his tongue."[40] Yet the very real legal measures and range of support Cola worked for could not possibly have been sustained by purely prophetic and oratorical means. He quite clearly shared certain of the apparatus and techniques of the signori of the northern city-states (with

---

and a longer, classicizing examination of Cola's profession and titles in a Paduan source: *Historia Cortusiorum de novitatibus Paduae et Lombardiae,* ed. Lodovico A. Muratori, in *R.I.S.* vol. 12 (Milan: Societas Palatinae, 1728), cols. 923–24.

36. Translated from *Storie Pistorese,* ed. Silvio A. Barbi, in *R.I.S.,* 2d ed., vol. 11, pt. 5 (Città di Castello: S. Lapi, 1907–27), 226.

37. Agnolo di Tura, *Cronica,* 551.

38. *Signore* is an Italian term, of course: it is possible that the Latin term *dominus,* used of Cola in the Latin-composed chronicles, occupies an analogous semantic region.

39. A curious antimagnatial element shared by a large number of chronicles (Rome, Florence, Bologna, Modena, Pistoia, Ferrara) is the seemingly gleeful listing of the barons who died at the Porta San Lorenzo battle on November 20, 1347. The probable source was supplied by Cola himself in his circular to various communes (III:46).

40. Partner, *Lands,* 333.

whom he was, of course, in contact, as these very chronicles demonstrate). There were occasions where his own closest supporters used the term of him;[41] is it not then fair to use the term *signore* of Cola?

The second circular to the cities of Italy was sent out on 19 September 1347. This declared an imperial election for the following Pentecost, and restated the legal claims of the Roman People to Italian hegemony. Yet there was a clear gap between the reality, and Cola's perception, of his position in "Italy." The document, read carefully, exposes the weakness of Cola's aims regarding Roman control over Italy: a complete absence of technical propositions. Precisely how would Italy in 1350 be federally united under imperial Roman control?

The strength of the claim to rule was legal, not political: Cola based his argument upon universal rights sanctioned by tradition and law, then enjoying a high profile because of the re-escalation of the debate between popes' lawyers and rebel imperial claimants after the 1320s. Strength lay also in the correspondence of Cola's schemes with the frequent calls for inter-city unity both from intellectuals and from the operators of civic economies across the peninsula. This lack of strategic, political and constitutional precision, however, was almost Petrarchan (see below), and very much in contrast, of course, to the admirable administrative measures proposed and implemented within Rome, and the military operations conducted within Rome's hinterland. In a local, city-*contado* sense, Cola's position did in fact come close to identification with that of the contemporary signore; it is ironic that his imperial ambitions were more grandiose than his signorial achievements. This irony was not, perhaps, lost, on the Roman and Florentine chroniclers.[42]

At home in Rome, however, the notion of signoria may have had less resonance. An examination of the use of the term *signore* by the Chronicler suggests that in Roman circles its semantic range was less precise; the term had no contemporary governmental implications. True, the term is applied explicitly in the Chronicler's own perception of Cola's role; even before his coup, when he is mocked by the barons, Cola warns them: "I shall be a great signore or emperor. I shall persecute all of these barons."[43]

---

41. IV:3, 39; IV:5, 66, 70.

42. Nor indeed on the *Chronicon Estense,* which is, as usual, a very precise source, noting the submission of Arezzo, of the *signore* of Orvieto, of Viterbo, Anagni, and "also of all the cities within fifty-four miles of the City of Rome, except the commune of Fani" (Bertoni and Vicini, *Chronicon Estense,* 151).

43. *ARC,* 109.

There are further examples throughout the Roman chronicle, where the author describes Cola as signore;[44] in 1354 Cola executed his former ambassador, Pandolfuccio, because he "desired the signoria of the people."[45] Elsewhere, however, the term *signore,* quite simply, translates as "lord." The Chronicler applies it as readily to the barons whom Cola castigates: "Thus the Signori desired to set up a conspiracy against the Tribune."[46] In the same chapter, the term is used of Cola's local "liege-lord" in Regola ("his particular Signore"), Francesco Savelli. Elsewhere it is applied to the lords of Montagna and Molise, and to the Carrara dynasty (whereas the della Scala, Gonzaga, Ordelaffi, Malatesta, Visconti, and Taddeo Pepoli are all called tyrants, rather than signori. Cola himself had become a "tyrant" by the end of 1347 and is described as such throughout his short rule in 1354). The vagueness of the term *signore* as "lord" is also evident in usages such as *nostro signore Jesu Christi;* the Chronicler even applies it to the pope.

So we may conclude that cities at some distance from Rome slotted Cola into a pattern emerging elsewhere across central and north Italy; and indeed Cola shares many characteristics with signorial figures like Castruccio Castracane of Pisa.[47] On the other hand, the Estense chronicle, surprisingly well informed on the subtle constitutional shifts in the city of Rome during 1347, tellingly avoids using the term *signore* of Cola (although elsewhere referring to his relations with "the *Signori* and communes of Italy"),[48] and the Chronicler's use of the term is inconclusive given the modern historiographical notion of the Italian late-medieval signore. There is no evidence that Cola copied a signorial role model from peers in other cities, just as there is no precise context for his peculiar, self-awarded title, the *Zelator* (striver, enthusiast, or hero) of Italy.[49]

Yet most contemporary signorie were the products of local circumstances, and this is as true in Rome as anywhere else. The peculiar prophetic and historic features of Cola's de facto "signorial" rule may well be ascribed to the very peculiar features of Rome—city of the past and the future—as a civic entity in the contemporary world. As we will see in the next chapters, Cola certainly attempted to map conventional economic

---

44. E.g. *ARC,* 114; note the term *solo signore* at 131.
45. Ibid., 193.
46. Ibid., 115.
47. See Louis Green, *Castruccio Castracane: A Study in the Origins of a Fourteenth Century Italian Despotism* (Oxford: Clarendon Press, 1986).
48. Bertoni and Vicini, *Chronicon Estense,* 149.
49. III:27, 12, 28, 201; 29/30/33/36/41, 2.

and security measures onto the government of the Eternal City; he clearly tried to build conventional signorial powers, both legal and military, into the foundations of a series of "less realistic" roles and titles. Cola was no more a typical Trecento signore than Rome was a typical Trecento city; but up to a point it was just that.

The View from Vaucluse

Contemporary "Avignon-centric" accounts of Cola's activities, generally ecclesiastical in origin, retained their own angle on events.[50] Petrarch is discussed in the first chapter;[51] in fact, the scholar-*litterato,* who enjoyed a love-hate relationship both with Avignon and the papacy, and with Rome and Cola, provides little objectively useful evidence in terms of the reconstruction of Cola's political ambitions. Some indication of the lack of Petrarch's comprehension of Cola's constitutional subtlety may be gained from an examination of his response to a later request, in 1351, from papal policy advisers, to act as a consultant in the matter of the reform of the institutions of civic government in Rome. Petrarch's solution was distinctly lacking in practical application: he recommended the revitalization of that ancient Roman moral quality, *virtus,* and moved swiftly from a vague recommendation of imitating antique Roman heroes into a prolonged and unhelpful version of the "contemporary decline" trope.[52]

A rather better-informed narrator of the events of Cola's career was Jean Hocsème ("Hocsemius," 1279–1348), a canon and humanist scholar at Lièges, compiler of the *Gesta pontificum Leodiensium,*[53] acquaintance of Rainaldo Orsini, papal protonotary, and personal correspondent with Cola.[54] Hocsemius introduces his subject with the information that he has seen the very letters of Cola both to the pope and to the protonotary (several of which are reproduced in his narrative, which therefore includes

---

50. There are in fact four accounts (not all contemporary, however) of the life of Clement VI (see bibliography) that mention Cola, but these contribute little to our knowledge of the social and constitutional structures of Trecento Rome, or the working context of the revolution.

51. As are Giovanni Colonna and Giovanni Cavallini, whose "records" of Cola are equally patchy.

52. *Familiari,* 11.16; November 1351. Cosenza, *Petrarch,* 155–67.

53. Jean d'Hocsème, *Gesta Pontificum Leodinensium,* ed. Jean Chapeauville, in *Qui Gesta Pontificum Leodinensium scripserunt auctores praecipui,* 2 vols. (Lièges, 1613), 2:272–514.

54. III:40.

more original material than any other account of events in Rome in 1347).
He sheds no further light on the issues of Roman political or social life, but
undeniably supplements our knowledge of events at one place, where he
reports that Cola went into exile in Naples, allied with Lewis of Hungary,
who took Naples in late January 1348, and become "more powerful than
ever."[55] This piece of double-dealing is not proven, though highly plausible. It is not, obviously, mentioned in Cola's own account of events. Earlier, in October, he did inform Avignon that Hungarian ambassadors had
made overtures to him in Rome; the Chronicler confirms Cola's account,
echoing Cola's assertions of impartiality; at least, while still in power.[56]
Hocsemius also claims that Cola's Tribunate had the support—expressed
in a general Italian pogrom of magnates—of over sixty Italian cities. The
exaggeration probably reflects anxieties in Avignon over Cola's threat to
papal control in Rome and beyond; an anxiety that may also explain the
accusation of alliance with the Hungarians. It certainly demonstrates a
peculiar Avignonese diplomatic perspective on events in the Italian peninsula, which located Cola and his influence at a political level beyond the
local and civic in Rome and its *Destretto.*

Bene me ne ricordo: The Roman Chronicler

The Roman chronicle is, on the other hand, unashamedly Rome-centric,
claiming first of all to be a *speziale livro e narrazione* of events in the City,
from 1329 to 1355; an account of the rest of Italy, next; and finally, of
other parts of Europe.[57] As we will see, the Chronicler's own perspective
was both civic and ecclesiastic, as well as both Roman and pan-European;
hence we place it here precisely between the evidence from "afar" and that
from "within." The perceived status of this chronicle as a contemporary
"witness" of events is already ratified in this study by its use as a control,
that is, a source against which to match evidence garnered from other documentary materials. Here we assess the Chronicler's value and importance
as a historical source for mid-Trecento Rome and the events surrounding
Cola's experience of, and effect upon, his city. The following remarks will
be limited, given the existence of an increasingly substantial critical and

---

55. Hocsème, *Gesta,* 510. The Hungarians' prompt departure, in the face of the plague, is
supposed to have left Cola stranded and forced him to retreat to his Roman Orsini allies.

56. III:43, 141–68; Wright, *Life,* 65–69.

57. *ARC,* 4.

historiographical bibliography,[58] to an analysis of the extrinsic value of the chronicle for its representation of contemporary Roman politics; the detailed prosopographical, constitutional, and institutional material it contains appears elsewhere throughout this study.

This chronicle's literary importance was not properly recognized until 1940.[59] The last half-century has seen its reintegration into the mainstream of Trecento Italian chronicles, and it has enjoyed several new editions. These include the excellent critical version by Giuseppe Porta in 1979, which in turn sparked off a new series of critical analyses. The most exhaustive and stimulating of these is that of Gustav Seibt, published in 1992; this involves a full-scale adoption of the techniques of literary criticism, combined with a sensitivity to historical context that has permitted the author to reconstruct both the intellectual framework and internal agenda of the chronicle. Seibt argues, essentially, that the Chronicler's leitmotiv is not conformity to a rigid, anachronistic, "annalist" genre of historical chronicle, but, rather, typological portraiture; *esemplarità* (exemplarity), as Anna Modigliani has neatly translated the concept.[60] What message to readers is, then, contained in these thematic "exemplars"? To paraphrase Seibt, the message to contemporaries is that Cola di Rienzo wasted his opportunity. Starting well, in exemplary fashion indeed—the Chronicler appropriates a series of classical models, good and bad, as analogues—Cola then proceeded down the path to the delusion and paranoia of a fractured tyranny, an "antimodel," or model not to imitate.

Seibt, however, does not attempt to locate the chronicle within the macrocosm of Roman contemporary social and political developments. He makes a number of cutting remarks about the modern historian's tendency to privilege content over form, in harvesting a source. While taking on board this criticism, the importance of external context in understanding the construction of a record of, and dialogue with, events must not be

---

58. Scholars have tended to privilege the literary, stylistic, and linguistic aspects of the chronicle over its historiographical status (see bibliography). Of course, these aspects do, tangentially, also shed light on particular interpretative lines associated with the Chronicler, and therefore his account of the circumstances surrounding Cola's career.

59. Gianfranco Contini, "Invito a un capolavoro," *Letteratura* 4 (1940): 3–6. Until this point it had been often dismissed as a naive, confused account in a barbaric dialect.

60. Anna Modigliani, "La cronica dell'*Anonimo Romano*," *Roma nel Rinascimento* (1992), 19–30. Miglio's subsequent description of *novitate* in the Chronicler also bears a strong resemblance to Seibt's concept (Massimo Miglio, "Anonimo Romano," *Il Senso della Storia nella cultura medievale italiana (1100–1350)* (Pistoia: Centro italiano di studi di storia e d'arte, 1995), 175–87.

underestimated: this is precisely the purpose of the present study. A sophisticated contextual reading, set against the circumstances of the late 1350s,[61] supplements Seibt's position well; the logical extension of Seibt's case but incorporating the broader historical context he somewhat disparages, is to suggest that the Chronicler was claiming that Cola ruined not just his own opportunity to rule but, more cogently, that Cola spoiled an occasion for the consolidation of the political position of the Chronicler's audience. That opportunity was now again available, in 1357–58; Cola's example should not be imitated.

The Chronicler's constituency was the *bona iente,* the so-called good folk with whom he clearly identified, referring to his own *ientilezza,* "gentility"; an urban "middle class," probably involved in government and the economy, definitely not baronial, nor sympathetic to the baronial class. He designed his "special book" to appeal to "the merchants" and "other excellent people," not students of literature or barons;[62] precisely those social types who came to the fore in Cola's regime, but were then outraged by Cola's inconsistent policy toward the traditional, aristocratic dominators of Rome.[63] At this chronological juncture, 1357–58, it is impossible for a historian (Seibt is primarily a journalist and literary critic) to ignore the "coincidence" of the composition of the chronicle, and a contemporary concerted attempt to forge a new antimagnatial regime; the most serious attempt since Cola's, in fact, a decade before.[64] It certainly explains the attachment of the Chronicler to the more discernibly antimagnatial elements of *popolo* ideology and policy in Cola's polity, and his disgust at Cola's evolution into what he describes as "an Asian tyrant."[65]

The justice-cruelty dialectic neatly identified, by Seibt, as running throughout the chronicle[66] does, in fact, tap into precisely this ideological and political discourse. The Chronicler exposes the potential frailty of new

---

61. The growth in authority of the *popolo,* particularly the maturing of the power of the Felice Società, their Bandaresi, and the debt this process owed to Cola's own regime are described in the introduction to part 2, and more extensively in chapter 5.

62. Wright, *Life,* 23.

63. Cola's release and promotion of various barons in September 1347 provoked a sharp reaction and clear indication of the Chronicler's allegiance to the *descreti,* "discreet men," whom he immediately identifies with *la iente,* "the people" versus "the few citizens," *aicuni cittadini,* who had persuaded Cola to back off from his strict antimagnatial policy: "I would remind him of the proverb which says that a man ought to shit or get off the pot" (Wright, *Life,* 75–77; *ARC,* 140–41).

64. See the introduction to part 2 of this study for the sequence of popular revolutions.

65. Wright, *Life,* 91.

66. Seibt, *Anonimo Romano,* 99.

popolaresco governmental structures of the late 1350s, by showing what happened a mere decade before. He highlights the need for military and economic stability, for balance and control within the power to punish, and thus demonstrates how not to abuse, and lose, that power. Hence again the Chronicler uses Cola as a negative example. Cola's lapses into unjust, tyrannical persecution, his frequent compromises with the magnates, his evident attempts to imitate or join the aristocracy despite his "popular" rhetoric, and his insistence on policies that transcended the exigencies of the commune, very quickly lost him the support of the "good folk," that is, the merchants and other urban gentry. His vacillation and deviation from *popolo* criteria spoiled the chance in 1347 to build a safe and thriving commune; a chance, if we read between the lines of the chronicle, that was being offered again, "now" in 1357–58, by the new regime of the Bandaresi.

This pinpoints another crucial issue, of course: if our reconstruction of this agendum is correct, how accurate, then, and objective a source may we consider the Chronicler, especially for the earlier events of 1347–54? The problem is twofold: selective bias and actual ignorance. On the one hand, there is the problem of rival contexts; the possibility of the deliberate retrospective contamination of the account by a political agendum relevant to 1357. On the other hand, there is a simpler, but also potentially upsetting, factor: the all-too frequent evidence for the Chronicler's distance from the subject, both in time and in space. How reliable a witness can the "narrator" have been?

To deal with the latter difficulty first: despite frequently asserting the "eyewitness" veracity of his account, the author was, clearly, not always in Rome, and in any case, probably composed the greater part of his account (the events of 1347, which occupy two-thirds of the narrative space) a decade after their occurrence. However, Seibt weaves a complicated, generally persuasive, theory, explaining the relationship between the "subjective" versus the "narrative" first persons in the chronicle; an argument that stresses the personal sincerity of the writer's claim to have had eyewitness experience of events—"I recall it as vividly as a dream"—and thus, by implication, the authenticity of his account. Seibt's case is that this was an internally generated feature of the chronicle, with a precise and discrete function, bearing no relation to modern, anachronistic historiographical concepts of empirical data-gathering, but nonetheless valid according to the Chronicler's own logic. Moreover, in support of this theory of "sincerity therefore authenticity," Seibt argues that the eidetic elements of the chronicle are so strongly articulated that the points at which the writer's focus is less acute, in contrast, are obvious. He seems to claim that with this device the Chronicler makes a tacit admission of noneyewitness status at these points, though not actually admitting his absence from the scene of events. This is, perhaps, a less convincing argument on Seibt's part.

The most valuable contribution to our knowledge of the literal location(s) of the Chronicler is the new research of Giuseppe Billanovich.[67] He has traced the itinerary of the Chronicler by the reflection of episodes, and the relative depth of their reflection, in the events of the chronicle itself, and has matched it to a particular social-intellectual circle. The internal evidence of the chronicle has permitted scholars over the years to extrapolate that the author was a little older than Cola, had had training as a medical student in the schools at Bologna, that he had traveled extensively across the peninsula and beyond, but was a Roman citizen; that he placed himself socially within the *bona iente,* but as one whose *ientilezza* was no obstruction to the articulation of a particularly antimagnatial *popolo* ideology; and that, despite a distinct political viewpoint, he was not himself a *politico.* Of course this still leaves in doubt the precise identity and occupation of a Chronicler who has been anonymous for over six hundred years. However, Billanovich's recent thesis attaches—and not in the least tentatively—a name: Bartolomeo di Iacovo da Valmontone. Most startlingly, Billanovich "reveals" that Bartolomeo was not a secular medic, but a cleric, long in the *familia* of Bishop Ildebrandino Conti of Segni,[68] eventually (certainly by 1351, Billanovich asserts, drawing upon papal archival evidence) occupying the bishopric of Trau in the Balkans, where, he argues, the composition of the never-finished Roman chronicle was begun.

The Conti bishop could well have offered the Chronicler better access to records of local papal policy in the Roman *Destretto.* Indeed, Billanovich theorizes that Bishop Ildebrandino, a much-traveled papal diplo-

---

67. Giuseppe Billanovich, "Come nacque un capolavoro: Il non più Anonimo Romano," *Rendiconti dell'Accademia Nazionale dei Lincei,* 9th ser., 6 (1995): 195–211; reviewed by Massimo Miglio in *Roma nel Rinascimento* (1996), 239–42.

68. A family that generated popes in the previous century; see chapter 3. One branch resided at Valmontone: Billanovich, "Come nacque un capolavoro," 196. Ildebrandino was certainly acquainted with Petrarch; hence the encomium at *Familiari,* XV.14 (Francesco Petrarca, *Letters on Familiar Matters: Rerum familiarum libri IX–XVI,* ed. Aldo S. Bernardo [Baltimore: Johns Hopkins University Press, 1982], 284–90). Billanovich is convinced, moreover, that Petrarch knew Bartolomeo, although neither apparently wrote, nor referred, to each other. Both, however, held benefices at Monselice; but both, however, in absentia.

mat, left Bartolomeo between 1343 and circa 1350 to be his eyes and ears in Rome; an ecclesiastical spy, like Cochetus de Cochetis. Astonishingly Billanovich fails to note a piece of evidence that would support his hypothesis: Ildebrandino was in Valmontone in 1347, near Rome; his letter of July 30, to his vicar in Padua, describes the events of Cola's rule to date in terms readily comparable to the account of the Chronicler.[69] Of particular significance is Ildebrandino's reference to the two August festivals; he describes the knighting about to take place on August 1, 1347. He then immediately says that Cola has planned an "unprecedented" Tribunician coronation for August 15.[70] We might thereby push Billanovich's thesis further, to suggest that the Chronicler's account might well have followed this very letter: both conflate a prefatory description of the knighting with the coronation. The sequence, scope, and pace of Ildebrandino's entire narrative is, arguably, closer to that of the Chronicler than any other narrative account of Cola's life.

The impact of Billanovich's provocative hypothesis upon the analysis of the Chronicler's account of Cola has not yet been fully tempered. Although his theory would explain the differing levels of accuracy, it does not, of itself, solve the reliability and credibility problems that result from the Chronicler's periodic absences from the scenes he was describing.[71] The "cleric" thesis would certainly help to explain why the Chronicler could not be, legally, a participant in his native administration; and why he appears to have made a number of strange leaps across the peninsula ("postings" beyond his control, not places visited by choice). However, Billanovich does not explain the general (though not total) absence of reference to the papacy, or to papal authority in the city. Of course, if the Chronicler were in fact an adherent of the governmental measures proposed by the regime of the Bandaresi—this in my opinion is the direction

---

69. See Burdach and Piur, *Briefwechsel*, V:1. Another Valmontone connection should be noted: *Dominus Paulus de Comite* of Valmontone was one of the co-signatories of Cola's declaration of the sovereign power of the *Romanus Populus* (III:27, 81) (although he also co-signed the protest of the same day against Cola's actions: IV:7, 41–42).

70. V:1, 155–66.

71. Billanovich does not draw out the geographical and familial connections between the Conti, Rome, Anagni (where Cola grew up), and Valmontone, which lies halfway between Rome and Anagni in the Ciocaria. He does not mention the Chronicler's reference to "Janni conte de Vallemontone,"—*Conti,* surely, contra Porta's reading?—captain of the troops of the Roman *popolo* in 1353, fighting Cola's old enemy Giovanni di Vico in Viterbo alongside the Papal Legate Albornoz, whose own troops included Cola himself (Wright, *Life,* 110; *ARC,* 166). See chapter 3 for the cultural importance of this subregion of Lazio, its relationship to Rome generally, and to Cola specifically.

in which the evidence of the Chronicler's political attachments points—then a clerical occupation could have meant for him a severe conflict of loyalties: the Bandaresi were notoriously keen to assert Rome's political independence from the papacy. It is possible that the Chronicler's silence on papal matters indicates the existence of such a dilemma. Clerical status was by no means always an index of support of papal politics, of course. Membership of an episcopal household, however, where the head—Ildebrandino—was working toward papal diplomatic goals, would surely imply that the Chronicler was operating within a politically restricted milieu.[72]

The other difficulty with this source, as identified above—that is the possibly partisan nature of the chronicle—cannot be resolved satisfactorily without further information regarding the Chronicler's circumstances at the time of the events and at the time of writing. His choice of whom to name, as the friends, enemies, or killers, of Cola, may illustrate the delicacy of his circumstances. It is notable that despite his sympathy with *popolo* causes, and implied criticism of the *aicuni cittadini* who persuaded Cola to release the barons he held hostage, the Chronicler, nevertheless, named neither the Colonna nor the Savelli as the forces behind Cola's ousting in 1347 or murder in 1354. Instead, the Chronicler lays the blame in 1347 on an anarchic Neapolitan aristocrat, Pipino, and in 1354 on an obscure relative of Cola, Locciolo Pelliciaro, and on two notaries (see chap. 6): the last group of people, on the face of it, to work for Cola's destruction. However, this is surely the point: to express how far Cola had alienated his "natural" supporters, men with whom, it is obvious, the Chronicler felt a sense of community (and a shared disappointment in Cola).[73] Quite logically, the Chronicler may have wished to avoid the possible recriminations of openly identifying the barons involved in the sordid affair of Cola's slaughter. He does note, however, that the Colonna seized Cola's body and had it exposed and ridiculed; this could have been read as reasonable revenge for Cola's abuse of the bodies of Colonna scions in November 1347. In any case the chronicle disappeared (was it suppressed?)[74] for two hundred years.

---

72. Scurrilous tales concerning a number of churchmen have also earned the Chronicler an anticlerical reputation; this is certainly an issue for Billanovich's followers to resolve.

73. Notaries and the individuals involved in Cola's rise and fall will be discussed in chapter 6.

74. See the preface to Porta's 1979 critical edition of the *Cronica*, x–xi; also discussion by Massimo Miglio, "La *Cronica* dell'Anonimo Romano," *Roma nel Rinascimento* (1992), 30–37.

An equally important problem is that of retrospective ideological, rather than factual, contamination. Could the Chronicler's accounts of Cola's constitutional measures, for example, be a "memory" of details somewhat "enhanced" by more recent *popolo* governmental theories and initiatives in the later 1350s? Are the measures ascribed to Cola drawn from what the Chronicler in or after 1357 thought Cola ought to have done, rather than what Cola in 1347 actually did? This is impossible to answer definitively; however, we should note immediately that the majority of the other evidence of Cola's own political and constitutional measures does correspond with that presented by the chronicle.[75] There are gaps between Cola's constitutional innovations and "popular" measures recorded in other sources, and those policies attributed to him by the Chronicler; but these are no more dramatic than any of the Chronicle's other inaccuracies and lacunae.

A more interesting disjunction lies between the Chronicler's perception of Cola's exercise of Roman power, and Cola's own pan-Italic perception of his position and authority. In this context the factual misinformation of the Chronicler is precisely an index to, and reflection of, the ideological distance between author and subject. The "factual misinformation" in question is the failure of the Chronicler to record certain events crucial to a comprehension of Cola's ambitions beyond Rome: Cola's early call for an all-Italian congress of jurists; the banner-giving ceremony of Italian "fraternity" on August 2, 1347; the Tribunician coronation of August 15; and the declaration of September 19 (that there would be an imperial election the following Pentecost, when Rome would assert its authority to withdraw the *translatio imperii* from the Germans). In short, the Chronicler fails to record, or to analyze sufficiently, anything relating to Cola's desired resurrection of the Italian or global hegemony of the city of Rome.

Seibt's persuasive theory concerning such "missing" passages is that these were neither lost nor censored lacunae, but were simply never added in, because the chronicle was never finished. He suggests that these events were left out in the first Romanesco draft because the Chronicler found it hard to reach a judgment concerning Cola and his ambitions, understanding neither the legal nor ideological reasoning behind Cola's claim that

---

75. Although it is, regrettably, the case that the fifteen constitutional reforms of the early Tribunate (Wright, *Life,* 42–43) are not elaborated in Cola's diplomatic communiqués, nor in other narrative sources. These will be discussed in chapter 5; see also chapter 1 for the analogy to powers conferred by the antique Vespasianic *lex de imperio* tablet.

Rome was at the head of all, or at least all Italian, cities.[76] The gaps are particularly curious given the Chronicler's evident attachment to the ritualistic and visually stunning aspects of the Tribunate. Seibt argues that the Chronicler is less clear concerning, and therefore puts off describing, Cola's pan-Italic ideological motivation, because he, the Chronicler, reads the festivities of the Tribunate as episodes in a civic rather than national or imperial ideology. The Chronicler observed a display of power from citizens of equal status from different cities; a social, rather than a political, message. He read Cola's gestures, particularly the banner-giving ceremony, as a form of competition with, not a display of control over, the representatives of other city-states (certain "foreign" chroniclers were more sensitive, as we have seen). According to Seibt, the Chronicler failed, therefore, to comprehend Cola's message to Italy: that is, that Rome was superior to all other cities.[77]

This different understanding of high-powered semiotic codes by the Chronicler and by his subject, Cola, exposes the mental gap between them. The Chronicler understood Cola's *popolo* gestures as having certain conventional, contemporary goals analogous with those in evidence in other cities. For Cola they were only part of a wider, "supra-urban," ambition. As chapter 5 explicates, Cola certainly introduced *popolaresco* measures within the City; but he used other, overarching, ideological markers when it came to his plans for the reestablishment of Roman hegemony within the Italian peninsula; a policy that led to the falling-off of the support of the *popolani,* those for whom the Chronicle was later composed.

His "political agenda" was, therefore, ultimately and crucially prejudicial in the Chronicler's assessment of the Tribune and helps explain certain of the inconsistencies in his portrayal of Cola's character. Where the Chronicler fails (or refuses) to comprehend the peculiar logic behind Cola's diplomatic overtures toward other cities, he tends to dismiss these gestures as evidence of the Tribune's growing "madness." Surely, Cola's ambitions for *Italia una* were overimaginative, and not realizable, while those of the *popolo* in Rome—as the 1350s and 1360s were to prove—were

---

76. This cannot have been aided by the constant slippage we find in Cola's own position, between declaring Rome head of a federal Italy (a "national" ideology), and head of the world (his "global" polity).

77. Seibt's impression is somewhat ingenuous; the Chronicler certainly failed to include Cola's extra-Roman activities, but perhaps this was a deliberate refusal to acknowledge even the basis of a pan-Italic union.

within reach in the short term. The accusation of insanity was, however, unwarranted. It was generated by the Chronicler's very narrow perception of the economic and political potential of the Trecento Roman commune; ironically, a more realistic contemporary perception than Cola's own but, essentially, a different viewpoint from Cola's. The damage wreaked by these accusations upon the historical image of Cola di Rienzo was to be extensive beyond measure.

Cola from Within

From such a distinctly individual witness, we move to the entirely impersonal source material of the fourteenth-century city of Rome itself. One of the major problems that has beset the study of Cola di Rienzo has been the difficulty of recovering evidence of the social context of Trecento Rome. Unlike other cities of the late Middle Ages, Rome failed to preserve a governmental archive; a fact that has contributed greatly to the image of the city in the Trecento as an anarchic and inscrutable urban entity. Cola's revolution is thereby "naturally" isolated as a brief period for which a comparatively broad range of sources is available. More recent work has sought to repair the fractured image of civic organization left by the considerable lacunae in source material; but as yet, the results of these studies have not been incorporated into a broad social history of "Rome during Avignon." Nor have they been used systematically to throw light on Cola's revolution, although in fact chapter 6 will show how evidence from guild and confraternity records helps reconstruct the social profile, even the precise identities, of the men who participated in or militated against Cola's revolution. On the other hand, institutional records have allowed certain historians to begin to reconstruct the sophisticated mechanisms by which private and public organizations were administered, while the notarial evidence demonstrates the importance of that profession—Cola's own—within the economy and culture of mid-Trecento Rome.

Rome was a "late starter," as we have described, in the race to civic bureaucratic specialization. The process of diversification and the laying down of civic and corporate statutes only came to fruition with the relative autonomy of the fourteenth century, in the absence of the curia. Even so, political administration after 1305 was dominated by a handful of overmighty papal subjects, the great baronial families of the City, which slowed the process considerably. However, it bears repetition that some sort of "republic" had been in operation, rarely autonomous but frequently vociferous, for over two centuries by the time of Cola's revolution, as described in the introduction to part 2. There is corresponding evidence to suggest that the structures of civic government in Rome were established, although at a less mature stage of formation, well before the thirteenth century.

The form of Cola's "revolution"—the attempted assertion of *popolaresco* constitutional, military, and antipapal autonomy within a self-consciously "Roman" identity—therefore had ample precedent. Cola's administrative policies were not themselves without earlier roots. One series of administrative documents in particular, that of the *magistri edificorum,* has survived.[78] The contents demonstrate that governmental mechanisms of Rome from the early thirteenth century did exist, albeit stunted, compared to Tuscan communes, by the dominating presence and operation of older, more powerful curial administrative machinery. There was clearly a sense of Roman municipal responsibility and identity comparable to that in the majority of contemporary Italian towns; a common culture that will be seen to have informed every aspect of Cola's regime in 1347.

Notarial Material

The richest evidence for the social history of Rome comes from private notarial archives. It is from 1348—or, more precisely, from Christmas 1347, a couple of weeks after Cola's abdication—that the earliest collection of these documents survives. It is, of course, no coincidence that Cola di Rienzo was a notary, although records of his personal practice no

---

78. Urban "surveyors" who policed construction within the City and enforced the Trecento equivalent of planning regulations: see Cristina Carbonetti Vendittelli, "Documentazione inedita riguardante i *magistri edificorum urbis* e l'attività della loro curia nei secoli XIII–XIV," *ASRSP* 113 (1990): 169–88; "La curia dei magistri edificorum Urbis nei secoli XIII e XIV a la sua documentazione," in *Roma nei secoli XIII e XIV. Cinque Saggi,* ed. Etienne Hubert, 1–42 (Rome: Viella, 1993). Other codifications existed, though they do not survive; there is evidence for a *cartularium* for senatorial consultation, from 1229. For 1346 there is a reference *de libro et archivio Cancellarie Urbis* (B.A.V. Vat. Lat. 7931, 181r–182r; ed. Paola Supino, *La Margarita Cornetana* [Rome: Società romana di storia patria, 1969], 327–28). The same document describes the payment of fines to the Roman Camera Urbis—at that time supervised by Cola as official notary—which are recorded in its *Liber Introitum.* The Margarita Cornetana, first compiled in the seventeenth century, contains around seventy documents related to (and many rogated in) Rome, of which twenty-six date from the fourteenth century. These documents almost all concern the huge fines and military action imposed on the Cornetans for daring to export their grain to cities other than Rome.

longer exist. Only a small number of notarial collections, seventeen, do survive for the period 1348–1400, out of the collections of the hundreds of notaries for whose existence there is evidence. Yet just these seventeen notaries' records together present over seven thousand folios of *abbreviature* (brief, formulaic reference copies of documents "rogated" for customers). The organization of these *protocolli*,[79] their condition, accessibility, and general legibility range from abysmal to admirable. These factors have been almost as extensively described as the material itself has been examined; that is, by a small number of people, but very thoroughly.[80] In two cases, only a single document survives.[81] In another two cases, we have a collection of over twenty protocols, which span thirty-five years or more.[82]

The acts of notaries are of inestimable value for the study of both the public and private lives of Roman inhabitants, and particularly of the notaries themselves, in the second half of the fourteenth century. A public notary's basic business was to give legal force to all transactions concerning individuals or institutions. These transactions covered all conceivable aspects of social and economic intercourse[83] and establish a set of para-

---

79. One "protocol" represents the bound collection of a year's business.

80. See the work of two state archivists: Anna-Maria Corbo, "Relazione descrittiva degli archivi notarili Romani dei secoli XIV–XV nell'Archivio di Stato e nell'Archivio Capitolino," in *Sources of Social History: Private Acts Of the Late Middle Ages,* ed. Paolo Brezzi and Egmont Lee (Toronto: Pontifical Institute of Medieval Studies, 1984), 49–67; and Maria-Luisa Lombardo, "Sprunti di vita privata e sociale in Roma da atti notarili dei secoli XIV e XV," *Archivi e Cultura* 14 (1980): 61–100; "Nobili, mercanti e popolo minuto negli atti dei notai romani del XIV e XV secolo," in Brezzi and Lee, *Sources of Social History,* 291–310. The scholars Isa Lori-Sanfilippo and the late Renzo Mosti (see bibliography) are responsible for the bulk of transcription to date, and the former has written a series of excellent analytical papers; the growing numbers of social historians in the field of late medieval Rome have also developed differing levels of experience and expertise in the field (see for example Anna Modigliani, "I protocolli notarili romani per la storia del secondo Trecento," *Roma nel Rinascimento* [1995], 151–58). The particular difficulties inherent in tracking down, and then reading, the Roman material partly explains the dearth of scholarship before the late 1960s; this period also witnessed a sharp rise in interest in social historiography in neo-Marxian circles of Italian academia, bringing this unstudied material into relief.

81. Angelo di Nicola Grivelli; Nicola del fu Nuzio di Pietro di maestro Raynaldo.

82. Antonio dei Scambi; Nardo Venettini.

83. Including matrimony and dowry negotiations and settlements; wills, money deposits and loans, labor contracts and apprenticeships, emancipation of minors; investitures with legal representative authority, and the appointment of agents and *procuratores;* the sale of manufactured and agricultural goods and raw materials; arbitrations and reconciliations between enemies or factions; private dealings with governmental *enti* ("agencies," or "structures") in cases such as the purchase of trading monopolies, and with ecclesiastical foundations regarding, for example, the construction of family chapels; donations charitable and

digms for Cola's own "experience" as a notary. The importance of notaries and their work, and the nature and range of a notary's relationship to his broader society and culture, applies equally to Cola's own career as a notary; this is further discussed in chapter 6. It is only by understanding the uniquely powerful position of the notary in Rome that the profession can be understood as a springboard into governmental administration and political authority for Cola and others like him in the same city, during the same period. Moreover, both his social "climbing" and the technical and legal precision of the measures of Cola's regime may also be seen as, in part, a product of his professional background.

Institutional Archives and Familial Sources

The *magistri edificorum* documents, noted above, are a rare and valuable archival source; even so, they suffer a considerable Trecento lacuna (1305–61). Public administrative records barely survive from this period in Rome.[84] However, considerable evidence for the administration of private organizations can be extrapolated from archival collections in and around Rome,[85] for the period up to 1380.[86] My research, combined with a thorough reading of the work of archival scholars of the eighteenth, nineteenth, and early twentieth centuries,[87] indicates that Rome, in fact, has extensive collections of *non*-public documentary material for the fourteenth century. Much of it has never been edited (some barely seen); little of it has been studied systematically for its implications regarding the

---

personal; oaths; property rentals and concomitant descriptions; artistic-architectural commissions; the enforcement or execution of *apodisse* (written undertakings not made initially before a notary).

84. A rare exception, garnered from all sorts of sources, is the not always reliable Salimei, *Senatori e statuti.*

85. My own research (1994–99) was conducted in the Archivio Capitolino (in the Borromini Chiesa Nuova complex), the Archivio Storico di Roma (at the Sapienza palace), in the Vatican Library, the Vatican Archives, and in a series of private family archives (e.g. the Cenci and Odescalchi archives and the Colonna archive at Subiaco; the Orsini parchments are readily accessible in the Archivio Capitolino).

86. I concentrated, although not exclusively, on records dating from before 1380, since the situation—economic, political, cultural—after the definitive return of the papacy underwent considerable change. I did not, therefore, thoroughly examine Antonio dei Scambi's protocols after 1383; the records of Nardo Venettini (working 1382–1428), although an invaluable source for the Schism period, also received only a brief examination (his impressive career, however, is noted in chapter 6).

87. There was a flurry of interest in necrologies and similar sources in the later nineteenth century, during the post-Risorgimento heyday of civic pride in Rome.

broader, that is, public-political, context. There are numerous direct references to Cola's period of power amid these records (which will be discussed in chapter 6); they also provide models for the internal administration of institutions, of family holdings and interfamilial politics, and demonstrate crucial aspects of the distribution of power in the Roman local community.

Such records include the parchment (and, occasionally, paper) records of over twenty religious communities or organizations. To this religious/institutional evidence one may add the administrative and onomastic information of the Catalogue of Turin (dating to after 1313), a list of the parish churches of the City, divided into the three administrative sectors of the *Romana Fraternitas.*[88] There are also the published necrologies; the most important are the *Libri Anniversorum* of the Vatican Basilica and of the Arciconfraternità dei Raccomendatori della Sant' Immagine del Santissimo Salvatore *ad Sancta Sanctorum* (the "Confraternity of the Savior").[89] These collections have more relevance to the institutional than the social history of Rome, but are still almost as valuable as the notarial resources. The necrologies, for example, provide essential prosopographical information, for notaries themselves certainly, and also for an entire sector of the citizen body of Rome. They reveal aspects of the identity and social status of members of religious foundations and their self-perception in terms of public responsibility: hence their sponsorship of charitable foundations, especially hospitals, for the populace of the City. These dominant social groups, and some of the individuals comprising them, it will be seen, were closely involved in Cola's revolution.

The majority of this "institutional" evidence consists of over a thousand parchment copies (the tidy *in mundum* version of the *abbreviatura,* for the client) of acts, rogated (i.e., drawn up) by hundreds of notaries, on behalf of the ecclesiastical foundations of medieval Rome; several hundred more exist in Roman family archives (some still privately maintained, others on permanent deposit in the public archives).[90] Most of those are concerned with property, usually land and agriculture, or housing and leasing, but also the exchange or testamentary distribution of valuable goods in

---

88. The body responsible for the governance of parochial Rome: edited in Mariano Armellini, *Le Chiese di Roma dal secolo IV al XIX* (Rome, 1891), 45–59. See Susanna Passigli, "Geografia parrocchiale e circoscrizioni territoriali nei secoli XII–XIV: Istituzioni e realtà quotidiana," in Hubert, *Roma nei secoli XIII e XIV,* 43–86.

89. See Egidi, *Necrologia.*

90. For example, the Arciconfraternità della Santissima Annunziata archive contains fifty-nine documents, of which thirty-six relate to the Trecento.

precious metals, paper, stone, or fabric, and particularly, in the case of the familial collections, dowry- or inheritance-related business. This provides fascinating material for the relationship of religious communities with one another and with the economic and commercial life of the City, which helps to contextualize, for example, Cola's dealings with both urban ecclesiastical foundations and the local aristocracy during his periods in power. Various lists of goods, possessions, and incomes from rentals have been extracted from these documents and used to compare the economic structure and social profile of certain organizations.[91] Meanwhile, the high profile of the secular notary, out in the community, as representative and agent of these institutions or families, is also very obvious in this material.

Statutory Evidence

Guild, in addition to civic, statutes are also an important source of information for the notaries of fourteenth-century Rome. The notaries whose names appear in documents that relate to these *arti,* the semipoliticized secular organizations based on profession, were often what might today be called "public sector" or "state" employees. The titles these men bore within the civic administration are regularly appended to their names, where mentioned, particularly in the cases of those responsible for the act of official communal reconfirmation of guild statutes. Cola, in fact, as Notary of the Civic Chamber, 1344–46, falls into this category (see cover illustration).[92] So, in addition to describing the activities of the corporation and its members, this material provides considerable assistance in the process of uncovering which notaries held public office, and during which periods in the City's history, enjoying *cursus honorum* analogous to Cola's own.

The guild statutes themselves date from the early fourteenth century (apart from those of the notaries' and fish-sellers' guilds), which helps to balance the later Trecento bias of the notarial evidence. These organiza-

91. See e.g. Etienne Hubert, "Un censier des biens romains du monastère du S. Silvestro in Capite (1333–1334)," in Etienne Hubert and Marco Venditelli, "Materiali per la storia dei patrimoni immobiliari urbani a Roma nel Medievo. Due censuali di beni del secolo XIV," *ASRSP* 111 (1988): 93–140; Etienne Hubert, "Economie de la propriété immobilière: Les établissements religieux et leurs patrimoines au XIVe siècle," in *Roma nei secoli XIII e XIV,* 177–230.

92. March 28, 1346; from *Archivio del Collegio dei Commercianti,* 47v; ed. Giuseppe Gatti, *Statuti dei Mercanti di Roma* (Rome: Della Pace, 1885), 80 and figure opposite. Both the guild and these documents, sadly, have disappeared since 1900.

tions were arguably central to the social changes then under way and are of particular relevance to the study of Cola's regime and its backers: in 1343 he had used the title *consul,* suggesting that he then held, or at least identified, high office in a guild context, with guild language (these organizations were often governed by "consuls").

Finally, the city statutes are an invaluable constitutional (and cultural) resource; they describe the sixty or so permanent governmental offices of the commune,[93] employing around 150 men, including seventeen administrative notaries, in addition to between fifty and over a hundred *conestabiles.* Although these date from 1363,[94] there is evidence that earlier versions existed, and were consulted.[95] The fifteen *ordinamenti* of Cola's regime in 1347 are closely related to this statutory material, as will be discussed in chapter 5. The statutes of 1363 were not introduced to fill a vacuum, but written rather to supplement and clarify the body of preexisting civic statutes. Those of the measures of 1363 that refer to different social "classes" are also of particular interest and will merit careful attention; the same social divisions encapsulated in the constitution of 1363 will be shown to have been crucial in Cola's regime.

These three categories of source material—comprising forty-two separate sources of notarial, institutional/familial, and statutory documentation—demonstrate, first, changes in social and economic hegemony in the city and *Destretto,* which have a direct bearing upon the course, the short-term failure, and the long-term effects of Cola's revolution. The next chapter will draw heavily upon this evidence in a reconstruction of the political, social, and economic impact of Cola's reconstruction. Second, the study of

---

93. See Maria Luisa Lombardo, *La Camera Urbis. Premesse per uno studio dell'organizzazione amministrativa della città di Roma durante il pontificato di Martino V,* Fonti e studi del Corpus membranarum italicarum 6 (Rome: Centro di Ricerca, 1970) for a reconstruction of the situation after 1368; the distribution of power at the top, however, had already slightly changed twice between the period of Cola's rule and the definitive return of the papacy in 1378 (see chap. 5).

94. Re, *Statuti.*

95. An antimagnatial statute fragment of 1305 (described in A. Rota, "Il Codice degli *Statuta Urbis* del 1305 e i caratteri politici della sua riforma," *ASRSP* 70 [1947]: 147–62) is accepted by Brentano, *Rome before Avignon,* 115–16, but discredited by Agostino Paravicini-Bagliani, "Alfonso Ceccarelli, gli Statuti Urbis del 1305 e la famiglia Boccamazza," in *Xenia Medii Aevi Historiam Illustrantia oblata T. Kaeppeli O.P.,* ed. R. Creytens and Pius Künzle, Storia e Letteratura 141 (Rome: Edizioni di storia e letteratura, 1978), 1:317–50, as the work of a notorious sixteenth-century forger. My own research has uncovered previously unnoted references to civic statutes from 1279 (B.A.V. Vat. Lat. 7931, 163r–v = Supino, *Margarita Cornetana,* 288–89) and from 1317, 1338–41, and 1359, in the merchant guild's statutes: Gatti, *Statuti dei Mercanti,* xxv–xxxix.

this material highlights the social and political importance of notaries, both in the public and private spheres; this will inform the analysis of Roman notarial status in chapter 6. Such insights, applied to Cola's own career, show him to be far from the social and political anomaly traditionally presented by historians. The latter part of chapter 6 will present new evidence from these notary-written sources for Cola's activities as senior communal magistrate; and it will be used to investigate the lives and careers of the men who participated in his revolution, in order to demonstrate that Cola, his supporters, and his detractors emerge from a very distinctive Trecento Roman social context.

Chapter 5

Ad perpetuam rei memoriam:
The New Social History of
Fourteenth-Century Rome

The popular notarial formula in the title of this chapter ("as a permanent record of affairs"), found in many Trecento Roman documents, was added to legal contracts to supply both a sense of historic timelessness and to guarantee the future of a new dispensation. Ironically, despite this injunction, Rome's civic life and the social profiles of its leaders remained among the shadows of the "den of thieves" until only a few years ago. From the extensive but patchy documentary records of Trecento Rome, described in chapter 4, a handful of Italian and French social historians, following the pioneering work of Clara Gennaro and Jean-Claude Maire-Vigueur around 1970,[1] began to produce a series of invaluable theses and articles.[2] These, in

---

1. Jean-Claude Maire-Vigueur has spent much of his career examining the material circumstances of the ecclesiastical foundations of Rome, especially their landed investments in the *Destretto;* the encroachments of secular agriculturalists; and how changes in the pattern of land tenure both affect and reflect the changing social and economic conditions of Rome and its hinterland—agriculture, infrastructure, regional autonomy, and local toponymy—in the second half of the Trecento. Maire-Vigueur's own point of departure was earlier research into the changing social profile of the *mercanti* and *bovattieri,* the two "noble guilds" of fourteenth-century Rome (Chiara Gennaro, "Per lo studio della composizione sociale della popolazione di Roma nella seconda metà Trecento," Ph.D. diss., University of Rome "La Sapienza," 1963); "Mercanti e bovattieri nella Roma della seconda metà del Trecento," *Bulletino dell'Istituto storico italiano per il Medio Evo* 78 [1967]: 155–87). Maire-Vigueur's results, similarly, proved to be an essential foundation and the first point of departure for the social analysis offered here: see especially "Classe dominante et classes dirigeantes à Rome à la fin du Moyen Age," *Storia della Città* 1 (1976): 17–22.

2. These not only serve as evidence of the rise of the *popolo,* but also have an impact on our knowledge of Cola, and the social and spatial mechanics of his revolution, though this is rarely acknowledged. The new studies encompass investigations of the physical and social

the broadest possible sense, provide a social, economic, and physical context for the period circa 1350–1500 in Rome and its hinterland. The crucial social shifts of the Roman Trecento occurred with the development and extension of the local power of social classes that closely resembled the better-documented *popolo grasso* and *popolo minuto* of Tuscan and other northern city-communes. This evolution has been delineated in the course of thirty years of social historiography; and yet the material and cultural authority of these new social groups within Cola's own revolution has been presented, at best, as a by-product of the process. It will be argued here that the social-economic shift that has been observed by historians was, in part, a cause of the revolution in 1347 that brought Cola to power. Nonetheless, the continued drive of the new groups toward material security, through antimagnatial politics and constitutional reform, must also be seen, in part, as an effect of Cola's regime. In short, the policies of 1347 were also connected intimately and essentially with events in Rome particularly in the two decades following Cola's death in 1354.

The following examination is designed to demonstrate the dynamism, mobility, and innovation inherent in the Roman economy circa 1350–80. The most striking process that emerges from research in the notarial archives is the gradual takeover, by these *popolani,* of the agrarian bases of the Roman economy:[3] their inexorable acquisition of many of the great estates of the *contado,* formerly owned partly by the great barons, partly by the ecclesiastical organizations of medieval Rome. The dowries offered by these upwardly mobile groups[4] never, however, approached the thousands of florins exchanged by the *vires magnifici,* the baronial "superelite" (a narrow caste of between a dozen and twenty or so families with its own

---

geography of the City, its topography, toponymy, demography, and microeconomies; the administrative techniques employed by its larger *enti;* credit, money, and the grain supply; industry, the guilds, and material culture; the existence of a range of religious organizations; and linguistic, cultural, and intellectual resources, including the revitalization of the university during Cola's Tribunate (noted in chap. 1). Each of the preceding aspects of social historical research might inform the absolute reconstruction of Cola's context; one would, however, require considerably more space to plunder each fully.

3. Seventy-five percent of the *Districtus,* by the later fourteenth century (Maire-Vigueur, "Classe dominante," 5).

4. Compare the average *Ars Bobacteriorum* dowry of ca. three hundred florins, with dowries offered by shopkeepers, fish merchants, notaries, and certain skilled tradesmen, of one hundred to two hundred florins: Maire-Vigueur, "Classe dominante," 17. Artisans and less well off notaries or shopkeepers tended to leave bequests or arrange dowries in the tens, or dozens, of florins.

internal hierarchy).[5] The relatively high status of barons in Rome, and their impressive, almost untouchable, ability to disrupt the city from their *fortilitia* (fortified complexes) inside the *abitato* (the "inhabited" zone radiating from the Tiber, well within the ancient walls and hills) is a phenomenon anomalous in contemporary Italy. Of course, the particularly powerful position of barons in Rome also reflects the fact that these were the families who supplied the senior personnel of those, institutions uniquely powerful and rich in all Christendom, the Curia and papacy.

Nominally (not always) present in Rome until the death of Boniface in 1303, the cardinal-deacons of Rome's ancient basilicas each exercised a degree of "local" municipal influence. This was much more difficult to manage from Avignon (indeed, Cola "bearded" Cardinal Giovanni Colonna—first enemy, then patron in Avignon, then enemy again—in Giovanni's own deaconry, S. Angelo in Pescheria). By the later fourteenth century necrological records show that the major basilicas of the City, pilgrim centers of all Christendom, were now "staffed" by men from the newly powerful social classes.[6] The roots of the wealth of these groups lay in the "boom" period of the thirteenth century, and it is likely that their control of the municipal churches of Rome began to develop then, alongside the evolving parochial hegemony of the *Romana Fraternitas.* However, their opportunity to rise to dominance over the whole civic economy and all of its institutions only came with the departure of the curia in 1305, when the lines of communication—that is, between curial office-holders from the old Roman elite, now in France, and their baronial bases of wealth in the City and *Destretto*—stretched to breaking point.

The barons of Rome, though unusual in Italy, are thus relatively straightforward to identify and describe; any attempt, however, to delineate the new groups within the urban social hierarchy, by status- or rank-defined stages, tends to mask the fluidity of the situation; nor is the image

---

5. Now analyzed in detail: Franca Allegrezza, "Trasformazioni della nobiltà baronale," in *Roma Medievale. Aggiornamenti,* ed. Paolo Delogu (Florence: All'Insegna del Giglio, 1999), 211–20; Sandro Carocci, *I Baroni di Roma. Dominazione signorili e lignaggi aristocratici nel duecento e nel primo Trecento* (Rome: École Française, 1993); also "Baroni in città. Considerazioni sull'insediamento e i diritti urbani della grande nobiltà," in Hubert, *Roma nei secoli XIII e XIV,* 137–73; Maire-Vigueur, "Classe dominante," 16–17. *Magnificus* is a legal definition used by notaries (thus also by Cola in official despatches). The Chronicler tends to describe barons as *potienti* (and) *baroni,* although he does once use the term *mannifichi* of the Colonna (*ARC,* 108). His term *nuobili* refers to a much broader sector of society.

6. Argued by Ian Robertson, in reference to capitular reform in the fifteenth-century Lateran (paper presented in the Italian history seminar series of the University of London Institute of Historical Research, London, November 2, 1995).

of a social-economic spectrum, though better than a ladder, entirely satisfactory, since the social progress of certain individuals or groups is
"three-" and not "two-dimensional"; that is, some moved through different "stages" at different speeds, or bypassed these artificial markers altogether. With these considerable reservations in mind, it should yet be useful to present a necessarily simplistic snapshot or "cross-section" of
Roman society in Cola's time.

The most distinctive and powerful of the new groups were the cattle-
raisers or *bovattieri,* working as individuals or syndicates to buy up vast
tracts of lands to herd their livestock, and consequently operating as chief
suppliers to the meat industry. The *Ars Nobilis Bobacteriorum* (Noble
Guild of Stock-Raisers) dominates the new social hierarchy and was
indeed a self-proclaimed aristocracy. The groups that sought to emulate
them, mostly also styling themselves *nobiles,* were clearly economically
distinguishable, as the dowries show, from the *magnifici.* However, it is
much harder to make such distinctions between the *bovattieri* and the
other "nobles" below them within the ranks of new civic aristocracy, such
as their near rivals the "merchants," who had their own noble guild.
Despite the occupational titles, it is clear that both merchants and *bovattieri* did considerably more than trade goods and farm beef cattle, respectively. The absence of the papacy favored the rise of entrepreneurial
groups who created wealth in a sudden economic vacuum; the concomitant faltering in Rome's communal self-definition may also be seen to have
encouraged the development of this new class with the financial resources
to train its own bureaucrats. The Ars Bobacteriorum became the elite of
that group; its members lived primarily in the colonnaded street-palaces of
the medieval city, and many bore the honorific title *nobilis vir.* They
formed an urban squirarchy; a landed gentry only in the sense of possess-
ing agrarian holdings (cattle *non*-barons, one might say).

These high-class guildsmen enjoyed the status of *nobilis,* whether they
came from newer or older Roman families; there is no clear demarcation
between them. However, some powerful men whose interests did not
include the intensive raising of livestock or commodities trading are also
described as *viri nobiles* in notarial documents: not all urban aristocrats
derived their standing from "new" money. There is a distinction we, from
a distance, may draw between "new men" and older families within the
traditional sub-baronial "nobility": that is, between those whose families
had been established (and thus ennobled, sometimes self-ennobled) over a
century or so—the Cenci, Boccamazzi, de' Rustici, Pappazuri, Capozuc-

chi, Cerroni—and the more recent nobles, whose names—Baccari, Porcari (cowboys, swineherds)—betray their less than noble ancestral relationship to the land.[7] However, there is no contemporary category into which this distinction slots; it does not appear to have caused resentment in Rome (in contrast to the antiarriviste snobbery of Florentine writers), nor a consequent re-articulation or identification as a discrete social group. To complicate these axes (old standing, new wealth) of social grouping, however, there was another further high-status group, the *cavalerotti.* These men were not exactly the traditional, semioccupational military *cavalieri,* knights; both the statutes of 1363 and the Chronicler use the term *cavalerotto* as distinct from *miles* or *cavaliere.* It was certainly not intended of the new entrepreneurial businessman, denoting, rather, men of aristocratic, sometimes (though not necessarily) of baronial origin. Unique to Rome, these individuals were seemingly accepted, and even "elected" as knights, by the new social groups of the *popolo,* especially the *popolo grasso;* they enjoyed a superior or super-"knightly" status (recalling the modern paradoxical notion of Diana, the [British] "People's Princess"). Therefore *viri nobiles* as a description covers a wide range of newly powerful groups, embracing both the newer and older powerful urban families.[8]

Meanwhile, "below" these *nobiles,* but still within the constant stream of upward mobility in the mid–fourteenth century, there was a vast group of more definitely "new," commercially active, families clinging onto the tails of the greater merchants. These families included, for example, the Tordoneri of the *rione* S. Angelo, still remembered in the mid-Trecento as millers. By now, however, the interests of the *consorterie* under the Tordoneri umbrella had diversified into mill ownership and the management of numerous shops and workshops *(botteghe).* The Grassi and Ponziani, who dominated the later Trecento fish and game market, were similarly important. These men, I suggest, were the *vulgari mercatanti,* the merchants who read no Latin, who were not noble, and to whom the Chronicler addressed his dialect narrative.[9] Their local, but extensive business interests were organized in familial *consorterie* or guild networks, in order

---

7. Names as unpretentious as those attached to the Roman Forum and the Capitoline hill in the period: Campo Vaccino and Monte Caprino (Cow Field and Goat Hill respectively).

8. The *viri nobiles* of Rome ca. 1350 had reached a similar point, I suggest, to that reached by the Guelf "urban aristocracy" of Tuscan communes in the later Duecento, just before this Guelf-*grasso* entity split further into the slightly newer White and rather older Black factions. Such internal evolution within the group was only starting to happen in Cola's Rome (see the *aicuni cittadini* debate below).

9. Wright, *Life,* 23.

to pursue the commercially related activities that dominate the surviving notarial material from circa 1350. They were, increasingly, the backbone of the new economic drive in Rome, as the more elevated urban "aristocrats" moved inevitably into politics, land-ownership, international commerce, and high finance (as similar types had done in, e.g., Florence, almost a century earlier).

"Below" these men in social origin, but, through personal success, also a part of the spearhead of economic change in fourteenth-century Rome, it is possible to identify another influential group, made up of individual operators whose names and thus family origins are relatively obscure: Pietro Renzicoli, Nicola Valentini, Lello Maddaleno, Piero Matteo di Giovanni *Judicis Angeli,* the Dello Preyte family, and an especially important man in Trecento Rome, Nucio Gibelli. Yet by becoming a major player in the late-fourteenth-century economy and politics of Rome, Nucio effectively joined the ranks of the *bovattieri.* A supreme businessman, Nucio, like Francesco Datini of Prato, even employed an in-house notary. These individuals, of course, are the exceptional figures; not exactly stereotypes, since many of their social peers remained "small" and anonymous, but archetypical examples highlighting the potential mobility even of this socially less advantaged group. These men might be considered the influential elements of the Roman version of the *popolo minuto.* In Rome the political power this part of society came to exercise in the City was generally expressed in the more conservative terms of military, rather than commercial, hegemony (the Bandaresi were to succeed where the cobbler Pocadota's revolution of 1362 failed).[10] These men may correspond to the anonymous, non-noble *bona iente* whom the Roman Chronicler also addresses but distinguishes from the merchants and *nuobili.* The value-loaded term *boni* is used in many sources to describe the unnamed lesser-guild and rional representatives who fronted municipal agitation against baronial and sometimes, later, against the civic-noble, *popolo grasso*-style government. On one occasion the description *iustissimi puopolari* follows and appears to qualify another, *buoni uomini;*[11] the Chronicler may be referring to two slightly different groups, such as the two "lower" sections of the three *popolo* groups tentatively outlined here: nobles, merchants, "good men"; in reality these categories overlapped. All

---

10. Matteo, *Cronica,* 2:623–24 (11:25); Matteo Villani is the only source for this episode; a revolution of the *popolo minuto,* under one "Bonadota," which expelled both *possenti cittadini* and *cavallerotti.* See also Dupré-Théseider, *Roma dal Comune,* 665–66.

11. *ARC,* 116.

discussion of hierarchy involves speculative and artificial delineation; the reality was far more fluid in a period of economic growth and its concomitant social mobility.

Finally, "below" these men we may locate the "mob": not so large at Rome, which attracted crowds of pious pilgrims to holy sites rather than agitated ex-rural workers to industrial factories, although baronial anarchy in civic administration and the consequent breakdowns in the food supply were particularly problematic in Rome and led to rioting more frequently than in most Italian cities (indeed Cola rode to power on the back of one such crisis).

The activities of a few men like Gibelli manifest the kind of social mobility one might expect to see in a Tuscan industrial town like Florence, whereas Rome had no manufacturing output, depending primarily on its production of meat and grain (and income from pilgrims) and relying heavily on imported goods. The fact that certain individuals from obscure social origins were able to carve out a niche among their social superiors is evidence, then, of the vitality of the Roman social-economic situation, combined with its unusual geographic and demographic factors.[12] Social status took a while to catch up with the generation of wealth, but by 1390 Lello Maddaleno had reached the top: his timely delivery of grain in that

---

12. In the first decades of the fourteenth century, the population declined to an all-time low of approximately seventeen to twenty-five thousand. The figures remain vague; a new study, possibly edited by E. Sonnino, still in the course of publication, will hopefully cast new light on the issue. See also Anna Esposito, "Note sulla populazione Romana dalla fine del secolo XIV al Sacco (1527)," in *Un Altra Roma* (Rome: Il Calamo, 1995), 19–30. This depopulation appeared in especially shocking contrast to those who had experienced the Bonifatian city of 1300, such as Dante; it helped prompt contemporary and later overstatement of Rome's Trecento ills. In fact the resident medieval population (as opposed to pilgrims, or envoys to the papal court) had probably never topped thirty thousand, even in the later thirteenth-century ecclesiastical heyday, and decline everywhere was a feature of the period. The slump in river trade and the lower density of population in Rome than in other cities perhaps even saved Rome from the worst ravages of the Black Death; certainly the Roman earthquake of 1348 was a disaster more widely commented upon than the arrival of plague. After Cola's Tribunate, and certainly following the 1350 Jubilee, the City's population began slowly to rise. Notarial evidence suggests the gradual and exponential reinhabitation of the Fora, Colosseum, Lateran, and S. Maria Maggiore zones during the next decades, areas often under the influence of the newer families though still within the anomalous ancient walls of the city; see Jean-Claude Maire-Vigueur and G. Broise, "Strutture familiari, spazio domestico e architettura civile a Roma alla fine del Medio Evo," in *Monumenti di architettura,* Storia dell'arte italiana, vol. 12 (Turin: Einaudi, 1983), 99–160; Etienne Hubert, "Rome (Moyen Age: Ville e population)," in Levillain, *Dictionnaire historique de la Papauté,* 1463 (his bibliography is exhaustive). By 1527 the population had risen to 53,689 (though only following a surge in the later fifteenth century): Egmont Lee, *The "Descriptio Urbis": The Roman Census of 1527* (Rome: Bulzoni, 1985), 13–20.

year earned him the title "Savior of the Roman People." Already, in 1365, Nucio Gibelli had become one of the Seven Reformers (these government offices are described below), and in 1370, a Conservator. In 1382 he is cited as a contender for the post of podestà of Rieti.[13] Both Lello and Nucio, in 1370, were present alongside the senators, canons, and *caporioni,* at the symbolic "municipal" installation in the *Sancta Sanctorum* of the new reliquaries of Peter and Paul.[14] As a classic feature of an economy on the upturn, the *trasversalità* of Cola's career is comparable (albeit more extreme): from plebeian innkeeper's son, provincially educated, to notary, to municipal official, to noble knight and senior magistrate.

However, while historians have discussed at length the mechanisms by which the various "levels" of *popolani* of medieval Rome, described above, achieved hegemony in the second half of the Trecento, less energy has been expended explaining why this was so. This apparent privileging of mechanics over reasons reflects the nature of the notarial evidence (though possibly also the interests, methodologies, and assumptions of social historians). This context is obviously too limited to describe, let alone explain, the rise of the *popolo* in Italy or Europe as a whole. It would, however, be appropriate to draw attention to those factors that differentiate Rome in the fourteenth century; here the process began considerably later, but then took hold much more quickly than was the case in other Italian cities.

With the move of the curia, and its many consumers, to Avignon, the valuable, long-established market for the agricultural produce of the *Destretto* lands of the barons evaporated. Simultaneously, the Roman aristocracy lost a role within the Curia as favored political intermediaries between the Lateran enclave and the rest of the City. Papal appointments proved to be very difficult to enforce from Avignon, leaving an effective vacuum in civic control. The senatorial office was filled from various sources, with varying degrees of cooperation and hostility toward Avignon; by papal representatives, frequently Angevin appointees, such as King Robert and his vicars; by leaders of the commune itself, in small rushes of military self-assertion;[15] by counterbalanced pairs of Roman barons; and even by "Roman emperors" on two brief occasions, in

---

13. Arcangelo Natale, "La Felice Società dei Balestrieri e dei Pavesati a Roma (1358–1408)," *ASRSP* 62 (1939): 140–41, 147–48.

14. Recorded officially by Antonio dei Scambi: B.A.V. S.A.P. 6/1370, 31v–32v.

15. See Carole M. Small, "The District of Rome in the Early Fourteenth Century," *Canadian Journal of History* 16 (1981): 193–213.

1312–13 and 1327. The financial downturn that struck the baronial land-holders after the departure of the Curia was combined with appalling internal discord and factional warfare, though also an unprecedented degree of autonomy and opportunity sized by some; a recent case has been made for the "survival of the fittest" in the case of the Orsini.[16]

This threatened to drag down the newly enriched "urban nobility" too. In 1300 the sub-baronial elements of Roman society enjoyed the results of economic boom; politics was a route to retain this new standing. It became imperative to establish a politically secure system to guarantee Rome's already limited markets. This spurred the mercantile elements of Roman society into the rapid assumption of increasing control of all spheres of economic and political activity; a process that proved unstoppable for decades, given the chaos at the top. A series of shifts that may have taken two hundred years in Florence was telescoped in Rome, once released from papal control, into less than fifty; namely, the definitive start of the wresting of economic control from magnates and the beginnings of a con-sequent hegemony by a new elite (this is an overstatement and an over-simplification, but serves to illustrate the process). Among the political factors in the process of *popolo* enrichment and empowerment, Cola's own attack on the barons was central. His antimagnatial gestures had an effect; his policy measures, initially unsuccessful but constantly resurrected after his death, sealed the economic fate of the barons, while boosting the strength of their opponents.

Other contemporary events played their part. First, Florentine bankers had created a new climate of venture capitalism, but after the financial crises of the 1330s and the shrinking of the Florentine loans industry,[17] the gap had to be filled by locals; the need to finance their own business deals gradually led Roman merchants to diversify into more sophisticated credit operations.[18] Second, the Jubilee of 1350, pushed very hard by Cola, did bring wealth to investing groups within a relatively small urban popula-

---

16. Allegrezza, "Trasformazioni della nobiltà baronal," 219, uses the analogy of the process of natural selection.

17. The Peruzzi bank was finally dissolved in the year of Cola's revolution. See Edwin S. Hunt, *The Medieval Super-Companies* (Cambridge: Cambridge University Press, 1994), esp. 212–42, for a detailed recent treatment.

18. See Isa Lori-Sanfilippo, "Operazioni di credito nei protocolli notarili romani del Tre-cento," in *Credito e sviluppo economia in Italia del Medio Evo all'Età Contemporanea* (Verona: Società italiana degli storici dell' Economia 1988), 53–66; Ivana Ait, "Aspetti del mercato del credito a Roma nelle fonti notarili," in Chiabò et al., *Alle origini della nuova Roma*, 479–500. The pawn and loans market in Rome was relatively small-scale until the return of the cash-hungry papacy in the 1370s.

tion.[19] Cola was adamant that the food supply and the safety of pilgrims should be guaranteed, and attempted to set up appropriate provisioning and security arrangements. His stress on the Jubilee as early as 1343, and the economic measures proposed in 1347 to manage the Jubilee, allowed the City's merchants and property owners to visualize (indeed many were to reap) its potential rewards.[20]

However, just as there are political factors in the economic equation,[21] it may be seen that the evolving social position of certain groups in turn affected the political structures of the city. If the *causes* of the changing role of the *popolo* are difficult to extrapolate from the documentary evidence, the same cannot be said of its *effects* on the constitution and politics of Trecento Rome. The new economic power-brokers, as we have seen, displayed a social mobility that was also wholly characteristic of the fluidity, adaptability, and intensity of the capital generation techniques the same operators applied to land and property.[22] Their political activities both reflected and represented an extension of their business operations: there is clear evidence, in the protocols and elsewhere, that certain elements within the *popolo* attempted, over and over, to assume governmental power, sometimes against other sectors of the newly powerful group.[23]

It would be inappropriate, however, to speak of partisan groups with clearly defined political aims. The earliest social historiography (of Gennaro, Macek, Palermo, and Miglio) often manifested an older Marxist view of society with a terminological and analytical rigidity pursued beyond the outer markers of its usefulness.[24] In place of this reductionist,

---

19. See especially Paolo Brezzi, "Holy Years in the Economic Life of the City of Rome," *Journal of European Economic History* 4 (1975): 673–90.

20. This is nicely analyzed by Luciano Palermo, *Il Porto di Roma nel XIV e XV secolo. Strutture socio-economiche e statuti* (Rome: Il Centro di Ricerca, 1979), 71–79.

21. A third political factor led to a gradual takeover of ecclesiastical land-holdings by the new classes: from the 1350s right through to the end of the Schism we see a somewhat heavy-handed papal fiscality imposed on religious institutions in order to finance the continual fight for the restoration of the Roman Patrimony. As Roman monasteries sold their lands and their own patrimonies, to enable the Roman pontiff to retain his, so they were purchased by secular investors; dozens of examples survive in the notarial protocols of the 1370s.

22. See especially Hubert, "Economie de la propriété immobilière."

23. An overall reading of Salimei, *Senatori e Statuti,* demonstrates the onomastic shift from the thirteenth century (dominated by baronial names) to the fifteenth (where the *bovattieri* come into their own, but only to be edged out, swiftly, by curial imports from Florence, Naples, and beyond).

24. Even Maire-Vigueur's excellent work on the social politics of Trecento Rome is peppered with "class" analysis: the very title—"Classe dominante et classes dirigeantes"—is witness to an assumption of class identity/hostility.

two-dimensional approach there has emerged a need to review the evidence for the existence of networks that were vertical as well as horizontal. Terms such as *elite* and *popular,* language used in more recent Marxian analyses, serve a useful purpose, but the idea of a deliberate political hostility on the basis of economic hegemony—or the quest for it—is often a misleading way to assess medieval society. While artificial horizontal divisions can be used to demonstrate Cola's ability to draw support from groups with different social-economic profiles, and differing attitudes to their social superiors, we must be aware of the danger of thereby over-politicizing these groups and attributing greater group cohesion and class identity than was ever the case in reality. Political and economic gain by the individual Roman Trecento *popolano* was generally achieved by means of aspiration, ambition, and swift social assimilation rather than class warfare, although some element of group, if not "class" identity does, nevertheless, inform the relationship between the civic elite and the militia-based power-brokers in the late 1350s, as evident in the Roman Statutes of 1363 (reviewed below). Success for the individual was not generally viable without the backing both of patrons, and clients in a system of acknowledged, socially "vertical" relationships. The one recorded occasion in Rome of what would appear to have been an uprising by the Roman equivalent of the *popolo minuto* (Pocadota in 1362) was abortive, and hardly identical to the activity of the Florentine *Ciompi* of the 1380s.[25] Rome did not have the wide industrial economic basis of her Tuscan counterparts, nor a corresponding "proletariat"; group authority, where expressed, tended to draw on local and/or military loyalty. Instead the City had an exceptionally large "service sector," particularly consisting of lawyers and notaries (whose social origins, as Cola's case demonstrates, could be humble, but were generally from the upper echelons of the *popolo*). While the "solidarity" of the new groups may be witnessed crystallizing around organizations such as the new Roman confraternities,[26]

---

25. Even so, class-bound analyses of the more powerful Florentine *popolo minuto* are no longer convincing: see e.g. Carol Lansing, *The Florentine Magnates: Lineage and Faction in a Medieval Commune* (Princeton: Princeton University Press, 1991), preface, xiii–xiv.

26. The earliest of these lay religious organizations date from the later thirteenth century; exactly the period when the mid-Trecento elite began their rise to economic and political hegemony. By the mid-Trecento some, particularly the Confraternity of the Savior, operated more like chambers of commerce or Rotary clubs in terms of the social standing of their membership and the organization's charitable and political activities. See Maire-Vigueur, "Classe dominante," 15; Paola Pavan, "Gli statuti della Società dei Raccomendati del Salvatore *ad Sancta Sanctorum* (1331–1496)," *ASRSP* 101 (1978): 35–96, and "La confraternita del Salvatore nella società romana del Tre-Quattrocento," *Ricerche per la Storia Religiosa di*

nonetheless networks of support in Rome had a particularly steep social gradient, reflecting the relatively large gap between the barons and the crowd. Lawyers particularly enjoyed this mobility, as we will see in chapter 6, drawing clients from barons to butchers: Cola's career, with its diverse axes of support—from Orsini scions to mob rallies—is representative of the fortunes of the newly powerful Roman *popolo.*

The mechanics of the creation of wealth by these newly powerful groups were, arguably, protocapitalistic. But the Roman *bovattieri* and their imitators hardly appear to be the nouveaux riches exponents of a self-consciously entrepreneurial new business culture so despised by Dante and, in contrast, endorsed as "bourgeois" by nineteenth-century historians. Indeed the aesthetic conservatism of the Roman equivalent of the *popolo grasso,* as well as the very traditional areas of their investments, contrasts with—to the point of apparent contradiction—new administrative techniques being employed by lay, confraternal, and ecclesiastical managers in order to maximize agricultural productivity or property rental returns.[27] A similar paradox—archaism of form combined with up-to-date political practice—occupies the gap between Cola's titles and techniques, suggesting again that his regime is only comprehensible within the context of Trecento social politics. Instead of "class war," the social and political ramifications of the changes occurring in the fourteenth-century economy were expressed as short-term coalitions "across the ranks"; opportunistic conspiracies and temporary coalescences; cooperation, consent, and, for some individuals, upward mobility involving magnatial emulation and imitation. This same breadth of support from ranks across

---

Roma 5 (1984): 81–90; Giulia Barone, "Il movimento francescano e la nascita delle confraternite romane," *Ricerche per la storia religiosa di Roma* 5 (1984): 71–80.

27. Maire-Vigueur has addressed this "contradiction," discussing Roman *popolano* "cultural conservatism," in terms both of architecture and investment ("Capital économique et capital symbolique. Les contradictions de la société romaine à la fin du Moyen Age," in Brezzi and Lee, *Sources of Social History,* 213–24; with Maire-Vigueur and Broise, "Strutture familiari," 159–60). In architecture, the weighty presence of the past had more of an impact in Rome than anywhere else; instead of using new money to sponsor new techniques and styles, as was happening in Tuscany, the new elite in Rome showed a greater tendency to reinforce their status with definitive endorsements of traditional aesthetic styles (there is a marked contrast in the administrative techniques used by newly arrived property-owners in the 1360s and their long-established "rivals": see the cases outlined by Hubert, "Economie de la propriété immobilière"). Rome's manufacturing industry was embryonic. Imports of relative luxuries, especially wine and cloth, were extremely high (see Palermo, *Il Porto di Roma,* 100, 111). Most reinvestment before 1400, certainly, was directed at the traditional areas of internal consumption, namely the meat and grain markets.

society, and combination of idealism and opportunism, was undeniably at work in Cola's own revolution.

By 1350, many important administrative and judicial offices had already come to rest in the hands of the men whose families, at the same time, were coming to dominate the agrarian-mercantile economy. This was a process contemporary with, and reflective of, the increasing economic power of the *bovattieri, mercanti,* and the various ranks of citizen described as *nobiles, descreti,* or *boni.* Again, this is not exactly the same as the Tuscan *grasso-minuto* range, because of the different economic conditions of Rome, but the analogy is useful. This is not to imply that the "new classes" approached government in an egalitarian style among themselves; markers of distinction such as *nobiles, descreti, boni,* alert the observer to the differential terminology employed by contemporaries, such as the Roman Chronicler, within Rome. In the years directly after Cola's revolution, men from these groups achieved a considerable degree of political control, their relative seniority reflecting the hierarchy outlined above. The elite of the *popolani* consolidated their position by thrashing out a set of civic statutes. These were distinctive and apparently effective (at least in terms of governmental control)[28] in their circumscription of the baronial elite. Baronial names simply fail to appear in the governmental lists after the late 1350s.[29] The notarial protocols contain many cases of barons selling off their property, just as they show ecclesiastical organizations alienating their patrimonies. The new classes became the backbone of the administration and the most powerful of the *popolani* occupied the senior magistracies of the commune.[30]

One figure who epitomized the new elite and whose career unfolded alongside that of Cola himself, was the "new" nobleman Matteo di don Francesco de Baccariis, friend and in-law of the notary Antonio di Lorenzo Impoccia de Scambiis, whose early protocols Matteo dominates. A considerable number of documents were rogated at Matteo's house, not all concerning the Baccari personally: Matteo was clearly a local *gran padrone.* The name Baccari, as mentioned previously, reveals the basis of the family's wealth (from *vacca,* cow); they were in fact originally butchers

---

28. Allegrezza ("Trasformazioni della nobilità baronal," 219) questions the efficacy of the antimagnatial statutes of 1363 in terms of "real" power, but accepts that far fewer baronial families enjoyed authority in 1400 than in 1300.

29. See Salimei, *Senatori e Statuti,* 112–38.

30. This of course was a general rule, to which exceptions may be found, e.g. among the three Conservators of 1370 (Salimei, *Senatori e Statuti,* 139–40).

who moved into the raising and supply of the livestock for slaughter.[31] Success and concomitant status in the vanguard of the Ars Nobilis Bobacteriorum was reflected in the family's increased use of the patronymic name form—*de Baccaris*—after the midcentury.[32] Matteo was a particularly ambitious urban "aristocrat" and enjoyed a professional career far distant from the ancestral fields.[33] His first wife had come to him with a dowry of a hundred florins, but by the end of his career, he could afford the best dowry rates (apart from those of the magnates) for his daughters: three hundred florins.[34] In his will of September 7, 1367, he left his daughters (he had no sons) two and seven hundred florins respectively.[35]

Matteo's business deals reveal techniques and acumen[36] similar to those of Nucio Gibelli, for example operating informal syndicates among friends for speculative investment: in one case (it also serves to illustrate the expansion of the landed possessions of the civic upper class at the expense of the baronial elite) on May 24, 1368, Antonio dei Scambi rogated a sale of property[37] by the appointed agents of two Savelli barons. Matteo purchased an *integram medietam* (i.e., a half share in each of the buildings and territories) for eight hundred florins. It was a good time to buy, with Pope Urban V and his court about to return to Rome from Avignon: rental incomes and property values increased by as much as 25 percent with a pope in town.[38]

---

31. Giuseppe Marchetti-Longhi, "Il *Mons Fabiorum*. Note di topografica medioevale di Roma," *ASRSP* 99 (1976): 54, mentions a Baccari or Vaccari in 1247. Brentano selected Matteo to exemplify local authority in post-Avignon Rome: *Rome before Avignon,* 41–42, 282–83.

32. The same process may be seen throughout the ranks of the new "nobility."

33. Even so, his will shows he still owned cattle worth five hundred florins, and two horses for visiting them; very traditional investments.

34. B.A.V. S.A.P. 3/1367, 70r–77r. Maire-Vigueur and Broise, "Strutture familiari," 139, illustrates brilliantly the local network of the Baccari.

35. B.A.V. S.A.P. 3/1367, 99r–104r.

36. Matteo was not above forging documents within property transfer deals, even among his associates, possibly to avoid ecclesiastical censure and incrimination under canon law as a usurer: this is confessed in his will (see also Lori-Sanfilippo, "Operazioni di credito," 58–59).

37. B.A.V. S.A.P. 4/1368 66r–70v, 71r–78r, 79r–80r. The property consisted of forty-four houses all near the Tiber, three fishing areas in the river, a (water-)mill, and a piece of the *prata Sabellorum*. Maire-Vigueur and Broise, "Strutture familiari," 124, note that, unusually among their peers, the Baccari had no tower to their name (they do not mention that the Baccari had nonetheless commissioned the extraordinarily outsized bell-tower of S. Maria in Cosmedin in the late thirteenth century).

38. There are numerous cases (Capanna's inn is noted below) in Antonio dei Scambi's protocols and elsewhere, of rental agreements stipulating the right of the owner to charge more in the event of the presence of the papacy, often unpredictable until after 1420.

Yet Baccari roots lay deeper still, within the structures of the community: literally, in the church of S. Angelo. Matteo's will earmarked four hundred florins to found a Baccari family chapel, dedicated to Ss. Cosma Damiano, and to pay for masses.[39] Some time after his death in 1368,[40] a dispute over the payment for these masses led to the alienation—to the canons of S. Angelo—of one house in Matteo's extensive patrimonial portfolio. There were still plenty of other local properties left in the hands of the Baccari after this, as the inventory compiled after Matteo's death makes clear.[41] He also owned a typical *bovattiere* estate (a *casale* at Pulvis Role, beyond the Porta Portese) and a string of small vineyards and pieces of land.

Most impressive, however, was Matteo's town residence. His daughter (Mattea) in her will of 1371 left her sons "that palace with the two grand levels and the colonnade with the Archangel," plus the house next door, fronted with marble stairs, all within the *reclaustro* (the enclosed area or "cloister") of the Baccari property. In 1376 one of the "lesser" houses of this complex was rented out, by Matteo's brother or nephew, Mascio: even this possessed two floors, three rooms, an enclosed open area, a covered walkway, and access via the archway "which is called the Gate of the Baccari and via the marble stairs to the side of the house of habitation." The Porta dei Baccari was the name then popularly given to the right-hand brick archway of the classical portico in front of the church of S. Angelo, part of the eighth-century reinforcements made to Augustus's monument as it crumbled. Regrettably, the nineteenth-century "isolation" of the Theatre of Marcellus[42] punched out many of the houses to the right of the Portico, where this complex may have stood.[43] The house to the right of the gap is an elegant, if heavily restored, town house of the later medieval period and may serve as something of a model, though it lacks the fine features of the *accasamenta* of the Baccari.[44]

---

39. His neighbor Nucio Gibelli, not to be outdone, also decided to found a chapel in the church of S. Angelo, dedicated to S. Maria Annunziata; B.A.V. S.A.P. 3/1367, 109v.

40. 18 October; B.A.V. S.A.P. 4/1368, 118v–120v, 131r–132v.

41. B.A.V. S.A.P. 1/1363, 162v; 3/1367, 129r–130v; 4/1368, 97v–98r.

42. Luckily, urban projects from the early 1940s, involving the further destruction of the nearby buildings (including the synagogue) to create an open zone down to the river, came to nothing: see "La mostra di sistemazione urbanistica al Centri di studi di Storia dell'Architettura," *Capitolium* 16 (1941): 151–53.

43. The building attached to the side of S. Angelo in Pescheria, built right into the Portico, must have been the cardinal's palace (the description of the location of the future chapel suggests this strongly).

44. This isolated survival, which bears a plaque commemorating the persecuted Jewish population and is now the headquarters of one of Rome's archaeological authorities, perhaps belonged to the Baccari family's neighbor, Nucio Gibelli (see B.A.V. S.A.P. 9/1376, 39r).

The notarial information therefore provides a clear idea of Matteo's social and economic status. His will, moreover, gives an idea of the intellectual and cultural ambience of the world in which he worked: it lists twenty-one named and priced codices[45] and refers to a further fourteen, with a cumulative value of 342 florins.[46] It should be no surprise that Petrarch bought books in Rome, or that Cola had a library to bequeath,[47] although these details hardly substantiate the humanist line on the decadence of Rome. Yet Matteo's collection of legal texts, as a *sapiens vir,* a doctor of both civil and canon law, was not merely for show. His career as a businessman was complementary, if not secondary, to his political career. In 1349 a copy of a document of 1289 was authorized and subscribed by Matteo, as *judex palatinus* (occupying the most senior Roman bench).[48] He still occupied this position in the years before his death: in 1365, he is found as *judex palatinus* and *judex collateralis domini Senatoris* (judge "at the side" of the lord Senator);[49] in 1367, as *judex*

---

45. 1 *codicillum* worth 12 florins.
  2 *Digesta Vetera,* 23 fl., 6 fl.
  1 *Infortiatum,* 12 fl.
  1 *Digestum Novum,* 12 fl.
  1 lectures of *dominus Bartoli, in papiro super* ff. *nono,* 20 fl.
  2 lectures of *dominus Cinus,* 36 fl., 15 fl.
  1 lectures of *Dinus super Infortiato &* ff. *veterum,* 6 fl
  2 "Volumes," 18 fl., 10 fl.
  1 *Decretales,* 25 fl.
  1 *Decretum,* currently on loan to the rector of S. Spirito
  1 *Speculum Judiciale,* 40 fl.
  1 *Summas Hostiensis,* 28 fl.
  1 *Innocentium et Compostellanum,* 12 fl.
  1 *Archdiaconis super* [?]*vi,* 8 fl.
  2 *Summas Aczonis,* 12 fl.
  1 *Liber Sextum, et clementinas,* 36 fl.
  1 *Evangelistarum, et multos alios libros juribus canonicis et civilis et aliarum scriptarum*
    (no price given)

The second inventory of his possessions, made on June 25, 1368 (B.A.V. S.A.P. 4/1368, 97v ff.) i.e., some days after his death, mentions "thirty-five volumes, of canon and civil law et al." (the latter noted briefly by Miglio, "Et rerum facta est," 52).

46. A contemporary town house cost between forty and a hundred florins.

47. III:64, 126

48. B.A.V. S. Maria in Via Lata, box 308, document 4; a 1349 copy of 1289 original document. The statutes of 1363 make it clear that for a copy of a dead notary's work to be authenticated, it had to be signed by two other notaries and a serving judge; in this case Matteo was the judge.

49. Renzo Mosti, *Il Protocollo Notarile di Anthonius Goioli Petri Scopte (1365)* (Rome: École Française, 1991), 114.

palatinus[50] and *judex collateralis* of the Seven Reformers.[51] Matteo must be regarded, simply, as one of the most important political figures in Trecento Rome. There is evidence for his career before 1349, too: Matteo lived next door to the church of S. Angelo; Cola's all-night vigil (May 19–20, 1347) and the start of the procession to the Capitol took place under Matteo's nose. Did it, in fact, take place under his aegis?

The case is very strong. Several passages in the chronicle mention the "learned men" of Rome;[52] the Lateran exhibition was designed for them, as much as for the magnates. Cola's description and reading of the *lex* tablet in 1346 owed its legal weight to a combined knowledge of Roman law and contemporary juristic thought. Several references to Cola's "privy council" survive, though with little guide as to its composition (the *dramatis personae* are discussed in chapter 6). Cola is described, by a papal spy, as acting "on the advice of the learned men of the City";[53] his confirmation, as civic governor, of the statutes of the Lana guild, is rogated "by mandate of the Lord Tribune and his *assectamentum* [privy council]."[54] Cola's legal ordinances were almost certainly composed with the aid of his council, which was primarily composed, we may presume, of his earlier coconspirators, since such plans were unlikely to have sprung suddenly fully armed from the newly enlarged head of the People's Tribune and Liberator in May 1347.

Matteo Baccari's connection to Cola's regime as a legal adviser and political sponsor is, however, easily confirmed. In a letter (III:11) of late June 1347 Cola mentioned the four ambassadors he had despatched to the Florentine government. Naturally, the economic and cultural status of Florence required the most highly qualified diplomats.[55] "Matheus de Becchariis" was one of the four. If his speeches, which do not survive, were similar to those of the other diplomats, Francesco Baroncelli or Pandolfuccio dei Franchi, then we would be justified in adding cultural distinction to the political and economic status of this lawyer from Cola's locale. An éminence grise of Cola's revolution, Matteo survived the collapse of

---

50. B. Trifone, "Le carte del monastero di San Paolo di Roma," *ASRSP* 32 (1909): 32.

51. Subsignatory to a copy made by Giovanni di Nicola di Paolo, one of our "surviving" notaries; A.S.R. Ospedale di S. Maria della Consolazione, doc. 9.

52. Wright, *Life,* 35–36, 45.

53. IV:8, 24–25.

54. Enrico Stevenson, ed., *Statuti delle arti dei merciai e della lana di Roma* (Rome: Della Pace, 1893), 166.

55. The delegation was not successful, as chapter 4 described.

the regime with seeming impunity. He had probably abandoned Cola well before the end of 1347.

The life and career of Matteo, then, gives us an idea of the retrospective value for the political historian of the notarial and other material surviving after Cola's death (described in chap. 4) in assessing the 1347 events. It shows how Cola drew support from the spearhead of political and economic change in his period and gives us an idea of the political and social status of one such supporter. The notarial evidence, however, tends to be filled with men such as Matteo Baccari by dint of their economic activity, somewhat swamping the question of where else Cola's backers came from *across* the hierarchical social and political landscape of Trecento Rome. This is of immense importance for our understanding of how the revolution happened at all, let alone the social and economic aims expressed in the ideology of the regime; it also impacts upon the subsequent history of Roman politics.

Cola and the Roman *Popolo*

In 1346, Cola met his fellow conspirators in a church on the Aventine; scholars have homed in on the passage in which the Chronicler sketches the outline of Cola's backers:

> Roman *popolari,* discreet and good men, and also among them *cavalerotti* and men of good lineage, many discreet and rich merchants . . .[56]

The implication of this passage is clear: the conspirators were neither barons, nor of *vasso lenaijo,* "base lineage" (a term that the Chronicler used earlier to describe Cola, an innkeeper's son). There are three distinct groups: the lowest social grouping are the *popolani* and *buoni uomini;* then he ranks the dominant economic group—the *ricchi mercanti*—and then adds a smattering of the "top" social class, the *cavalerotti* (the distinction is of note, although *descreti* is used of two of the groups). The historiographical concentration on the new mercantile aristocracy, the Baccari types who surrounded Cola before his revolution, has drawn attention away from Cola's successful efforts to recruit support both further down and farther across Roman society.[57] In fact, the economic heterogeneity of

---

56. Wright, *Life,* 39; *ARC,* 111.

57. Scholars in the field have often overlooked the fact that the relatively few surviving notarial protocols of the period after 1350 are not necessarily representative of all notaries'

Cola's supporters revealed in this one chronicle sentence is all the more marked when other passages from the same source are taken into consideration. Notarial evidence does not serve to elucidate Cola's association with the illiterate plebs: his use of popular iconographic themes in pictorial media not requiring literacy (themes and color schemes that were seen later in the Florentine Ciompi revolt, for example); his rhetorical style and emphasis on public spectacle (in the Lateran exhibition of 1346, and the processions, judicial proceedings and parties of 1347); his self-styled title "consul of the poor, widows, and orphans" in 1343, and his deliberate self-identification with the mob that killed him in 1354 ("As if to say 'I am a citizen and a plebeian like you . . .'").[58] At the opposite end of the social ladder, individual barons, too, played a essential role in raising—and dropping—Cola at crucial stages, though this was more to do with self-interest and internecine feud than ideological adherence. Cola thus had natural enemies but also rather fickle friends among the Orsini. Interestingly, he moved "laterally" too, into different areas of Roman society: for example Cola worked hard and often successfully to derive support from certain ecclesiastical organizations in 1347.[59] He was to uphold more than one convent's rights against baronial intrusion (a case is noted in chapter 6); his ordinances also specified communal assistance for impoverished monasteries. The initial inclusion of the papal vicar (the bishop of Orvieto) in Cola's regime, and the participation at his coronation of a string of leading local churchmen—the bishop of Ostia's vicar, the priors of the Vatican, the Lateran, S. Maria Maggiore, S. Spirito, the deacon of S. Paolo *fuori le Mura,* and the abbot of S. Lorenzo[60]—demonstrate Cola's initial appeal to the representatives of local ecclesiastical interests. Cola had a special relationship with the wealthy S. Spirito (see chap. 6). He was evidently on sufficiently good terms with the Franciscans at the Araceli and the canons at the Lateran[61] to stage the sacro-political extravaganzas of

---

business in this period: I suggest they survive precisely because they were connected with *bovattieri* and barons' affairs. Scholars extrapolating evidence from collections such as those of Antonio dei Scambi and Nardo Venettini to create an image of the balance of economic power must proceed with caution.

58. Wright, *Life,* 149.

59. Massimo Miglio, "Gli ideali di pace e di giustizia in Roma a metà del Trecento: Gruppi sociali e azione politica nella Roma di Cola di Rienzo," in *Per la Storia del Trecento,* 55–87, mentions, although consistently underplays, Cola's ecclesiastical support.

60. IV:13, 4–5, 21–36.

61. Men increasingly drawn from mercantile and *bovattieri,* rather than baronial families, as noted previously.

1346–47. The four groups present at the feast of the ceremony of knight-hood, on August 1, 1347, were, in order, abbots, clerics, knights, mer-chants. Cola, like civic leaders elsewhere in contemporary Italy (uncom-mon in papal Rome, however), extended his judicial authority over churchmen, even executing a notorious friar of S. Alessio.[62] This action does not seem to have done him much harm: one of his clerical correspon-dents, in 1351, was the abbot of S. Alessio. By this stage, however, ecclesi-astical support was the exception, rather than the rule; after the Porta S. Lorenzo victory in November 1347, as Cola faced a cash crisis, "it became clear that he wanted to rule by force and tyranny; he began taking money from the abbeys' revenues."[63]

It is clear that while Cola's regime both relied upon, and boosted the authority of, the group in Rome that roughly corresponded to the Tuscan *popolo grasso*—the Baccari-type urban aristocrats—he also drew support from a wider cross-section of society. There is an obvious overlap between the economic interests of the Baccari types and Cola's governmental ideals. However, if Cola's regime has been seen as predominantly repre-sentative of the interests of the new *popolo* elite, it is because, as we have discussed, the notarial protocols of later Trecento Rome somewhat distort the picture. They do not give an absolutely reliable account of social trends, and their political effects, across the whole of the Roman economy. The evidence that survives is filled with the doings of the more economi-cally powerful Baccari-type individuals, and tends to be less representative of the less elevated *popolo*—the guilds, artisanal confraternities, and the military—which, nonetheless, challenged the *bovattieri* for political con-trol in the 1350s and 1360s. The evidence notaries provide generally—and perhaps particularly those notaries whose documents survived the Roman Trecento—for the reconstruction of a sociopolitical hierarchy needs to be supplemented. We must extract the information contained in the new statutes of 1363, and in the surviving documents of the militarized regime of the so-called Bandaresi (Latin *bandarenses,* "banner-holders"), the two joint leaders of the Felice Società dei Balestrieri e Pavesati (Joyous Society of Archers and Shield-Bearers). The latter group is particularly important, because the greatest boost to its political power, it will be argued here, stems precisely from 1347. Cola held the attention of barons and plebs, church officials and *bovattieri:* but he also reorganized the City's military

---

62. Wright, *Life,* 45.
63. Ibid., 91.

forces on a district-by-district basis, drawing his soldiers from a social background comparable to that of the lesser guildsmen.[64] They were never disbanded.

The power of the Bandaresi from the 1350s was not based on financial expansion within a social set, yet this was as clear a feature of latter half of the Trecento as the economic hegemony of the *bovattieri*. In the years immediately following Cola's revolution, there is evidence that the balance of power among the groups that composed the Roman *popolo* shifted around and gave a less elite group, the *minuto* equivalent, a share in political power. This is not readily noticeable in the notarial material (Gennaro's early work missed the process altogether, for example); the primarily economic evidence tends not to reflect the entrance of the less economically powerful into politics, because it had little effect on ongoing economic trends and practices both created and exploited by the agricultural and mercantile operations of the *bovattieri* and *mercanti*. In the governmental and administrative aftermath of Cola's revolt, though this does not show up in notarial documentation, the *bovattieri* and their peers may have been forced to concede that the only immediate solution to the disruptive effects of continued baronial interference was to back a local militia such as Cola had organized. Or perhaps they were forced to make political concessions to a militia that could not be disbanded, or that was, in part, controlled by the richer businessmen.[65] The *bovattieri* themselves

---

64. Hence, for example, Paolo Bussa, a *balestriero* in 1347 (Wright, *Life,* 83), from a family then starting its rise into the ranks of the *popolo grasso;* he was possibly a forefather of the Roman patron saint Francesca (ca. 1384–1440). The City had previously had a "police" force of *milites,* especially those imported under the control of Angevin vicars, although there is evidence of a municipally maintained outfit. As for continuity, in 1327 the Chronicler (*ARC,* 10) describes Sciarra Colonna's attempt to organize the *popolo:* he summoned a popular assembly, appointed *caporioni,* then *fece capo vinticinque* [*sic*], then *conestavili.* Cola was, as ever, building on a situation already familiar in late medieval Rome. But he radically upgraded the militia, specifically ordaining the equipping with a *pavese* (a long shield) and payment of a hundred foot soldiers and twenty-five cavalrymen for each of the thirteen *rioni* (Wright, *Life,* 42, 54–55). A chance reference in notarial protocols from 1365 (Mosti, *Anthonius Goioli,* 114) to the election of a new *Capud XXV* for the *contrada* (district) of Pappaçuris in Regola, by other members of the "Top 25," sheds light on the mechanics of rional representation and suggests that the constitution of the militia had changed little since Cola put his weight behind the institution.

65. This is also Maire-Vigueur's opinion ("Classe dominante," 19–21). He makes a subtle case for the political interpenetration of the *bovattieri* elite and the leading figures of the Felice Società in the 1360s, though assuming—dialectically—that the two "classes" would "naturally" be hostile to one another. He does not explore the background to the relationship between these groups, a relationship in which, I shall argue, Cola's sociopolitical alliances in 1347 played an essential role. The case is for consensus and cooperation rather than class-based political hostility and rivalry.

were not yet sufficiently politically dominant in the early 1350s to sustain and manipulate such a militia, with power still oscillating between papal legates, baronial senators, and their "own" candidates such as Cerroni in 1351 and Baroncelli in 1352 (both high-profiled "noble" supporters of Cola in 1347). This militia, therefore, enjoyed a degree of control over the City that the mercantile elite could not challenge; to the extent that the city companies, unified during the 1350s as the Felice Società dei Balestrieri e Pavesati, sometimes operated with an autonomy more typical of roving mercenary companies elsewhere in contemporary Europe.

The Felice Società was led by two Bandaresi and four deputies, drawn from the leadership of the local *rione*-based militia. Their names do not correspond with those of the *popolo grasso* entrepreneurs,[66] suggesting that the social origins of the organization's powerful leaders were distinctly "inferior" in *popolo* terms. By 1358 this militia was working sometimes apparently independently, sometimes as the "strong-arm" element in an alliance with the *popolo grasso,* the Roman civic nobility such as Baccari. By this alliance the Bandaresi and their lieutenants retained a constitutionally guaranteed role in the election of new senators, and the selection of the Seven Reformers of the Camera Urbis.[67] In return the Bandaresi ensured the conditions of peace and security vital to an economy geared primarily to the interests of the *bovattieri* and their imitators, but ultimately, in "trickle down" terms, for the benefit of the whole populace. Naturally, the Felice Società's response to baronial faction-fighting across the ruins of the City in the chaos of the 1350s was one of military standoff, while the more economically and politically powerful groups of the *popolo,* with their notaries and bureaucrats, worked toward a constitutional solution to magnate interference: the Statutes of 1363 were a obvious step in this process. Such a combination—the balance of military guarantees and economic growth, seemingly parallel to a balance in the operation of upper and lower *popolo* influence in Rome's government—had of course

---

66. Natale, "La Felice Società," presents lists of the names of the men involved; names that rarely appear throughout several thousand notarial mercantile-*grasso* documents, and which are clearly less elite: for example, among the *antepositi* (counselors) of 1374 is listed Nutius Pauli Pecudis, and for 1376, Iacobellus Pecoronis; one of the *executores*/Bandaresi of 1385 is called "Sutor," and one of his *antepositi,* Antonis Factoris; in 1391, one of the Bandaresi was Iacobellus Tutii *calsolarius;* his replacement later in the year was called Andreoctus Tuctobuono. The notaries of the Felice Società were, however, drawn from the more socially elite.

67. The mechanisms by which this influence functioned are not visible, unfortunately, beyond the frequent appearance of the Felice Società in the statutes, as one of the legitimating authorities of the City. Urban V dissolved the Bandaresi in 1368, upon his short-lived return to Rome, but they were effectively reconstituted as the "Executors of Justice" in 1370.

been attempted under Cola's regime a few years earlier; it took more time than Cola had, for this process to come to fruition. By the early 1360s, it would appear, the lessons had been learned.[68] Further shifts in this balance of power occurred with the return of the papacy, and its attempt to quash the semiautonomous activities of the Felice Società.[69] Still, as the guarantors of the circumstances under which economic and political activity could flourish, the Bandaresi retained considerable power, exercised particularly over public order, dealings with other communes, and the relationship of the City with rival papal troops after 1378.

So whose interests did Cola, ultimately, best serve? Not his own, clearly, since he died in the process. It is fair to say, along with Miglio and other social historians, that the guarantee of the Jubilee business, control of the food supply, and the anchor ruthlessly attached to the autonomy of barons, were all features of Cola's government that aided the long-term process of the rise of the entrepreneurial civic elite. But it is equally appropriate to make a claim for Cola's contribution to the establishment and

---

68. See chapter 4 for the Chronicler's attempts to highlight those lessons to the various social groups among his fellow Romans ca. 1357. Maire-Vigueur ("Classe dominante," 17) implies that the Chronicler's lists of different civic status reflects his difficulty in finding a term for Cola's backers: I suggest, on the contrary, that his groups were well defined.

69. The Statutes nonetheless show the direct influence which, by 1363, the Bandaresi were able to exercise in the administration of the City: their powers appear alongside those of the Senator and Reformers/Conservators, the senior executive Roman magistracies: note Statute III:137 (Re, *Statuti,* 272), with reference to the appointment of the magistrates of the grain supply: "We decree and ordain that all of the above official posts shall be filled by order of the Lords Conservators of the Civic Chamber *tantum salvo iure balisteriorum et pavesatorum Urbis.*" Their position was confirmed not merely through their part in the elective process, but in two other areas. First, they were written into the constitution from a financial perspective; the *Societas Executorum Iustitiae et quattuor consiliarum balestrierum et pavesatorum* (the title after 1370) had responsibility for all incoming urban dues. Gregory XI had to accept, in 1376, that the *executores iustitiae* would, *more solito,* continue to administer the "emoluments of the Civic Chamber" (Augustin Theiner, *Codex diplomaticus dominii temporalis S. Sedis. Recueil de documents pour servir à l'histoire du gouvernement temporel des États du Saint-Siège. Extraits des Archives du Vatican* [Rome: Imprimerie du Vatican, 1861–62], 2:590). Second, the influence of the less elite is evident in the tight statutory reins of 1363 on the political influence of those closest in status to the barons: namely the upper ranks of the civic aristocracy, the "knights." Even after 1368, when the Seven Reformers of 1358 were replaced by three papally appointed Conservators and the Bandaresi were temporarily disbanded, the pressure to lower the social profile of the Conservators is still there in a statutory revision, demanding a proportion of no more than one *cavalerotto* (see the role of Paolo Vaiani in chapter 6) to two *popolani* Conservators: III:25 (Re, *Statuti,* 213). After 1368 prosopographical evidence for the identity of Conservators demonstrates that the balance between knights, the representatives of *bovattieri*-mercantile families, and the *buoni* below these, became less favorable to the class from which the Bandaresi were drawn.

maintenance of the power of those of lower *popolo* rank. The continued difficult relationship of the Bandaresi and the *bovattieri,* and the shifting balance of constitutional power through the 1350s and 1360s, after Cola's death, demonstrates how tricky an alliance this really was. Cola's long-term failure to secure that alliance—that is, to bridge the gap between the upper and lower *popolo,* between the commercial entrepreneurs and the militia men, both in ideological aims and in the techniques of civic control—contributed directly to the collapse of his regime. The real turning point of Cola's career in 1347 came with an impasse caused by the friction of these two groups within the *popolo* over opposing policies toward the barons.

The critical episode was Cola's imprisonment of, and then, after their submission, his release of a number of Colonna and Orsini notables, including the young Giovanni Colonna, whom he had previously favored. The Chronicler describes Cola's obvious ambivalence,[70] and again, a careful reading of the chronicle suggests a quandary that went beyond any accusation of personal indecisiveness on Cola's part:

> Several Roman citizens *(aicuni cittadini),* thinking over the judgment which Cola wanted to carry out [i.e., executing the barons], stopped him with honeyed words. . . . This deed was most displeasing to the discreet men. People *(la iente)* said: "He has lit a flame . . . which he will not be able to put out."[71]

Cola faced the strain of holding together such disparate elements as the *aicuni cittadini* on the one hand, who persuaded him not simply to release, but to elevate various barons to bogus duchies and real civic office; and a different group, the *descreti,* on the other hand, who were then "very displeased" with the turn of events, their sentiments echoed by *la iente.* We must recall here the distinction the Chronicler makes between *Romani popolari discreti e buoni uomini,* a lower class of *popolani;* his *descreti e ricchi mercatanti,* presumably the *popolo grasso* guildsmen rising toward the noble social ranks of the *bovattieri;* and a third, specifically less numerous and clearly more established aristocratic element that the Chronicler also

---

70. In a subsequent letter to an Orsini contact in Avignon (III:40, 11–30), Cola tried to persuade his reader that he never had any real intention of executing the barons; it is unconvincing.

71. *ARC,* 141; Wright, *Life,* 76–77.

lists among Cola's conspirators of 1346: *cavalerotti e di buono legnaggio.*[72] On the occasion in 1347 of the imprisonment of the magnates (after his own knighting and thus elevation to the aristocracy), probably in late September,[73] Cola vacillated alarmingly and then did a U-turn. He thereby sacrificed the support of the *descreti,* the socially inferior and more noisily antimagnatial of his supporters, for that of a small group of only "several" *(aicuni)* citizens, arguably identifiable with the "noble" *cavalerotti.*[74] This group subsequently betrayed him: the Chronicler follows a comment on Cola's inability to pay his troops in October–November with the note that the *cavalerotti* of Rome at this point wrote to Stefano Colonna and asked him "to come with soldiers,"[75] which led to the Porta S. Lorenzo massacre. This may have been more satisfying to the popular militia, which played the most active part in the slaughter of Cola's old banqueting acquaintance, Giovanni Colonna. However, the knighting of Cola's son Lorenzo in Stefano's blood outraged not so importantly the *cavalerotti,* presumably already lost to Cola's cause, but specifically the *cavalieri* and *conestavili da cavallo* of Cola's "sacred army," who "refused to carry arms for him again." He had still been obliged to pay them in the first place, and as the heavy taxation and military demands gradually alienated the remnants of his support, the Chronicler states, "The people began to hate the Tribune."[76] The entire spectrum of Cola's support—the noble *cavalerotti,* the elite businessmen and judges, and the popular, locally generated militia, the *bona iente*—had started to disintegrate; within a very few weeks Cola was forced into abdication.[77]

His regime, however, had certainly had the effect of drawing distinctions more clearly within the new powerful social groups. The continued success of the upper class of the *popolo* is evident throughout the notarial material: but we must also credit Cola with the reinforcement and extension of the authority of the "lesser" *popolo,* the men who made up the Felice Società. His refurbishment[78] of the rional militia, in May–June

---

72. *ARC,* 111.

73. The *terminus ante quem* is Clement's complaint to Cola dated October 6: III:42.

74. See chapter 6 for an attempt to name the men who occupied these varying, even opposing, positions vis-à-vis the barons of Rome.

75. Wright, *Life,* 81.

76. Ibid.

77. Despite his return to power, in 1354, Cola never enjoyed the same range and depth of support his Tribunate had attracted.

78. As mentioned previously there were precedents in 1327 for the rional militia (see also Small, "District of Rome"; Egidi, *Intorno all'Esercito del Comune).* The connections between Cola's polity and the role of a rional militia are strengthened by the remarkable similarity of

1347, included giving the levied troops a powerful sense of their own importance. He described them as a holy army, the *sacra milizia*,[79] guarantors of Cola's new age of righteousness, conquerors of the enemies of the people of Rome (it is also reminiscent of the army in Revelation 19 led by the Rider Faithful and True). The rional cavalry actually preceded the civic magistrates in Cola's processions, and shared the watchword(s) "knights of the Holy Ghost." The archers of the 1347 militia were called *valestrieri* in both the chronicle and Cola's own correspondence.[80] By October the *cavalerotti* had deserted Cola and invited the Colonna to return; but Cola's own *cavalieri,* the mounted element of the militia, remained fervently antimagnatial (indeed, Cola played little strategic role in the riotous slaughter of the Colonna in November; the *popolo* army ran amok). Though they deserted him after the knighting of his son in blood, Cola's militia certainly continued to flourish after his exile in 1347. A later chronicle passage refers to a riot in 1350 against the Papal Legate led by armed men from one district, described as armed with various weapons, including, interestingly, *pavesi* and *valestre*.[81] There is no apparent discontinuity between this militia and the Felice Società dei Balestrieri e Pavesati of the later 1350s, which came to be notorious for its antipapal agitation well into the fifteenth century. It even retained a constitutional relationship with the organization of the thirteen *rioni* of Rome: a meeting of the city council was called in 1360 "to make new *bandarenses* and *capiregiones* (Caporioni)."[82]

Other features of Cola's regime also seem to have been continued or resurrected by the Bandaresi: Cola's "House of Justice and Peace," run in 1347 by the "most just *popolari,*" the "*buoni uomini* peacemakers,"[83] appears to survive in the role, or at least the title, of the *Gubernatores pacis et libertatis rei publice Romane,* of 1376;[84] one of them was also an "Execu-

---

Cola's "popularizing" iconography to the figure of the archangel, trampling and lancing his diabolic enemy, at the side of a long graffito engraved at the S. Sebastiano gate to mark the 1329 victory of the army of the *popolo* (and used later by the Ciompi of Florence, too). The accounts of the levy of 1327 and the organization of the army under Cola (*ARC,* 10–11, 123; Wright, *Life,* 54) are also comparable in terms of their ranks and arms.

79. *ARC,* 152.
80. E.g. *ARC,* 146; III:35, 56.
81. *ARC,* 158.
82. Natale, "La Felice Società," 125.
83. Wright, *Life,* 46.
84. Natale, "La Felice Società," 133–34. Also see Supino, *La Margarita Cornetana,* 365–66, which revels that another *gubernator* was an important notary, Nicola Porcari.

tor of Justice" or Bandarese.[85] Obviously, this description is in Latin, in accordance with notarial practice, but another area of continuity between Cola (and the Chronicler) and the regime of the Bandaresi was the persistent ideological adherence to the *volgare* in public contexts, explicitly to communicate with a broader populace: the majority of the surviving documents of the Felice Società are not in Latin.[86]

Another possible point of contact between Cola, the militia, and the Statutes of 1363, otherwise remarkable for an absence of reference to spiritual and ecclesiastical matters, is that an annual mass, dedicated to the Holy Spirit, was written into the new codification. After Cola's regime any reference to the authority of the Holy Spirit combined with "real" Roman power must have invoked the memory of Cola's bypassing papal authority. In fact the Felice Società were to became notorious in their hostility to papal pressure. The balance of the relative influence of the two *popolo* groups shifted in 1363, with the completion of the Statutes, and again in 1368 with the interference of the pope and the substitution of the three Conservators for the Senator and Reformers of 1358. The papal factor was crucial: generally speaking, Bandaresi and *bovattieri* views on the desirability of the papal presence were poles apart, as were their techniques for reducing magnatial influence. The Bandaresi militantly opposed any compromise of urban political autonomy with the returning pope; the latter were more interested in economic priorities, particularly the accommodation of the valuable curial market.

Again we see the continuity of the economic and political situation addressed by Cola's measures into the next twenty years and beyond. Certainly a direct relationship between the policies of Cola's regime and the statutes of 1363 may be hypothesized. Cola's early reform measures were designed to address the issues of food supply, peace, the exercise of justice, and military security. The food supply and peace were relevant to the long-term position of the *bovattieri,* the *popolo grasso* types; justice and security,

---

85. In 1380 the notary Francesco di Stefano Capogalli recorded the election "of those to sit on the tribunal on the podium before the House of the Lovers of Peace and Justice" (Renzo Mosti, *Un notaio Romano del '300. I Protocolli di Francesco di Stefano de Caputgallis (1374–1386)* [Rome: École Française, 1994], 270) though no such organization appears in the 1363 Statutes.

86. Though also like Cola, if and when required, the Bandaresi could speak the language of humanist scholars: ergo the Vergilian flourishes of one diplomatic communiqué—in Latin—to Florence in 1362, describing the historic role of the Roman People, "cui est parcere subjectis et debellare superbos": a rather clichéd tag, but revealing (Natale, "La Felice Società," 125).

however, were issues more relevant to the progenitors of the Felice Società. Both these streams of influence, and a working compromise, may be detected in the Statutes of 1363. If a particular wariness of the *cavalerotti,* the reference to the Holy Spirit, and the constitutional absence of the papacy, all smack of the influence of a *popolo minuto* pressure group, nonetheless there is little reference to the militia per se; on the other hand, considerable emphasis is given to the mechanics of administration and the civil judicial concerns of the Baccari types, the *popolo grasso.* However, the central correspondence between Cola's political measures and those of the Statutes of 1363 lies in the fundamentally antimagnatial polity each attempted to establish. Cola failed, in the short term, to impose his reforms; but the impetus was not lost. Four years after his death, the socially inferior section of his *popolo* supporters still maintained a civic force with political clout, independent of baronial or *grasso* patronage; five years after that, the more socially elite and economically dominant of Cola's original partisans codified a new political order that excluded barons for ever.

This, then, was the essential contribution of Cola's regime to the antimagnatial Statutes of 1363 and to the subsequent history of the City: his preliminary moves toward the curtailment of the power of the barons, while also incorporating them within a new polity; simultaneously Cola was responsible for unleashing a militant popular backlash that probably went somewhat beyond his control and was to cause the deaths of dozens of young barons connected to the Colonna family in November 1347. This effectively cleared the decks, removing a proportion of the next generation of barons and thus considerably lowering local magnate resistance to the inevitable process of their exclusion from social and economic dominance.

There are also more subtle features of Cola's *Buono Stato* that may be seen to go on influencing the municipal administration of Rome: here we will examine the continuity of Cola's administrative measures, the "Ordinances of the Good State," into the City's statutes of 1363 (which were not in turn drastically altered until the 1440s). Cola's *Ordinamenti dello Buono Stato* ran as follows in the account of the Chronicler:[87]

1. Those who kill were to receive death.
2. Lawsuits were to be concluded within fifteen days.

---

87. Wright, *Life,* 42–43.

3. The houses of convicted criminals were not to be destroyed, but placed in the hands of the commune.
4. A militia of twenty-five horse and a hundred infantry was to be established in each of the thirteen *rioni.*
5. The commune was to assist widows and orphans.
6. A coast guard boat was to patrol the mouth of the Tiber to protect merchant shipping.
7. All income from hearth taxation, salt gabelles (i.e., the right to collect taxes from salt imports), punitive fines and gate tolls was to go to the *Buono Stato.*
8. The Rector of the People, not a baron, was to control access routes to the city.
9. No noble fortresses were to be permitted.
10. Barons were to ensure roads to the City were safe, or receive a fine of a thousand marks.
11. Monasteries were to receive financial aid from the commune.
12. Each *rione* was to have a granary, to ensure the food supply.
13. The families of soldiers killed were to be compensated.
14. The Roman People were to have authority over all *Destretto* towns.
15. False accusations were to attract the penalty of the accused's crime.

These fifteen ordinances, as reported, were not of themselves the basis of a constitution: indeed we must question the reliability of the Chronicler in the light of possible retrospective contamination of his account from his time of writing, 1357–58, which saw a period of constitutional reform prior to the codification in 1363. The list in question is not confirmed by any nearer contemporary source: moreover, it is obviously disorganized (different administrative categories overlap), and by the Chronicler's own admission, not complete: "Many other things were written in this document." We may suggest, instead, that the Chronicler is here summarizing a set of reforms gradually introduced during the early weeks of the Tribunate: reforms to a preexisting order. As noted (in chap. 4), there is evidence of a body of statutes predating the 1363 redaction. Those may not have had the clarity and exhaustive nature of the five hundred ordinances of 1363 but must surely have been more comprehensive than Cola's package of measures. Cola's measures were not designed to replace, but to supplement, the status quo, where that was unsatisfactory. Nonetheless continuity into the complex measures of 1363 may be posited in a whole range of examples. Cola's first ordinance, for example, clarifies what may have been an ambiguity, cutting through the corruption and influence in the system that he had criticised so vehemently in the months before the revolution. The Statutes of 1363 would seem to echo this need for clarity around the issue of unlawful killing, with a division of the crime of murder into "homicide" and "assassination" (Statutes II:8, II:9). The second ordinance, on the conclusion of lawsuits within fifteen days, says nothing about the structure or function of the judicial system, merely about its inefficiency; this strengthens the contention that Cola's ordinances were complementary, or supplementary. By the mid–fourteenth century, the process had become so expensive, lengthy, and unreliable that notaries had invented a new formula. When presenting cases for small institutions or individuals, they requested an accelerated trial on the grounds of poverty.[88] The Statutes of 1363 did not limit the time of the process itself, but many other circumscriptions are introduced, including a "statute of limitations" (II:105) on accusations.[89]

Moreover, Cola's legislation and social measures did not stop with the issuing of the fifteen ordinances. There are several other areas in which policy promoted by Cola made its way into the 1363 redaction. One may compare the intense criticism, and the punishments handed out for bribery and falsification by Cola,[90] to the long stream of prohibitions on forms of corruption in 1363, though this might be considered a feature common to most statute books. On a more precise note, Cola's attack on the conspiracy of the barons "against the Tribune and the Good Estate"[91] is echoed very nearly by II:167, "Concerning those who conspire against the good state of the City." Other specifically antimagnatial gestures, in addition to those of Cola's ordinances, also seem to have lasted into 1363: one of

---

88. Cola as notary does so himself: the case of the nuns of S. Cosimato is described in chapter 6.

89. In another crucial area of civic administration, certain statutes echo Cola's provisions regarding the grain supply (II:124–25: Re, *Statuti*, 154). They do not express a need for rional granaries; Cola had had these constructed already, according to his ordinance 12 (the Vicolo dei Granai in Parione with its two-story medieval houses dates from this period). Other approximate correspondences also exist in the case of Ordinance 3 and Statute II:16, II:81 (Re, *Statuti*, 94, 130–32); 5, and I:122 (Re, *Statuti*, 152); ordinance 6, and II.118 (Re, *Statuti*, 150); ordinance 8–9, and II.66 (Re, *Statuti*, 117); ordinance 10, and II:68 (Re, *Statuti*, 119–21); ordinance 13, and I:117 (Re, *Statuti*, 149); ordinance 14, and III:73 and II:114 (Re, *Statuti*, 238, 148); ordinance 15, and II:33, III:68–72, and III:99–100 (Re, *Statuti*, 104, 236–37, 252). See also Seibt, *Anonimo Romano*, 96–98, for an account of connections between the Chronicler's list of Cola's measures and the 1363 codification.

90. Wright, *Life*, 50 (*ARC*, 120), on Tortora; the cases of Poncelletto and Tommasso Fortifioccha appear in chapter 6.

91. Wright, *Life*, 44.

Cola's letters of July 1347 outlines a series of new security and administrative measures, including an attack on feudal vassalage, and a ban on the depiction of baronial arms on partisans' houses.[92] This is practically identical to Statute II:150, which criminalizes oaths of vassalage given by a citizen to the inhabitant of a *roccha* or *castrum*, and warns factions not to *despingere arma* on their houses.[93] Oaths to the *bonum statum* by civic magistrates were already a statutory requirement before 1363 but now also had to be made by magnates and *cavalerotti* (III:110); just as Cola had demanded in 1347.

Like most new revolutionary governments, Cola introduced new weights and measures, to stabilize exchange mechanisms;[94] if the Chronicler can be believed, he was successful in preventing traders from swindling customers: "Each guild simply told the truth."[95] Similar reforms were introduced by the regime of the Felice Società after 1358; their arms appear on the side of a classical funerary urn (now in the courtyard of the Museo dei Conservatori) that was given a more prosaic function under their regime as a unit of grain measurement. Trading standards, of course, appear throughout the second book of the Statutes of 1363.

Certain social mores, and the disapproval thereof, connect Cola and the compilers of the statutes. Cola banned the playing of dice and punished blasphemers;[96] both were prohibited in 1363 at II:69 and II:102 respectively.[97] At a council meeting in 1346, following his complaints about their administration, Cola was slapped by the chamberlain and insulted with an obscene gesture from a senatorial scribe. Comparable acts of public infamy are to be fined according to the statutes at II:52 ("On making the

---

92. III:15, 44; except for the arms of the commune, or the pope, as Cola assured Clement.

93. Cola also banned the use of those partisan terms *Guelf* and *Ghibelline* (III:35, 35); this ban does not appear in the 1363 Statutes, but does, in the *(volgare)* statutes applied across the patrimony and Roman *Destretto* by the Papal Legate Albornoz in the 1350s and early 1360s; see Paolo Colliva, *Il Cardinale Albornoz, lo stato della chiesa, le Constitutiones Aegidiane (1353–57)* (Bologna: Publicaciones del Real Colegio de España, 1977). On Albornoz, see Mercurino Antonelli, "La dominazione pontificia nel Patrimonio negli ultimi venti anni del periodo Avignonese," *ASRSP* 30 (1907): 269–332; *ASRSP* 31 (1908): 121–68, 315–55; "Il Cardinal Albornoz e il governo di Roma nel 1354," *ASRSP* 39 (1916): 587–601. The Chronicler, writing in the late 1350s (*ARC,* 14), describes the terms as *quelle maladette parte.* Cola, writing from Prague after the end of his regime, somewhat hypocritically used the term Ghibelline when writing the Florentines to reassure them that their interests would not be harmed by his new proimperial position (III:52, 53).

94. III:15; see also Mosti, *Johannes Nicolai Pauli,* 34.

95. Wright, *Life,* 68.

96. III:18, 13–15.

97. Re, *Statuti,* 113–14, 143.

gesture of the fig"), and II:53 ("On slapping with the palm of the hand").[98] The last grand artistic gesture of Cola's Tribunate was the depiction of an armed angel in the piazza of the Castel S. Angelo,[99] but after his abdication this was contemptuously splattered in mud; interestingly, Statute II:154 introduces a severe fine for the "vituperation" or destruction of public *armaturae et picturae*.[100] More historically minded, the civic pride, and an awareness of the classical heritage, demonstrated by Statute II:191, "Concerning the nondestruction of ancient edifices," echoes Cola's own antiquarian pursuits and his attempt to remind the population of the City of the glories of its classical past.

The statutes, finally, show an enormous interest in the magistracies of the commune, and their function. Even the particulars of the dress code of various officials, addressed in III:1, recall immediately the extraordinary level of interest displayed by the Chronicler in the outfits on show during Cola's official engagements. Particular constitutional attention is given, however, to a small number of offices, and of those, obviously, the key position in the commune was occupied by the newly *unicus* Senator: precisely the sort of one-man role played by Cola in 1347, and the stand-alone title he was actually awarded in 1354. Nevertheless, there was a wariness and circumscription of the statute's description of the sole Senator's duties and rewards (II:208, 209; III:1): under no circumstances was he to seek from the people what the statute describes as *liberam arbitriam seu gratiam*. Presumably the compilers remembered recent disastrous precedents and experiments:

> The people have granted us [Cola] full and free authority to reform the peaceful state of the said City and the whole Roman province, and has granted this full jurisdiction in its public and most solemn meeting.[101]

However, there was certainly one of Cola's "senatorial" impositions with which the compilers appear to have agreed heartily. Cola decided to make the "official" Senators of 1347 pay a sum of a hundred florins each, in a

---

98. Ibid., 111–12. Admittedly the statutes ban "making the fig," whereas Tommaso Fortifioccha "made the tail" at Cola (Wright, *Life,* 33).

99. Wright, *Life,* 125.

100. Re, *Statuti,* 172.

101. Burdach III:7, 104; also III:27, 24. Cola's personal powers were not addressed in the fifteen ordinances recorded by the Chronicler; these were constructed around more complicated and long-standing Roman legal traditions (see chap. 1).

scheme to finance the restoration of the Capitoline palace.[102] In the last lines of the long statute (III:1) on the duties and salary of the Senator, in 1363, exactly the same requirement is laid down.

Finally, and curiously, the office that occupied the most space in the statutes seems to have been that of the Notary of the Camera Urbis. His oath, salary, incorruptibility, and extensive financial duties and responsibility are all given an extremely detailed and thorough examination; not a fraction of this attention is paid to the Senator's protonotary, or to the *camerarius* himself. Cola occupied this very post in 1344–47: "He said that his office was so noble that his pen ought to be of silver."[103] Could it be that an extraordinary emphasis on, and circumscription of, this magistracy, in 1363, may reflect a perceived potential for its "abuse" and for "tyranny," after its occupation by Cola di Rienzo? Certainly its profile, at the very heart of the communal administration of the City of Rome, had been raised for ever.

To conclude: Cola's regime depended on a broad range of support. The circuses of his performance-driven public spectacles were complemented by the bread that his regime ensured arrived in the mouths of the poor; he improved relations with grain-funneling towns on the Lazio coast and built local storage facilities inside the City. Those who provided the most, in terms of individual and material support, were also those who stood to gain the most: the entrepreneurial elite, the *popolo grasso*. Yet Cola also used the same iconography found elsewhere in *popolo minuto* manifestations, manipulating antipapal sentiment and stressing the *volgare* aspects of his regime; he instituted administrative and military reforms that have a direct connection to the later power of the Bandaresi. The input Cola had into the constitutional reform of Roman urban government may still be traced in the 1363 law code, itself a product of the combined influence of Bandaresi and *bovattieri*. Fifteen years after Cola's regime this was still no easy alliance. Back in 1347 it had collapsed under the strain of Cola's refusal to slaughter barons en masse (the "people" and its militia took matters into their own hands at the Porta S. Lorenzo in November). It was an alliance, nonetheless, that continued to be crucial in the decades following Cola's revolution: and after his revolution, it was that much easier, since Cola had effectively both legislated, at the *grasso* end, and militated,

---

102. Wright, *Life,* 54.
103. Ibid., 35.

with the *minuto* army, against his baronial enemies. It is a tribute to Cola's skill at political maneuvering that the "alliance" against the barons worked for as long as it did. His broad popular appeal may be seen as a product of plebeian social origins skillfully exploited and combined with *popolo grasso*–style education and notarial training; this will be investigated in the next chapter. His attempt to harness the different elements of society into a new, "popular" regime was, in the long run, the foundation of the successful antimagnatial Roman regime of the 1360s. Had the papacy never returned to Rome from Avignon, then perhaps Cola would have been remembered rather differently: this is a piece of useless speculation, of course. Yet hopefully the new evidence and analysis presented here will ensure that Cola's legacy is remembered and presented rather differently in the future.

Chapter 6

Ut per oblivionem veritas non mutetur: The Professionals, Politicians, and Prosopography of Trecento Rome

In vastly generalizing language the social history of fourteenth-century Italy may be characterized as the maturing of the economic assertion of the urban *popolo;* in cultural terms, it was the period of evolution of the political culture of civic humanism. One powerful factor that linked these tectonic shifts was the rising importance of notaries, keepers of "the truth, so that it is not altered by being forgotten." Notaries played a considerable role in the formation of urban identity in the later medieval period. Indeed, their social fluidity, wealth generation, technical and professional training, but also their cultural interests, especially in the Roman past, could be said to have made the notary the ideal citizen of the Trecento city. For Rome, however, despite what I will argue was the particular importance of its notarial class, the cultural importance of the group is rarely discussed by scholars. No one, moreover, has properly explicated Cola's participation, as a notary, in this process; how his occupation connected him to a political culture and a political process flourishing both within and far beyond the City of Rome.

Trecento notaries became politicians, chroniclers, scholars, poets, or all or any of these: men such as Dino Compagni, Salimbene de'Adam, Francesco da Barberino, and Coluccio Salutati;[1] Petrarch's father was a notary, and he himself was pushed in that direction as a youngster. Late

---

1. See *Il Notaio nella civiltà Fiorentina: secoli XIII–XVI. Biblioteca Medicea Laurenziana, Firenze 1984. Atti del XVII Congresso Internazionale del Notariato Latino* (Florence: Vallecchi 1984), esp. 40–48; see 122 for a notary translating Boethius, Cola's hero; 219–22 on one notary's interest in astrology (Jacks, *Antiquarian and Myth,* 59–60, offers a somewhat overstated account of Cola's similar interests).

medieval Rome was typical: the City's two most valuable late-fourteenth-and fifteenth-century chronicle sources (besides that of the Chronicler of Cola's career) were composed by notaries. Some of Paolo di Lello Petroni's protocols survive; he also wrote the chronicle *La Mesticanza*, spanning circa 1388–1447.[2] Stefano Infessura, the Roman Pepys, whose sometimes gossipy "diary" spans the latter half of the fifteenth century, was also a *scribasenatus* or senatorial scribe, and very likely a trained notary.[3] Nicolò Signorili (died 1427), humanist scholar and author of one of the earliest Renaissance antiquarian works, the *Descriptio Urbis Romae eiusque excellentiae* (once in fact thought to have been the work of Cola di Rienzo), was also a central government *scribasenatus,* a local Monti *caporioni,* and secretary of the influential Confraternity of the Savior. These men were the heirs of the notarial culture of fourteenth-century Rome, and clearly passionate about preserving the words and deeds of the past, as the Statutes of 1363 demanded.[4]

The problem in the case of Rome is that while there is ample evidence of notarial participation in economic and political affairs, our sources for the City's cultural life in the mid-Trecento period (see chap. 1) are extremely limited. Cola was not, however, the only notary of this generation with humanist connections. Another powerful mid-Trecento notary, Francesco di Pietro ("Cecco") Rosani, appears in a large proportion of the surviving documentary sources consulted for this study: the merchants' guild records, for example, reveal that he was notary of the Camera Urbis (i.e., Cola's post ca. 1345–47) in 1359 and 1367.[5] He appears in a document of Cola's regime as a protonotary, already occupying a senior position within the administration Cola headed.[6] The necrologies of the Confraternity of the Savior show that he was one of its rectors, in or after 1367; a little-known inscription in the Lateran Hospital (see below) informs us he was already one of the two guardians nearly twenty years earlier, in 1348.[7] Cecco was one of the seventeen men who drew up the Statutes of 1363; one of the Seven Reformers of 1365, and one of the three Conservators of 1370. But he was also friend of Coluccio Salutati, humanist, notary, and

2. *La Mesticanza di Paolo di Lello Petrone (c. 1388–c.1447),* ed. F. Isoldi in *R.I.S.,* 2d ed., vol. 24, pt. 2 (Città di Castello, 1912).

3. *Diario di Stefano Infessura,* ed. Oreste Tommassini, Fonti per la Storia d'Italia 5 (Rome: Istituto Storico Italiano, 1890).

4. "Notarius scribat, ut per oblivionem veritas non mutetur" (I:113; Re, *Statuti,* 74–75).

5. Gatti, *Statuti dei Mercanti,* 87, 97.

6. Stevenson, *Statuti delle arti,* 166.

7. The full significance of this inscription is explicated below.

chancellor of Florence, whose correspondence reveals that while he was living in Rome (1368–70), Cecco Rosani lent him a copy of Seneca's tragedies.[8]

Notaries constituted an important element of the cultured elite, but the *publica fides* with which the notary was invested also lent itself to a personal authority that could be wielded across all of society. An engaging witness to the received image of the authority of the notary is the Sassetta painting of the bargain driven by St. Francis with the wolf of Gubbio (fig. 5). The seated, writing figure, rendering the stuff of miracles into a legally binding agreement, is, of course, a notary; he signifies the triumph of civic authority over the wicked beasts of the wilderness beyond the walls. Wolves were a real problem in Rome as well as a common allegory:[9] Cola, among others (including Petrarch), used the image of the wolf to represent baronial intrusions into "the common good" of Rome from their strongholds in the *Destretto*. The Italian municipal notary, as repository and representative of the statutory authority of the city and its antimagnatial polity, could be readily depicted as the natural enemy of the lawless "suburban" tyrant, the baron (though barons were also the successful notary's best customers).

The notary's individual jurisdiction was, nevertheless, circumscribed by those same statutory regulations, and by the statutes of the notarial guild itself. In this context, however, the position of the Roman notary, compared to his peers in other cities, was exceptional. The historic absence of a clear *popolo* mandate until the fourteenth century, owing to the papal presence (among other factors already discussed), meant that the municipal bureaucracy of Trecento Rome was less advanced, in terms of the exercise of authority and self-regulation, than in communes to the north. It was, put simply, more difficult on the streets of Rome than elsewhere to know who possessed legal authority. This, paradoxically, enhanced the position of the Roman notary, in local quotidian society, as a sort of mobile, semiautonomous repository and distributor of legally binding social and economic contracts (some within more elevated socially circles than others). It may also explain why, in a period that saw overall demographic shrinkage,[10] my prosopographical research nonetheless revealed

---

8. Noted in chapter 1, from Eugenio Dupré-Théseider, *Roma dal Commune di Popolo alla Signoria Pontificia (1252–1377)*, Storia di Roma, vol. 11 (Bologna: Cappelli, 1952), 669, 702.

9. Hence the 1363 statute rewarding the killing of a wolf: II:147 (Re, *Statuti*, 170).

10. Described in the notes to chapter 5.

Fig. 5. Sassetta, *St. Francis and the Wolf of Gubbio* (1437/44)

the names of over a thousand notaries, living and working between circa 1300 and 1400. At the same time, there was less circumscription in Rome—in comparison to the rigid "checks and balances" of the Florentine constitution, for instance[11]—of the jurisdiction of the individual notary. The result of these two factors was that the *publica fides* of a Roman notary was particularly meaningful: in the absence of tight regulation and other local sources of legitimate authority, their status and power was, logically, higher in Rome than elsewhere.

The social and political opportunities available to the Roman notary were considerable. Once again, of course, it is the direct and indirect evidence provided by the work of the notaries themselves that provides the clearest examples of the process under way. Cola, as a young notary, enjoyed all the advantages and bore all the responsibilities of the notaries described here; this is the context in which his own activities must be set. At the same time, one may also argue that his own career set new parameters for the ambitions and the status of the notary, particularly the notary of relatively low social origins, after 1350.

Notaries within Roman Society

The high profile of notaries within the "public spaces" of the City gave them the opportunity to influence local politics—including fomenting discontent—in the course of their daily work. In terms of individual social origins, notaries were generally representative of the *popolo* as a whole—that is, of the *popolo minuto* in addition to the *popolo grasso*. We have noted the tendency, among the seventeen Trecento notaries whose professional documents survive, toward the representation of the business/family interests of the upper range of *popolani;* a factor that probably helps explain the survival of these few notaries' work. Several possessed names ending in the elite patronymic form: *de Scambiis, de Astallis, de Caputgallis, de Venectinis.*[12] There are, of course, many cases with which these men

---

11. See esp. John M. Najemy, *Corporatism and Consensus in Florentine Electoral Politics, 1280–1400* (Chapel Hill: University of North Carolina Press, 1982).

12. Not all sources used the form consistently, however. Paolo Serromani was less than generous in his use of the patronymic form in his 1348–55 protocols; he referred to "Tucius Baccari" (Matteo's brother) in 1348 (A.C./I 649 1/1348, 4v), whereas in 1363 Antonio dei Scambi mentioned the widow of Tucio "de Baccariis" (B.A.V. S.A.P. 1/1363, 64r). Perhaps Cola's revolution had led to a hike in the notary's status: the younger Paolo's protocols, from 1359, use patronymic forms more frequently; and he calls himself Paolo de Serromanis (Lori-Sanfilippo, "I protocolli notarili romani," 114–16).

dealt, involving artisans, fishermen, and other affairs far from the business interests of the elite, such as the *briga* cases: street brawls, resolved by the combatants' performance of highly theatrical, usually *volgare* symbolic orchestrations; a secular penance of sorts.[13] The less dramatic but more frequent arbitration cases still offered the public the spectacle of notarial justice literally on the street, sometimes issued from a (possibly purpose-built) *podium* or tribunal.

The notarial guild was indeed a broad church; at the opposite end of the social scale, barons knew well the importance of drawing up legally binding contracts. In January 1372, the prefect Francesco di Vico came to Rome to invest new notaries;[14] but, more importantly, to have notarized the renewal of his betrothal to Perna Orsini, sister of the knight and baron Francesco di Giordano Orsini of Monte Giordano.[15] Interestingly the *Chronicon Estense* for December 1347, as noted in chapter 5, reveals that this alliance was first mooted during Cola's regime in one of his attempts at compromise with the barons.[16] As a guarantee for her dowry of thirty-five hundred florins (NB: the initial budget of Cola's entire revolution was four thousand), Francesco now offered the fortified *castrum* of Breda, near Vetralla, south of Viterbo. Antonio dei Scambi's social contacts, it is evident, reached to the very top of Roman society; but the list of witnesses to the act of betrothal is even more revealing. It includes a fascinating, entire whole cross-section of society in the *rione* S. Angelo, all gathered together: Orsini *magnifici viri;* Ylperini *nobiles viri;* the son of the previous chancellor of Rome, Angelo Malabranca; a Bussa, that is, the *popolano* family connected (through S. Francesca Romana) with those other *pescivendoli,* the Ponziani;[17] and, last and most definitely least, Cecco, alias "Capanna," the innkeeper.[18]

Capanna, in fact, appears as a witness to a number of his neighbor Antonio dei Scambi's acts. His inn was at a good location for local busi-

---

13. See e.g. Mosti, *Johannes Nicolai Pauli,* 258, 261, 266.

14. B.A.V. S.A.P. 7/1372, 17r–21v. Notarial authority had to be rubber-stamped by representatives of the emperor, the pope, or the Prefect; this, while adding little to their real powers, offered the cultural *imprimatur* of Roman antiquity.

15. B.A.V. S.A.P. 7/1372, 12v–16v.

16. Bertoni and Vicini, *Chronicon Estense,* 157–58.

17. Paolo Bussa was one of the men of Cola's militia (see chap. 5).

18. Another example of mobility is found at A.C./I 649 1/12 1383, 68r: the daughter of the self-made *bovattiere* Lello Maddaleno (see chap. 5) married an Arcione notary; as honorary guests, the Orsini headed the list of witnesses. Another daughter was married into the noble Cerroni family. Both received a dowry of five hundred florins (A.C./I 649 1/13 1389, 45r–47r), the highest of any *bovattiere* noted in this research.

ness: in 1368, the canons of S. Angelo rented him a towered house *ubi sit taberna,* right below the cardinal's house next door to the church.[19] It must have been the local "bar" of the Baccari, Nucio Gibelli, and the fish merchants of the piazza below the Portico. The rent "while the pope and his retinue reside in the City" was twenty florins, fifteen florins otherwise. Innkeeping was a lucrative business, but as an occupation it had a very bad press[20] and, socially, a low status. Notaries—except for the notary of the guild of taverners—were banned from entering inns by their own guild statutes.[21] Still, as this particular case demonstrates, innkeepers were not banned from the company of notaries. Indeed, one innkeeper's son from the neighboring *rione* Regola, therefore originally "of base lineage," became a notary and went on to have a spectacular social and political career: Cola himself.

While it seems unlikely that Antonio dei Scambi used this opportunity to introduce the innkeeper to the signore of Viterbo, nonetheless it offers an interesting paradigm of the notarial process as a social interface and of the notary's own social contacts as extraordinarily wide-ranging. It recalls Cola's political ability to hold together, albeit temporarily, a support group of lesser and greater *popolani,* as well as his capacity for attracting the support of large crowds, big institutions, and individual barons. The betrothal case also conjures up the presence of a popular audience outside the Portico of Octavia—the starting post of Cola's own revolution—attracted by the baronial entourage, and participating, certainly on the part of the local innkeeper, in the transaction of business that had public and political as well as private and economic ramifications, for city as well as *contado.*

Notaries in Economic Life

In a large number of cases notaries inherited their occupation (along with records and custom) from their fathers, or other close male relatives.[22]

---

19. B.A.V. S.A.P. 4/1368, 35r

20. One visitor's scathing opinion of Roman innkeepers is quoted in chapter 4. The hotel trade, however, did very well, from the 1350 Jubilee onward (there are no earlier records). One particularly impressive establishment on the Campo de' Fiori, the Albergo della Corona, was worth 1,440 florins in 1426; its rent was 144 ducats per year (Maire-Vigueur and Broise, "Strutture familiari," 108).

21. A.C. Credenza IV/88, ch. 46.

22. The Scriniarii family (*scrinarius* was an old-fashioned, late-antique alternative term for *notarius*) were one of dozens of cases: Pietro Scriniarii, his son Giovanni, and his son Pietro all appear in the sources consulted here. See also the Vecchi clan described below.

Their immediate families, however, as well as the extended kin group, display a range of different occupational and economic interests. Maire-Vigueur cites an example of a notary investing in a *societas taverne* (notwithstanding the ban mentioned above).[23] A Pantaleone in 1372 was not the only fishmonger's son to become a notary; the Ponziani and Sisti families share the distinction. In 1377 Antonio dei Scambi mentions a notary not simply acting as legal adviser to his *consorteria,* but trading as a fish merchant in his own (family) right; he was thus a major businessman by medieval Roman standards, not far below the *bovattieri* in status.[24] Another interesting example of a notary exploiting economic advantage with the rest of the *popolo* was Matteo dei Baccari's purchase of 50 percent of a Savelli property agglomeration in the Velabro and outside the City, a case mentioned in chapter 5. Meanwhile another notary, Omodeolo dei Buccabelli, and a partner had just bought the other half of this baronial estate for eight hundred florins.[25]

A later Trecento case powerfully illustrates the involvement of notaries at the highest levels of Roman politics and economics, and the overlap of these areas of operation, again showing Cola as not atypical in his career.[26] In 1390 the governing Conservators awarded a salt gabelle in favor of the Hospital of S. Spirito, one of the richest and most powerful ecclesiastical institutions of medieval Rome (Cola had made identical concessions to this institution). The document is rogated by their official notary, Nardo Venettini, one of the most important notaries of the period.[27] It is addressed to the magistrates of the Camera Urbis, the "customs officials" of the ports and gates of the City, the consuls of the millers' guild, the Felice Società and its officials, the *Magistri Edificorum* and their officials, and "anyone else" whom they, the Conservators, feel should know, that from now on the Hospital is exempt from the payment of customs dues. "Anyone else" is then defined as the *emptores gabelle:* thirty-

---

23. Maire-Vigueur, "Classe dominante," 12 n. 40: B.A.V. S.A.P. 8/1374, 72r–v.

24. Isa Lori-Sanfilippo, "Per la storia dell'arti a Roma; da una ricerca sui protocolli notarili. I: L'*Ars Pescivendulorum* nella seconda metà del XIV secolo," *ASRSP* 115 (1992): 110–12.

25. B.A.V. S.A.P. 4/1368, 71r–80r.

26. S. Malatesta, *Statuti delle gabelli di Roma* (Rome: Della Pace, 1886), 129–34; January 10, 1390, from Archivio S. Spirito, cass. III, no. 73. Parchment copy at A.S.R. S. Spirito, collection B, box 62, doc. 192.

27. His tombstone, interestingly, with a summary of his political career—almost as impressive as Cola's—may be found on the outside wall of the church of S. Francesca Romana, on the edge of the Roman Forum (see also Lori-Sanfilippo, "Il protocolli notarili," 138).

four named individuals who were not magistrates of the commune, but entrepreneurial monopolists holding the government concession. Among these we find only one so-called merchant, but eight guild officials, the two *Magistri Edificorum,* four officers of the Camera Urbis including its notary, and no fewer than nine other notaries, including Antonio dei Scambi, four of whom are given their current official governmental titles; this variant on insider trading was clearly the norm. The men who managed the commune were, to a large extent, notaries by training; they also participated in its economy, both on their own behalf as *popolani* investors, and on behalf of their *popolani* peers and families.

Notaries and Trecento Politics

As I have sought to emphasize, the greater proportion of that notarial evidence which survives comes from the protocols of an "upper class" of notaries; men who were personally involved either in the administration of Trecento Rome, or of its richest and most powerful organizations: Giovanni di Nicola di Paolo, Paolo dei Serromani, Antonio dei Scambi, and Nardo Venettini all enjoyed top-flight political careers. Our "survivors," therefore, tend either to have come from, or ended up within, the elite core of the *popolo.* Yet the majority of Roman notaries, according to statistical evidence (from my research across the spectrum of documentary evidence, as described in chapter 4) fall into a humbler political-economic band. It is not possible to draw absolute lines of demarcation, but an examination of bequests and dowries reveals, for instance, bequests of twenty-two florins (rather than in the hundreds);[28] the infrequent participation in government of the majority of notaries;[29] and an absence of titles or patronymic name forms.[30] Not even every one of our "survivors" had elite contacts: Marino di Pietro Milçonis's clients in 1357 were almost exclusively small traders—builders, butchers—each operating on a small capital base; neither artisans, nor rich merchants, but lesser guildsmen, *popolo minuto* types. This definition would seem to be appropriate for Marino himself; the Statutes of 1363 on notarial charges[31] permit scholars to calculate a

---

28. E.g. in the will of the notary Francesco di Pucio, at B.A.V. S.A.P. 1/1363, 62r.

29. According to the information in Salimei, *Senatori e Statuti.*

30. Fewer than 40 of the 350 whose names appear more than once in my archival research were given (and not always consistently, then) the patronymic form; an index, arguably, of the aspirant "noble" who claims *bovattieri*-style social status.

31. Notaries acting in private matters, at I:113; employed by the commune in various magistracies, in III:20, 42, 44, 46 (Re, *Statuti,* 74–75, 97–98, 107, 108).

notary's rough income on the basis of the value of the work each turned over. On the other hand, as over, there is a clear discontinuity between the list of names of the Bandaresi of the nonelite Felice Società, and their notarial employees and "councilors."

My archival research turned up the names over a thousand named notaries who lived between 1300 and 1400. From these I compiled a database of the 350 notaries better known and/or more active professionally (using, as a rough criterion, the appearance of their names in more than one archive's documents). It is, of course, no coincidence that a higher proportion of these 350 names correspond to the names of notaries involved in the exercise of civic authority in the fourteenth century than of the thousand names I found overall. And the broader the evidentiary range is established—that is, the more sources in which the name "had to appear" to fall within a given set—the more cases emerge where that notary was upwardly mobile, within the office-holding political elite.[32] Most of the more powerful notaries of fourteenth-century Rome appear in this narrower list. There is a generally clear correspondence between the distinction of the notary's career, and his appearance in a wide range of the sources, though the chance nature of documentary survival means that this is by no means a universal rule. It could be argued that the most politically active individual notaries would be the least likely to leave large amounts of written notarial business: only one document rogated by Cola di Rienzo survives, for instance, and that from his early administrative-political career as notary of the Camera Urbis. Francesco di Stefano dei Capogalli, on the other hand, evidently less politically ambitious, "got on with" his work and, consequently, left more business behind him.[33]

This is not true, however, of the careers of Paolo dei Serromani and Antonio dei Scambi, who have left vast amounts of documentary evidence; they themselves also appear in the most other sources; and in their time, these two enjoyed most impressive notarial careers in politics. Both appear among the necrological records of the Confraternity of the Savior,

---

32. Though they were not necessarily aspirant *bovattieri* or politicians, it should be emphasized. Francesco di Puzio appears in no fewer than twelve of the sources examined, but was hardly as well off and powerful as the notary who drew up his will, Antonio dei Scambi. Antonio, incidentally, appears in ten sources, including his own protocols. Giovanni di domini Jacobi Jordani dei Bulgamini (or Bulgarii) appears in fifteen sources, yet does not seem appear to have had a high-profile political career: unlike Cecco Rosani, who will be discussed in the prosopographical section following; he appears in ten sources.

33. Mosti's edition of Francesco di Stefano Capogalli's protocols runs to 660 pages.

along with Nardo di Pucio Venettini and Lorenzo Staglia,[34] two of the other seventeen "surviving" notaries. There is no room here for a full biography of either, but one example of the political role and the close-knit nature of the notarial governmental community may be cited, from early 1386.[35] In the early throes of the Schism, a powerful company of pro-Clementine Breton mercenaries held the Castel S. Angelo and denied Urban VI access to the Vatican. A joint embassy from the Felice Società and the *Romanus Populus* was sent to Francesco di Vico in Viterbo, to request military aid against the intruders. The mission was composed of a team of skilled political negotiators: of the five representatives, three— Lorenzo Staglia, Paolo dei Serromani, and Antonio dei Scambi—are notaries familiar to us. The record of the embassy's report was rogated by the notary of the Felice Società: Nardo Venettini.

Cola di Rienzo, *Notaio*

Notaries "ran" Rome, then, sometimes as political leaders—Conservators, diplomats, financial administrators, judges—and staffing almost exclusively the less exalted bureaucratic posts. Cola was one of them, yet little scholarly attention has been given to his chosen career, that is, to his training as a notary. We should recall that even Cola's title, Tribune, demonstrates an ideological progression as well as a practical heritage from the career of notary.[36] In his pursuit of the "high justice" of the Romans[37] (and arguably in imitation of the divine justice of the Son of Man and Rider Faithful and True) Cola sat on his Tribunal throne and exercised supreme judicial power. Many other Roman judges, including Cola's prime supporters, had also begun their careers as notaries.

As the penultimate stage in the reconstruction of Cola's context (we will examine his "personnel" last), we should take into account the professional expectations of notaries outlined in this chapter: their ambitions, social connections, and aspirations; the juridical and frequently political authority they exercised; the legal education and humanist culture associated closely with the notarial profession, and the sense of the past and its

---

34. Egidi, *Necrologia*, 1:325–26, 2:493.
35. Cited by Lori-Sanfilippo, "Il protocolli notarili," 136, slightly at odds with Natale, "La Felice Società," 150–51; she supplies full details of these men's careers.
36. Chapter 1 reviews the origins of the title *Tribunus*.
37. Wright, *Life*, 31.

preservation for the future—*ad perpetuam rei memoriam*—that so often accompanied and informed their work.[38] Apart from the Church, where attention, scholarship, and patronage in varying degrees could also allow a gifted man of "low" birth to rise to a position of power and influence,[39] the career of a notary was one of very few in which a talented "plebeian" could rise to overt political authority.

No external testimony to Cola's career before 1344 exists, and such information as we have comes from the retrospective angles of the chronicle and Cola's own letters. Cola's father, as a Regola innkeeper, may have been a person like Antonio dei Scambi's Capanna, enjoying a local standing despite the stigma of the occupation. At any rate, Cola's father had relations in Anagni who were financially, or socially, sufficiently well placed to support a lengthy classical education for at least one of his sons, perhaps at the bishop's school. It is, however, difficult to imagine Anagni as a center of legal training; and tempting to call to mind evidence that exists, albeit sketchily (see chap. 1), for the survival of Boniface's Roman Studium.

After Cola's return to the City, around 1333, and his (presumed) investiture as a notary, it would seem he married well, into a family of important notaries, the Mancini or Martini, one of whom appears in no fewer than eight of the sources examined here. Since his wife was described as "very young" in 1347,[40] when Cola was thirty-three or thirty-four, he may not have married until around or even after his return from the Avignon trip 1343–44. Leaving Rome with an emotive, populist "guildish" title ("consul of orphans and widows and sole representative of the poor") and returning as arguably the most highly placed notary of the City undoubtedly reinforced his new social status. The political promotion to the office of Notary of the Civic Chamber, along with "plenty of emolu-

---

38. For an idea of how legal practitioners assessed change over time, see Chris Wickham, "Lawyer's Time: History and Memory in Tenth- and Eleventh-Century Italy," in *Studies in Medieval History presented to R. H. C. Davies,* ed. Henry Mayr-Harting and R. I. Moore (London: Hambledon, 1985), 53–71, esp. 64. The notary's handbooks were legal codifications: in Rome notaries had to undergo a statutory examination on the City's code in order to qualify: A.C. Credenza IV.88, chap. 36, 145r. Of course, only the heads of the guild of notaries, the elite of the legal profession, men like Matteo dei Baccari—or Cola, for that matter—would be versed in canon and Roman civil law collections (including issues such as the *lex regia*) and become the judges and *doctores* of the City.

39. Though not as a city magistrate in Rome: III:21 (Re, *Statuti,* 98–99).

40. Wright, *Life,* 63.

ments and benefits,"[41] added the perfect circumstances for conspiracy to the new social network.

The frequent failure to contextualize Cola's professional political background would seem to reflect a general lack of interest, among scholars who have worked on Cola, in the details of the Roman constitution of the fourteenth century; yet the evidence is there, and some is even published. The office of Notary of the Chamber, that is, of the civic finances, was absolutely central to the financial administration of the City. Cola and his silver pen occupied one of these posts for three years, subordinate in rank only to the *camerarius,* or chamberlain, of the City himself, who was, in turn, accountable only to the executive officer (one or more Senators) and to the judicial authority of the college of six "Palatine" and a small number of "other" judges. Cola explicitly requested the post of cameral notary from Clement;[42] the request was granted, the office apparently conferred in April and reconfirmed in June 1344.[43] Cola's awareness of the covert potential of his position is demonstrated by his knowledge of and control over the revenues of the City: he boasted of the money available to his conspirators in 1346, his Chronicler listing them, interestingly, in proper legal fashion: *item . . .*[44] His manipulation and understanding of the financial duties of the post is revealed in the dealings of his 1347 Tribunate, particularly in the administrative precision of his ordinances. The same is true of the initially overwhelming success of his fiscal policy; the hearth tax, gathered from all corners of the *Destretto,* paid for the militia, and in his first report to Clement VI, Cola claimed, inter alia, to have substantially increased the revenues from the salt taxes.[45]

Outside his own evidence and that of the chronicle, scattered direct references to Cola, and even documents written by or for Cola, do survive. We have his rogation, as Notary of the Camera Urbis, of the senatorial confirmation of the statutes of the Guild of Merchants, which provides a sample of his flamboyant script and signature (cover illustration).[46] It shows Cola fulfilling the obligations of his notarial office in the same manner as dozens of other notaries of the Camera whose names crop up

---

41. Ibid., 32.

42. III:4, 10–16.

43. See III:5, III:6.

44. Wright, *Life,* 39.

45. Ibid., 55; III.15, 168–70. Cola also stabilized the exchange rate in Rome between the various currencies circulating in central Italy: III:18, 84–92. For the general problems of tax collection in the region, see G. Tomassetti, "Del sale e focatio del commune di Roma," *ASRSP* 20 (1897): 313–68.

46. Fully noted in chapter 4.

throughout the Trecento, including, for example, Cecco Rosani, or the long-established Egidio Angilerii, Cola's own "herald" and cameral notary in 1347.[47]

Another piece of evidence of Cola's judicial and administrative impact appears in the protocols of Giovanni di Nicola di Paolo, dated August 19, 1348: Donna Francesca, abbess of S. Maria in Selce, and her senior nuns, rent land outside the City to Pietro Cerroni, who promises to "pay" them in return "ten *rubla* of grain in accordance with the former measures in effect before Cola took over the Capitol."[48] This illustrates the confusion that followed the rejection of Cola and the apparent attempt to overturn the new systems he had introduced, which in turn led to the renewed chaos he was sent back to deal with in 1354.

Other evidence, sifted from thousands of ecclesiastical folios (and considerable numbers of nineteenth-century secondary sources), relates to the granting of privileges or concessions, and to the exercise of civil jurisdiction, by Cola in 1347. One concession concerns the rights held by the Vatican basilica to mine salt;[49] the second, more interesting case revolves around the Trastevere convent of S. Cosimato *in mica aurea,* and their dispute with the Stefaneschi.[50] In the 1290s, their Roman heyday, the Stefaneschi had obtained an emphyteotic (transgenerational) contract from the nuns of S. Cosimato, for lands around Porta; the terms were extremely unfavorable to the community.[51] Nonetheless it was renewed in 1317 by

---

47. Egidio first appeared in 1317 as one of the newly approved *scrinarii mercatantiae,* the notaries of the Guild of Merchants; he appears again frequently in this context between 1333 and 1344 (Gatti, *Statuti dei Mercanti,* 70–72, 76–79), when he gains an additional title, *notarius camere urbis et dictator* . He occupied this post again in 1347 and 1348 (presumably "ousted" by Cola in the meantime, 1344–46), where he rogated the confirmation of the guild's statutes, on behalf of Cola's regime (Gatti, *Statuti dei Mercanti,* 81–82). In 1354 (Malatesta, *Statuti delle gabelli,* 86) Egidio was still notary and *dictator* of the Civic Chamber, and again in 1356 in the records of the Lana, the cloth merchants' guild (Stevenson, *Statuti delle arti,* 168–69). Small, "District of Rome," 205, mentions that in 1346 the Velletrans attempted to bribe the Roman Capitoline "notary and *dictator,*" presumably Egidio, if not Cola. Was this standard practice in *Destretto* administration?

48. Mosti, *Johannes Nicolai Pauli,* 34.

49. L. Schiaparelli, "Un nuovo documento di Cola di Rienzo," in *Scritti di Storia, di Filosofia e d'arte* (Naples, 1908), 135–46. The original document has, on the back, in a fourteenth-century hand, "Litteras Tribuni Urbis pro sale basilicae 'nostre.'" Also ed. Burdach and Piur, *Briefwechsel,* IV:16.

50. Pietro Fedele, "Un giudicato di Cola di Rienzo fra il monastero di S. Cosimato e gli Stephaneschi," *ASRSP* 26 (1903): 437–51. The original is at A.S.R. SS. Cosma e Damiano, doc. 357 (also = IV:20).

51. Automatic renewal every nineteen years, in return for one florin and several pounds of candle wax.

Francesco, father of Martino.[52] After Cola's execution of Martino Ste-faneschi di Porta[53] the nuns evidently seized their opportunity to end the sixty-year situation.

The document is also interesting insofar as it preserves information concerning Cola's judicial processes; this does not survive in either the chronicle or in the epistolary evidence. It contains a very common formu-laic plea for the speeding up of the process;[54] that this was a common problem is evidenced not by its existence, but by the second of Cola's *ordinamenti* of May 1347, which specifically addressed the problem of the length and expense of court procedure. It is another clear example of the manner in which Cola's notarial career influenced his administration of the City, and it acts as an external confirmation of the Chronicler's claims that Cola's unrelenting commitment to law and justice actually pene-trated, albeit temporarily, much of Rome and its *Destretto*.[55]

A final document directly relating to Cola's regime is a copy from 1368 of Cola's sentence from September 16, 1354, in favor of S. Spirito, one of the most powerful institutions of later medieval Rome.[56] A *Parlamentum* was summoned by mandate of the "excellent" Nicolas, defender and "Knight of the Roman People," papal Senator, captain, and syndic. Egidio Angilerii, Notary of the Camera Urbis, by special commission of the Senator, has researched, *ad perpetuam rei memoriam publicum,* and now confirms, the exemption of S. Spirito from gabelle, forced loans, and all forms of taxation, as a reward for helping the Senator in his fight against the enemies of the people of Rome (i.e., the Colonna). Giacomo, the previous preceptor of S. Spirito, recently dead, had been a friend of Cola, a colleague on Cola's council, and assistant at Cola's coronation. Rather earlier, the statue of the pope, which Cola called for in 1343—to celebrate Clement's decision for a Jubilee in 1350—had actually been com-missioned and erected in S. Spirito by Giacomo.[57] The Chronicler tells us that Giacomo was one of the "official" Roman ambassadors to Avignon in 1343 (Cola was an embassy of the "unofficial" coup); perhaps this was

52. Senator in 1340; Antonio Vendettini, *Serie cronologica dei senatori di Roma* (Rome, 1778), 31.

53. Wright, *Life,* 48–50.

54. "And on these matters the plaintiffs supplicate that the case may proceed summarily, openly, without delaying tactics or challenges to the judgment, and free from all *suspitione* and counterappeals."

55. The most striking examples in the chronicle are at Wright, *Life,* 68–69.

56. Malatesta, *Statuti delle gabelli,* 122–25 (also = IV:71). The 1368 copy was drawn up to specify that other properties of the hospital were equally exempt from the payment of the var-ious taxes specified.

57. See Schwartz, "Images and Illustrations," 154–55.

where they met, though other official envoys of 1343 became Cola's sworn enemies.[58] Cola seems to have had an equally close acquaintance in Giacomo's 1348 successor, Giovanni di Lucca; the Chronicler describes Giovanni, *commannatore* of S. Spirito, quieting the Romans during a protest in 1350 against the Papal Legate.[59] The decision of 1354 describes the new preceptor of S. Spirito as "fervid *zelator* for the honor and standing of the Roman People," a phrase interestingly similar to Cola's title of 1347, *Zelator* of Italy.

The effect of the grant of 1354 was to strengthen considerably the influence of S. Spirito; the same can be posited of the copy of 1368 and the grand reformulation of 1390, described above, which offers stunning confirmation of the importance of notaries generally, the political careers open to the most skilled among them, and the networks available to those who achieved such prominence. Cola's place within the network, as a notary and moreover as Notary of the Civic Chamber, may now be illustrated by an examination of that network in microcosm.

The *Dramatis Personae* of the Revolution

Chapter 5 offers a profile of Cola's revolution in broad brush-strokes based on the evidence discussed in chapter 4; the following section will use that same source material to sharpen the focus on the identities, origins, and loyalties of both Cola's allies and his enemies, unraveling the political careers of the very men who made, and unmade, Cola's career.[60] We will

---

58. Giovanni Colonna the Elder, whose family was cut to pieces at the Porta S. Lorenzo battle, and Francesco Orsini, son of Giordano and nephew of Rainaldo, the "dog knights" Cola besieged at Marino. On Giacomo see *ARC*, 66; H. Schmidinger, "Die Gesandte der Staat Rom nach Avignon vom Jahre 1342/3," *Romische Historische Mitteilungen* 21 (1979): 24.

59. *ARC*, 158; Wright, *Life*, 99 translates the term incorrectly as a military "commander of the Holy Ghost," though the mistake is understandable: the term conjures up the image of militia "of the Holy Ghost" more readily than that of a monastery.

60. In 1975 Massimo Miglio published what he called "a first attempt" to expose some of the dramatis personae, but this attempt was barely supplemented for republication in 1991 ("Gli ideali," 82–87, from which subsequent references are made here). It has not been appended since. Miglio mentions Cola's supporters among the *popolani,* but not those among the baronial magnates, nor all of those who would count as nobles. He notes few, and discusses none, of the numerous characters named in the chronicle who militated against Cola's rule. He does not note, or investigate, the names of many of the men who appear in Cola's correspondence. His primary sources are the published necrologies and the notarial material ready-edited by Gennaro and Maire-Vigueur. Here I have focused on the Romans involved in Cola's regime, and not on his "foreign" allies in Avignon or Bohemia (such as Cardinal Guido of Bologna or Imperial Chancellor Johan von Neumarkt).

begin with his early partisans, investigating the group that included the conspirators of 1346, the councilors and ambassadors of 1347, and the much smaller group of "faithful" between 1348 and 1354.

In 1349, Cola referred to his ascension to the Capitol in 1347, with twenty-five *socios* (allies),[61] a group that, as we know from the Chronicler's account, contained knights, nobles, merchants, and "good men" (city guildsmen or rional political and military leaders). The character with the highest profile among the sources examined here must have been Matteo dei Baccari, one of Cola's ambassadors to Florence in 1347, discussed in chapter 5. Another member of this delegation was Francesco dei Baroncelli, who stepped into power as *Tribunus Secundus,* self-appointed successor to Cola, in 1353. His ambassadorial speech (unlike that of Matteo) survives in all its rhetorical finery[62] and provides an impressive example of the cultural milieu of Cola's court, "where the jesters played and poets composed songs about his deeds."[63] The Baroncelli were a noble Florentine family, with a rich and well-established cadet branch in Rome; references to Baroncelli merchants and notaries abound in our sources, particularly throughout Antonio dei Scambi's protocols, and in the *Liber Anniversorum* of the Confraternity of the Savior. The civic status of the Baroncelli is clear; their ecclesiastical affiliation was with a church no less important than S. Maria Maggiore.[64] References to Francesco's career—apart from a bogus sixteenth-century "life"—are rare,[65] although there is a epitaph (he died in 1353). Matteo Villani referred to Baroncelli's request for con-

---

61. III:50, 202.

62. IV:4. The Vergilian flourishes are mentioned in chapter 1.

63. Wright, *Life,* 48.

64. Silvester dei Baroncelli's 1352 will (A.C./I 649 3/1352, "46r–49v") shows him to have been a canon and artistic patron of the basilica; he was also the son and brother of two Lorenzos. The elder Lorenzo appears as a notary in the records of S. Maria in Via Lata and the Hospital of S. Maria della Consolazione (B.A.V. S. Maria in Via Lata, cass. 306, doc. 108 (1355); A.S.R. Consolazione doc. 4, 1348); the younger, as notary to the *judex appelationum* in 1386 (B.A.V. S. Maria in Via Lata cass. 302, doc. 10). One of them also rogated the confirmation of the statutes of the cloth merchants in 1346 (Vendettini, *Serie cronologica dei senatori,* 36) and appears as one of the Seven Reformers in 1362 (Vendettini, *Serie cronologica dei senatori,* 42; also Salimei, *Senatori e statuti,* 131). Another Baroncelli, Stefanello, possessed an estate outside Porta Maggiore (A.C./I 649 3/1352, 40v; B.A.V. S.A.P. 4/1368, 30v). An older relative, Baroncello dei Baroncelli, was notary to the regime of Thirteen Good Men in 1335 (Vendettini, *Serie cronologica dei senatori,* 30).

65. Ingeborg Walters, "Francesco Baroncelli," *Dizionario Biografico degli Italiani* (1964), 6:437–38; Egidi, "Per la vita di Francesco Baroncelli"; "Privilegio di Francesco Baroncelli in favore di Vitorchiano," *Scritti storici in memoria di Giovanni Monticolo* (Venice, 1922), 333–36.

stitutional advice from Florence in 1353, as ruler of Rome. Two documents, both unfortunately difficult to date, survive among the disparate
parchment collections of S. Maria *in Via Lata;* neither proves, but both
suggest, that Baroncelli was a notary: one mentions Francesco as one of
the two senatorial scribes, while the other mentions Cecchus Johannis
Baroncelli as a *judex super appelationum.*[66] His sons Paolo (a notary) and
Domenico did not seem to have suffered from their father's association
with Cola nor from Francesco's own political machinations.[67]

The source material is almost silent concerning the third ambassador,
Stefanello dei Boezi,[68] and the other of the four, the noble Pandolfuccio di
Guido dei Franchi; we do know of the latter that he was not so fortunate
as Matteo or Francesco, nor in 1347 so grandiloquent.[69] In 1354, during
his brief second period in power, Cola's behavior toward his peers was
unpredictable: first, fearing a counterrevolution, he executed Fra Moreale,
captain of the largest, most dangerous army of mercenaries in the
mid–fourteenth century Italy, namely, the Great Company. The same
merciless fate overtook Pandolfuccio, who, according to the Chronicler,
"desired the *signoria* of the People."[70]

One of Cola's most trusted *nobiles,* and colleague in office before 1347,
was the chancellor of the City, Angelo Malabranca. Malabranca was yet
another neighbor of Matteo Baccari, Antonio dei Scambi, and Nucio
Gibelli in the *rione* S. Angelo, around the church from where Cola led his
followers to the Capitol. Cola, describing him as "Lionheart," sent him
against the rebellious Giovanni Gaetani, count of Fondi, on the Lazio-
Campania border, with twelve hundred cavalry and archers *(balistarii).*[71]

---

66. B.A.V., S. Maria in Via Lata, cass. 317, doc. 35; 306, doc. 109.

67. B.A.V. S.A.P. 5/1369, 109r, for Paolo: Isa Lori-Sanfilippo, *Il Protocollo Notarile di
Pietro di Nicola Astalli (1368),* Codice diplomatico di Roma e della regione romana 6
(Rome, 1989), doc. 47, for Domenico.

68. A.C./I 649 8/1366, 29v mentions one Stefano *de Boczi,* a notary of Pigna, who may fit
the bill.

69. His short peroration to the Florentines (IV:3) has a few biblical and one Dante reference, but otherwise seems to act solely as a preface to the (nonexistent) speech by "Matteo . . .
and these other ambassadors." He also provided a brief summation and thanks (IV:5) that
incorporated a Caesar story, borrowed from Dante, who was in turn had paraphrased Lucan
(Burdach's notes have the full references).

70. *ARC,* 193.

71. III:35, 56. Military leadership is not the immediately obvious role of a "chancellor;"
still, Cola the notary-knight had both led his own army and captained a small corps in the
papal army of Albornoz. Giovanni dei Cenci, Malabranca's replacement as chancellor, was
appointed by the *gubernatores pacis* of 1376 to lead an army, as *capitano del popolo,* with soldiers, counselors, and notaries in his train (Supino, *Margarita Cornetana,* 365–66).

Later, in exile in Prague, Cola corresponded with Angelo regarding plans for his proposed return to power in Rome. Angelo was to be the recipient of official communications on Cola's part—a letter from the king of France, for example—after Cola fled.[72] Angelo was also, like Cola, connected with the property dealings of S. Spirito.[73] The Chronicler, interestingly (and misleadingly), describes Angelo (and his son Matteo)[74] as "barons." Certainly the noble Angelo numbered barons among his acquaintance; on the other hand, he had already demonstrated himself to be an anti-Colonna partisan in 1338.[75] He could well have been one of the Good Men of 1343 who picked Cola as mouthpiece to send to Avignon, where Giovanni Colonna, cardinal-deacon of S. Angelo, wielded enormous influence.

Another noble name that crops up is that of *dominus* Gottifredus Scoctus, a *cavalerotto* of Cola's own *rione,* Regola, who played a central part in Cola's coronation ritual. The Scotti, like the Malabranca, were old Roman noble stock who had wielded political influence for well over a century. Miglio notes his appearance in the *Liber Anniversorum* of the Confraternity of the Savior. In fact, Gottifredo was also a major benefactor of S. Spirito, where Cola and other of his partisans had close ties. Despite the claims of his father Oddo and brother Pietro, Gottifredo's will of 1371 bequeathed to the hospice his *casale* (estate) "La Bocticella."[76] We should also note the letter in which Cola declared the sovereignty of the Roman People, which was, significantly, signed in the presence of a number of senior magistrates: the Papal Legate (Cola's co-rector), Don Paolo del Conte (the official papal Vicar), Don Gottifredo Scoto, Fra Giacomo (preceptor of S. Spirito), three Latian judges, a Dominican friar, a Foschi de' Berta *bovattiere,* and a "plebeian" called Grannelli.[77] These were surely the men of Cola's *assectamentum* (privy council), and probably among the

---

72. Wright, *Life,* 66, 88.

73. B.A.V. Vat. Lat. 7931, 47v (1355); also as over, A.S.R. Ospedale del S. Spirito, coll. B, cass. 60–62, doc. 136 (1360).

74. B.A.V. S.A.P. 12/1383, 53r–v. In a strange turn of political allegiances—or economics—Angelo's son Paolo later sold a string of properties in central Rome to the *magnificus vir* Onorato Gaetani of Fondi (B.A.V. S.A.P. 9/1376, 3r); though Onorato was presumably the son of Giovanni, Paolo's father Angelo's military target in 1347. Onorato's agent for the purchase was Giovanni Cenci, Angelo's "heir" as Roman chancellor. Paolo was also one of the witnesses to the di Vico-Orsini betrothal in 1370, noted previously.

75. Alongside Savelli and Orsini factions that year Angelo participated in a violent attack on the Colonna-controlled zone and church of S. Angelo; Mercati, "Nell'Urbe"; Marchetti-Longhi, "Il *Mons Fabiorum*," 35.

76. A.S.R. Spirito B. cass. 60–62, doc. 152 (1371).

77. III:27, 80–85.

socios of his initial revolution. Some of them may have become the *aicuni cittadini* who dissuaded Cola from executing the barons. When Raymond of Orvieto complained to the pope about his dismissal as co-governor and the arrogance of Cola's knighting ceremony, his letter to Clement, too, was witnessed by the same men.[78] This may not necessarily indicate their entire disapproval of Cola's actions: Gottifredo Scotto had just that moment returned from his central role in the ceremony itself.

An equally important and interesting figure participated not in the knighting, but in Cola's coronation of August 15, 1347: Paolo Vaiani (or "Vagiano"), a knight, *doctor legum,* and judge, who was also an ambassador to Florence in August, for Cola's new policy of Italian brotherhood.[79] Miglio notes his collusion in the purchase of gabelle rights in 1379,[80] and his burial in SS. Celso e Giuliano, taken from an unspecified *Liber Anniversorum* (presumably that of the Confraternity of the Savior).[81] Other sources, however, provide a broader frame of reference. The earliest archival reference to Paolo comes from 1342, when he was already being described as appeals judge, *judex appelationum;*[82] in this year he and another judge actually governed the City as vicars of the absent Senators.[83] The regime of XIII that supplanted these Senators, shortly afterward in 1342, elected Cola in 1343 as their representative in Avignon; perhaps, like Malabranca, Vaiani helped engineer the coup of 1342 just as, later, he supported the 1347 regime. The *Casa delli Vaiani* on the Via dei Banchi Vecchi is mentioned by the Chronicler in the year 1345.[84] References from 1348 include Vaiani as *iudex palatinus* for appeals.[85] Paolo's name appears in association with that of the chancellor, Angelo Malabranca, in 1360

---

78. IV:7, 41–47.

79. III:41, 107.

80. From Gennaro, "Per lo studio della composizione sociale della popolazione di Roma," 793: AC/I 649, 14/72v–80v.

81. In fact corresponding to Egidi, *Necrologia,* 1:324.

82. B.A.V. S. Maria in Via Lata cass. 300–301, doc. 11 (1339 and 1342). The legal profession was in the family; S. Maria in Via Lata cass. 303, doc. 15 refers to *Petrus Vaiani* as *judex palatinum* in 1335; the same name appears as one of the Seven Reformers of 1365, alongside Cecco Rosani and Nucio Gibelli. Both references are from Vendettini, *Serie cronologica dei senatori,* 36, who also notes Bartolomeo Vaiani and Andrea de Maximis as Palatine judges and regents for the Senators of that year, out of town (in Corneto) for the confirmation of the statutes of what Vendettini describes as the *Mercanti de' panni.*

83. Salimei, *Senatori e statuti,* 35.

84. *ARC,* 100. The location is provided by Pasquale Adinolfi, *Roma nell'età di mezzo* (Narni, 1857–60), 3:40–41.

85. Mosti, *Johannes Nicolai Pauli,* 60 (in 1348); Isa Lori-Sanfilippo, *Il Protocollo Notarile di Lorenzo Staglia (1372),* Codice diplomatico di Roma e della regione romana 3 (Rome, 1986), 127 (she also mentions his appearance in the archive of S. Maria in Monastero).

S. Spirito business;[86] he appears again in 1372 as a witness.[87] In 1379, in a document concerning property in the *prati Sancti Petri*[88] neighboring lands are described by Antonio dei Scambi as belonging to *dominus Paulus Vaiani milex*.[89] Among the most curious evidence is the proof of his close ties to Cola's bêtes noires, the Marino-based Orsini. In the registers of the Hospital of S. Spirito,[90] on July 23, 1347, the *nobilis vir dominus* Paolo Vaiani of Ponte, *milex* and *judex*, witnessed the sale of a *casale* in Sabina, by the Orsini brothers against whom Cola went to war in late August 1347. This Orsini faction was not at odds with Cola until shortly after the imprisonment episode; so until August, association with the Marino Orsini was not necessarily incompatible with loyalty to Cola's regime. However, Vaiani retained the connection: among the *pergamene* of the Hospital of the Savior there is a copy of the will of 1372[91] of Rainaldo Orsini, Giordano's brother (and fellow "dog knight," according to Cola's symbolic drowning of the brothers).[92] The will is not merely witnessed but in fact rogated by Paolo Vaiani, who was of course yet another trained notary. Paolo Vaiani could well have been another of the *aicuni cittadini* who persuaded Cola not to execute but instead to release the barons he had captured, and put them in control of the very titles, supplies, and territories they had traditionally dominated. Paolo was a knight and a nobleman with baronial connections. Yet this has to be set against another important aspect of Vaiani's political career: he appears as the first named compiler of the new Roman civic statutes of 1363. Clearly, despite his earlier association with Cola, Paolo remained a senior and influential member of the Capitoline curia for at least the next sixteen years.

Various people are mentioned playing significant parts in the ceremonials and processions staged by Cola di Rienzo during the Tribunate. A striking example is Buccio di Jubileo, who walked before Cola to St. Peter's, holding a naked sword to symbolize justice. His *bovattiere* career was not in the least harmed by his association with Cola, even although he,

---

86. A.S.R. S. Spirito, coll. B, cass. 60–62, doc. 136 (1360); also B.A.V. Vat. Lat. 7931, 48v.

87. Lori-Sanfilippo, *Lorenzo Staglia,* 127. She refers to Paolo's appearance in the statutes of the Lana as a guild judge for 1321 (Stevenson, *Statuti delle arti,* 141); this would be an appropriate early career position, but even so a sixty-year political career seems unlikely.

88. The intensely developed area north and east of the Vatican City still bears the now inappropriate name *Prati,* "open fields." It has been traversed since the 1870s, curiously enough, by the Via di Cola di Rienzo.

89. B.A.V. S.A.P. 11/1379, 99r–v.

90. A.S.R. S. Spirito, coll. B, cass. 60–62, doc. 112.

91. A.S.R. Confraternity of the Savior, cass. 453, docs. 4A–C (1372).

92. Wright, *Life,* 79.

like Angelo Malabranca, was one of the few supporters in 1347 to remain overtly loyal to Cola between 1348 and 1354: he was sent as part of an unsuccessful two-man embassy to parley with the Colonna at Palestrina in September 1354 (the men were imprisoned and "fined": one lost a tooth).[93] Miglio provides a useful paragraph on Buccio's co-envoy, "Ianni Cafierello";[94] he mentions Paulo Serromani's reference to the *nobilis vir Johannes de Cafarellis, miles* in 1363, and news of his death and burial in S. Maria *sopra Minerva* in 1373. He does not note the curious reference from the Monaldesco chronicle for 1339, which mentions the murder of one Giovanni dei Giudici (presumably not the ambassador of 1347, then) by one Giovanni Cafarelli.[95] The latter is also given the strange title *miles camerae Urbis* in 1356.[96] For Buccio himself Miglio borrows nine references from the protocols of Paolo dei Serromani, cited by Gennaro, to the noble Buccio's business operations between 1363 and 1366, and one from Antonio dei Scambi in 1376, referred to by Maire-Vigueur. My own research further reveals that Buccio's father—"Petrus, dictus alius Jubilleus"—and Buccio acted as joint procurators in 1348.[97] There are a further ten Serromani references to Buccio (including three references to his son, Petruccio), mainly descriptions of property both in town and in the *contado,* between 1367 and 1372.[98] The latter shows Buccio as witness to a document rogated in his house but concerning another party, suggesting a close acquaintance with the notary, Paolo dei Serromani (who was at that time Notary of the Camera Urbis). The most interesting case, however, is from 1376: Buccio appears as a guarantor, in the purchase of properties by Giovanni Cenci as a baron's agent. Buccio's full name, given here—*Buccius quondam Iubilei de Cinthiis of Trastevere*—reveals he was a member of the Cenci family, nobles as well established (and still around today) as the Malabranca and Scotti. Many of the Cenci, of course, were Cola's neighbors, from the Monte dei Cenci on the Regola–S. Angelo boundary.

---

93. Ibid. 136.

94. Wright, *Life,* 129.

95. Muratori, *Fragmenta Annalium Romanorum,* 541A. There is no mention either, in Miglio's appendix, of Cola's 1354 *capitano del popolo,* "Liccardo Imprennente delli Annibaldi" for whom, unfortunately, I have found no further information.

96. Stevenson, *Statuti delle arti,* 169.

97. A.C./I 649: 1/1348, 7r.

98. A.C./I 649: 8/1367, 126v; 9/1368, 97v; 10/1369, 18r; 11/1371, 13v, 32r–36r, 66r, 71r; 12/1372, 8v, 27r, 39v. See also A.S.R. *collezione pergamene* Ospedale di S. Maria Annunziata, doc. 29 (1362) rogated by *Paulus de Sorromanis;* S. Maria della Consolazione, doc. 12 (1373), by Giovanni di Nicola di Paolo.

Other figures in Cola's inner circle include *magister* Giovanni dei Giudici, sent as an ambassador to Avignon in September 1347,[99] where he received the post of *doctor in primitiviis scientiis* to the Roman Studium. "Messer Giovanni's excellent performance," praised by Petrarch, has remained generally unnoticed.[100] Little is known of the Trecento family: one notary from Trastevere of the name appears in the protocols of Antonio dei Scambi for 1368.[101] The name is an old one: there was a senator in 1238 called Giovanni dei Giudici.[102] Another "old" aristocratic name belonged to Cola's envoy to the emperor to announce Cola's imperial descent, Eunufrio dei Ilperini.[103] Naturally, older families reinforced the legitimacy of Cola's regime in the ancient courts of pope and emperor. The Ilperini were *cavalerotti* who appear throughout the Trecento evidence.

Then there was "Cola Guallato" (Nicola dei Vallati), one of the men who bore the symbolic banners on the day of Cola's ascent of the Capitol. Like the Baccari, and of a similarly ennobled mercantile social rank,[104] the Vallati were concentrated in S. Angelo.[105] One of their houses, at Via del Portico d'Ottavia 29, may still be seen; and there are extensive records for Vallati canons of S. Angelo.[106] Both these points are noted by Miglio, along with evidence for the occasional Vallati in government (e.g. in 1358) and other references to the family, culled from Maire-Vigueur and Gennaro. My research actually revealed a number of notaries with the name Vallati. There is, in fact, a passage in Antonio dei Scambi's protocols that draws the net much more tightly around the individual concerned: a 1370 reference to a notary, Nicola "de Vallatis" himself, of the *rione* S. Angelo.[107] He is described as "Cola Guallato, the good speaker" in the chronicle, where he is followed by another standard bearer, a notary.[108]

---

99. Thus far also mentioned by Miglio, "Gli ideali," 85.

100. *Variae* 40, postscript; Cosenza (*Petrarch,* 67–72) presents a careful examination of Giovanni's identity.

101. B.A.V. S.A.P. 4/1368, 17v.

102. Vendettini, *Serie cronologica,* 8. There was also a "Angelo Malabranca" in 1235 and 1247 (Vendettini, *Serie cronologica,* 7; Salimei, *Senatori e statuti,* 68, 74); and a Giovanni Cenci in 1228 and 1284 (Vendettini, *Serie cronologica,* 6; Salimei, *Senatori e statuti,* 67, 86); names and offices clearly ran for generations in these older families.

103. III:50, 225.

104. B.A.V. S.A.P. 3/1367, 70r–77r reveals their marital alliances.

105. As in the case of the Cenci, the modern Lungotevere, although running through "baronial" Savelli territory, pays tribute to the historic profile of the Vallati.

106. And a family chapel, dedicated by Gregorio dei Vallati (B.A.V. S.A.P. 1/1363, 52r).

107. B.A.V. S.A.P. 6/1370, 97r.

108. Miglio, "Gli ideali," 87, supplies corroborative identification evidence for this supporter, Stefaniello Magnacuccia, but the 1402 dating seems rather unlikely.

The odd-sounding description has potential notarial precedents however: in Latin sources the "titles" *notary* and *dictator,* "speaker," appear together, in the context of government, as in the case of Egidio *Angilerii,* the "herald" who declared Cola's new Italian brotherhood and world rule polity, on August 1, 1347.[109] Cola Vallati, therefore, may well have been a notary as well as a good speaker, like Cola di Rienzo himself, or even a formal *dittatore;* he certainly belonged to the same list of new and old prominent S. Angelo and Regolan families, placing him nicely within the group supporting the revolution.

It is possible to find evidence of the Mancini family, Cola's "in-laws,"[110] who were not noble, although clearly important *popolani.* The Chronicler talks of Cecco Mancini, Cola's "notary and chancellor," and mentions Conte Mancini, whom Cola instructed to read out the measures for the *Buono Stato.* Miglio offers one Serromani reference to a *discretus vir* Cecchus Mancini, but there is considerably more to be extracted from the sources. Both these Mancini were closely associated with Cola's regime; Cola gave Conte the rule of Civitavecchia, no less. The association was evident to Cola's enemies, who had both Mancini depicted, inverted, alongside a *pittura infamante* of Cola, after the collapse of the Tribunate.[111] The father, at least, remained loyal after the abdication: in a letter of 1350 Cola indirectly asks his father-in-law Francesco to look after Cola's son.[112] Other Mancini joined the government of 1347: the Tribune's protonotary who drew up the S. Cosimato privilege was one Johannes Francisci de Mancinis, presumably another of Cecco's sons. Paolo dei Serromani also mentions Joanna, daughter of Cecco Mancini; could this have been Cola's wife?[113] Cecco appears in Paolo dei Serromani's protocols in 1363, but also in those of Antonio Goioli in 1365, and Antonio dei Scambi in 1368, where he is described as "Cecchus Nicolai Lelli Mancini" (of Campitelli, the *rione* between S. Angelo and the Capitol). Cola's wife's grandfather must, therefore, have been Nicola Mancini; obligingly, Paolo

---

109. IV:7, 9.

110. Evidence for the marriage itself, however, is fragmentary (see Burdach and Piur, *Briefwechsel,* 5:159–60). The evidence that will be cited in the paragraphs following relates to the name Mancini, but in paleographical terms this proved indistinguishable from *Martini;* this should be taken into account for the identifications and connections asserted here. Again the name is old: Benedetto Carushomo had a Mancini councilor in 1191 (Salimei, *Senatori e statuti,* 51). Transcriptions of the fifteenth-century manuscripts of the chronicle might easily have suffered a similar paleographical confusion, Mancini for Martini.

111. Wright, *Life,* 93.

112. III:52, 31.

113. A.C./I 649 10/1369, 59r.

dei Serromani mentions, in early 1348, one *Nicolaus Mancini,* of S. Angelo: a protonotary. Nicola Mancini was also the very first notary to be mentioned in the protocols of Antonio dei Scambi (he goes on to appear in another six sources). He was one of the most widely mentioned and important notaries of mid-Trecento Rome, and S. Angelo in particular, and was yet another notary "with portfolio." His son also became a notary and then protonotary and political appointee of Cola; one grandson also appears to have been a protonotary in 1347/48, while the other ruled an important Latian grain-port on Cola's behalf. For Cola di Rienzo to have married a Mancini daughter on his way up is entirely plausible: the Mancini were not noted businessmen, or a noble family; they belonged entirely to the educated *popolo,* the level "below" the Vallati, Baccari, Malabranca, and so on, but operated in precisely the same geographical, as well as social and political, circles.[114]

Other men who took part in Cola's processions, on various occasions in 1347, prove more difficult to pinpoint: men such as Cecco di Alessio; or Cola's uncle, "Janni Varviervi," barber by name and profession. Miglio has no evidence for "Janni de Allo" (or Giovanni di Aldo); a reference found in the Margarita Cornetana to the 1310 *hostarius* of the Senator's palace, one Iacopus di Allo,[115] is hardly conclusive (perhaps the family retained a connection in the service of the ruler's court). In a letter to one remaining partisan, the abbot of S. Alessio, in 1350, Cola tried to reassure and encourage—"May all my *socios* remain well!"—mentioning specifically Fra Nicola, the superior at S. Eufemia.[116] For the man who scattered coin to the crowds in Cola's processions, Lello Migliaro, Miglio cites Gennaro, who notes Paulus Milgiarus of Campo Marzio. Neither scholar notes the extensive evidence for Paolo's son, a notary called Sabba, mentioned in two of the seventeen surviving notarial archives.[117]

Miglio fails to mention one of Cola's 1354 counselors, Cecco di Peru-

---

114. The chronicler Henrik of Diessenhoven comments on Cola's financial resources, namely that he had accumulated a sum of 350 florins from his wife's dowry and his notarial income; Henrik's contemporary Mathias of Neuenburg makes a similar comment, although lowers the figure to 50 (Henrik of Diessenhoven, *Chronica,* 57; Adolf Hofmeister, ed., "Mathias of Neuenburg: *Chronik,*" Monumenta Germaniae Historia [Scriptores], n.s., 4, 2d ed. [Berlin, 1955], 242).

115. Supino, *Margarita Cornetana,* 302–3.

116. III:52, 38–39.

117. The name is also recorded in a Corneto document of 1409 (Supino, *Margarita Cornetana,* 326).

gia, although a 1368 document records the occupation of a man by this name (a miller), and his appointment as a procurator.[118] He may have been previously one of the Perugian councilors flattered by Cola in 1353, who, according to the Chronicler, "Allowed themselves to be licked like honey."[119]

Cola's military relationship with members of the Roman aristocracy in 1347 has been described, as have his concessions to the preceptor of Hospital of S. Spirito in 1347 (who sat on his council) and his successor in 1354. Other pro-Cola characters from 1347 emerge from the chronicle, and there are cross-references elsewhere (noted by Miglio). When the Colonna attempted to enter the Porta S. Lorenzo, they were abused by a *popolano* guard and archer, *valestrieri,* named Paolo Bussa (noted in chap. 5), who later appears among the *fratelli* of the Confraternity of the Savior.[120] Others again leave no information beyond their names: "Fonneruglia" of Trevi, the first to attack the young Colonna baron at the Porta S. Lorenzo battle; and the militia constable Scarpetta, who died in the counterrevolution at the very end of Cola's 1347 Tribunate, apparently causing Cola to lose his nerve and abdicate. One of Cola's senior governmental colleagues not discussed by Miglio, the notary and humanist Cecco Rosani, falls into a curious category: he will be discussed along with Cola's enemies.

One figure who did, indirectly, become involved in Cola's military and peacekeeping activities and deserves further investigation is Fra Acuto, a popular preacher from Franciscan Assisi, in whose name the Hospital of the Cross, near the Pantheon, was established (it was still thriving in 1380).[121] We should note, then, the Chronicler's mention of "Brother Acuto the Hospitaller."[122] Acuto's Roman followers and hospice may be identifiable as the Confraternity of the Magdalene; it is likely that he founded the penitential group that was one of four or five *sodalizi* later to unite as a single Marian confraternity.[123] Although a direct connection between the confraternity and Cola's polity is not evident, this was the organization that, in 1351, sponsored a Cavallini noble, Giovanni Cer-

---

118. Lori-Sanfilippo, *Lorenzo Staglia,* 97 n. 1.

119. Wright, *Life,* 129.

120. Miglio, "Gli ideali," 87, referring to Egidi, *Necrologia,* 2:483.

121. Mosti, *Francesco di Stefano Capogalli,* 387.

122. *ARC,* 48, 125.

123. Anna Esposito, "Le 'confraternite' del Gonfalone (secoli XIV–XV)," *Ricerche per la storia religiosa di Roma* 5 (1984): 99.

roni,[124] in a new antimagnatial regime; a very unusual direct involvement in political action for a confraternity. The connection with Fra Acuto might explain its exceptional politicization, however: the chronicle also mentions Fra Acuto's intervention in the fund-raising in 1344 for the Ponte Milvio reconstruction after its destruction in baronial warfare, as well as his central role later in the diplomatic process between Cola and the Viterbese tyrant Giovanni di Vico.[125] Fra Acuto and his confraternity were, evidently, among the éminences grises of mid-fourteenth-century Roman politics.

These, then, are the supporters of Cola whose names appear in the documents relating to the regime, and their identities slot well into the social categories more broadly delineated in the previous two chapters. It illustrates the case that Cola derived his earlier support—that which sent him first to Avignon on behalf of the anonymous *popolani* of 1343, the Good Men of the thirteen *rioni*—from notarial and administrative personnel: his in-laws, the antibaronial chancellor, the *popolo* militia, guild, and confraternal circles who, presumably, approved his first title (consul—i.e., guild head—of widows, orphans, and the poor). This was the long-standing support that he retained after abdication and exile. The more glamorous noble merchants, judges, and *cavalerotti* in whose elite company Cola moved only after 1345—the Scotti, Vaiani, and Baccari of Rome—lent their immense authority to the conspiracy and then to Cola's ruling council. They, the "few citizens," pressured Cola, however, when he went too far and threatened the lives of their personal contacts among the baronial superelite. When Cola's popular militia then shredded the Colonna in November, their support was lost for good: these men do not reappear in 1354, when Cola was forced to find financing from Perugia, not from within Rome itself. However, Cola's dithering over executing the barons when he had the chance in summer 1347 had also weakened his position with the "discreet men" and *la iente*, his *popolo minuto* supporters: as the Chronicler graphically reminds readers, Cola failed to "shit or get off the pot."[126]

Thus Cola's supporters, in some cases, became his enemies. We cannot

---

124. Presumably a close relative of the *litterato* and canon, Giovanni Cavallini dei Cerroni, author of *Polistoria* (see Laureys, "Giovanni Cavallini's *Polistoria*"); see chapter 1. For his will see Mosti, *Johannes Nicolai Pauli*, 25–26. The dynastic strategies of the Cerroni are nicely described by Maire-Vigueur and Broise, "Strutture familiari," 118–21.

125. *ARC*, 48, 125–26; Wright, *Life*, 57–58.

126. Wright, *Life*, 77.

prove that Matteo Baccari or Gottifredo Scotti turned on him, but there is in fact compelling evidence of the individual and social identities of those who sought to undermine him. As well as his enemies from 1344, we have seen some of the turncoats and counterrevolutionaries of 1347, and we will discuss his assassins in 1354. The magnate element among Cola's backers has been discussed in chapter 5, and in any case motives for their participation in Cola's regime were more typically based on internal social politics—which prevented the immediate formation of an alliance against Cola in 1347, as the Chronicler notes[127]—rather than in commitment to Cola's dream of the *Buono Stato*. His enemies among the Colonna were of course implacable. Cola could not trust even the Orsini barons of Castel S. Angelo who claimed to support him, after their initial submission. However, as described in chapter 5, Cola's regime played a catalytic role in undercutting baronial wealth and autonomy, a gradual process in the later Trecento. One non-Roman baron whose persistent provocation helped drive Cola into abdication in 1347 was the Neapolitan count Giovanni Pipino, a former favorite of King Robert, and contact of Cardinal Giovanni Colonna, Petrarch, and Clement VI in Avignon. His antipathy to the Hungarians earned him the affections of Joanna and Lewis of Taranto in 1347–48, but subsequent overmighty behavior led to his execution in 1354; in 1356 his hanged body was portrayed in a classic *pittura infamante* on the walls of his own castle, and among his ironically depicted titles was one of Cola's own: "Liberator of the Roman People."[128] The majority of Cola's enemies—and victims—were baronial: and not just at home in Rome, but in Avignon, of course. A less well known case was Petrarch's friend "Laelius," Lello dei Stefaneschi dei Tosetti, a Colonna partisan and absentee syndic of Rome, deprived by Cola of his official post; when Lello's property was also confiscated, he complained to the pope himself (and probably to Petrarch).[129]

There are significant exceptions to the rule, however. Miglio's work on the supporters of the regime does not attempt to encompass those of nonaristocratic origins: he mentions one figure only, Cola's relative, Locciolo Pelliciaro (an occupation-based *minuto* name, "fur-dealer"). He is

---

127. Ibid., 44.
128. Ibid., 92–94.
129. See Cosenza, *Petrarch,* 148–49. Lello was in fact a member of the "official" embassy of 1342–43 to Clement VI (see Schmidinger, "Die gesandte," 28–29, 32–33) and quite possibly the author of the ecstatic Jubilee announcement that Burdach attributed to Cola (i.e., III:1); see Fedele's 1914 review, "Konrad Burdach und Paul Piur—*Briefwechsel,*" 388–93.

described by the Chronicler as ultimately responsible for Cola's death, by betraying him to the mob at the end: not much of a supporter, one might suggest, and so I rank him among Cola's enemies. Miglio does not of course mention the man who is then explicitly named in the chronicle as the first man to stab Cola: Cecco dello Viecchio. Yet Cecco's story is intriguing, and, I would argue, could be extrapolated to understand the wider-spread hostility to Cola that developed in late 1347.

In 1909 Pietro Egidi, having discovered an interesting reference in the necrological sources he was editing, published an article entitled "Who Killed Cola di Rienzo?"[130] In 1348, one Francesco del Vecchio, a notary from Parione, became prior or "guardian" of the Confraternity of the Savior; it is noted in the confraternity's necrology that the same Francesco gave the church of S. Angelo a marble statue of an archangel.[131] Egidi hypothesized that because the Confraternity of the Savior had been founded by a Colonna, in the 1280s, and since the Colonna were responsible for smashing Cola in October 1354, Cecco must, therefore, have been a Colonna partisan. This is not necessarily the case, however: by the mid–fourteenth century the Confraternity's members can be seen (as a result of prosopographical analysis) as a cross-section of the new groups who exercised economic and political hegemony. My research reveals that Cecco was among the more important notaries of the City; this echoes the centrality of his position in the most important noncommercial organization of the City, the Confraternity of the Savior. Apparently, murdering the man who in 1347 ruled Rome did Cecco's career no harm at all; he went on as a lawyer, as a political appointee in the civic administration, and, as a private businessman, accumulating a stack of city properties, frequently at the expense of local barons; all of which undermines Egidi's claim that Cecco was a Colonna pawn. In fact Francesco di Simone del Vecchio appears in no fewer than seven (and his notary son, Pietro, in five) of the archival sources investigated here. Two other sons, Vecchiarello and Lello Cecchi Vecchi, appear in the Confraternity's *libro dei fratelli* as Parione lay members.[132] Other confraternity

---

130. Pietro Egidi, "Chi era l'uccisore di Cola di Rienzo," *Miscellanea per le Nozze Crocioni-Ruscelloni* (Rome, 1908), 141–46.

131. Egidi, "Chi era l'uccisore," 142, cites Armellini, *Le Chiese di Roma,* 112–14; perhaps replacing the angel whose arm was knocked off in the anti-Colonna scuffle of 1338 at S. Angelo in Pescheria. An illustration of this statue (mentioned in chap. 2) within the Lateran Hospital is found at Filippini, *La Scultura del Trecento,* illust. 29 (facing 98); the inscription reads "HOC OPUS FIERI FECIT FRANCISCUS VECHI NOTARIUS DE PARIONE PRO ANIMA SUA."

132. Egidi, *Necrologia,* 2:483.

records show Cecco was still alive and working in 1361; when he died, he was buried in the church of SS. Lorenzo e Damiano. In 1365, the protocols of Antonio Goioli reveal that Vecchiarello, son of the now deceased Cecco, was also a notary, working in Regola; Goioli's protocols also mention another brother Angelo, who was a canon of the Regolan church of S. Salvatore de Caccabariis.[133] Paolo Serromani and Goioli both provide yet another son's name: Saba.[134] Another grandson of Cecco, Lorenzo di Pietro, appears in the protocols of Francesco di Stefano dei Capogalli;[135] his brother Silvestro di Pietro Vecchie became one of the Seven Reformers of 1367.

Yet Cecco dello Vecchio was already close to the center of power during Cola's Tribunate, nearly a decade before the assassination: in 1348 Cecco had a colleague in the guardianship of the Confraternity of the Savior, whose name is carved alongside Cecco's on the medieval archway leading into what was then the Hospital of the Salvatore (it is now the mortuary chapel area of the modern-day Lateran Hospital): Franciscus Rosani. Cecco Rosani we have met before: he was both a governmental colleague of Cola's and a cultural fellow-traveler. Yet within weeks, possibly, of Cola's abdication, Cola's past supporter and future assassin were co-governing one of the most socially and economically active and influential lay organizations of Rome. The two of them, evidently wealthy and cultured men, commissioned the monumentally fine—and rare, in Trecento terms—marble portal: the inscription reads, TEMPORE GUARDIANATUS FRANCISCI VECCHI & FRANCISCI ROSANI PRIORUM SUB ANNO DOM [INI .M.CCC.XLVIII.] ([This work was undertaken] in the time of the guardianship of *Franciscus Vecchi* and *Franciscus Rosani,* priors, in the year of our Lord [1348, in the seventh indiction, in the month of September]) (see fig. 6).

Finally, there is even evidence that Cecco dello Vecchio assisted in the government of the City in the very period of Cola's ascension: in the confirmation of the statutes of the merchant guild for 1345, Cecco appears as one of the witnesses, who are all notaries.[136] In 1346 the same confirmation document was drawn up by the Notary of the Camera Urbis, that is, by Cola di Rienzo himself, and in the next year, by Egidio Angilerii, for Cola to authorize as ruler.

Cola, therefore, was very likely to have known the man who killed him;

---

133. Mosti, *Anthonius Goioli,* 194.
134. A.C./I 649 4/1359, 1v; Mosti, *Anthonius Goioli,* 207–9.
135. Mosti, *Francesco di Stefano Capogalli,* 218, 409.
136. Gatti, *Statuti dei Mercanti,* 79–80.

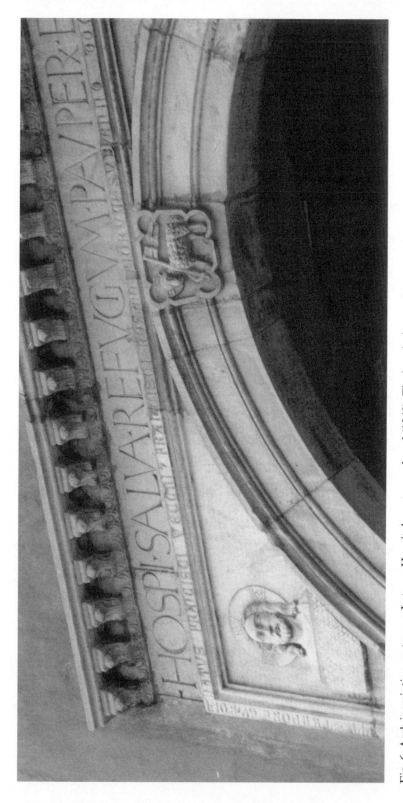

Fig. 6. Arch inscription, entrance, Lateran Hospital mortuary chapel (1348). The inscription reads, TEMPORE GUARDIA / NATUS FRANCISCI VECCHI & FRAN-CISCI ROSANI PRIORUM SUB ANNO DOM[INI .M.CCC.XL VIII.

and to have known him for a number of years. Cola and Cecco dello Vecchio clearly moved in very similar professional, geographical, social, and political circles. One may see, then, how Cola's supporters and enemies could come from the same economic and political milieu. This does not explain Cecco's personal motivation, of course. My theory is that he represented a particular *popolo* economic and political interest group in their desire in 1354 to see the pope's Senator, Cola, destroyed, so that he would stop spending money and men on his obsessive, personal war with the Colonna, and so they could get on with forging a new popular regime: there had already been similar attempts since 1347, with Cerroni in 1351 and Baroncelli in 1353. The second person to strike Cola in 1354 was another notary, Lorenzo of Trevi.[137] Egidi can only suggest, as motive, what he calls *gelosia di mestiere,* but if my hypothesis is correct, then it was because by 1354 a number of Cola's professional colleagues—the more radical *descreti,* the guild and confraternity *minuto* types, and his logical supporters—became impatient of Cola's obsession with the past at the expense of present good government, and with his baronial vendettas at the expense of the taxpayer. The *popolo grasso* types had already jumped ship by the end of 1347. Cola had become expendable. The men who supported him in 1347 and then (or later) dropped him, continued to reinforce their political and economic authority at the expense of the baronial elite, though not necessarily in harmony with less elite groups among the *popolo.*

Cola did, therefore, make enemies among his peer group, as well as among the barons. Just as when in 1346 he punished the barons who laughed at him, his memory for insult from his peers was long, too. A chronicle passage from 1347 demonstrates that when Cola was mocked, in the Roman council, in 1346, one of the senatorial scribes, described as *Tomao de Fiortifioccha,* made an obscene gesture, *la coda,* at him: the same character who was thought by seventeenth-century publishers to have penned the "biography" of the Tribune. Some months later, in June 1347, after his procession to St. Peter's, Cola had two senatorial scribes arrested, "mitred"[138] as forgers, and fined a thousand *librae* each. They are described in the chronicle as "very powerful *popolani.*" Both appear among the documentary records of the period: Tommaso's wife Una, of

---

137. Egidi and Wright read "Lauriento"; Porta suggests it was a nickname, "lo ventre" (*ARC,* 258 n. 349).

138. "Mitred": made to wear a false hat, with the crime written on it; a great public infamy.

the *rione* Colonna—the family were possibly clients of the chancellor in 1346, the Colonna-cadet Andrea dei Normanni, who slapped Cola on the same occasion—is mentioned by Paolo Serromani; his relative Giacomo, also of Colonna, by Giovanni di Nicola di Paolo; Tommaso himself is seen in his role as scribe in a guild confirmation of 1345.[139] Poncelletto "della Cammora" (of the Camera) of the chronicle also appears in the S. Spirito archives for 1338, where the senators passed judgment against some Orsini in a case of property rights; the document was rogated by *Poncellettus quondam Jacobi Johannis de Petiis notarius scriba sacri senatus.*[140] If these two *popolani,* who occupied senior magistracies in the administration, really did side with the Colonna chamberlain, one might hypothesize a personal "anti-Colonna" motive behind Cola's public humiliation of these two figures: this was Egidi's theory about Cecco dello Vecchio. Cola, however, did not act—for the most part—from personal malice or for revenge for his brother, as demonstrated by his critique (in both visual satire and legal ordinance) and his severe punishment of corrupt elements within his own administration; he even branded a messenger called Tortora for taking a bribe.[141]

Conclusion

This case demonstrates, in microcosm, the aspects of Cola's polity and administration upon which the second half of this study has focused. Cola was both supported and opposed by men from all parts of his society. Those who gave him the most support, and formed his government, correspond broadly to the social groups then evolving into the most powerful in contemporary Rome; these included knights such as Paolo Vaiani, *bovattieri* nobles like Buccio di Jubileo, lawyers and judges such as Matteo Baccari; but also *balestrieri* like Paolo Bussa. There are very good reasons for seeing Cola's revolt in terms of the expression of the interests of a new "class" or even classes: but not exclusively. Cola also received encouragement from parts of the ecclesiastical hierarchy of the City, and from certain fickle *magnati,* and an even more fickle populace. The same cross-section of origin and of motivation applies to his enemies. His own policies

---

139. Mosti, *Johannes Nicolai Pauli,* 54; AC/I 1/1347–48, 6r; Stevenson, *Statuti delle arti,* 165.

140. B.A.V. Vat. Lat. 7930, 46v. A Poncelletto is also recorded as Notary of the Camera Urbis in 1318: Gatti, *Statuti dei Mercanti,* 63.

141. Wright, *Life,* 50.

were, occasionally, equally inconsistent, and even tainted with the desire for personal glory or vengeance. His alliances were, moreover, not merely convenient associations based on a common economic background or even social and ideological convictions, but also based on personal factors; hence his choice of advisers from among his in-laws, the Mancini, and from the worthies of S. Angelo, his main zone of reference; an amalgam of new and previous staff.

It was in fact a very sincere and serious attempt at a new and incorruptible administration, focused on the niceties of justice, based firmly on the precedent of law, while basking in the glory of the classical past and anticipating the renewed sanctity of a world to come. Corruption and crime was punished within Cola's personnel: an admirable tenet for a regime in the broadest conceivable context of Roman politics. There was even an attempt to render politics answerable to the *populus,* by the *pittura infamante* of the governors of Rome, sneakily erected on the Capitol at some point in 1346. Immediately after the angry slapping episode in the *Parlamentum,* in council, the chronicle describes a giant visual allegory painted on the Capitol at Cola's instigation. This depicted all of the various social groups of Trecento Rome in pejorative "bestial" terms, singling out three groups for censure. Two of these fell into Cola's "own class": respectively "the bad councilors, followers of the nobles," and "the false officials, judges, and notaries." Another barely noted passage also confirms that Cola was not necessarily the darling of either his profession or, more broadly, his "own class" in 1347. After the account of his popular acclamation and installation as Tribune, the Chronicler describes the initially aggressive responses of the barons, and then their oaths of obedience. Only after this act of affirmation by the *magnifici* did the "natural" supporters of the new regime express their commitment: "A few days later the judges of the City came and swore fidelity. . . . Then the notaries came and did the same, then the merchants. In short, one by one . . . every man came and swore to the Good Estate."[142]

The passage demonstrates how great a struggle Cola faced, even from the very sector of Roman society that was to provide the mainstay of his support. Calling them—albeit pictorially—dogs, pigs, cats, goats, and monkeys may not have served his cause, for all that it expressed his conviction. It is unsafe to make sweeping assumptions about Cola's supporters, presuming a solidarity based on economic "class distinctions," as we

---

142. Ibid., 45.

saw in chapter 5. He had just stood up and accused them—not the barons, but his fellow citizens who were councilors—of "sucking the blood of the poor."[143] Similarly it would be unwise to dismiss the relationship of Cola with the magnates of the City, during his governmental career, as unswervingly hostile. It was his career as a notary, and from this position as a politician, diplomat, and senior financial magistrate, that allowed Cola access to exalted aristocratic banquets and acquaintances, at least in the early part of the regime.

However, while Cola focused on vertical as well as horizontal networking, it is nonetheless undeniable that the mainstay of Cola's rise to power was the attraction of his proposed measures to a broadly defined *popolo*. The impasse of the imprisoning episode, caused by the clash of those Romans who would work with or for the *magnifici* (men, we must assume, like Antonio dei Scambi and Matteo de Baccariis), with those who would have killed the barons (the Chronicler, perhaps; Cola's militia, certainly) is described in chapter 5. The only reason such a coalition held together, I have argued, was because Cola straddled these two groups within the *popolo:* by dint of his role as Notary of the Civic Chamber, on the one hand, and his "low" origins, and early public self-identification as champion of the poor and needy, on the other. Meanwhile Cola's official status, a result of his notarial career, allowed him, the son of an tavern keeper, access to the pinnacles of Roman society. The Chronicler describes how he was jeered at by the barons—"when he attended banquets with Janni Colonna and the nobles of Rome"[144]—presumably in his capacity as Notary of the Chamber. His professional career offered, then, at one end of the scale, the necessary entrée to the entourage of the barons, but at the other, the opportunity, and the skills, to address the broadest conceivable audiences in the public spaces of the City: just like a notary giving an arbitration in a street tribunal, but writ large. However, it was Cola's career as a notary that brought him well before 1347 into the ranks of the *popolo* and up through this to the forefront of the administrative culture of Rome, and it was from here that he derived the backbone of his support.

Cola's ability to mediate between the top and the bottom ranks of society veered all too often precariously close to its limit. The loss of the social elements at either extreme of the social spectrum followed swiftly after the

---

143. Ibid., 33.
144. Ibid., 37.

collapse at the center of Cola's support. True of the political career of *popolani* in general, success for the notary in politics tended to follow the forging of vertical alliances of reciprocal clientage and economic symbiosis in both directions. In this sense Cola was treading ground familiar to those of the rank—the elite of the notaries of Rome—into which he had climbed; but the fact that he was always something of a social outsider may have made it all the easier to drop him. He proved expendable, as the long-term success of the *popolo* during the second half of the fourteenth century was to demonstrate. Yet for a period, back in 1347, Cola di Rienzo carried off a coalition unique in its social range, of which his own career should be seen as an index: innkeeper's son, *popolano* notary, noble knight. His position offers historians a curious paradox: a professional paradigm and a social anomaly, at one and the same time. The particular social cachet of the Roman notary helped Cola reach a position from which he could built contacts and seize power, moving up and down the ranks of society secure in his personal status and the *publica fides* of the notary. The majority of the skills that guaranteed his authority, for as long as it lasted, were the skills he had learned as a notary: diligent administration, personnel supervision, legal expertise in both theory and practice, good financial management with precise resource analysis and budget allocation, fiscal extension and implementation, strategic political maneuvering and social networking, all combined with considerable scholarly, rhetorical, and forensic ability.

Combined with his visionary appeal to the future of the New Jerusalem, and his legalistic yet also heroic resurrection of classical Rome, Cola's temporarily overwhelming success is readily comprehensible; and even if his personal triumph was short-lived, we should not lose sight of his revolution in the context of broader shifts in society and culture in the late medieval period. The most diligent of Cola's historians, Konrad Burdach, saw Cola as occupying the twin roles of religious and political leadership on the eve of both the Renaissance and the Reformation, and thus carrying the world forward into a new era. That claim is overstated in the extreme (though Cola might well have liked it). Nonetheless, both the Roman regime of 1347 and its leadership deserve to take their place as both an effect and in turn, by reinforcing the effect, as a further cause of change in the medieval relationship between Roman Church and European Christendom, as well as in the relationship between the papacy and the City of Rome. Cola and his revolution therefore deserve to be relocated within the processes of cultural change between 1300 and 1500. This period of change affected forever the concept and exercise of power in the forms of national identity, ecclesiastical authority, civic autonomy, and social status. The rehabilitation of the Roman revolution in 1347 both as an integral part and as a reflection of the world that it shook—if just for one historical moment—has long been overdue.

Bibliography

Manuscript Sources

London, British Library

Additional 17333 (Apocalypse, thirteenth century)
Add. 35166 (Apocalypse, thirteenth century)
Add. 14801 (necrology, S. Maria in Trastevere, fourteenth century)
Royal 6.E.IX (Anjou panegyric, ca. 1340)
Add. 19587 (Dante's *Divine Comedy,* later fourteenth century)
Add. 21965 (Dante's *Divine Comedy,* later fourteenth century)
Royal 10. D. I. (Dante's *Divine Comedy,* later fourteenth century)
Add. 20040 (*Vita di Cola di Rienzo,* sixteenth century)
Harley 3543 (*Vita di Cola di Rienzo,* sixteenth century)

Malibu, Getty Museum

Getty Apocalypse (thirteenth century)

Oxford, Bodleian Library

Auct. D.IV.17 (Apocalypse, thirteenth century)
Douce 180 (Douce Apocalypse, thirteenth century)
Douce 58 (fols. 140r–146v: *Vaticinia de Summis Pontificis,* fifteenth century)

Paris, Bibliothèque Nationale

Fr. 4274 (Statutes, Order of the Knot or Holy Spirit, ca. 1354–55)
Ital. 81 (Fazio degli Uberti, *Dittamondo,* fifteenth century: 18r, *Roma vedova*)

Rome, Archivio Capitolino

Sezione I, 649/1–3*bis* (Paolo Serromani, notarial protocols, 1348–55)

Sez. I, 649/4–14, 650/1 (Paolo dei Serromani, 1359–87)
Sez. I, 763 (Lello dei Serromani, 1387–98)
Sez. I, 785/1–11, 785bis/1–3 (Nardo di Pucio Venettini, 1382–1427)
Credenza IV/88 (fols. 143r.–146v: Statutes, notaries' guild, early fifteenth century)
Archivio Orsini (all fourteenth-century parchment documents)
Archivio Boccapaduli, Mazzo Supplementario, 4–5 (later copy of so-called account of Nardo Scocciapile, ?1372)

Rome, Archivio Cenci

All fourteenth-century documents

Rome, Archivio Odescalchi

All copies of fourteenth-century documents

Rome, Archivio Storico di Stato

Notaries' Protocols

Collegio dei notai capitolini 1181 (Angelo di Nicola Grivelli, 1337)
Collegio dei notai capitolini 849, 1163, 1236 (Giovanni di Nicola di Paolo, 1348–79)
Collegio dei notai capitolini 1236 (Marino di Pietro Milçonis, 1357)
Collegio dei notai capitolini 1163 (Paolo di Nicola di Paolo, 1362)
Collegio dei notai capitolini 849 (Antonio Goioli di Pietro Scopte, 1365)
Collegio dei notai capitolini 138 (Pietro di Nicola Astalli, 1368)
Collegio dei notai capitolini 1703 (Lorenzo di Giovanni Staglia, 1372)
Collegio dei notai capitolini 475, 476 (Francesco di Stefano dei Capogalli, 1374–86)
Miscellanea notarile 1 (Nardo di Pucio Venettini, 1382–1427)
Collegio dei notai capitolini 477 (Giacomello di Stefano Capogalli, 1385–1400)
Collegio dei notai capitolini 1236 (Nicola di Giovanni di Giacomo, 1391)
Collegio dei notai capitolini 270 (Nicola del fu Nucio di maestro Raynaldo, 1394)
Collegio dei notai capitolini 849 (Giovanni Paolo di Antonio Goioli, 1397)

Ecclesiastical Institutions

Collezione pergamene, cassette 1 (S. Agostino)
Coll. perg. cass. 1 (Confraternità di S. Maria Annunziata)
Coll. perg. cass. 2–3 (SS. Alessio e Bonifacio)
Coll. perg. cass. 8 (SS. XII Apostoli)
Coll. perg. cass. 9 (S. Cecilia in Trastevere)
Coll. perg. cass. 18–19 (SS. Cosma e Damiano)

Coll. perg. cass. 21 (S. Crisogono)
Coll. perg. cass. 25 (S. Filippo Neri)
Coll. perg. cass. 31 (S. Martino ai Monti)
Coll. perg. cass. 34 (S. Paolo fuori le Mura)
Coll. perg. cass. 36 (S. Ononfrio)
Coll. perg. cass. 39–40 (S. Silvestro in Capite)
Coll. perg. cass. 42 (S. Suzanna)
Coll. perg. cass. 43–46 (Ospedale di S. Giacomo al Colosseo)
Coll. perg. cass. 49 (Ospedale di S. Maria della Consolazione, collezione C)
Coll. perg. cass. 54, 60–62 (Ospedale di S. Spirito in Sassia, coll. A & B)
Coll. perg. cass. 92 (Raccolta Gunther, *miscellanea*)
Coll. perg. cass. 73 (Orsini family land transactions)
Coll. perg. cass. 404–511 (Ospedale del Ss.mo Salvatore *ad Sancta Sanctorum*)

Subiaco, Monastery of S. Scholastica, Archivio Colonna

All fourteenth-century documents

Vatican City, Biblioteca Apostolica Vaticana

Barberini Lat. 2733 (Grimaldi, drawing of Giotto's *Navicella,* seventeenth century)
Chigiani L.VIII. 296 (Giovanni Villani, *Cronica,* illustrated ca. 1360)
Ottobon. Lat. 2615 (*Vita di Cola di Rienzo,* illustrated, 1610)
Pal.Gr. 431 ("Joshua Roll," fourth century)
S. Angelo in Pescheria 1, 1–27 (Antonio di Lorenzo di Stefanello "Impoccia" dei Scambi, notarial protocols, 1363–1427)
S. Maria Maggiore 1
S. Maria in Via Lata & S. Ciriaco, cass. 300–317 (*Varia* 1–150, 151–274)
Vat. Lat. 1927 (Valerius Maximus, *Facta et dicta memorabilia,* 1320s)
Vat. Lat. 2044 (Platina, *De Vitis Pontificarum,* ca. 1475)
Vat. Lat. 4029 (Inquisitorial records, 1334)
Vat. Lat. 6823 (*Ordine e Magnificenza. . . ,* fols. 23–31, after 1368/fifteenth century)
Vat. Lat. 7817 ("Francesco Baroncelli," *Vita,* sixteenth–seventeenth centuries)
Vat. Lat. 7929–31, 8029, 8043 (Don Pier Luigi Galletti, 1724–1790: transcriptions of Antonio dei Scambi and other fourteenth-century material incl. Margarita Cornetana)
Vat. Lat. 12503 (Bohemian collection of Cola's letters, later fourteenth century; prev. Archivo Segreto Vaticano, Misc. Arm. XV no. 45)

Published Sources

Adinolfi, Pasquale. *Roma nell'età di mezzo.* 3 vols. Narni, 1857–60.
Agnolo di Tura del Grasso. *Cronica.* In *Chronache Senesi,* edited by Alessandro Lisini and Fabio Iacometti. *R.I.S.,* 2d ed., vol. 15, pt. 6. Bologna: Nicola Zanichelli, 1935.

Ait, Ivana. "Aspetti del mercato del credito a Roma nelle fonti notarili." In *Alle origini della nuova Roma*. *Martino V (1417–1431)*, edited by Maria Chiabò, Giusi d'Alessandro, Paola Piacentini, and Concetta Ranieri, 479–500. Rome: Istituto Storico Italiano per il Medio Evo, 1992.

Allegrezza, Franca. "Trasformazioni della nobilità baronale." In *Roma Medievale. Aggiornamenti*, edited by Paolo Delogu, 211–20. Florence: All'Insegna del Giglio, 1999.

Amor, Anne Clark. *William Holman Hunt: The True Pre-Raphaelite*. London: Constable, 1989.

Amore, O. "L'apporto degli atti privati alla conoscenza della società medievale." *Studi Romani* 27 (1980): 459–67.

Andreiu, Michel. *Le Pontifical Romain au Moyen Age*. Studi e Testi 86–88. 3 vols. Vatican City, 1940.

Anonimo Romano. *Cronica*. Edited by Ettore Mazzali. Milan: Rizzoli, 1991.

———. *Cronica*. Edited by Giuseppe Porta. Critical ed. Milan: Adelfi, 1979. Text only ed. 1981.

Anselmi, Gian Mario. "Il tempo della storia e quello della vita nella Cronica dell'Anonimo romano." *Studi e problemi di critica testuale* 21 (1980): 181–94.

———. "La Cronica dell'Anonimo romano." *Bulletino dell'Istituto storico Italiano* 91 (1984): 423–40.

Antal, Frederick. *Florentine Painting and Its Social Background*. London: Kegan Paul, 1947.

Antonelli, Mercurino. "Vicende della dominazione pontificia nel patrimonio di S. Pietro in Tuscia; dalla traslazione della sede alla restaurazione dell' Albornoz." *ASRSP* 25 (1902): 355–95; 26 (1903): 249–341; 27 (1904): 109–46, 312–49.

———. "La dominazione pontificia nel Patrimonio negli ultimi venti anni del periodo Avignonese." *ASRSP* 30 (1907): 269–332; 31 (1908): 121–68, 315–55.

———. "Il Cardinal Albornoz e il governo di Roma nel 1354." *ASRSP* 39 (1916): 587–601.

Armellini, Mariano. *Le Chiese di Roma dal secolo IV al XIX*. 1891; reprint, Rome: Pasquino, 1982.

Arnaldi, Girolamo. "Il notaio-cronista e le cronache cittadine in Italia." In *La storia del diritto nel quadro delle scienze storiche*. Florence: Società italiana di storia del diritto, 1966.

Aulus Gellius. *Noctes Atticae*. Edited by Peter K. Marshall. Oxford: Clarendon Press, 1968.

Barbi, Silvio A., ed. *Storie Pistorese*. In *R.I.S.*, 2d ed., vol. 11, pt. 5. Città di Castello: S. Lapi, 1907–27.

Barone, Giulia. "Il movimento francescano e la nascita delle confraternite romane." *Ricerche per la storia religiosa di Roma* 5 (1984): 71–80.

———. "Il potere pontificio e la città di Roma tra XIII e XIV secolo." In *Dal Patrimonio di San Pietro allo Stato Pontificio. La Marca nel Contesto del Potere Temporale*. Ascoli Piceno: Premio internazionale Ascoli Piceno 1991.

Barone, Giulia, and A. M. Piazzoni. "Le più antiche carte dell'archivio del Gonfalone (1267–1486)." In *Le Chiavi della Memoria*. Vatican City: Scuola vaticana de paleografia, diplomatica e archivistica, 1984.

Bartoloni, Franco, ed. *Codice Diplomatice del Senato Romano dal MCXLIV al MCCCXLVII.* Fonti per la storia d'Italia 87. Rome: Istituto Storico Italiano, 1948.

Barzini, Luigi. "Cola di Rienzo or the Obsession of Antiquity." In *The Italians.* London: Hamish Hamilton, 1964.

Baudrillart, M. *Dictionnaire d'Histoire et de Géographie Ecclesiastique.* Paris, 1914.

Bayley, C. C. "Petrarch, Charles IV, and the *renovatio imperii.*" *Speculum* 17 (1942): 323–41.

Bazano, Giovanni. *Chonicon Mutinense.* Edited by Tommaso Casini. *R.I.S.,* 2d ed., vol. 15, pt. 4. Bologna: Nicola Zanichelli, 1919.

Beer, Jeanette M. *A Medieval Caesar.* Geneva: Librarie Droz, 1976.

Belting, Hans. "The New Role of Narrative in Public Painting of the Trecento: Historia and Allegoria." *Studies in the History of Art* (National Gallery, Washington, D.C.) 15–16 (1985): 151–68.

Beneše of Weitmühl. *Chronica.* Edited by Josef Emler. Fontes Rerum Bohemicarum, vol. 4. Prague, 1884.

Bernardo, Aldo S. *Petrarch, Scipio, and the "Africa": The Birth of Humanism's Dream.* Baltimore: Johns Hopkins Press, 1962.

Bertoni, Giulio, and Emilio Vicini, eds. *Chronicon Estense. R.I.S.,* 2d ed., vol. 15, pt. 3. 2d ed. Città del Castello: S. Lapi, 1907.

Bignami-Odier, Jeanne. *Études sur Jean de Roquetaillade.* Paris, 1952.

Billanovich, Giuseppe. "Gli umanisti e le chronache medioevale. I: *Liber Pontificialis,* le *Decadi* di Tito Livio e il primo umanesimo a Roma." In *Italia Medioevale e Umanistica.* 2 vols. Bologna: Antenore, 1958.

———. "Come nacque un capolavoro: La 'cronica' del non più Anonimo Romano." *Rendiconti dell'Accademia Nazionale dei Lincei,* 9th ser., 6 (1995): 195–211.

Blanc, P. "La construction d'une utopie néo-urbaine: Rome dans la pensée, l'action et l'oeuvre de Petrarque de 1333 à 1342." In *Jérusalem, Rome, Constantinople. L'image et le mythe de la ville en Moyen Âge,* edited by Daniel Poirion. Paris: Presses de l'Université de Paris-Sorbonne, 1986.

Bologna, Ferdinando. *I Pittori alla Corte Angioina di Napoli (1266–1414).* Rome: Ugo Bozzi, 1969.

Bona-Fellini, P. "Cola; un figlio del popolo nella passione di Roma." *Capitolium,* 3d ser., 41 (1966): 166–71.

Boskovits, Miklòs. "Gli affreschi del Duomo di Anagni." *Paragone: Arte* 30, no. 2 (1979): 3–41.

Bourel de la Roncière, Charles, J. de Loye, A. Coulon, and C. de Cenival, eds. *Registres d'Alexander IV.* 4 vols. Paris, 1902–59.

Brandi, Carl. "Konrad Burdach. Vom Mittelalter zur Reformation. . . ." Review of *Briefwechsel des Cola di Rienzo,* by Konrad Burdach and Paul Piur. *Göttingen Gelehrte Anzeigen* 7–12 (1923): 187–98.

———. *Cola di Rienzo und sein Verhältnis in Renaissance und Humanismus.* Darmstadt: Vorträge der Bibliothek Warburg, 1965.

Brentano, Robert, *Rome before Avignon.* 2d ed. London: British Museum Press, 1991.

Brezzi, Paolo. "Holy Years in the Economic Life of the City of Rome." *Journal of European Economic History* 4 (1975): 673–90.

———. "Il sistema agraria nel territorio romano alla fine del Medio Evo." *Studi Romani* 2 (1977): 153–68.

———. "Roma medioevale: la realtà e l'idea." *Studi Romani* 30 (1983): 16–30.

Brigante Colonna, G. "Cola di Rienzo tribuno di Roma." *Vie d'Italia* 8 (1943): 641–46.

Brizzolara, Giuseppe. "Il Petrarca e Cola di Rienzo." *Studi Storici* 8 (1899): 239–51, 423–63.

———. "Ancora Cola di Rienzo e Francesco Petrarca." *Studi Storici* 12 (1903): 353–411; 14 (1905): 69–101, 243–77.

Brunt, Peter A. "Lex de Imperio Vespasiani." *Journal of Roman Studies* 62 (1972): 95–116.

Buccio di Rannallo. *Chronicon Aquilana.* Edited by V. De Bartolomeis. Fonti per la Storia d'Italia 41. Rome: Istituto Storico Italiano, 1907.

Bulwer-Lytton, Edward. *Cola di Rienzo. The Last of the Tribunes.* 2d ed. London: Routledge, 1848.

Burdach, Konrad, and Paul Piur. *Briefwechsel des Cola di Rienzo.* Vol. 1, *Rienzo und die geistige Wandlung seiner Zeit* (1912). Vol. 2, *Kritische Darstellung der Quellung zur Geschichte Rienzos* (1928). Vol. 3, *Kritischer Text: Lesarten und anmerkung* (1912). Vol. 4, *Anhang: Urkundliche quellen zur Geschichte Rienzos* (1912). Vol. 5, *Nachlese zu den Texten: Kommentar.* Vom Mittelalter zur Reformation. Forschungen und Geschichte der Deutschen Bildung, no. 2. 5 vols. Berlin: Weidmann, 1912–29.

Buzzi, G. "Konrad Burdach und Paul Piur, Briefwechsel des Cola di Rienzo. Dritter Teil. . . ." Review of *Briefwechsel des Cola di Rienzo,* by Konrad Burdach and Paul Piur. *ASRSP* 35 (1912): 638–42.

Byron, George Gordon, Lord. *Childe Harold's Pilgrimage.* Edited by John D. Jump and Frederick Page. Rev. ed. Oxford: Oxford University Press, 1970.

Calisse, C. "I prefetti di Vico." *ASRSP* 10 (1887): 1–136, 353–594.

———. "Costituzione del Patrimonio di S. Pietro in Tuscia nel secolo XIV." *ASRSP* 15 (1892): 1–70.

Canning, Joseph. *The Political Thought of Baldus de Ubaldis.* Cambridge: Cambridge University Press, 1987.

Carbonetti Venditelli, Cristina. "Documentazione inedita riguardante i *magistri edificorum urbis* e l'attività della loro curia nei secoli XIII–XIV." *ASRSP* 113 (1990): 169–88.

———. "La curia dei magistri edificorum Urbis nei secoli XIII e XIV a la sua documentazione." In *Roma nei secoli XIII e XIV. Cinque Saggi,* edited by Etienne Hubert, 1–42. Rome: Viella, 1993.

Carocci, Sandro. "Baroni in città. Considerazioni sull'insediamento e i diritti urbani della grande nobiltà." In *Roma nei secoli XIII e XIV. Cinque Saggi,* edited by Etienne Hubert, 137–73. Rome: Viella, 1993.

———. *I Baroni di Roma. Dominazione signorili e lignaggi aristocratici nel duecento e nel primo Trecento.* Rome: École Française, 1993.

Castelfranchi, Luisa. "Le storie apocalittiche di Stoccarda e quelle di Giusto da Padova." *Prospettiva* 33–36 (1983–84): 33–44.

Castellani, Arrigo. "Note di lettura: La Chronica d'Anonimo romano." *Studi linguistici italiani* 13 (1987): 66–84.

———. "Ritorno a l'Anonimo romano." *Studi linguistici italiani* 18 (1992): 238–50.

Cenchetti, Giorgio. "Giovanni da Ignano *Capitaneus populi et Urbis Romae.*" *ASRSP* 63 (1940): 145–71.

Chadabra, R. "Der 'Zweite Konstantin': Zum verhältnis von Staat und Kirche in der Karolischen kunst Böhmes." *Umeni* 26, no. 6 (1978): 505–20.

Cherniss, Michael D. *Boethian Apocalypse: Studies in Middle English Vision Poetry.* Norman, Okla.: Pilgrim Press, 1987.

Chocholousek, Prokop. *Cola di Rienzi: Povídka. Karl IV a Tribun rimeskeho lidu.* Prague, 1856.

Clemente, Vittorio. "Cola di Rienzo nella leggenda e nella tradizione d'Abruzzo." *Capitolium* 17 (1942): 406–9.

Clementi, Filippo. *Il Carnevale Romano.* Rome, 1899.

Clifton-Everest, J. "Johann von Neumarkt und Cola di Rienzo." *Bohemia* 28 (1987): 25–44.

Coccanari, O. C. "Cola di Rienzo e la congiura di Fra Moriale." *Bolletino di Tivoli e regione* 18 (1936): 2693–95.

Cohn, Norman. *The Pursuit of the Millenium: Revolutionary Millenarians and Mystical Anarchists of the Middle Ages.* Rev. ed. London: Temple Smith, 1970.

"Cola di Rienzo." In *Il notariato nella civiltà italiana,* 190–201. Milan: Consiglio nazionale der notariato, 1961.

Collins, Amanda. "Cola di Rienzo: The Revolution in Historical Perspective." D. Phil. thesis, Oxford University, 1996.

———. "Cola di Rienzo, the Lateran Basilica, and the *Lex de Imperio* of Vespasian." *Mediaeval Studies* 60 (1998): 159–83.

Colliva, Paolo. *Il Cardinale Albornoz, lo stato della chiesa, le Constitutiones Aegidiane (1353–57).* Bologna: Publicaciones del Real Colegio de España, 1977.

Colombe, G. "Nicholas Rienzi au Palais des Papes d'Avignon. Le lieu de sa détention." *Memoires de l'Académie de Vaucluse* (1911): 323–44.

Conti, A. "Cola di Rienzo esule e prigioniero a Praga." *Latina* 17 (1939): 28–30.

Contini, Gianfranco. "Invito a un capolavoro." *Letteratura* 4 (1940): 3–6.

Corbo, Anna Maria. *Artisti e artigiani in Roma al tempo di Martino e di Eugenio IV.* Rome: De Luca, 1969.

———. "Relazione descrittiva degli archivi notarili Romani dei secoli XIV–XV nell'Archivio di Stato e nell'Archivio Capitolino." In *Sources of Social History: Private Acts of the Late Middle Ages,* edited by Paolo Brezzi and Egmont Lee, 49–67. Toronto: Pontifical Institute of Mediaeval Studies, 1984.

Corsi, Domenico. "La 'crociata' di Venturino da Bergamo nella crisi spirituale di metà Trecento." *Archivio Storico Italiano* 147 (1989): 697–747.

Cortonesi, Alfio, *Terre e signori nel Lazio medioevale.* Naples: Liguori, 1988.

Cosenza, Mario E. *Petrarch: The Revolution of Cola di Rienzo.* 1913; reprint, New York: Italica Press, 1986.

Coste, Jean. "L'archivio Liberiano." *ASRSP* 96 (1973): 5–77.

―――. "La famiglia De Ponte di Roma tra secoli XII–XIV." *ASRSP* 111 (1988): 49–73.

Crawford, Michael. *Roman Statutes.* 2 vols. London: Institute of Classical Studies, 1996.

D'Achille, Paolo. "Note sur l'epigrafia volgare a Roma nel Trecento e nel Quattrocento." In *Il Romanesco ieri e oggi,* edited by Tullio de Mauro, 3–12. Rome: Ignoto Editore, 1989.

D'Annunzio, Gabriele. *La Vita di Cola di Rienzo.* Florence, 1905.

Dante. *Dantis Alagheris Epistolae.* Edited by Paget Toynbee. 2d ed. Oxford: Clarendon Press, 1966.

―――. *Opere Minori.* Edited by Domenico de Robertis and Gianfranco Contini. Milan: R. Ricciardi, 1984.

D'Arrigo, Giuseppe. "Ricordo di due grandi; Francesco Petrarcha e Cola di Rienzo." In *Fatti e Figure del Lazio Medievale.* Roma: Palombi, 1979.

Davis, Charles T. *Dante and the Idea of Rome.* Oxford: Clarendon Press, 1957.

―――. "Rome and Babylon in Dante." In *Rome in the Renaissance: The City and the Myth,* edited by P. A. Ramsay, 19–40. Binghampton: Center for Medieval and Early Renaissance Studies, SUNY, 1982.

De Angelis, P. *L'Ospedale di Santo Spirito in Saxia.* 2 vols. Rome: Academia Laneisiana, 1960–62.

De Blasi, J. "Cola di Rienzo tragico Tribuno dei Romani." *Historia* 8 (1964): 58–65.

De Boispreaux, [Bénigne Dujardin]. *Histoire de Nicolas Rienzy, Chévalier, Tribun et Sénateur.* Paris, 1743.

De Boüard, Alain. "Les notaires de Rome au Moyen Age." *MEFRM* 31 (1911): 291–307.

―――. *Le Régime politique et les institutions de Rome au Moyen-Age 1252–1347.* Paris, 1920.

De Broqua, Joseph Jean, *Cola di Rienzo, Tribun de Rom. Une Drame Democratique au XIVième siècle.* Paris, 1925.

De Castris, Pierluigi. *Arte di Corte nella Napoli Angioina.* Florence: Cantini, 1986.

De Cupis, Cesare. "Regesto degli Orsini e dei Conti Anguillara." *Bolletino della Società Patria Anton Lodovico Antinori negli Abruzzi,* 15, n.s. 29 (1903–38).

De Rossi, Gian-Battista. *Inscriptiones Christianae urbis Romae.* Rome, 1857–88.

D'Onofrio, Cesare. *Un popolo di Statue Racconte. Storie, Fatti, Leggende della Città di Roma antica, medievale, moderna.* Rome: Romana società editrice, 1990.

Du Cerceau, Jean. *Conjuration de Nicholas Gabrini dit de Rienzo.* Paris, 1733.

Duncalf, F., and A. Krey. "The Coronation of Cola di Rienzo." In *Parallel Source Problems in Medieval History.* New York, 1912.

Dupré-Théseider, Eugenio. "L'impresa di Cola di Rienzo e Firenze." *Illustrazione Toscana* 2 (1940): 23–26.

―――. *Roma dal Commune di Popolo alla Signoria Pontificia (1252–1377).* Storia di Roma, vol. 11. Bologna: Cappelli, 1952.

————. "L'attesa escatologica durante il periodo avignonese." In *Mondo Cittadino e Movimenti Ereticali nel Medio Evo.* Bologna: Pàtron, 1978.

Egidi, Pietro. *Intorno all'Esercito del Comune di Roma nella prima metà del secolo XIV.* Viterbo, 1897.

————. "Per la vita di Francesco Baroncelli." In *Scritti di Storia, di filosophia e d'arte.* Naples, 1908.

————. "Chi era l'uccisore di Cola di Rienzo." In *Miscellanea per le Nozze Crocioni-Ruscelloni.* Rome, 1908.

————. "Privilegio di Francesco Baroncelli in favore di Vitorchiano." In *Scritti storici in memoria di Giovanni Monticolo.* Venice, 1922.

————. *Necrologia e libri affini della provincia Romana.* Fonti per la Storia d'Italia, 44–45. 2 vols. Rome: Istituto Storico Italiano, 1908–14.

Ehrle, Franz. "Die Spiritualen und ihr verhältnis zum Franziskenorden und die Fraticellen." *Archiv für Literatur- und Kirchen-Geschichte des Mittelalters* 4 (1888): 1–190.

Elliott, Janis, "The Last Judgement Scene in Central Italian Painting, ca. 1266–1343: The Impact of Guelf Politics, Papal Power, and Angevin Iconography." Ph.D. thesis, Warwick University, 2000.

Engels, Friedrich. *Cola di Rienzi.* Edited by Michael Knieriem, *Cola di Rienzi: Ein Unbekannter Dramatischer Entwurf.* Trier: Hammer, 1974.

Esch, Arnold. "Dal Medioevo al Rinascimento. Uomini a Roma dal 1350 al 1450." *ASRSP* 94 (1971): 1–10.

————. "La fine del libero comune di Roma nel giudizio dei mercanti fiorentino." *Bulletino dell' Istituto Storico Italiano per il Medio Evo* 86 (1977): 235–77.

Esposito, Anna. "Un inventario di beni in Roma dell'Ospedale di S. Spirito in Sassia (1322)." *ASRSP* 99 (1976): 71–115.

————. "La documentazione degli archivi di ospedali e confraternite come fonte per la storia sociale di Roma." In *Sources of Social History: Private Acts of the Late Middle Ages,* edited by Paolo Brezzi and Egmont Lee, 69–79. Toronto: Pontifical Institute of Mediaeval Studies, 1984.

————. "Le 'confraternite' del Gonfalone (secoli XIV–XV)." *Ricerche per la storia religiosa di Roma* 5 (1984): 91–136.

————. "I protocolli notarili per gli studi di topografia: un esempio romano dal rione Parione." In *Scritti in Memoria di Giuseppe Marchetti Longhi,* edited by Gioacchino Giammaria and Giampiero Raspa. Biblioteca di Latium 10–11. Anagni: Istituto di storia e di arte del Lazio meridionale, 1990.

————. "Note sulla populazione Romana dalla fine del sec. XIV al Sacco (1527)." In *Un Altra Roma.* Rome: Il Calamo, 1995.

Fedele, Pietro. "Un giudicato di Cola di Rienzo fra il monastero di S. Cosimato e gli Stephaneschi." *ASRSP* 26 (1903): 437–51.

————. "Konrad Burdach und Paul Piur—*Briefwechsel des Cola di Rienzo.* Kritischer Text. . . ." Review of *Briefwechsel des Cola di Rienzo,* by Konrad Burdach and Paul Piur. *Giornale Storico della Letteratura Italiana* 44 (1914): 386–405.

————. "Una lettera di Cola di Rienzo al comune di Padova." *ASRSP* 43 (1920): 429–31.

Federici, Vincenzo. "Regesto del monastero di S. Silvestro in Capite." *ASRSP* 22 (1899): 213–300; 23 (1900): 67–128, 489–538.

Federici, Vincenzo, Raffaello Morghen, Pietro Egidi, F. Tommassetti, O. Montenovesi, A. Diviziani, and P. Fontana, eds. *Statuti della Provincia Romana.* Fonti per la Stori d'Italia 48, 69. 2 vols. Rome: Istituto Storico Italiano, 1910–30.

Felici, Lucio. "'La Vita di Cola di Rienzo' nella tradizione chronacista Romana." *Studi Romani* 25 (1977): 325–43.

Filippini, Francesco. "Cola di Rienzo e la Curia Avignonese." *Studi Storici* 10 (1901): 241–87; 11 (1902): 3–35.

Filippini, Laura. *La Scultura del Trecento in Roma.* Turin, 1908.

[Fiortifioccha, Tomao.] *La Vita di Cola di Rienzo.* Bracciano: Andrea Fei, 1624.

Fleischer, Victor. *Rienzo: The Rise and Fall of a Dictator.* London: Aiglon Press, 1948.

Flutre, Louis-Fernand, and K. Sneyders de Vogel. *Li Fet des Romains.* 2 vols. Paris, 1937–38.

Franceschini, M. "*Popolares, cavallarocti, milites vel doctores.* Consorterie, fazioni e magistrature cittadine." In *Alle origini della nuova Roma. Martino V (1417–1431),* edited by Maria Chiabò, Giusi d'Alessandro, Paola Piacentini, and Concetta Ranieri, 291–300. Rome: Istituto Storico Italiano per il Medio Evo, 1992.

Františka of Prague. *Chronica.* Edited by Josef Emler. Fontes Rerum Bohemicarum, vol. 4. Prague, 1884.

Frova, Carla, and Massimo Miglio. "*Studium Urbis* e *Studium Curiae* nel Trecento e nel Quattrocento: Linee di politica culturale." In *Roma e lo Studium Urbis: Spazio Urbana e Cultura dal Quattro al Seicento. Atti del convegno. Roma, 7–10 giugno 1989,* edited by Paolo Cherubini, 26–39. Rome: Istituto Storico per il Medio Evo, 1992.

Frugoni, Arsenio. "Cola di Rienzo *Tribunus sompniator.*" In *Incontri nel Rinascimento.* Brescia: La Scuola, 1954.

———. "Cola di Rienzo." *Humanitas* 54 (1954): 362–70.

Fuhrmann, Horst. *Das Constitutum Constantini (Konstantinische Geschenk).* Fontes Iuris Germanici Antiqui, vol. 10. Hannover: Hahnsche Buchhandlung, 1968.

Gabrielli, A. "L'epistole di Cola di Rienzo e l'epistolografia medievale." *ASRSP* 11 (1888): 379–479.

———. *Epistolario di Cola di Rienzo.* Fonti per la Storia d'Italia 7. Rome: Istituto Storico Italiano, 1890.

———. "Cola di Rienzo e la theatro." *Nuova Antologia* 136 (1908): 201–12.

Gabrini, Tommaso. *Osservazioni storico-critiche sulla Vita di Cola di Rienzo.* Rome, 1806.

———. *Commento sopra il poemetto "Spirito Gentile" che il Petrarca indirezzo a Nicola di Rienzo tribuno e poi senatore di Roma colla interpretazione del lapide che l'istesso fece apporre al torrione di Ponte Rotto ivi ancora esistente.* Rome, 1807.

Gatti, Giuseppe. *Statuti dei Mercanti di Roma.* Rome: Della Pace, 1885.

Gennaro, Chiara. "Per lo studio della composizione sociale della popolazione di Roma nella seconda metà Trecento." Ph.D. diss., University of Rome 'La Sapienza,' 1963.

———. "Mercanti e bovattieri nella Roma della seconda metà del Trecento." *Bulletino dell'Istituto storico italiano per il Medio Evo* 78 (1967): 155–87.

———. "Giovanni Colombini e la sua 'compagnia.'" *Bulletino Italiano dell'Istituto Storico per il Medio Evo* 81 (1970): 237–71.

———. "Venturino da Bergamo e la peregrinatio romana del 1335." In *Studi sul medioevo cristiano offerti a Raffaello Morghen*. Rome, 1974.

———. "Venturino spirituale." *Rivista di Storia e Letteratura Religiosa* 23 (1987): 434–66.

Gessa, C. "La vicenda di Cola di Rienzo." *Rassegna Lazio* 54 (1962): 9–10.

Gherardius, Petrus Hercules. "Historia Romanae Fragmenta . . . Vita Nicholai Laurentii (sive di Cola di Rienzo) Tribuni Romanorum." In *Antiquitates Italicae Medii Aevi,* edited by Lodovico A. Muratori, 247–548. Vol. 3. Milan: Societas Palatinae, 1740.

Gibbon, Edward. *The History of the Decline and Fall of the Roman Empire.* 3 vols. London: Penguin, 1994.

Guidoni, Enrico. "Roma e l'urbanistica del Trecento." In *Storia dell'arte italiana. Dal Medioevo al Novecento.* Vol. 1, *Dal Medioevo al Quattrocento,* edited by Federico Zeri, 309–83. Turin: Einaudi, 1983.

Gori, Fernando. *La torre del Monzone presso il Ponte Rotto di Roma non fu mai casa del Tribune Cola di Rienzo e nuova spiegazione d'una tavola enigmatica del XII secolo.* Rome, 1872.

Grabner, Sigrid. *Traum von Rom. Historischer Roman um Cola di Rienzo.* Berlin: Buchverlag Der Morgen, 1988.

Graf, Arturo. *Roma nella memoria e nelle imaginazione del medioevo.* 2 vols. Turin, 1882.

Gratzer, C. "Cola di Rienzo." In *Miscellanea in Onore di A. Hortis.* Trieste, 1910.

Green, Louis. *Chronicle into History.* London: Cambridge University Press, 1972.

———. *Castruccio Castracane: A Study in the Origins of a Fourteenth Century Italian Despotism.* Oxford: Clarendon Press, 1986.

Gregorovius, Ferdinand. *The History of the City of Rome in the Middle Ages.* Translated by A. Hamilton. 6 vols. London: G. Bell and Sons, 1894–98.

Gregory the Great. *In primum regum expositio.* Edited by J.-P. Migne. Biblioteca Patrum Latinum, vol. 79. Paris, 1849.

Gregory, Master. *The Marvels of Rome.* Edited by John Osborne. Toronto: Pontifical Institute of Mediaeval Studies, 1987.

Grundmann, Herbert. "Die Papstprofetien des Mittelalters." *Archiv für Kulturgeschichte* 19 (1929): 77–159.

———. "Die *Liber de Flore.* Eine schrift der Franziskaner-Spiritualen aus dem Anfang des 14. Jahrhunderts." *Historisches Jahrbuch* 49 (1929): 33–91.

Hardorp, G. "Die Politischen Ideen des Cola di Rienzo." Ph.D. diss., University of Marburg, 1922.

Heinrich von Taube of Selbach. *Chronik.* Edited by Harry Bresslau. Monumenta Germania Historiae (Scriptores), n.s., 1. Hannover: Hahn, 1922.

Henrik of Diessenhofen. *Chronica.* Edited by J. F. Böhmer and J. Hüber. Fontes Rerum Germanicum, vol. 4. Stuttgart, 1868.

Hobhouse, John. *A Historical Illustration of the Fourth Canto of Childe Harold.* 2d ed. London, 1818.

Hocsème, Jean d'. *Gesta Pontificum Leodinensium.* In *Qui Gesta Pontificum Leodinensium scripserunt auctores praecipui,* edited by Jean Chapeauville. 2 vols. Lièges, 1613.

Höfele, K. *Rienzi, das Abenteuerliche Vorspiel de Renaissance.* Munich: Unbekannt, 1958.

Hubert, Etienne. "Un censier des biens romains du monastère du S. Silvestro in Capite (1333–1334)," in "Materiali per la storia dei patrimoni immobiliari urbani a Roma nel Medievo. Due censuali di beni del secolo XIV," edited by Etienne Hubert and Marco Venditelli, 93–140. *ASRSP* 111 (1988): 75–160.

——. "Patrimoines immobiliers et habitat à Rome au Moyen-Age: La *regio Columnae* de XIe au XIVe Siècle." *MEFRM* 101 (1989): 133–75.

——. "Economie de la propriété immobilière: les établissements religieux et leurs patrimoines au XIVe siècle." In *Roma nei secoli XIII e XIV. Cinque saggi,* edited by Etienne Hubert, 177–230. Rome: Viella, 1993.

——. "Le *rioni* de Rome." In *Dictionnaire historique de la Papauté,* edited by Philippe Levillain. Paris: Fayard, 1994.

——. "Rome (Moyen Age: ville e population)." In *Dictionnaire historique de la Papauté,* edited by Philippe Levillain. Paris: Fayard, 1994.

Hugenholz, F. W. N. "The Anagni Frescoes: A Manifesto." *Mededelingen van het Nederlands Institut te Rome* 41 (1979): 139–72.

Hunt, Edwin S. *The Medieval Super-Companies.* Cambridge: Cambridge University Press, 1994.

Il Notaio nella civiltà Fiorentina: Secoli XIII–XVI. Biblioteca Medicea Laurenziana, Firenze 1984. Atti del XVII Congresso Internazionale del Notariato Latino. Florence: Vallecchi, 1984.

Infessura, Stefano. *Diario della Città di Roma di Stefano Infessura, scribasenato.* Edited by Oreste Tommassini. Fonti per la Storia d'Italia 5. Rome: Istituto Storico Italiano, 1890.

Jacks, Philip. *The Antiquarian and the Myth of Antiquity: The Origins of Rome in Renaissance Thought.* Cambridge: Cambridge University Press, 1993.

James, Montague Rhodes. *The Dublin Apocalypse.* Cambridge: Camridge University Press, 1932.

Jean de Roquetaillade (Johannes de Rupescissa). *Vade Mecum in Tribulatione.* In *Appendix ad Fasciculum Rerum Competendarum et Fugiendarum,* edited by Edward Brown, 493–508. London, 1690.

——. *Liber Secretorum Eventum.* Edited by Robert E. Lerner, translated by Christine Morerod-Fattebert. Fribourg: Éditions Universitaires Fribourg Suisse, 1994.

Joachim of Fiore. *Abbot Joachim of Fiore. Liber de Concordia Novi ac Veteris Testamenti.* Edited by E. Randolph Daniel. Philadelphia: American Philosophical Society, 1983.

Joachimsen, Paul. "Vom Mittelalter zur Reformation." *Historische Vierteljahrsschrift* (1920–21): 426–70.

Joubert, Marie. "Rienzi and Petrarch." *Contemporary Review* 166 (1944): 37–42.

Juhar, Monika-Beate. "Der Romgedanke bei Cola di Rienzo." Ph.D. diss., Kiel University, 1977.

Kantorowicz, Ernst H. *The King's Two Bodies: A Study in Medieval Political Theology.* 2d ed. Princeton: Princeton University Press, 1981.

———. *Frederick the Second.* Translated by E. O. Lorimer. London: Constable, 1957.

Karlowa, Otto. *Römisches Rechtgeschichtes.* 2 vols. Leipzig: Von Veit, 1885–1901.

Kirner, Rudolph. *Cola di Rienzi: Trauerspiel.* Leipzig, 1845.

Koltay-Kastner, Jeno. *Cola di Rienzo.* Szeged, 1949.

Krautheimer, Richard. *Rome: Profile of a City, 312–1305.* Princeton: Princeton University Press, 1980.

Kristeller, Paul O. *Renaissance Thought.* 2 vols. New York: Harper and Bros., 1961.

Kühn, Fritz. *Die Entwicklung der Bündnispläne Cola di Rienzos im Jahre 1347.* Berlin, 1905.

"La mostra di sistemazione urbanistica al Centri di studi di Storia dell'Architettura." *Capitolium* 16 (1941) 146–56.

Labanca, Baldassare. *Cola di Rienzo.* Palermo, 1912.

Lanconelli, A. "Gli *Statuti Pescivendolorum Urbis* (1405). Note sul commercio del pesce fra XIV e XV secolo." *ASRSP* 108 (1985): 83–131.

Lansing, Carol. *The Florentine Magnates: Lineage and Faction in a Medieval Commune.* Princeton: Princeton University Press, 1991.

Laureys, Marc A. "An Edition and Study of Giovanni Cavallini's *Polistoria de virtutibus et dotibus Romanorum.*" Ph.D. diss. Harvard University, 1992.

———. *Iohannes Caballini de Cerronibus Polistoria de virtutibus et dotibus Romanorum,* Stuttgart: Teubner, 1995.

Law, John E. *The Lords of Renaissance Italy: The Signori, 1250–1500.* London: Historical Association, 1981.

Lee, Egmont. *The "Descriptio Urbis": The Roman Census of 1527.* Rome: Bulzoni, 1985.

Lerner, Robert E. "On the Origins of the Earliest Latin Pope Prophecies: A Reconsideration." In *Fälschungen im Mittelalters.* Monumenta Germaniae Historia, n.s., 33. Hannover: Hahn, 1988–90.

Livy. *The Early History of Rome: Rome and Italy.* Edited and translated by Aubrey de Sélincourt. London: Penguin, 1960, 1982.

Loevinson, E. "Documenti del monastero di S. Cecilia in Trastevere." *ASRSP* 49 (1926): 355–404.

Lombardo, Maria Luisa. *La Camera Urbis. Premesse per uno studio dell'organizzazione amministrativa della città di Roma durante il pontificato di Martino V.* Fonti e studi del Corpus membranarum italicarum 6. Rome: Centro di Ricerca, 1970.

———. "Sprunti di vita privata e sociale in Roma da atti notarili dei secoli XIV e XV." *Archivi e Cultura* 14 (1980): 61–100.

————. "Nobili, mercanti e popolo minuto negli atti dei notai romani del XIV e XV secolo." In *Sources of Social History: Private Acts of the Late Middle Ages,* edited by Paolo Brezzi and Egmont Lee, 291–310. Toronto: Pontifical Institute of Mediaeval Studies, 1984.

Lombroso, Cesare. "Cola di Rienzo monomane." *Fanfulla della Dominica* 46 (1880).

————. *Due Tribuni (N. Gabrino di Rienzi e F. Coccapieller) studiati da un alienista.* Rome, 1883.

Lori-Sanfilippo, Isa. "Roma nel XIV secolo. Riflessioni in margine alla lettura di due saggi usciti nella storia dell'arte italiana Einaudi." *Bulletino dell' Istituto Storico Italiano per il Medio Evo* 91 (1984): 281–316.

————. *Il Protocollo Notarile di Lorenzo Staglia (1372).* Codice diplomatico di Roma e della regione romana 3. Rome: Società Romana di Storia Patria, 1986.

————. "I protocolli notarili romani del Trecento." *ASRSP* 110 (1987): 99–150.

————. "Operazioni di credito nei protocolli notarili romani del Trecento." In *Credito e sviluppo economia in Italia del Medio Evo all'Età Contemporanea.* Verona, 1988: 53–66.

————. *Il Protocollo Notarile di Pietro di Nicola Astalli (1368).* Codice diplomatico di Roma e della regione romana 6. Rome: Società Romana di Storia Patria, 1989.

————. "Appunti sui notai medievali a Roma e sulla conservazione dei loro atti." In *Notariato e Archivi dei notai in Italia: Archivi per la Storia. Rivista dell'Associazione nazionale archivistica italiana* 3 (1990): 21–39.

————. "Per la storia dell'arti a Roma; da una ricerca sui protocolli notarili. I: L'*Ars Pescivendulorum* nella seconda metà del XIV secolo." *ASRSP* 115 (1992): 79–114.

————. Review of *Roma nei secoli XIII e XIV. Cinque saggi,* edited by Etienne Hubert. *ASRSP* 116 (1993): 414–24.

————. "Un 'luoco famoso' nel Medioevo, una chiesa oggi poco nota. Notizie extravaganti su S. Angelo in Pescheria (V–XX secolo)." *ASRSP* 117 (1994): 231–68.

Lucan. *Pharsalia.* Edited by R. Mayer. Warminster: Aris and Phillips, 1981.

Macek, Josef. "Pétrarque et Cola di Rienzo." *Historica* 9 (1965): 5–51.

————. "Racines sociales de l'insurrection de Cola di Rienzo." *Historica* 6 (1963): 45–107.

Machiavelli, Niccolò. *Florentine Histories by Niccolò Machiavelli.* Edited by Laura F. Banfield and Harvey Mansfield Jr. Princeton: Princeton University Press, 1988.

Maddalò, Silvia. *In Figura Romae. Immagini di Rome nel Libro Medioevale.* Rome: Viella, 1990.

Maire-Vigueur, Jean-Claude. "Les casali des églises romaines à la fin du Moyen Age." *MEFRM* 86 (1974): 63–136.

————. "Classe dominante et classes dirigeantes à Rome à la fin du Moyen Age." *Storia della Città* 1 (1976): 4–26.

————. "I registri notarili del Tre-Quattrocento." *Ricerche per la storia religiosa di Roma* 4 (1980): 22–27.

———. "Cola di Rienzo." *Dizionario Biografico degli Italiani* (1982), 26:662–75.

———. "Capital économique et capital symbolique. Les contradictions de la société romaine à la fin du Moyen Age." In *Sources of Social History: Private Acts of the Late Middle Ages,* edited by Paolo Brezzi and Egmont Lee, 213–24. Toronto: Pontifical Institute of Mediaeval Studies, 1984.

———. "Jean de Roquetaillade ou la rencontre de l'imaginaire." *MEFRM* 102 (1990): 381–89.

Maire-Vigueur, Jean-Claude, and G. Broise. "Strutture familiari, spazio domestico e architettura civile a Roma alla fine del Medio Evo." In *Monumenti di architettura,* 99–160. Storia dell'arte italiana, vol. 12. Turin: Einaudi, 1983.

Malatesta, S. *Statuti delle gabelli di Roma.* Rome: Della Pace, 1886.

Mariani, Marisa. "Il concetto di Roma nei Cronisti fiorentini." *Studi Romani* 4 (1956): 15–27, 153–66.

———. "Cola di Rienzo nel giudizio dei contemporanei fiorentini." *Studi Romani* 8 (1960): 647–60.

Mariano del Moro. *Cronica.* Edited by A. Fabretti. In *Cronaca della città di Perugia dal 1309 al 1491.* Archivio Storico Italiano, o.s., vol. 16, pt. 1. Florence, 1850–51.

Marle, R. van. *Iconographie de l'Art Profane au Moyen-Age et à la Renaissance.* Vol. 2, *Allegories and symboles.* The Hague, 1932.

Masetti-Zannini, L. "L'agricoltura nello stato Pontificio e le costituzioni Egidiane; Cola di Rienzo e la politica annonaria." In *El Cardenal Albornoz y el Collegio de Espana,* edited by Evelio Verdera y Tuells. Studia albornotiana nos. 11–13. Bologna: Real Colegio de España en Bolonia, 1973.

Mathias of Neuenburg. *Chronik.* Edited by Adolf Hofmeister. Monumenta Germaniae Historia (Scriptores), n.s., 4. 2d ed. Hannover: Hahn, 1955.

Mazzei, Francesco. *La Fantastica Vita e l'Oribile Morte del Tribuno del Popolo Romano.* Milan: Rusconi, 1980.

McGinn, Bernard. *Visions of the End: Apocalyptic Traditions in the Middle Ages.* New York: Columbia University Press, 1979.

———. "Teste David cum Sibylla: The Significance of the Sibylline Tradition in the Middle Ages." In *Women of the Medieval World: Essays in Honor of John H. Mundy,* edited by Julius Kirshner and Susan F. Wemple, 7–35. Oxford: Blackwell, 1985.

———. "Pastor Angelicus: Apocalyptic Myth and Political Hope in the Fourteenth Century." In *Santi e Santità nel secolo XIV.* Perugia: Università di Perugia, Centro di Studi Francescani, 1989.

———. *Antichrist: Two Thousand Years of the Human Fascination with Evil.* San Francisco: HarperSanFrancisco, 1994.

Meadly, G. W. "Two Pairs of Historical Portraits: Octavian Augustus and William Pitt; Rienzi and Buonaparte." *Pamphleteer* 18, no. 35 (1821): 129–41.

Meer, Frederic van der. *Maiestas Domini: Théophanies de l'Art Chrétien.* Rome, 1931.

———. *Apocalypse: Visions from the Book of Revelation in Western Art.* London: Thames and Hudson, 1978.

Mercati, A. "Nell'Urbe dalla fine di settembre 1337 al 31 gennaio 1338." *Miscellanae historiae pontificae* 10 (1945): 1–84.

Miglio, Massimo. "Gli ideali di pace e di giustizia in Roma a metà del Trecento: gruppi sociali e azione politica nella Roma di Cola di Rienzo." In *Scritture, Scrittori e Storia.* Vol. 1, *Per la Storia del Trecento a Roma.* Vecchiarelli: Rome, 1991.

―――. "Et rerum facta est pulcherrima Roma." In *Scritture, Scrittori e Storia.* Vol. 1, *Per la Storia del Trecento a Roma.* Vecchiarelli: Rome, 1991.

―――. "Il leone e la lupa; dal simbolo al pasticcio alla francese." In *Scritture, Scrittori e Storia.* Vol. 2, *Città e Corte a Roma nel Quattrocento.* Vecchiarelli: Rome, 1993.

―――. "Gli atti privati come contributo delle condizioni culturali di Roma nei secoli XIV–XV." In *Sources of Social History: Private Acts of the Late Middle Ages,* edited by Paolo Brezzi and Egmont Lee, 225–37. Toronto: Pontifical Institute of Mediaeval Studies, 1984.

―――. "Il progetto politico di Cola di Rienzo ed i comuni dell'Italia centrale." In *Scritture, Scrittori e Storia.* Vol. 1, *Per la Storia del Trecento a Roma.* Vecchiarelli: Rome, 1991.

―――. "La Cronica dell'Anonimo Romano." *Roma nel Rinascimento* (1992): 30–37.

―――. "Giuseppe Billanovich: 'Come nacque un capolavoro. . . .'" *Roma nel Rinascimento* (1996): 239–42.

―――. "Anonimo Romano." In *Il Senso della Storia nella cultura medievale italiana (1100–1350),* 175–87. Pistoia: Centro italiano di studi di storia e d'arte, 1995.

Mills, C. A. ed., *Ye Solace of Pilgrimes: A Description of Rome, circa 1450 A.D. by John Capgrave, an Austin Friar of King's Lynn.* Oxford: Oxford University Press, 1911.

Mitchell, John. "St. Sylvester and Constantine at the SS. Quattro Coronati." In *Federigo II e l'Arte del Duecento italiano,* edited by Angiola M. Romanini. 2 vols. Rome: Galatina, 1980.

Modigliani, Anna. "La cronica dell'Anonimo Romano." *Roma nel Rinascimento* (1992): 19–30.

―――. "Artigiani e botteghe nella città." In *Alle origini della nuova Roma. Martino V (1417–1431),* edited by Maria Chiabò, Giusi d'Alessandro, Paola Piacentini, and Concetta Ranieri, 455–77. Rome: Istituto Storico Italiano per il Medio Evo, 1992.

―――. *I Porcari: Storie di una famiglia romana tra Medioevo e Rinascimento.* Rome: Roma nel Rinascimento, 1994.

―――. "I protocolli notarili romani per la storia del secondo Trecento." *Roma nel Rinascimento* (1995): 151–58.

Mollat, Michel. *The Popes at Avignon, 1305–78.* Translated by Janet Love. 2d ed. London: Thomas Nelson and Sons, 1963.

Mollat, Michel, and Philippe Wolff. *The Popular Revolutions of the Later Middle Ages.* Translated by A. L. Lytton-Sells. London: Allen and Unwin, 1973.

Molnar, Amedeo. "Cola di Rienzo, Petrarca e le origini della riforma hussita." *Protestantismo* 4 (1964): 214–23.

Momigliano, Eucardio. *Tre tribuni: Jacques Artevelde, Étienne Marcel, Cola di Rienzo.* Milan, 1935.

Monaci, Ernesto. "Regesto dell'Abbazia di Sant'Alessio all'Aventino." *ASRSP* 28 (1905): 395–449.

———. *Storie de Troja et de Roma.* Rome: Società Romana di Storia Patria, 1920.

Monmerque, L. J. N. *Dissertation historique sur Jean 1er, Roi de France . . . suivre d'une charte par laquelle N. de Rienzi reconnaît Giannino, fils supposé de Guccius, comme roi de France.* Paris, 1844.

Montenovesi, O. "Archivi degli Ospedali Romani nell'Archivio di Stato in Roma." *Archivi d'Italia,* n.s., 2, no. 3 (1936): 165–72.

Morghen, Raffaello. "Il mito storico di Cola di Rienzo." In *Civiltà Medievale al Tramonto.* Biblioteca di cultura moderna, vol. 708. Bari: Laterza, 1971.

Mori, Elizabetta. "L'Archivio Capitolino e l'acquisizione di archivi familiare. Analisi di un percorso." In *Il Futuro della Memoria,* 767–82. Rome: Ministero per i Beni culturali e ambientali, Ufficio centrale per i Beni archivistici, 1997.

Mosti, Renzo. "L'eresia dei fraticelli nel territorio di Tivoli." *Atti e Memorie della Società Tiburtina di Storia ed Arte,* 38 (1965): 41–110.

———. *Un notaio Romano del '300. I Protocolli di Johannes Nicolai Pauli (1348–1379).* Rome: École Française, 1982.

———. "Due quaderne superstiti dei protocolli del notaio romano *Paulus Nicolai Pauli.*" *MEFRM* 96 (1984): 777–844.

———. *Il Protocollo Notarile di Anthonius Goioli Petri Scopte (1365).* Rome: École Française, 1991.

———. "Un quaderno superstite di un protocollo del notaio romano *Nicolaus Iohannis Iacobi* (1391)." *ASRSP* 116 (1993): 153–75.

———. *Un notaio Romano del '300. I Protocolli di Francesco di Stefano de Caput-gallis (1374–1386).* Rome: École Française, 1994.

———. "Un protocollo del notaio romano *Iohannes Paulus Iacobi* (1397)." *ASRSP* 117 (1994): 119–69.

Muñoz, A. "Un angolo di Roma mediovale." *L'Urbe* 4 (1942): 1–14.

Muratori, Lodovico A., ed. "Historia Cortusiorum de novitatibus Paduae, et Lombardiae ab anno MCCLVI usque ad MCCCLXIV." In *R.I.S.,* vol. 12. Milan: Societas Palatinae, 1728.

———. "*Fragmenta Annalium Romanorum.* Ludovico Bonconte Monaldesco." In *R.I.S.,* vol. 12. Milan: Societas Palatinae, 1728.

———. "Chronicon Regiense." In *R.I.S.,* vol. 18. Milan: Societas Palatinae, 1731.

———. "Bartolomeo of Ferrara: *Polyhistoria (Libro di Polistore).*" In *R.I.S.,* vol. 24. Milan: Societas Palatinae, 1738.

———. "Ordine e Magnificenze dei Magistrati Romani nel tempo la Corte del Papa stava in Avignone." In *Antiquitates Italicae Medii Aevi,* 856–61. Vol. 2. Milan: Societas Palatinae, 1739.

Musto, Ronald G. "Queen Sancia of Naples (1286–1345) and the Spiritual Franciscans." In *Women of the Medieval World: Essays in Honor of John H. Mundy,* edited by Julius Kirshner and Susan Wemple, 179–214. Oxford: Blackwell, 1985.

Musumarra, C. "Petrarca e Roma." *Critica Letteraria* 66–67 (1990): 155–67.

Natale, Arcangelo. "La Felice Società dei Balestrieri e dei Pavesati a Roma (1358–1408)." *ASRSP* 62 (1939): 1–168.

Nichols, Francis M., trans. *The Marvels of Rome: Mirabilia Urbis Romae.* 2d ed. New York: Italica Press, 1986.

Olschki, C. "Note bibliographiche su la Vita di Cola di Rienzo dell'Anonimo." *Roma* 11 (1924): 115–18.

Origo, Iris. *Tribune of Rome.* London: Hogarth Press, 1938.

Palermo, Luciano. *Il Porto di Roma nel XIV e XV secolo. Strutture socio-economiche e statuti.* Rome: Il Centro di Ricerca, 1979.

———. "Carestie e cronisti nel Trecento: Roma e Firenze nel racconto dell'Anonimo e di Giovanni Villani." *Archivio Storico Italiano* 142 (1984): 343–75.

Palma, M. "Giovanni Cavallini di Cerroni." *Dizionario Biografico degli Italiani* 22 (1979): 785–87.

Paludan-Müller, C. P. *Cola di Rienzo. Tribun og Senator i Rom. En historisk Skildring.* Odense, 1833.

Panofsky, Erwin. *Renaissance and Renascences in Western Art.* Stockholm: Almqvist & Wiksell, 1960.

Paolo di Lello Petrone. *La Mesticanza (c.1388–c.1447).* Edited by F. Isoldi. *R.I.S.,* 2d ed., vol. 24, pt. 2. Città di Castello: S. Lapi, 1912.

Paolucci, Giuseppe. *Cola di Rienzo. Appunti Storici.* Rome, 1883.

Papencordt, Felix. *Cola di Rienzo und Seine Zeit.* Hamburg, 1841.

Paravicini Bagliani, Agostino. "Alfonso Ceccarelli, gli Statuti Urbis del 1305 e la famiglia Boccamazza." In *Xenia Medii Aevi Historiam Illustrantia oblata T. Kaeppeli O.P.,* edited by R. Creytens and Pius Künzle. Vol. 1. Storia e Letteratura 141. Rome: Edizioni di storia e letteratura, 1978.

Partner, Peter. *The Lands of St. Peter.* London: Eyre Methuen, 1972.

Passigli, Susanna. "Urbanizzazzione e topografia a Roma nell'area dei Fori Imperiali tra XIV e XVI secolo." *MEFRM* 101 (1989): 273–325.

———. "Geografia parrochiale e circoscrizioni territoriali nei secoli XII–XIV: Istituzioni e realtà quotidiana." In *Rome nei secoli XIII e XIV,* edited by Etienne Hubert, 43–86. Rome: Viella, 1992.

Pavan, Paola. "Gli statuti della Società dei Raccomendati del Salvatore ad *Sancta Sanctorum* (1331–1496)." *ASRSP* 101 (1978): 35–96.

———. "La confraternita del Salvatore nella società romana del Tre-Quattrocento." *Ricerche per la Storia Religiosa di Roma* 5 (1984): 81–90.

Pepe, Gabriele. *Da Cola di Rienzo a Pisacane.* Rome, 1947.

Petrarch. *Scritti Inediti di Petrarca.* Edited by A. Hortis. Trieste, 1874.

———. *Poëmata Minora di Francesco Petrarca.* Edited by Dino De Rossetti. 3 vols. Milan, 1829–34.

———. *Petrarca: Vite degli Uomini Illustri.* Edited by Luigi Razzolini. 2 vols. Bologna, 1874.

———. *Le Rime di Francesco Petrarca.* Edited by G. Mestica. Florence, 1896.

———. *Invettiva contro un uomo di alta condizione ma senza dottrine e senza virtù.*

In *Petrarca: Prose,* edited by Guido Martellotti, Pier Giorgo Ricci, E. Carrara, and E. Bianchi, 695–709. Verona: Ricciardi, 1955.

———. *Petrarch: Bucolicum Carmen.* Edited by Thomas G. Bergin. New York: Twayne, 1970.

———. *Petrarch's Africa.* Edited by Thomas G. Bergin and Alice S. Wilson. New Haven: Yale University Press, 1977.

———. *Francis Petrarch: Letters of Old Age (Rerum Senilium Libri).* Edited by Aldo S. Bernardo, Saul Levin, and Reta Bernardo. Baltimore: Johns Hopkins University Press, 1992.

Petrucci, Armando. *Tabellioni, scriniarii e notai nella Roma del Medioevo.* N.p., n.d.

———. *Notarii. Documenti per la storia del notariato italiano.* Milan: Cosilio nazionale per il notariato, 1958.

Picchio, C. "Cola di Rienzo, l'eroe degli umili fu ucciso dalla plebe." *Storia Illustrata* 20 (1968): 40–46.

Pietrangeli, Carlo. "Il palazzo Senatorio nel Medioevo." *Capitolium* 35 (1960): 3–19.

———. "I palazzi Capitolini nel Medioevo." *Capitolium* 39 (1964): 191–94.

Piur, Paul. *Cola di Rienzo. Darstellung seines lebens und seines Geists.* Vienna: Seidel, 1931.

Pliny (the Elder). *Natural History.* Edited and translated (selections) by John F. Healy. London: Penguin, 1991.

Porena, Filippo. *Due Parole in Difesa di Cola di Rienzo.* Rome, 1873.

———. "L'ordinamento del Canzoniere petrarchesco e le due grandi canzoni politiche." *Rendiconti dell'Accademia dei Lincei,* 6th ser., 11 (1935): 129–234, 259–60.

Porta, Giuseppe. "Le vicende del Duca d'Atene e le gesta d'oltremare nella narrazione dell'Anonimo Romano." *Studi di Filologia Italiana* (1977): 1–28.

Potestà, Gian Luca. *Angelo Clareno: dai poveri eremiti ai fraticelli.* Rome: Istituto storico italiano per il Medio Evo, 1990.

Pozzi, Mario. "Appunti sulla 'Chronica' di Anonimo romano." *Giornale storico della Letteratura italiana* 99 (1982): 481–504.

Premoli, Beatrice. *Ludus Carnevaleschi. Il carnevale a Roma dal secolo XII al secolo XVI.* Rome: Guidotti, 1981.

Preston, Helen, and L. Dodge. "Cola di Rienzo." *Atlantic Monthly* 71 (1893): 62–78.

Pujmanova, O. "Bohemian Painting at the Time of Charles IV and its Relation to Naples." *Antichità Viva* 18, nos. 5–6 (1979): 15–25; 19, no. 3 (1980): 5–13.

Puschedsu, Gemma. "La fondazione dell'Universitaria di Roma." In *Roma e lo Studium Urbis: Spazio Urbana e Cultura dal Quattro al Seicento,* edited by Paolo Cherubini. Rome: Quasar, 1989.

Quaglione, Diego. *Politica e Diretto nel Trecento italiano: il "De Tyranno" di Bartolomeo da Sassoferrato (1314–57) con l'edizione critica dei trattati "De Guelfis et Gebellinis," "De Regimine civitatis" e "De Tyranno."* Florence: Olschki, 1983.

Re, Camillo, ed. *Statuti della citta di Roma dal secolo XIV.* Rome, 1880.

———. *Storia della città di Roma del secolo XIV.* Rome, 1883.

———. "Le regioni di Roma nel Medio Evo." *Studi e documenti di storia e diritto* 10 (1889): 349–81.

Reale, Ugo. *Cola di Rienzo.* Rome: Newton Compton, 1991.

Réau, Louis. *Iconographie de l'art Chrétien.* Paris: Presses universitaires de France, 1957.

Reeves, Marjorie. *The Influence of Prophecy in the Later Middle Ages: A Study in Joachimism.* Oxford: Oxford University Press, 1969.

———. "Some Popular Prophecies from the Fourteenth to the Seventeenth Centuries." In *Popular Belief and Practice.* Studies in Church History 8, 107–34. Cambridge: Cambridge University Press, 1972.

———. *Joachim of Fiore and the Prophetic Future.* London: SPCK, 1976.

———. "The *Vaticinia de Summis Pontificis:* A Question of Authority." In *Intellectual Life in the Middle Ages,* edited by Benedicta Ward and Lesley Smith, 145–56. London: Hambledon, 1992.

Ribera, Almerico. *Giovinezza dei Grandi: Il tribuno (Cola di Rienzo).* Rome, 1946.

Ricci, G. "La *Nobilis Universitas Bobacteriorum Urbis.*" *ASRSP* 16 (1893): 131–80.

Ricci, Pier Giorgio. "Il commento di Cola di Rienzo alla *Monarchia* di Dante." *Studi Medievali,* 3d ser., 6 (1965): 665–708.

Rice, Scott. *"It was a dark and stormy night": The Best (?) from the Bulwer-Lytton Contest.* London: Abacus, 1984.

Roberts, William J. *Mary Russell Mitford: The Tragedy of a Blue Stocking,* London: Andrew Melrose, 1913.

Robertson, Ian. ["Capitular Reform in the Fifteenth-Century Lateran."] Paper presented in the Italian history seminar series of the University of London Institute of Historical Research, London, November 2, 1995.

Romanini, Angiola M., ed. *Federigo II e l'arte del Duecento italiano.* 2 vols. Rome: Galatina, 1980.

———, ed. *Roma nel Duecento. L'arte nella città dei papi da Innocenzo III a Bonfacio VIII.* Turin: Edizioni Seat, 1991.

Romano, Serena, *Eclissi di Roma. Pittura Murale a Roma e nel Lazio da Bonifacio VIII a Martino V.* Rome: Argos, 1992.

———. *"Regio dissimilitudinis:* Immagine e parola nella Roma di Cola di Rienzo." In *Bilan et Perspectives des Études Médiévales en Europe,* 329–56. Louvain-la-Neuve: Fédération Internationale des Instituts d'Études Médiévales, 1995.

Rota, A. "Il Codice degli *Statuta Urbis* del 1305 e i caratteri politici della sua riforma." *ASRSP* 70 (1947): 147–62.

Rusconi, Carlo, and Nullo Amato. *I Tribuni. Masaniello, Cola di Rienzi, Ciceruacchio, Michele di Lando, Balilla.* Rome, 1890.

Salimei, A. *Senatori e statuti di Roma nel medio evo.* Rome: Biblioteca d'Arte, 1935.

Sanfilippo, Mario. "Dell'Anonimo e della sua e altrui nobilità." *Quaderni Medievali* 9 (1980): 121–27.

Savage, Alan. *Queen of Night.* London: Warner, 1993.

Savignoni, P. "A proposito di un documento relativo all'*exercitus Populi Romani Urbis.*" *ASRSP* 15 (1892): 217–27.

Saxl, Fritz. "The Classical Inscription in Renaissance Art and Politics." *Journal of the Warburg and Courtauld Institutes* 4 (1940): 19–46.

Schiaparelli, L. "Un nuovo documento di Cola di Rienzo." In *Scritti di Storia, di Filosofia e d'arte*. Naples, 1908.

Schiller, Friedrich von. "Revolution in Rom durch Nicholaus Rienzi im Jahre 1347." In *Geschichte der merkwürdigsten Rebellionen und Verschwörungen aus den mittlern und neuern Zeiten*. Leipzig, 1788.

Schmeidler, Bernhard. "Bemerkungen zu Konrad Burdach, *Vom Mittelalter zur Reformation*. . . ." Review of *Briefwechsel des Cola di Rienzo*, by Konrad Burdach and Paul Piur. *Zeitschrift für Kirchengeschichte* 49 (1930): 64–73.

Schmidinger, H. "Die Antwort Clemens' VI. an die Gesandtschaft der Stadt Rom vom Jahre 1343." In *Miscellanea in onore di Monsignore Martino Giusti*. Vol. 2. Vatican City, 1978.

———. "Die Gesandte der Staat Rom nach Avignon vom Jahre 1342/3." *Romische Historische Mitteilungen* 21 (1979): 15–33.

Schmitt, Anna-Liese. "Die Apokalypse des Robert von Anjou." *Pantheon* 6 (1970): 475–503.

Schmitz, Hermann. "Cola di Rienzo." *Sammlung historischer Bildnisse*, 5th ser., 4 (1879).

Schramm, Percy E. *Kaiser, Könige, und Päpste*. 4 vols. Stuttgart: Hiersemann, 1968–71.

Schwartz, Amy. "Images and Illustrations of Power in Trecento Art: Cola di Rienzo and the Ancient Roman Republic." Ph.D. diss., State University of New York, Binghampton, 1994.

Seibt, Gustav. *Anonimo Romano: Geschichtsschreibung in Rom an der Schwelle zur Renaissance*. Stuttgart: Klett-Cotta, 1992.

Sennuccio del Bene. *Epistola di Sennuccio del Bene della Incoronatione di M. Francesco Petrarca*. Edited by G. Marescotti. Florence, 1577.

Sensi, Guglielmo.*Vita di Cola di Rienzo*. Genoa, 1927.

Small, Carole M. "The District of Rome in the Early Fourteenth Century." *Canadian Journal of History* 16 (1981): 193–213.

Smith, M. Q. "Anagni: An Example of Medieval Typological Decoration." *Papers of the British School at Rome* 32 (1965): 1–47.

Sonnay, Philippe. "La politique artistique de Cola di Rienzo." *Revue de l'Art* 55 (1982): 35–43.

Sorbelli, Albano, ed. *Corpus Chronicorum Bononiensium*. In *R.I.S.*, 2d ed., vol. 18, pt. 1. Città di Castello: S. Lapi, 1911.

Sordi, Marta. "Il *pomerium* romano e l'*Italia giardin dell'impero* di Dante." *Atti del Accademia Peloritana* 48 (1951–67): 103–7.

———. "Cola di Rienzo e la clausole mancanti *della Lex regio de Imperio Vespasiani*." In *Studi in onore di E. Volterra*. Vol. 2. Milan: Giuffrè, 1971.

Staderini, T. "Cola di Rienzo notaro e iniziatore degli studi archeologici." *Strenna dei Romanisti* (1944): 170–74.

Stevenson, Enrico, ed. *Statuti delle arti dei merciai e della lana di Roma*. Rome: Della Pace, 1893.

Supino, Paola. *La Margarita Cornetana.* Rome: Società romana di storia patria, 1969.

Syme, Ronald. *The Roman Revolution.* Oxford: Clarendon Press, 1939.

Theiner, Augustin. *Codex diplomaticus dominii temporalis S. Sedis. Recueil de documents pour servir à l'histoire du gouvernement temporel des États du Saint-Siège. Extraits des Archives du Vatican.* 2 vols. Rome: Imprimerie du Vatican, 1861–62.

Toesca, Pietro. "Gli affreschi della Cattedrale di Anagni." In *Le Galleria Nazionale Italiane.* Vol. 5. Rome, 1902.

Toppani, Innocente. "Petrarch, Cola di Rienzo, e il mito di Roma." *Atti dell'Instituto Veneto di scienze, letteri, ed arti: Classe di scienze morali, lettere ed arti* 135 (1977): 155–73.

Tordi, Domenico. *La Pretesa Tomba di Cola di Rienzo.* Rome, 1887.

———. *Tribuno e Pontifice.* Rome, 1890.

Torraca, Francesco. "Cola di Rienzo e la canzone *Spirto gentile* di Francesco Petrarca." *ASRSP* 8 (1885): 141–222.

Torraca, L. "Nel sesto centario della morte di Cola di Rienzo." *Atti della Accademia pontaniana* 52–54 (1955): 173–86.

Trexler, Richard. "Rome on the Eve of the Great Schism." *Speculum* 42 (1947): 87–96, 489–509.

Trifone, B. "Le carte del monastero di San Paolo di Roma." *ASRSP* 32 (1909): 29–106.

Ullmann, Walter. *"De Bartoli sententia: Concilum repraesentat mentem populi."* In *The Papacy and Political Ideas in the Middle Ages.* London: Variorum, 1975.

———. *Medieval Foundations of Renaissance Humanism.* London: Elek, 1977.

Valentini, Roberto, and Giuseppe Zucchetti, eds. *Codice Diplomatico della città di Roma.* Fonti per la Storia d'Italia 81, 88, 90, 91. 4 vols. Rome: Istituto Storico Italiano, 1940–53.

Varisco, S. *Roma e i suoi ospedali. Caratteri e funzioni dei complessi ospedalieri nella Roma dei secoli XIII–XVII, e loro collocazione urbana.* Rome, 1969.

Vendemini, Francesco. *Discorso intorno alla vita e alle opere di G. Perticari con note illustrative ed un saggio della vita di Cola di Rienzo abbozzata dal medesimo.* Bologna, 1875.

Vendettini, Antonio. *Serie cronologica dei senatori di Roma.* Rome, 1778.

Venditelli, Marco. "Un censuale dei beni urbani della chiesa romana di S. Maria in Aquiro degli anni 1326–1329." *ASRSP* 111 (1988): 77–92.

Vielstedt, Herbert. *Cola di Rienzo. Geschichte des Volkstribun.* Berlin: S. Fischer Verlag, 1936.

Villani, Giovanni. *Cronica.* Edited by Giuseppe Porta. 3 vols. Parma: Ugo Guanda, 1990.

Villani, Matteo. *Cronica.* Edited by Giuseppe Porta. 2 vols. Parma: Ugo Guanda, 1995.

Vinay, Gustavo. "Cola di Rienzo e la crisi dell'universalismo medievale." *Convivium: Raccolta nuova* 17 (1948): 96–107.

Waetzoldt, Stephan. *Die Kopien des 17. Jahrhunderts nach Mosaiken und Wand-*

malereien im Rom. Römische Forschungen der Bibliotheca Hertziana, vol. 18. Vienna, 1964.

Waley, Daniel. *The Papal State in the Thirteenth Century.* New York: Macmillan, 1961.

Walters, Ingeborg. "Francesco Baroncelli." *Dizionario Biografico degli Italiani* (1964) 6: 437–38.

Weider, J. "Cola di Rienzo." In *Kaiser Karl IV Staatsman und Mäzen,* edited by Ferdinand Seibt. Munich: Prestel, 1978.

Weiss, Roberto. "Barbato da Sulmona, il Petrarca e la rivoluzione di Cola di Rienzo." In *Studi Petrarcheschi,* edited by E. Calcaterra. Vol. 3. Bologna, 1950.

Werner of Bonn. *Vitae Clementis VI.* In *Vitae Papae Avenionensium,* edited by Étienne Baluze. Paris, 1693.

Wickham, Chris. "Lawyer's Time: History and Memory in Tenth- and Eleventh-Century Italy." In *Studies in Medieval History presented to R. H. C. Davies,* edited by Henry Mayr-Harting and R. I. Moore, 53–71. London: Hambledon, 1985.

Wood, Diana. *Clement VI: The Pontificate and Ideas of an Avignon Pope.* Cambridge: Cambridge University Press, 1989.

Wright, John. *The Life of Cola di Rienzo.* Toronto: Pontifical Institute of Mediaeval Studies, 1975.

Zeller, Jean. *Les Tribuns et les Revolutions en Italie.* Paris, 1874.

Index

Page numbers for figures appear in italics.